T0360893

# Support Vector Machines

## Optimization Based Theory, Algorithms, and Extensions

# Chapman & Hall/CRC
# Data Mining and Knowledge Discovery Series

## SERIES EDITOR
### Vipin Kumar
University of Minnesota
Department of Computer Science and Engineering
Minneapolis, Minnesota, U.S.A.

## AIMS AND SCOPE

This series aims to capture new developments and applications in data mining and knowledge discovery, while summarizing the computational tools and techniques useful in data analysis. This series encourages the integration of mathematical, statistical, and computational methods and techniques through the publication of a broad range of textbooks, reference works, and handbooks. The inclusion of concrete examples and applications is highly encouraged. The scope of the series includes, but is not limited to, titles in the areas of data mining and knowledge discovery methods and applications, modeling, algorithms, theory and foundations, data and knowledge visualization, data mining systems and tools, and privacy and security issues.

## PUBLISHED TITLES

ADVANCES IN MACHINE LEARNING AND DATA MINING FOR ASTRONOMY
**Michael J. Way, Jeffrey D. Scargle, Kamal M. Ali, and Ashok N. Srivastava**

BIOLOGICAL DATA MINING
**Jake Y. Chen and Stefano Lonardi**

COMPUTATIONAL METHODS OF FEATURE SELECTION
**Huan Liu and Hiroshi Motoda**

CONSTRAINED CLUSTERING: ADVANCES IN ALGORITHMS, THEORY, AND APPLICATIONS
**Sugato Basu, Ian Davidson, and Kiri L. Wagstaff**

CONTRAST DATA MINING: CONCEPTS, ALGORITHMS, AND APPLICATIONS
**Guozhu Dong and James Bailey**

DATA CLUSTERING IN C++: AN OBJECT-ORIENTED APPROACH
**Guojun Gan**

DATA MINING FOR DESIGN AND MARKETING
**Yukio Ohsawa and Katsutoshi Yada**

DATA MINING WITH R: LEARNING WITH CASE STUDIES
**Luís Torgo**

FOUNDATIONS OF PREDICTIVE ANALYTICS
**James Wu and Stephen Coggeshall**

GEOGRAPHIC DATA MINING AND KNOWLEDGE DISCOVERY, SECOND EDITION
**Harvey J. Miller and Jiawei Han**

HANDBOOK OF EDUCATIONAL DATA MINING
**Cristóbal Romero, Sebastian Ventura, Mykola Pechenizkiy, and Ryan S.J.d. Baker**

INFORMATION DISCOVERY ON ELECTRONIC HEALTH RECORDS
**Vagelis Hristidis**

INTELLIGENT TECHNOLOGIES FOR WEB APPLICATIONS
**Priti Srinivas Sajja and Rajendra Akerkar**

INTRODUCTION TO PRIVACY-PRESERVING DATA PUBLISHING:
CONCEPTS AND TECHNIQUES
**Benjamin C. M. Fung, Ke Wang, Ada Wai-Chee Fu, and Philip S. Yu**

KNOWLEDGE DISCOVERY FOR COUNTERTERRORISM AND LAW ENFORCEMENT
**David Skillicorn**

KNOWLEDGE DISCOVERY FROM DATA STREAMS
**João Gama**

MACHINE LEARNING AND KNOWLEDGE DISCOVERY FOR
ENGINEERING SYSTEMS HEALTH MANAGEMENT
**Ashok N. Srivastava and Jiawei Han**

MINING SOFTWARE SPECIFICATIONS: METHODOLOGIES AND APPLICATIONS
**David Lo, Siau-Cheng Khoo, Jiawei Han, and Chao Liu**

MULTIMEDIA DATA MINING: A SYSTEMATIC INTRODUCTION TO CONCEPTS AND THEORY
**Zhongfei Zhang and Ruofei Zhang**

MUSIC DATA MINING
**Tao Li, Mitsunori Ogihara, and George Tzanetakis**

NEXT GENERATION OF DATA MINING
**Hillol Kargupta, Jiawei Han, Philip S. Yu, Rajeev Motwani, and Vipin Kumar**

RELATIONAL DATA CLUSTERING: MODELS, ALGORITHMS, AND APPLICATIONS
**Bo Long, Zhongfei Zhang, and Philip S. Yu**

SERVICE-ORIENTED DISTRIBUTED KNOWLEDGE DISCOVERY
**Domenico Talia and Paolo Trunfio**

SPECTRAL FEATURE SELECTION FOR DATA MINING
**Zheng Alan Zhao and Huan Liu**

STATISTICAL DATA MINING USING SAS APPLICATIONS, SECOND EDITION
**George Fernandez**

SUPPORT VECTOR MACHINES: OPTIMIZATION BASED THEORY, ALGORITHMS,
AND EXTENSIONS
**Naiyang Deng, Yingjie Tian, and Chunhua Zhang**

TEMPORAL DATA MINING
**Theophano Mitsa**

TEXT MINING: CLASSIFICATION, CLUSTERING, AND APPLICATIONS
**Ashok N. Srivastava and Mehran Sahami**

THE TOP TEN ALGORITHMS IN DATA MINING
**Xindong Wu and Vipin Kumar**

UNDERSTANDING COMPLEX DATASETS:
DATA MINING WITH MATRIX DECOMPOSITIONS
**David Skillicorn**

# Support Vector Machines

## Optimization Based Theory, Algorithms, and Extensions

Naiyang Deng

Yingjie Tian

Chunhua Zhang

CRC Press
Taylor & Francis Group
Boca Raton London New York

CRC Press is an imprint of the
Taylor & Francis Group, an **informa** business

A CHAPMAN & HALL BOOK

CRC Press
Taylor & Francis Group
6000 Broken Sound Parkway NW, Suite 300
Boca Raton, FL 33487-2742

© 2013 by Taylor & Francis Group, LLC
CRC Press is an imprint of Taylor & Francis Group, an Informa business

No claim to original U.S. Government works

Printed in the United States of America on acid-free paper
Version Date: 20121112

International Standard Book Number: 978-1-4398-5792-2 (Hardback)

**Visit the Taylor & Francis Web site at**
**http://www.taylorandfrancis.com**

**and the CRC Press Web site at**
**http://www.crcpress.com**

*Dedicated to my beloved wife Meifang*

Naiyang Deng

*Dedicated to my dearest father Mingran Tian*

Yingjie Tian

*Dedicated to my husband Xingang Xu and my son Kaiwen Xu*

Chunhua Zhang

# Contents

# List of Figures

# List of Tables

# Preface

*Support vector machines* (SVMs), which were introduced by Vapnik in the early 1990s, have proven effective and promising techniques for data mining. SVMs have recently made breakthroughs and advances in their theoretical studies and implementations of algorithms. They have been successfully applied in many fields such as text categorization, speech recognition, remote sensing image analysis, time series forecasting, information security, and so forth.

SVMs, having their roots in Statistical Learning Theory (SLT) and optimization methods, have become powerful tools to solve the problems of machine learning with finite training points and to overcome some traditional difficulties such as the "curse of dimensionality", "over-fitting", and so forth. Their theoretical foundation and implementation techniques have been established and SVMs are gaining quick popularity due to their many attractive features: nice mathematical representations, geometrical explanations, good generalization abilities, and promising empirical performance. Some SVM monographs, including more sophisticated ones such as Cristianini & Shawe-Taylor [39] and Scholkopf & Smola [124], have been published.

We have published two books in Chinese about SVMs in Science Press of China since 2004 [42, 43], which attracted widespread interest and received favorable comments in China. After several years of research and teaching, we decided to rewrite the books and add new research achicvements. The starting point and focus of the book is optimization theory, which is different from other books on SVMs in this respect. Optimization is one of the pillars on which SVMs are built, so it makes a lot of sense to consider them from this point of view.

This book introduces SVMs systematically and comprehensively. We place emphasis on the readability and the importance of perception on a sound understanding of SVMs. Prior to systematical and rigorous discourses, concepts are introduced graphically, and the methods and conclusions are proposed by direct inspection or with visual explanation. Particularly, for some important concepts and algorithms we try our best to give clearly geometric interpretations that are not depicted in the literature, such as Crammer-Singer SVM for multiclass classification problems.

We give details on classification problems and regression problems that are the two main components of SVMs. We formated this book uniformly by using the classification problem as the principal axis and converting the regression problem to the classification problem. The book is organized as follows. In Chapter 1 the optimization fundamentals are introduced. The convex programming encompassing traditional convex optimization (Sections 1.1–1.3) and conic programming (Sections 1.4-1.5). Sections 1.1–1.3 are necessary background for the later chapters. For beginners, Sections 1.4 and 1.5 (marked with an asterisk *) can be skipped since they are used only in Subsections 8.4.3 and 8.8.3 of Chapter 8, and are mainly served for further research. Support vector machines begin from Chapter 2 starting from linear classification problems. Based on the maximal margin principal, the basic linear support vector classification is derived visually in Chapter 2. Linear support vector regression is established in Chapter 3. The kernel theory, which is the key of extension of basic SVMs and the foundation for solving nonlinear problems, together with the general classification and regression problems, are discussed in Chapter 4. Starting with statistical interpretation of the maximal margin method, statistical learning theory, which is the groundwork of SVMs, is studied in Chapter 5. The model construction problems, which are very useful in practical applications, are discussed in Chapter 6. The implementations of several prevailing SVM's algorithms are introduced in Chapter 7. Finally, the variations and extensions of SVMs including multiclass classification, semisupervised classification, knowledge-based classification, Universum classification, privileged classification, robust classification, multi-instance classification, and multi-label classification are covered in Chapter 8.

The contents of this book comprise our research achievements. A precise and concise interpretation of statistical leaning theory for $C$-support vector classification ($C$-SVC) is given in Chapter 5 which imbues the parameter $C$ with a new meaning. From our achievements the following results of SVMs are also given: the regularized twin SVMs for binary classification problems, the SVMs for solving multi-classification problems based on the idea of ordinal regression, the SVMs for semisupervised problems by means of constructing second order cone programming or semidefinite programming models, and the SVMs for problems with perturbations.

Potential readers include those who are beginners in the SVM and those who are interested in solving real-world problems by employing SVMs, and those who will conduct more comprehensive study of SVMs.

We are indebted to all the people who have helped in various ways. We would like to say special thanks to Dr. Hang Li, Chief Scientist of Noah's Ark Lab of Huawei Technologies, academicians Zhiming Ma and Yaxiang Yuan of Chinese Academy of Sciences, Dr. Mingren Shi of University of Western Australia, Prof. Changyu Wang and Prof. Yiju Wang of Qufu Normal University, Prof. Zunquan Xia and Liwei Zhang of Dalian University of Technology, Prof. Naihua Xiu of Beijing Jiaotong University, Prof. Yanqin Bai of Shanghai University, and Prof. Ling Jing of China Agricultural University for their valuable suggestions. Our gratitude goes also to Prof. Xiangsun Zhang and Prof. Yong Shi of Chinese Academy of Sciences, and Prof. Shuzhong Zhang of The Chinese University of Hong Kong for their great help and support. We appreciate assistance from the members of our workshop — Dr. Zhixia Yang, Dr. Kun Zhao, Dr. Yongcui Wang, Dr. Xiaojian Shao, Dr. Ruxin Qin, Dr. Yuanhai Shao, Dr. Junyan Tan, Ms. Yanmei Zhao, Ms. Tingting Gao, and Ms. Yuxin Li.

Finally, we would like acknowledge a number of funding agencies that provided their generous support to our research activities on this book. They are the Publishing Foundation of The Ministry of Science and Technology of China, and the National Natural Science Foundation of China, including the innovative group grant "Data Mining and Intelligent Knowledge Management" (♯70621001, ♯70921061); the general project " Knowledge Driven Support Vector Machines Theory, Algorithms and Applications" (♯ 11271361); the general project "Models and Algorithms for Support Vector Machines with Adaptive Norms" (♯ 11201480); the general project "The Optimization Methods in Multi-label Multi-instance Learning and its Applications" (♯10971223); the general project "The Optimization Methods of Kernel Matrix Learning and its Applications in Bioinformatics" (♯11071252); the CAS/SAFEA International Partnership Program for Creative Research Teams; the President Fund of GUCAS; and the National Technology Support Program 2009BAH42B02.

# List of Symbols

| | | | |
|---|---|---|---|
| $R$ | real numbers | w | weight vector in $\mathcal{H}$ |
| $x \in R^n$ | input and Euclidian space | $\mathrm{w}_i$ | the $i$th component of w |
| $y \in \mathcal{Y}$ | output and set of output | $b$ | threshold |
| $(x_i, y_i)$ | the $i$th training point | $K(x, x')$ | kernel function $(\Phi(x) \cdot \Phi(x'))$ |
| $T = \{(x_1, y_1), \cdots, (x_l, y_l)\}$ | training set | $K$ | kernel matrix (Gram matrix) |
| $l$ | number of training points | $\|\cdot\|_p$ | $p$-norm |
| $[x]_i, [x_i]_j$ | the $i$th component of the vector $x$, the $j$th component of the vector $[x_i]_j$ | $\|\cdot\|$ | 2-norm |
| | | $\|\cdot\|_1$ | 1-norm |
| | | $h$ | VC dimension |
| | | $C$ | penalty parameter |
| $\mathrm{x} = \Phi(x)$ | vector in Hilbert space and mapping from input space into Hilbert space | $\xi$ | vector of slack variables |
| $[\mathrm{x}]_i, [\mathrm{x}_i]_j$ | the $i$th component of vector x, the $j$th component of vector $\mathrm{x}_i$ | $\xi_i$ | the $i$th component of $\xi$ |
| | | $\alpha$ | dual variables, vector of Lagrange multipliers |
| $(x \cdot x')$, $(\mathrm{x} \cdot \mathrm{x}')$ | inner product between $x$ and $x'$, inner product between x and x′ | $\alpha_i$ | the $i$th component of $\alpha$ |
| | | $\beta$ | dual variables, vector of Lagrange multipliers |
| $\mathcal{H}$ | Hilbert space | | |
| $w$ | weight vector in $R^n$ | $\beta_i$ | the $i$th component of $\beta$ |
| $w_i$ | the $i$th component of $w$ | $P(\cdot)$ | possibility distribution or possibility |

# Chapter 1

## *Optimization*

As the foundation of SVMs, the optimization fundamentals are introduced in this chapter. It includes two parts: the basic part — Sections 1.1–1.3 and the advanced part — Sections 1.4–1.5. Sections 1.1, 1.2 and Section 1.3 are respectively concerned with the traditional convex optimization in Euclidian space and Hilbert space. For the readers who are not interested in the strict mathematical argument, Section 1.3 can be read quickly just by comparing the corresponding conclusions in Hilbert space and the ones in Euclidian space, and believing that the similar conclusions in Hilbert space are true. Sections 1.4–1.5 are mainly concerned with the conic programming and can be skipped for those beginners since they are only used in the later subsections 8.4.3 and 8.8.4. In fact they are mainly served for further research. We believe that, for the development of SVMs, many applications of conic programming are still waiting to be discovered.

## 1.1    Optimization Problems in Euclidian Space

### 1.1.1    An example of optimization problems

**Example 1.1.1**    *Suppose that there exist two closed line segments $u_1u_2$ and $v_1v_2$ on the plane $[x]_1 O[x]_2$ (see Figure 1.1). The distance between two points $u \in u_1u_2$ and $v \in v_1v_2$ is denoted as $d(u, v)$. Find the points $u^*$ and $v^*$ such that the distance $d(u, v)$ is minimized at $(u^*, v^*)$ under the restrictions $u \in u_1u_2$ and $v \in v_1v_2$.*

This problem can be formulated as an optimization problem. The points $u$ on the segment $u_1u_2$ and $v$ on $v_1v_2$ can be represented as

$$u = \alpha u_1 + (1 - \alpha)u_2, \quad \alpha \in [0, 1] \tag{1.1.1}$$

and

$$v = \beta v_1 + (1 - \beta)v_2, \quad \beta \in [0, 1] \tag{1.1.2}$$

respectively. Thus the distance between $u$ and $v$ is a function of $(\alpha, \beta)$

$$f(\alpha, \beta) = \|u - v\|^2 = a_{11}\alpha^2 - 2a_{12}\alpha\beta + a_{22}\beta^2 + b_1\alpha + b_2\beta + c, \tag{1.1.3}$$

1

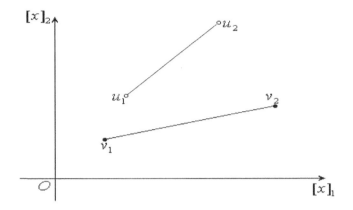

**FIGURE 1.1**: Two line segments in $R^2$.

where the coefficients are given by

$$a_{11} = \|u_1 - u_2\|^2, \qquad a_{12} = (u_1 - u_2)^{\mathrm{T}}(v_1 - v_2), \qquad a_{22} = \|v_1 - v_2\|^2,$$
$$b_1 = 2(u_1 - u_2)^{\mathrm{T}}(u_2 - v_2), \quad b_2 = 2(v_1 - v_2)^{\mathrm{T}}(v_2 - u_2), \quad c = \|u_2 - v_2\|^2.$$
$$(1.1.4)$$

We should find $(\alpha^*, \beta^*)$ at which the function $f(\alpha, \beta)$ obtains its minimum. Note that the variables $\alpha$ and $\beta$ are restricted in the intervals $\alpha \in [0, 1], \beta \in [0, 1]$ respectively. Therefore the problem can be formulated as

$$\min \quad f(\alpha, \beta) = a_{11}\alpha^2 - 2a_{12}\alpha\beta + a_{22}\beta^2 + b_1\alpha + b_2\beta + c, \quad (1.1.5)$$
$$\text{s.t.} \quad 0 \leqslant \alpha \leqslant 1, \qquad\qquad\qquad\qquad\qquad\qquad\qquad (1.1.6)$$
$$0 \leqslant \beta \leqslant 1, \qquad\qquad\qquad\qquad\qquad\qquad\qquad (1.1.7)$$

where the coefficients $a_{ij}$, $i, j = 1, 2$, $b_i$, $i = 1, 2$ and $c$ are given by (1.1.4). Here "min" stands for "minimize", and "s.t." stands for "subject to". The meaning of the problem is to find the minimizer $(\alpha^*, \beta^*)$ of the function $f(\alpha, \beta)$ under restrictions (1.1.6) and (1.1.7). Having got $(\alpha^*, \beta^*)$, the points $u^*$ and $v^*$ with nearest distance can be obtained by

$$u^* = \alpha^* u_1 + (1 - \alpha^*)u_2, \quad v^* = \beta^* v_1 + (1 - \beta^*)v_2. \quad (1.1.8)$$

What we are concerned with now is the problem $(1.1.5) \sim (1.1.7)$. Introducing a two-dimensional vector $x = ([x]_1, [x]_2)^{\mathrm{T}} = (\alpha, \beta)^{\mathrm{T}}$, the problem can be rewritten as

$$\min \quad f_0(x) = a_{11}[x]_1^2 - 2a_{12}[x]_1[x]_2 + a_{22}[x]_2^2 + b_1[x]_1 + b_2[x]_2 + c,$$
$$(1.1.9)$$
$$\text{s.t.} \quad -[x]_1 \leqslant 0, \qquad\qquad\qquad\qquad\qquad\qquad\qquad (1.1.10)$$
$$[x]_1 - 1 \leqslant 0, \qquad\qquad\qquad\qquad\qquad\qquad\qquad (1.1.11)$$
$$-[x]_2 \leqslant 0, \qquad\qquad\qquad\qquad\qquad\qquad\qquad (1.1.12)$$
$$[x]_2 - 1 \leqslant 0, \qquad\qquad\qquad\qquad\qquad\qquad\qquad (1.1.13)$$

where $a_{ij}$, $i,j = 1,2$, $b_i$, $i = 1,2$ and $c$ are given constants.

## 1.1.2 Optimization problems and their solutions

Extending the problem (1.1.9)$\sim$(1.1.13) by changing the two-dimensional vector $x$ into the $n$-dimensional vector $x$, the function involved into the general smooth function, 4 restrictive conditions with inequalities into $m$ ones, and adding $p$ restrictive conditions with equalities, the general optimization problem can be obtained as follows

$$\min \quad f_0(x), x = ([x]_1, \cdots, [x]_n)^{\mathrm{T}} \in R^n, \tag{1.1.14}$$

$$\text{s.t.} \quad f_i(x) \leqslant 0, \ i = 1, \cdots, m, \tag{1.1.15}$$

$$h_i(x) = 0, \ i = 1, \cdots, p. \tag{1.1.16}$$

Here the vector $x$ is called the (optimization) variable of the problem, the function $f_0$ in (1.1.14) is called the objective function. Restrictions (1.1.15) and (1.1.16) are called the constraints; the former the inequality constraints, the latter the equality constraints. $f_i(x), i = 1, \cdots, m$ and $h_i(x), i = 1, \cdots, p$ are called the constraint functions. Problem (1.1.14)$\sim$(1.1.16) is called an unconstrained problem if $m+p = 0$, i.e. there are no constraints; a constrained problem otherwise.

**Definition 1.1.2** *(Feasible point and feasible region) A point satisfying all the constraints is called a feasible point. The set of all such points constitutes the feasible region $D$*

$$D = \{x | f_i(x) \leqslant 0, i = 1, \cdots, m ; h_i(x) = 0, i = 1, \cdots, p ; x \in R^n\}. \tag{1.1.17}$$

**Definition 1.1.3** *(Optimal value) The optimal value $p^*$ of the problem (1.1.14)$\sim$(1.1.16) is defined as the infimum, i.e. the greatest lower bound, of the objective function $f_0$ in the feasible region $D$ when $D$ is not empty; and $p^*$ is defined as infinity, otherwise:*

$$p^* = \begin{cases} \inf\{f_0(x) | x \in D\}, & \text{when } D \neq \phi, \\ \infty, & \text{otherwise.} \end{cases} \tag{1.1.18}$$

**Definition 1.1.4** *(Global solution and local solution) Consider the problem (1.1.14)$\sim$(1.1.16). The point $x^*$ is called a global solution if $x^*$ is a feasible point and*

$$f_0(x^*) = \inf\{f_0(x) | x \in D\} = p^*, \tag{1.1.19}$$

*where $D$ is the feasible region. The point $x^*$ is called a local solution, or just a solution, if $x^*$ is a feasible point and there exists an $\varepsilon > 0$ such that*

$$f_0(x^*) = \inf\{f_0(x) | x \in D ; \|x - x^*\| \leqslant \varepsilon\}. \tag{1.1.20}$$

*The set of all global solutions and the set of all (local) solutions are called the corresponding solution set respectively.*

Obviously, a (local) solution is a point at which the objective function value is smaller than or equal to that at all other feasible points in its vicinity. The best of all the (local) solutions is the global solution.

Problem $(1.1.14)\sim(1.1.16)$ is a minimization problem. However, it should be pointed out that the choice of minimization does not represent a restriction since the maximization problem can be converted to minimization ones by reversing the sign of the objective function $f_0$. Similar consideration shows that a great many restrictive conditions can be written in the form $(1.1.15)\sim(1.1.16)$.

### 1.1.3   Geometric interpretation of optimization problems

For the optimization problems in $R^2$, the geometric interpretation is clear and can be illustrated by the following example.

**Example 1.1.5**   *Suppose that two line segments $u_1u_2$ and $v_1v_2$ are given by*

$$u_1 = (0,0)^T, \quad u_2 = (1,0)^T, \quad v_1 = (1,1)^T, \quad v_2 = (2,2)^T, \qquad (1.1.21)$$

*(see Figure 1.2). Optimization problem $(1.1.9)\sim(1.1.13)$ becomes*

$$
\begin{align}
\min \quad & f_0(x) = [x]_1^2 - 2[x]_1[x]_2 + 2[x]_2^2 + 2[x]_1 - 6[x]_2 + 5, & (1.1.22)\\
\text{s.t.} \quad & f_1(x) = -[x]_1 \leqslant 0, & (1.1.23)\\
& f_2(x) = [x]_1 - 1 \leqslant 0, & (1.1.24)\\
& f_3(x) = -[x]_2 \leqslant 0, & (1.1.25)\\
& f_4(x) = [x]_2 - 1 \leqslant 0. & (1.1.26)
\end{align}
$$

*Solve the above problem by graphical method.*

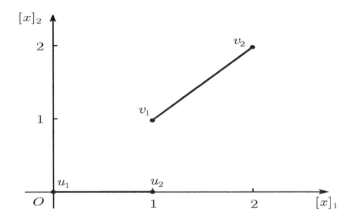

**FIGURE 1.2**: Two line segments $u_1u_2$ and $v_1v_2$ given by (1.1.21).

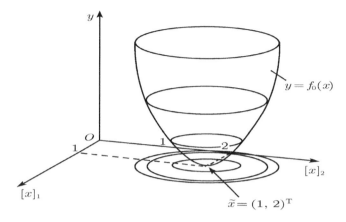

**FIGURE 1.3**: Graph of $f_0(x)$ given by (1.1.22).

The surface of the objective function is depicted in Figure 1.3. Its lowest point lies just on the coordinate plane $[x]_1 O[x]_2$ with the coordinates $(1,2)^{\mathrm{T}} = \tilde{x}$. This implies that $\tilde{x}$ is the global solution to the unconstrained problem

$$\min \quad f_0(x), x \in R^2. \tag{1.1.27}$$

However $\tilde{x}$ is not a solution to our constrained problem since the feasible region is the square $ABOC$ with its boundary by constraints $(1.1.23)\sim(1.1.26)$ and $\tilde{x}$ lies outside of it (see Figure 1.4), where the feasible square is shaded. Note that the contours of the objective function $f_0$, i.e. the set of points for which $f_0$ has a constant value, are a set of ellipses with center at $\tilde{x}$. So it can be observed that the vertex $x^* = B = (0,1)^{\mathrm{T}}$ of the feasible square is the global solution of the constrained problem since the ellipse with $f_0 = 1$ is tangent to one side $AB$ of the square at $x^*$.

In the optimization problem $(1.1.14)\sim(1.1.16)$, the objective function and the constrained functions are allowed to be any functions, see [40, 41, 78, 100, 164, 172, 183, 6, 54, 91, 111, 112]. Due to the lack of the effective methods for solving such general problems, we do not study it further and turn to some special optimization problems below.

## 1.2 Convex Programming in Euclidean Space

Among the optimization problems introduced in the above section, the convex optimization problems are important and closely related with the main topic of this book. They can be solved efficiently (see [9, 10, 17] for further reading).

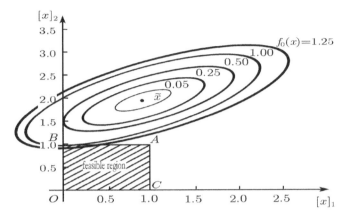

**FIGURE 1.4**: Illustration of the problem $(1.1.22)\sim(1.1.26)$.

## 1.2.1 Convex sets and convex functions

### 1.2.1.1 Convex sets

Let us introduce the convex set in $R^n$ first.

**Definition 1.2.1** *(Convex set) A set $S \subset R^n$ is called a convex set if the straight line segment connecting any two points in $S$ lies entirely in $S$, i.e. for any $x_1, x_2 \in S$ and any $\lambda \in [0, 1]$, we have*

$$\lambda x_1 + (1 - \lambda)x_2 \in S . \tag{1.2.1}$$

Intuitively, in the two-dimensional space $R^2$, the circle shaped set in Figure 1.5(a) is a convex set, while the kidney shaped set in Figure 1.5(b) is not since the line segment connecting the two points in the set shown as dots is not contained in this set. It is easy to prove the following conclusion, which

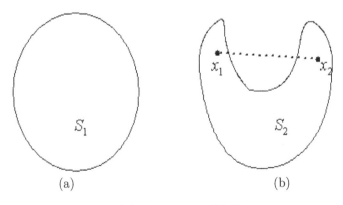

**FIGURE 1.5**: (a) Convex set; (b) Non-convex set.

shows that the convexity is preserved under intersection. This is illustrated in Figure 1.6.

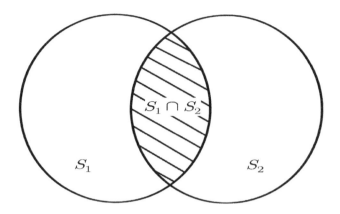

**FIGURE 1.6**: Intersection of two convex sets.

**Theorem 1.2.2** *If $S_1$ and $S_2$ are convex sets, then their intersection $S_1 \cap S_2$ is also a convex set.*

### 1.2.1.2 Convex functions

**Definition 1.2.3** *(Convex function) Let $f$ be a function defined on $R^n$. The function $f$ is called a convex function on $R^n$ if for any two points $x_1, x_2 \in R^n$, the graph of $f$ lies below the straight line connecting $(x_1, f(x_1))$ and $(x_2, f(x_2))$. That is, for any $\lambda \in [0, 1]$,*

$$f(\lambda x_1 + (1 - \lambda)x_2) \leqslant \lambda f(x_1) + (1 - \lambda)f(x_2) . \tag{1.2.2}$$

*The function $f$ is called a strictly convex function on $R^n$ if strictly inequality holds in (1.2.2) whenever $x_1 \neq x_2$ and $\lambda \in (0, 1)$.*

Intuitively, when $f$ is smooth as well as convex and the dimension $n$ is 1 or 2, the graph of $f$ is bowl-shaped, see Figures 1.7(a) and 1.8(a). The functions shown in Figures 1.7(b), 1.8(b), and 1.8(c) are not convex functions.

The following theorem gives the characteristic of a convex function.

**Theorem 1.2.4** *(Sufficient and necessary condition) Let $f$ be continuously differentiable on $R^n$. Then $f$ is a convex function if and only if for all $x, \bar{x} \in R^n$,*

$$f(x) \geqslant f(\bar{x}) + \nabla f(\bar{x})^{\mathrm{T}}(x - \bar{x}). \tag{1.2.3}$$

*Similarly, $f$ is a strictly convex function if and only if strict inequality holds in (1.2.3) whenever $x \neq \bar{x}$.*

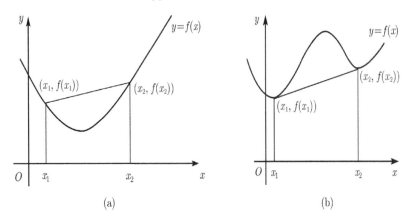

FIGURE 1.7: Geometric illustration of convex and non-convex functions in $R$: (a) convex; (b) non-convex.

**Corollary 1.2.5** *Consider the quadratic function in $R^n$*

$$f(x) = \frac{1}{2}x^{\mathrm{T}}Hx + r^{\mathrm{T}}x + \delta , \qquad (1.2.4)$$

*where $H \in R^{n \times n}$, $r \in R^n$, $\delta \in R$. If $H$ is positive semidefinite, then $f(x)$ is a convex function in $R^n$. Similarly, if $H$ is positive definite, then $f(x)$ is a strictly convex function in $R^n$.*

**Proof** We only show the conclusion when $H$ is positive semidefinite. Noticing $\nabla^2 f(x) = H$, we have

$$f(x) = f(\bar{x}) + \nabla f(\bar{x})^{\mathrm{T}}(x - \bar{x}) + \frac{1}{2}(x - \bar{x})^{\mathrm{T}}H(x - \bar{x}) \qquad (1.2.5)$$

for all $x, \bar{x} \in R^n$. As the semidefiniteness of $H$ implies that $(x - \bar{x})^{\mathrm{T}}H(x - \bar{x}) \geqslant 0$, the above equality leads to

$$f(x) \geqslant f(\bar{x}) + \nabla f(\bar{x})^{\mathrm{T}}(x - \bar{x}), \qquad (1.2.6)$$

which proves that $f(x)$ is a convex function by Theorem 1.2.4. ∎

### 1.2.2    Convex programming and their properties

#### 1.2.2.1    Convex programming problems

Instead of the general optimization problem $(1.1.14)\sim(1.1.16)$, we shall focus our attention on its special case: convex programming problems.

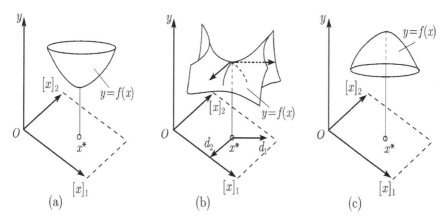

**FIGURE 1.8**: Geometric illustration of convex and non-convex functions in $R^2$: (a) convex; (b)(c) non-convex.

**Definition 1.2.6** *(Convex programming problem) A convex programming problem is an optimization problem in the form*

$$\min \quad f_0(x), \ x \in R^n, \tag{1.2.7}$$
$$s.t. \quad f_i(x) \leqslant 0 \ , \ i = 1, \cdots, m \ , \tag{1.2.8}$$
$$h_i(x) = a_i^T x - b_i = 0 \ , \ i = 1, \cdots, p, \tag{1.2.9}$$

*where $f_0(x)$ and $f_i(x), i = 1, \cdots, m$ are continuous convex functions on $R^n$, and $h_i(x), \ i = 1, \cdots, p$ are linear functions.*

The following theorem can be obtained from Corollary 1.2.5.

**Theorem 1.2.7** *Consider the quadratic programming (QP) problem*

$$\min \quad \frac{1}{2} x^T H x + r^T x, \ x \in R^n, \tag{1.2.10}$$
$$s.t. \quad \bar{A} x - \bar{b} \leqslant 0, \tag{1.2.11}$$
$$A x - b = 0, \tag{1.2.12}$$

*where $H \in R^{n \times n}$, $r \in R^n$, $\bar{A} \in R^{m \times n}$, $A \in R^{p \times n}$, $\bar{b} \in R^m, b \in R^p$. If $H$ is positive semidefinite, then the above problem is a convex programming, i.e. a convex quadratic programming problem.*

### 1.2.2.2 Basic properties

The following lemma leads to the property of the feasible region of a convex programming problem.

**Lemma 1.2.8**  *If $f(x)$ is a convex function on $R^n$, then for any $c \in R$, the level set*

$$S = \{x | f(x) \leqslant c, \ x \in R^n\} \qquad (1.2.13)$$

*is convex.*

**Proof** Suppose $x_1, x_2 \in S$. It is easy to see that $f(x_1) \leqslant c, f(x_2) \leqslant c$. Let $x = \lambda x_1 + (1 - \lambda)x_2$, where $\lambda \in [0, 1]$. Thus, the convexity of $f(x)$ implies that

$$f(x) = f(\lambda x_1 + (1 - \lambda)x_2) \leqslant \lambda f(x_1) + (1 - \lambda)f(x_2) \leqslant \lambda c + (1 - \lambda)c = c,$$
$$(1.2.14)$$

and hence $x \in S$. Therefore $S$ is convex. ∎

Lemma 1.2.8 and Theorem 1.2.2 lead to the following theorem.

**Theorem 1.2.9**  *Consider problem $(1.2.7)\sim(1.2.9)$. Then both its feasible region and solution set are convex closed sets.*

Thus solving a convex programming problem is just to find the minimal value of a convex function on a convex set.

**Theorem 1.2.10**  *Consider the problem $(1.2.7)\sim(1.2.9)$. If $x^*$ is its local solution, then $x^*$ is also its global solution.*

**Proof** Suppose that $x^*$ is a local solution, i.e. there exists an $\varepsilon > 0$ such that

$$f_0(x^*) = \inf\{f_0(x) | x \in D, \|x - x^*\| \leqslant \varepsilon\}, \qquad (1.2.15)$$

where $D$ is the feasible field. Now we show $x^*$ is a global solution by contradiction. If $x^*$ is not a global solution, there would be a $\bar{x} \in D$, such that $f_0(\bar{x}) < f_0(x^*)$ and $\|\bar{x} - x^*\| > \varepsilon > 0$ by (1.2.15). Now let us examine the objective value $f(z)$, where $z$ is defined by

$$z = (1 - \theta)x^* + \theta\bar{x}, \qquad \theta = \frac{\varepsilon}{2\|\bar{x} - x^*\|}. \qquad (1.2.16)$$

On one hand, according to Theorem 1.2.9, the feasible field $D$ is convex. Therefore, the convexity of $f_0(x)$ implies that

$$f_0(z) \leqslant (1 - \theta)f_0(x^*) + \theta f_0(\bar{x}) < f_0(x^*). \qquad (1.2.17)$$

On the other hand, noticing $\|z - x^*\| = \dfrac{\varepsilon}{2} < \varepsilon$, equality (1.2.15) yields

$$f_0(x^*) \leqslant f_0(z). \qquad (1.2.18)$$

This is a contradiction with inequality (1.2.17), and the conclusion follows. ∎

Note that general optimization problems may have local solutions that are not global solutions. However, the above theorem indicates that, for convex programming, there is not any difference between local solutions and global solutions. This is an important characteristic of convex programming because what we are concerned with in applications is usually global solution and the most efficient optimization algorithms seek only a local solution.

**Corollary 1.2.11** *Consider the problem (1.2.10)~ (1.2.12) where H is positive semidefinite. Then its local solution is its global solution.*

Next theorem is concerned with the relationship between the uniqueness of solution and the strict convexity of the objective function. It is a particular case of Theorem 1.2.15 below.

**Theorem 1.2.12** *Consider the problem (1.2.7)~(1.2.9), where the objective function $f_0(x)$ is strictly convex. Then its solution is unique when it has solution.*

Among the components of a solution $x^*$ to the problem (1.2.7)~(1.2.9), the main issue that concerns us may be only a part of them instead of all of them sometimes. In this case, the $n$-dimensional vector $x$ is partitioned into

$$x = \begin{pmatrix} x_1 \\ x_2 \end{pmatrix}, \quad \text{where } x_i \in R^{m_i}, \quad i = 1, 2, \quad m_1 + m_2 = n, \qquad (1.2.19)$$

and the following definition is introduced.

**Definition 1.2.13** *Consider the problem (1.2.7)~(1.2.9) with variable $x$ being partitioned into the form (1.2.19). Vector $x_1^* \in R^{m_1}$ is called its solution with respect to (w.r.t.) $x_1$ if there exists a vector $x_2^* \in R^{m_2}$, such that $x^* = (x_1^{*\mathrm{T}}, x_2^{*\mathrm{T}})^\mathrm{T}$ is its solution. The set of all solutions w.r.t. $x_1$ are called the solution set w.r.t. $x_1$.*

For the convex programming with partitioned variable, we have the following theorems.

**Theorem 1.2.14** *Consider the problem (1.2.7)~(1.2.9) with variable $x$ being partitioned into the form (1.2.19). Then its solution set w.r.t. $x_1$ is a convex closed set.*

**Proof** The conclusion follows from Theorem 1.2.9 and Definition 1.2.13. ∎

**Theorem 1.2.15** *Consider the problem (1.2.7)~(1.2.9) with variable $x$ being partitioned into the form (1.2.19). If*

$$f_0(x) = F_1(x_1) + F_2(x_2), \qquad (1.2.20)$$

*where $F_1(x_1)$ is a strictly convex function of the variable $x_1$, then the solution to the convex programming w.r.t. $x_1$ is unique when it has a solution.*

**Proof** It is sufficient to show by contradiction that if both $\bar{x} = (\bar{x}_1^\mathrm{T}, \bar{x}_2^\mathrm{T})^\mathrm{T}$ and $\bar{\bar{x}} = (\bar{\bar{x}}_1^\mathrm{T}, \bar{\bar{x}}_2^\mathrm{T})^\mathrm{T}$ are solutions, we have

$$\bar{x}_1 = \bar{\bar{x}}_1. \qquad (1.2.21)$$

In fact, if
$$\bar{x}_1 \neq \bar{\bar{x}}_2, \tag{1.2.22}$$

construct the vector

$$x(t) = (1 - t)\bar{x} + t\bar{\bar{x}}, \quad t \in [0, 1]. \tag{1.2.23}$$

Noticing that the solution set is convex and any local solution is a global solution by Theorem 1.2.9 and Theorem 1.2.10, vector $x(t)$ is always a global solution for any $t \in [0, 1]$, implying that

$$f_0(x(t)) = \text{constant}, \forall t \in [0, 1]. \tag{1.2.24}$$

However, according to (1.2.20) and (1.2.23), we have

$$f_0(x(t)) = F_1(x_1(t)) + F_2(x_2(t)), \tag{1.2.25}$$

where
$$x_1(t) = (1 - t)\bar{x}_1 + t\bar{\bar{x}}_1, \quad x_2(t) = (1 - t)\bar{x}_2 + t\bar{\bar{x}}_2. \tag{1.2.26}$$

Note that $F_1(x_1(t))$ is strictly convex by (1.2.22) and the strict convexity of $F_1(x_1)$. And $F_2(x_2(t))$ is convex since the convexity of $f_0(x)$ implies that $F_2(x_2)$ is convex. Therefore, according to (1.2.25), we conclude that $f_0(x(t))$ is strictly convex. This is a contradiction with (1.2.24) and the conclusion is obtained. ∎

## 1.2.3   Duality theory

### 1.2.3.1   Derivation of the dual problem

Consider the convex programming problem (1.2.7)~(1.2.9)

$$\begin{align}
\min \quad & f_0(x), x \in R^n, \tag{1.2.27} \\
\text{s.t} \quad & f_i(x) \leqslant 0, \ i = 1, \cdots, m, \tag{1.2.28} \\
& h_i(x) = a_i^T x - b_i = 0, \ i = 1, \cdots, p, \tag{1.2.29}
\end{align}$$

where $f_i(x), i = 0, 1, \cdots, m$ are continuously differentiable and convex in $R^n$. We start from estimating its optimal value $p^*$ defined by Definition 1.1.3

$$p^* = \inf\{f_0(x) | x \in D\}, \tag{1.2.30}$$

where

$$D = \{x | f_i(x) \leqslant 0, i = 1, \cdots, m; h_i(x) = 0, i = 1, \cdots, p; \ x \in R^n\}. \tag{1.2.31}$$

Introduce the Lagrangian function

$$L(x, \lambda, \nu) = f_0(x) + \sum_{i=1}^{m} \lambda_i f_i(x) + \sum_{i=1}^{p} \nu_i h_i(x), \tag{1.2.32}$$

where $\lambda = (\lambda_1, \cdots, \lambda_m)^{\mathrm{T}}$ and $\nu = (\nu_1, \cdots, \nu_p)^{\mathrm{T}}$ are Lagrangian multipliers. Obviously, when $x \in D, \lambda \geqslant 0$, we have

$$L(x, \lambda, \nu) \leqslant f_0(x), \qquad (1.2.33)$$

thus

$$\inf_{x \in R^n} L(x, \lambda, \nu) \leqslant \inf_{x \in D} L(x, \lambda, \nu) \leqslant \inf_{x \in D} f_0(x) = p^*. \qquad (1.2.34)$$

Therefore, introducing the Lagrangian dual function

$$g(\lambda, \nu) = \inf_{x \in R^n} L(x, \lambda, \nu), \qquad (1.2.35)$$

yields

$$g(\lambda, \nu) \leqslant p^*. \qquad (1.2.36)$$

The above inequality indicates that, for any $\lambda \geqslant 0, g(\lambda, \nu)$ is a lower bound of $p^*$. Among these lower bounds, finding the best one leads to the optimization problem

$$\max \quad g(\lambda, \nu) = \inf_{x \in R^n} L(x, \lambda, \nu), \qquad (1.2.37)$$

$$\text{s.t.} \quad \lambda \geqslant 0, \qquad (1.2.38)$$

where $L(x, \lambda, \nu)$ is the Lagrangian function given by (1.2.32).

**Definition 1.2.16** *(Dual problem) Problem* (1.2.37)~(1.2.38) *is called the dual problem of the problem* (1.2.27)~(1.2.29). *Correspondingly, problem* (1.2.27)~(1.2.29) *is called the primal problem.*

It is easy to show the following conclusion.

**Theorem 1.2.17** *Dual problem* (1.2.37)~(1.2.38) *is a convex programming problem.*

#### 1.2.3.2 Duality theory

**(1) Weak duality theorem**
The optimal value of the dual problem (1.2.37)~(1.2.38), which we denote $d^*$

$$d^* = \sup\{g(\lambda, \nu) | \lambda \geqslant 0\} \qquad (1.2.39)$$

is, by definition, the best lower bound on $p^*$ that can be obtained. In particular, we have the following theorem.

**Theorem 1.2.18** *(Weak duality theorem) Let $p^*$ be the optimal value of the primal problem* (1.2.27)~(1.2.29) *and $d^*$ be the optimal value of the dual problem* (1.2.37)~(1.2.38). *Then*

$$p^* = \inf\{f_0(x) | f_i(x) \leqslant 0, i = 1, \cdots, m; a_i^{\mathrm{T}} x - b_i = 0, i = 1, \cdots, p; \ x \in R^n\}$$
$$\geqslant \sup\{g(\lambda, \nu) | \lambda \geqslant 0\} = d^*. \qquad (1.2.40)$$

Note that the inequality (1.2.40) still holds when $p^*$ and $d^*$ are infinite. For example, if the primal problem is unbounded below, so that $p^* = -\infty$, we must have $d^* = -\infty$, i.e. the dual problem is infeasible. Conversely, if the dual problem is unbounded above, so that $d^* = \infty$, we have $p^* = \infty$, i.e. the primal problem is infeasible.

The following corollary is a direct conclusion of the above theorem.

**Corollary 1.2.19** *Let $\tilde{x}$ be the feasible point of the problem (1.2.27)~(1.2.29) and $(\tilde{\lambda}, \tilde{\nu})$ be the feasible point of the dual problem (1.2.37)~(1.2.38). If $f_0(\tilde{x}) = g(\tilde{\lambda}, \tilde{\nu})$, then $\tilde{x}$ and $(\tilde{\lambda}, \tilde{\nu})$ are their solutions respectively.*

**(2) Strong duality theorem**

Strong duality theorem concerns the case where the inequality in (1.2.40) holds with equality. For convex programming, this equality holds under some conditions. One of these conditions is Slater's condition.

**Definition 1.2.20** *(Slater's condition) Convex programming problem (1.2.27)~ (1.2.29) is said to satisfy Slater's condition if there exists a feasible point $x$ such that*

$$f_i(x) < 0, i = 1, \cdots, m; \qquad a_i^{\mathrm{T}} x - b_i = 0, i = 1, \cdots, p. \qquad (1.2.41)$$

*Or, when the first $k$ inequality constraints are linear constraints, there exists a feasible point $x$ such that*

$$f_i(x) = \bar{a}_i^{\mathrm{T}} x - \bar{b}_i \leqslant 0, i = 1, \cdots, k; \quad f_i(x) < 0, i = k+1, \cdots, m;$$
$$a_i^{\mathrm{T}} x - b_i = 0, i = 1, \cdots, p. \qquad (1.2.42)$$

**Theorem 1.2.21** *(Strong duality theorem) Consider the convex programming problem (1.2.27)~(1.2.29) satisfying Slater's condition. Let $p^*$ be the optimal value of the primal problem (1.2.27)~(1.2.29) and $d^*$ the optimal value of the dual problem (1.2.37)~(1.2.38). Then*

$$p^* = \inf\{f_0(x)|f_i(x) \leqslant 0, i = 1, \cdots, m; a_i^{\mathrm{T}} x - b_i = 0, i = 1, \cdots, p; \ x \in R^n\}$$
$$= \sup\{g(\lambda, \nu)|\lambda \geqslant 0\} = d^*. \qquad (1.2.43)$$

*Furthermore, if $p^*$ is attained, i.e. there exists a solution $x^*$ to the primal problem, then $d^*$ is also attained, i.e. there exists a global solution $(\lambda^*, \nu^*)$ to the dual problem such that*

$$p^* = f_0(x^*) = g(\lambda^*, \nu^*) = d^* < \infty. \qquad (1.2.44)$$

**Proof** See [17].                                                                    ∎

## 1.2.4　Optimality conditions

First introduce the famous Karush-Kuhn-Tucker (KKT) conditions:

**Definition 1.2.22** *(KKT conditions) Consider the convex programming problem* (1.2.27)~(1.2.29). *Point* $x^*$ *is said to satisfy the KKT conditions if there exist the multipliers* $\lambda^* = (\lambda_1^*, \cdots, \lambda_m^*)^{\mathrm{T}}$ *and* $\nu^* = (\nu_1^*, \cdots, \nu_p^*)^{\mathrm{T}}$ *corresponding to constraints* (1.2.28) *and* (1.2.29) *respectively, such that the Lagrangian function*

$$L(x, \lambda, \nu) = f_0(x) + \sum_{i=1}^{m} \lambda_i f_i(x) + \sum_{i=1}^{p} \nu_i h_i(x) \qquad (1.2.45)$$

*satisfies*

$$f_i(x^*) \leqslant 0, \quad i = 1, \cdots, m, \qquad (1.2.46)$$

$$h_i(x^*) = 0, \quad i = 1, \cdots, p, \qquad (1.2.47)$$

$$\lambda_i^* \geqslant 0, \quad i = 1, \cdots, m, \qquad (1.2.48)$$

$$\lambda_i^* f_i(x^*) = 0, \quad i = 1, \cdots, m, \qquad (1.2.49)$$

$$\nabla_x L(x^*, \lambda^*, \nu^*) = \nabla f_0(x^*) + \sum_{i=1}^{m} \lambda_i^* \nabla f_i(x^*) + \sum_{i=1}^{p} \nu_i^* \nabla h_i(x^*) = 0. \qquad (1.2.50)$$

It is not difficult to show from strong duality theorem that, for convex programming, the KKT conditions are the necessary condition of its solution:

**Theorem 1.2.23** *Consider the convex programming problem* (1.2.27)~(1.2.29) *satisfying Slater's condition. If* $x^*$ *is its solution, then* $x^*$ *satisfies the KKT conditions.*

**Proof** Noticing that $x^*$ is a solution to the primal problem (1.2.27)~(1.2.29) where Slater's condition is satisfied, we conclude by strong duality theorem that there exists $(\lambda^*, \nu^*)$ such that $x^*$ and $(\lambda^*, \nu^*)$ are the solutions to the primal problem (1.2.27)~ (1.2.29) and the solution to the dual problem (1.2.37)~(1.2.38) respectively, and their optimal values are equal. This means that

$$\begin{aligned}
f_0(x^*) &= g(\lambda^*, \nu^*) \\
&= \inf_x \left( f_0(x) + \sum_{i=1}^{m} \lambda_i^* f_i(x) + \sum_{i=1}^{p} \nu_i^* h_i(x) \right) \\
&\leqslant f_0(x^*) + \sum_{i=1}^{m} \lambda_i^* f_i(x^*) + \sum_{i=1}^{p} \nu_i^* h_i(x^*) \\
&\leqslant f_0(x^*). \qquad (1.2.51)
\end{aligned}$$

The second line and the third line follow from the definitions. The last line follows from $\lambda_i^* \geqslant 0, f_i(x^*) \leqslant 0, i = 1, \cdots, m$ and $h_i(x^*) = 0, i = 1, \cdots, p$. We conclude that the two inequalities in this chain hold with equality. This yields

$$\inf_x \left( f_0(x) + \sum_{i=1}^m \lambda_i^* f_i(x) + \sum_{i=1}^p \nu_i^* h_i(x) \right)$$
$$= f_0(x^*) + \sum_{i=1}^m \lambda_i^* f_i(x^*) + \sum_{i=1}^p \nu_i^* h_i(x^*) = f_0(x^*). \tag{1.2.52}$$

Now we are in the position to prove the conclusions. First, equations (1.2.46)~(1.2.48) are obvious. Second, equality (1.2.49) follows from the second equality in (1.2.52). At last, equality (1.2.50) is valid since $x^*$ is the minimal point of the Lagrangian function $L(x, \lambda^*, \nu^*)$ by the first equality in (1.2.52). ∎

The next theorem shows that, for a convex programming, the KKT conditions are also a sufficient condition of its solution.

**Theorem 1.2.24** *Consider the convex programming problem* (1.2.27)~(1.2.29). *If $x^*$ satisfies the KKT conditions, then $x^*$ is its solution.*

**Proof** Suppose that $x^*$ and $(\lambda^*, \nu^*)$ satisfy conditions (1.2.46)~(1.2.50). Note that the first two conditions (1.2.46)~(1.2.47) state that $x^*$ is a feasible point of the primal problem and condition (1.2.48) states that $(\lambda^*, \nu^*)$ is a feasible point of the dual problem. Since $\lambda_i^* \geqslant 0, i = 1, \cdots, m$, $L(x, \lambda^*, \nu^*)$ is convex in $x$. Therefore, condition (1.2.50) states that $x^*$ minimizes $L(x, \lambda^*, \nu^*)$ over $x$. From this we conclude that

$$g(\lambda^*, \nu^*) = \inf_{x \in R^n} L(x, \lambda^*, \nu^*) = L(x^*, \lambda^*, \nu^*)$$
$$= f_0(x^*) + \sum_{i=1}^m \lambda_i^* f_i(x^*) + \sum_{i=1}^p \nu_i^* h_i(x^*)$$
$$= f_0(x^*), \tag{1.2.53}$$

where in the last line we use conditions (1.2.49) and (1.2.47). Therefore, $x^*$ is a solution to the primal problem by (1.2.53) and Corollary 1.2.19. ∎

The above two theorems are summarized in the following theorem.

**Theorem 1.2.25** *Consider the convex programming problem* (1.2.27)~ (1.2.29) *satisfying Slater's condition. Then for its solution $x^*$, it is necessary and sufficient condition that $x^*$ satisfies the KKT conditions given by Definition 1.2.22.*

## 1.2.5 Linear programming

Among the optimization problems, linear programming (LP) is the simplest one. There are many excellent books on linear programming, including [188, 111, 154]. Here it is introduced briefly.

Linear programming in general form is

$$\min \quad c^T x, \ x \in R^n, \tag{1.2.54}$$

$$\text{s.t.} \quad \bar{A}x - \bar{b} \leqslant 0, \tag{1.2.55}$$

$$Ax - b = 0, \tag{1.2.56}$$

where $c \in R^n$, $\bar{A} \in R^{m \times n}$, $A \in R^{p \times n}$, $\bar{b} \in R^m$, $b \in R^p$.

Because linear programming belongs to convex programming, the conclusions concerning convex programming are also valid for linear programming. But these conclusions usually have simpler representations.

For linear programming, the Lagrangian function is

$$L(x, \lambda, \nu) = c^T x + \lambda^T (\bar{A}x - \bar{b}) + \nu^T (Ax - b) \tag{1.2.57}$$

by (1.2.32). Thus, we have the following theorem.

**Theorem 1.2.26** *Optimization problem*

$$\max \quad -\bar{b}^T \lambda - b^T \nu, \tag{1.2.58}$$

$$\text{s.t.} \quad \bar{A}^T \lambda + A^T \nu + c = 0, \tag{1.2.59}$$

$$\lambda \geqslant 0 \tag{1.2.60}$$

*is the dual problem of the linear programming* (1.2.54)~(1.2.56). *Furthermore, the optimal value $p^*$ of the primal problem is equal to the optimal value $d^*$ of the dual problem.*

**Proof** Since the linear programming (1.2.54)~(1.2.56) is a convex programming, its dual problem is

$$\max \quad g(\lambda, \nu), \tag{1.2.61}$$

$$\text{s.t.} \quad \lambda \geqslant 0, \tag{1.2.62}$$

by definition 1.2.16 and equality (1.2.57), where

$$g(\lambda, \nu) = \inf_{x \in R^n} L(x, \lambda, \nu) = \inf_{x \in R^n} (c^T x + \lambda^T (\bar{A}x - \bar{b}) + \nu^T (Ax - b)). \tag{1.2.63}$$

It is easy to see that

$$g(\lambda, \nu) = -\bar{b}^T \lambda - b^T \nu + \inf_{x \in R^n} (c + \bar{A}^T \lambda + A^T \nu)^T x$$

$$= \begin{cases} -\bar{b}^T \lambda - b^T \nu, & c + \bar{A}^T \lambda + A^T \nu = 0; \\ -\infty, & \text{else}, \end{cases} \tag{1.2.64}$$

and hence the problem (1.2.61)~(1.2.62) is equivalent to the problem (1.2.58)~(1.2.60).

Note that Slater's condition is always satisfied by linear programming. Therefore, we conclude that the optimal values $p^*$ and $d^*$ are equal from Theorem 1.2.21. ∎

There are several user-friendly software programs, such as LINDO and LINGO [171], that can be used to solve linear programming. For small-scale linear programming, MATLAB® is also a good choice due to its simplicity [20].

## 1.3    Convex Programming in Hilbert Space

The variable $x$ in the above optimization problems is an $n$-dimensional vector in Euclidian space

$$x = ([x]_1, \cdots, [x]_n)^{\mathrm{T}}. \tag{1.3.1}$$

It is interesting to extend the vector from the finite dimensional space $R^n$ into an infinite dimensional space $l_2$ where the variable $x$ can be expressed as

$$x = ([x]_1, [x]_2, \cdots)^{\mathrm{T}} \tag{1.3.2}$$

with the convergence condition

$$\sum_{i=1}^{\infty} [x]_i^2 < \infty. \tag{1.3.3}$$

Note that $l_2$ space is a Hilbert space. So, corresponding to the optimization problems in Euclidian space, we have also the optimization problems in Hilbert space, where the variable $x$ can be considered to have the expression (1.3.2). The task of this section is to study the convex programming in Hilbert space.

It should be pointed out that the convex programming problems in Hilbert space and in Euclidian space are very similar. In fact, almost all results for the former can be obtained by copying the corresponding ones for the latter given in the last section except their variables are different. Therefore, we only describe its main conclusions briefly below; see [162, 15] for details.

### 1.3.1    Convex sets and Fréchet derivative

The definitions of convex set and convex map in Hilbert space $\mathcal{H}$ are similar to the ones in Euclidian space $R^n$, and therefore are omitted here. The derivative of a function in $R^n$ is extended in the following definition.

**Definition 1.3.1** *(Fréchet derivative and differentiability) Let $\mathcal{H}$ and $R$ be Hilbert space and Real space respectively. A function $f : \mathcal{H} \to R$ is called Fréchet differentiable at $\bar{x} \in \mathcal{H}$ if there exists a bounded linear map $\mathcal{A}(h) = (a \cdot h)$, where $a \in \mathcal{H}$, such that*

$$f(\bar{x} + h) - f(\bar{x}) - (a \cdot h) = o(\|h\|). \tag{1.3.4}$$

*In this case, we call $a$ in (1.3.4) the Fréchet derivative of $f$ at $\bar{x}$ and denote $\nabla f(\bar{x}) = a$. In addition, a function $f$ which is Fréchet differentiable at any point of $\mathcal{H}$, and whose derivative is continuous, is said to be continuously differentiable.*

## 1.3.2 Convex programming problems

The following definition is an extension of Definition 1.2.6.

**Definition 1.3.2** *(Convex programming problem in Hilbert space) A convex programming problem is an optimization problem in the form*

$$\min \quad f_0(x), \quad x \in \mathcal{H}, \tag{1.3.5}$$

$$\text{s.t.} \quad f_i(x) \leqslant 0, \quad i = 1, \cdots, m, \tag{1.3.6}$$

$$h_i(x) = (a_i \cdot x) - b_i = 0, \quad i = 1, \cdots, p, \tag{1.3.7}$$

*where $f_0(x) : \mathcal{H} \to R$ and $f_i(x) : \mathcal{H} \to R, i = 1, \cdots, m$ are continuously differentiable convex functions, and $h_i(x) : \mathcal{H} \to R, i = 1, \cdots, p$ are bounded linear maps shown in (1.3.7).*

For the convex programming (1.3.5)~(1.3.7), the conclusions corresponding to Theorem 1.2.7~ Corollary 1.2.12 are also valid. For example, Theorem 1.2.7 can be extended as follows: Instead of the quadratic function $(x \cdot Hx) : R^n \to R$, consider the quadratic map $(x \cdot Hx) : \mathcal{H} \to R$, where $H : \mathcal{H} \to \mathcal{H}$ is a bounded linear map. Here $H$ is called positive semidefinite if $(x \cdot Hx) \geqslant 0$ for any $x \in \mathcal{H}$. Thus we have the following theorem:

**Theorem 1.3.3** *Consider the quadratic programming problem*

$$\min \quad \frac{1}{2}(x \cdot Hx) + (r \cdot x), \quad x \in \mathcal{H}, \tag{1.3.8}$$

$$\text{s.t.} \quad \bar{A}x - \bar{b} \leqslant 0, \tag{1.3.9}$$

$$Ax - b = 0, \tag{1.3.10}$$

*where $H : \mathcal{H} \to \mathcal{H}, \bar{A} : \mathcal{H} \to R^m$ and $A : \mathcal{H} \to R^p$ are bounded linear maps, $\bar{b} \in R^m, b \in R^p, r \in \mathcal{H}$. If $H$ is positive semidefinite, then the above problem is convex programming, i.e. a convex quadratic programming problem.*

The following Theorem and Corollary correspond to Theorem 1.2.10 and Corollary 1.2.11 respectively.

**Theorem 1.3.4** *Consider the problem (1.3.5)~(1.3.7) in Hilbert space. If $x^*$ is its local solution, then $x^*$ is also its global solution.*

**Corollary 1.3.5** *Consider the problem (1.3.8)~(1.3.10) in Hilbert space, where $H$ is positive semidefinite. Then its local solution is its global solution.*

### 1.3.3  Duality theory

For the problem $(1.3.5)\sim(1.3.7)$, corresponding to $(1.2.32)$, introduce the Lagrangian function

$$L(x, \lambda, \nu) = f_0(x) + \sum_{i=1}^{m} \lambda_i f_i(x) + \sum_{i=1}^{p} \nu_i h_i(x), \qquad (1.3.11)$$

where $\lambda = (\lambda_1, \cdots, \lambda_m)^{\mathrm{T}}$ and $\nu = (\nu_1, \cdots, \nu_p)^{\mathrm{T}}$ are Lagrangian multiplier vectors. Corresponding to Definition 1.2.16, the following definition is given.

**Definition 1.3.6** *(Dual problem) Problem*

$$\max \qquad g(\lambda, \nu) = \inf_{x \in \mathcal{H}} L(x, \lambda, \nu), \qquad (1.3.12)$$

$$\text{s.t.} \qquad \lambda \geqslant 0 \qquad (1.3.13)$$

*is called the dual problem of the problem $(1.3.5)\sim(1.3.7)$. Correspondingly, problem $(1.3.5)\sim(1.3.7)$ is called the primal problem.*

Here we also have the duality theory, including weak duality theorem and strong duality theorem corresponding to Theorem 1.2.18 and Theorem 1.2.21 respectively, where Slater's condition corresponding to Definition 1.2.20 is defined as follows:

**Definition 1.3.7** *(Slater's condition) Problem $(1.3.5)\sim(1.3.7)$ is said to satisfy Slater's condition if there exists a feasible point $x$ such that*

$$f_i(x) < 0, \ i = 1, \cdots, m; \quad (a_i \cdot x) - b_i = 0, \ i = 1, \cdots, p. \qquad (1.3.14)$$

### 1.3.4  Optimality conditions

Similarly, we have the theorems corresponding to Theorem 1.2.23$\sim$ Theorem 1.2.25:

**Theorem 1.3.8** *Consider the problem $(1.3.5)\sim(1.3.7)$ satisfying Slater's condition. If $x^*$ is its solution, then $x^*$ satisfies the KKT conditions:*

$$f_i(x^*) \leqslant 0, \quad i = 1, \cdots, m, \qquad (1.3.15)$$

$$h_i(x^*) = 0, \quad i = 1, \cdots, p, \qquad (1.3.16)$$

$$\lambda_i^* \geqslant 0, \quad i = 1, \cdots, m, \qquad (1.3.17)$$

$$\lambda_i^* f_i(x^*) = 0, \quad i = 1, \cdots, m, \qquad (1.3.18)$$

$$\nabla_x L(x^*, \lambda^*, \nu^*) = \nabla f_0(x^*) + \sum_{i=1}^{m} \lambda_i^* \nabla f_i(x^*) + \sum_{i=1}^{p} \nu_i^* \nabla h_i(x^*) = 0. \qquad (1.3.19)$$

**Theorem 1.3.9** *Consider the problem* $(1.3.5)\sim(1.3.7)$. *If* $x^*$ *satisfies KKT conditions* $(1.3.15)\sim(1.3.19)$, *then* $x^*$ *is its solution.*

**Theorem 1.3.10** *Consider the problem* $(1.3.5)\sim(1.3.7)$ *satisfying Slater's condition. Then for its solution* $x^*$, *it is necessary and sufficient condition that* $x^*$ *satisfies the KKT conditions* $(1.3.15)\sim(1.3.19)$.

---

## *1.4   Convex Programming with Generalized Inequality Constraints in Euclidian Space

The convex programming given in Section 1.2 was extended from the case in Euclidian space to the one in Hilbert space in Section 1.3. Now it will be extended from the case with usual inequality constraints to the one with generalized inequality constraints [17].

### 1.4.1   Convex programming with generalized inequality constraints

#### 1.4.1.1   Cones

**Definition 1.4.1** *(Cone and convex cone) A set* $K$ *in* $R^n$ *is called a cone if for every* $x \in K$ *and* $\lambda \geqslant 0$, $\lambda x \in K$. *A set* $K$ *in* $R^n$ *is called a convex cone if it is a cone and a convex set, which means that for any* $u, v \in K$ *and* $\lambda_1, \lambda_2 \geqslant 0$, $\lambda_1 x_1 + \lambda_2 x_2 \in K$.

**Definition 1.4.2** *(Proper cone) A set* $K$ *in* $R^n$ *is called a proper cone if it satisfies:*
   *(i)* $K$ *is a convex cone;*
   *(ii)* $K$ *is closed;*
   *(iii)* $K$ *is solid, which means it has nonempty interior;*
   *(iv)* $K$ *is pointed, which means that it contains no line (or, equivalently,* $x$ *must be null* $(x = 0)$ *if* $x \in K$ *and* $-x \in K$).

**Example 1.4.3** *The nonnegative orthant* $K = R_+^n$ *in* $R^n$

$$R_+^n = \{u = (u_1, \cdots, u_n)^{\mathrm{T}} \in R^n \mid u_i \geqslant 0, i = 1, \cdots, n\} \qquad (1.4.1)$$

*is a proper cone.*

#### 1.4.1.2   Generalized inequalities

A proper cone can be used to define a generalized inequality.

**Definition 1.4.4** *(Generalized inequality) Let $K$ be a proper cone and $u, v \in R^n$. The generalized inequality $u \preceq_K v$ or $v \succeq_K u$ means that $v - u \in K$; the strict generalized inequality $u \prec_K v$ or $v \succ_K u$ means that $v - u \in \text{int} K$, where $\text{int} K$ is the interior of the proper cone $K$.*

Obviously, when $K = R^n_+$, the generalized inequality $u \preceq_{R^n_+} v$ is reduced to the usual inequality $u \leqslant v$, which means $u_i \leqslant v_i, i = 1, \cdots, n$ if $u = (u_1, \cdots, u_n)^{\mathrm{T}}, v = (v_1, \cdots, v_n)^{\mathrm{T}}$. Corresponding conclusion holds for the strict generalized inequality.

The generalized inequalities have properties similar to the usual inequalities:

**Theorem 1.4.5** *(Properties of the generalized inequality) A generalized inequality $\preceq_K$ has the following properties:*

*(i) $\preceq_K$ is preserved under addition: if $u \preceq_K \tilde{u}$, $v \preceq_K \tilde{v}$, then $u + v \preceq_K \tilde{u} + \tilde{v}$;*

*(ii) $\preceq_K$ is transitive: if $u \preceq_K v$ and $v \preceq_K w$, then $u \preceq_K w$;*

*(iii) $\preceq_K$ is preserved under nonnegative scaling: if $u \preceq_K v$ and $\alpha \geqslant 0$, then $\alpha u \preceq_K \alpha v$;*

*(iv) $\preceq_K$ is reflexive: $u \preceq_K u$;*

*(v) $\preceq_K$ is antisymmetric: if $u \preceq_K v$ and $v \preceq_K u$, then $u = v$;*

*(vi) $\preceq_K$ is preserved under limits: if $u_i \preceq_K v_i, for\ i = 1, 2, \cdots,\ u_i \to u, v_i \to v\ as\ i \to \infty$, then $u \preceq_K v$.*

### 1.4.1.3 Convex programming with generalized inequality constraints

First, let us extend the convex function in $R^n$ given by Definition 1.2.3.

**Definition 1.4.6** *(K-convex function) Let $K \subseteq R^m$ be a proper cone. A function $f : R^n \to R^m$ is called a $K$-convex function if for all $x_1, x_2 \in R^n$ and $\lambda \in [0, 1]$,*

$$f(\lambda x_1 + (1 - \lambda)x_2) \preceq_K \lambda f(x_1) + (1 - \lambda)f(x_2). \qquad (1.4.2)$$

*The function is strictly $K$-convex function if for all $x_1, x_2 \in R^n, x_1 \neq x_2$ and $\lambda \in (0, 1)$,*

$$f(\lambda x_1 + (1 - \lambda)x_2) \prec_K \lambda f(x_1) + (1 - \lambda)f(x_2). \qquad (1.4.3)$$

Now we are in a position to define the convex programming with generalized inequalities.

**Definition 1.4.7** *(Convex programming with generalized inequality constraints) A convex programming with generalized inequality constraints is an* *optimization problem in the form*

$$\min \quad f_0(x), \ x \in R^n, \tag{1.4.4}$$

$$\text{s.t.} \quad f_i(x) \preceq_{K_i} 0, \ i = 1, \cdots, m, \tag{1.4.5}$$

$$h_i(x) = a_i^\mathrm{T} x - b_i = 0, \ i = 1, \cdots, p, \tag{1.4.6}$$

*where $f_0 : R^n \to R$ is convex and continuously differentiable, $K_i$ is a proper cone in $R^{m_i}$, $i = 1, \cdots, m$, $f_i(x) : R^n \to R^{m_i}$ is $K_i$-convex and continuously differentiable, $i = 1, \cdots, m$, and $h_i(x)$ is the linear function, $i = 1, \cdots, p$.*

## 1.4.2 Duality theory

### 1.4.2.1 Dual cones

In order to derive the dual problem of the problem (1.4.4)~(1.4.6), introduce the dual cone first.

**Definition 1.4.8** *(Dual cone) Let $K$ be a cone. The set*

$$K^* = \{v \in R^m \mid (v \cdot u) \geqslant 0, \forall u \in K\}, \tag{1.4.7}$$

*is called the dual cone of $K$, where $(\cdot)$ is the inner product between two vectors.*

As the name suggests, $K^*$ is a cone. It is not difficult to prove the following conclusion.

**Theorem 1.4.9** *(Properties of a dual cone) If $K$ is a proper cone, then its dual cone $K^*$ is also a proper cone.*

**Example 1.4.10** *Find the dual cone of the nonnegative orthant cone $R_+^m$ in $R^m$.*

It is easy to see that

$$(R_+^m)^* = R_+^m. \tag{1.4.8}$$

i.e. the cone $R_+^m$ is its own dual. We call such a cone self-dual.

### 1.4.2.2 Derivation of the dual problem

Now let us derive the dual problem of the problem (1.4.4)~(1.4.6) from estimating its optimal value $p^*$

$$p^* = \inf\{f_0(x) | x \in D\}, \tag{1.4.9}$$

where

$$D = \{x | f_i(x) \preceq_{K_i} 0, \ i = 1, \cdots, m; \ h_i(x) = 0, \ i = 1, \cdots, p; \ x \in R^n\}. \tag{1.4.10}$$

Introduce the Lagrangian function

$$L(x, \lambda, \nu) = f_0(x) + \lambda_1^{\mathrm{T}} f_1(x) + \cdots + \lambda_m^{\mathrm{T}} f_m(x) + \nu_1 h_1(x) + \cdots + \nu_p h_p(x), \quad (1.4.11)$$

where $\lambda = (\lambda_1^{\mathrm{T}}, \cdots, \lambda_m^{\mathrm{T}})^{\mathrm{T}}$ and $\nu = (\nu_1, \cdots, \nu_p)^{\mathrm{T}}$ are Lagrangian multiplier vectors. When $x \in D, \lambda_i \in K_i^*$, we have

$$L(x, \lambda, \nu) = f_0(x) + \sum_{i=1}^{m} \lambda_i^{\mathrm{T}} f_i(x) + \sum_{i=1}^{p} \nu_i h_i(x) \leqslant f_0(x), \quad (1.4.12)$$

then

$$\inf_{x \in R^n} L(x, \lambda, \nu) \leqslant \inf_{x \in D} L(x, \lambda, \nu) \leqslant \inf_{x \in D} f_0(x). \quad (1.4.13)$$

Therefore, introducing the Lagrangian dual function

$$g(\lambda, \nu) = \inf_{x \in R^n} L(x, \lambda, \nu), \quad (1.4.14)$$

yields

$$g(\lambda, \nu) \leqslant p^*. \quad (1.4.15)$$

Inequality (1.4.15) indicates that, for any $\lambda_i \in K_i^*, i = 1, \cdots, m, \nu \in R^p$, $g(\lambda, \nu)$ is a lower bound of $p^*$. Among these lower bounds, finding the best one leads to the optimization problem

$$\max \quad g(\lambda, \nu) = \inf_{x \in R^n} L(x, \lambda, \nu), \quad (1.4.16)$$

$$\text{s.t.} \quad \lambda_i \succeq_{K_i^*} 0, \ i = 1, \cdots, m, \quad (1.4.17)$$

where $L(x, \lambda, \nu)$ is the Lagrangian function given by (1.4.11).

**Definition 1.4.11** *(Dual problem) Problem* (1.4.16)~(1.4.17) *is called the dual problem of the problem* (1.4.4)~(1.4.6). *Correspondingly, problem* (1.4.4)~(1.4.6) *is called the primal problem.*

It is easy to show the following conclusion.

**Theorem 1.4.12** *Dual problem* (1.4.16)~(1.4.17) *is a convex programming problem.*

**Example 1.4.13** *Find the dual problem of the convex programming with generalized inequalities*

$$\min \quad c^{\mathrm{T}} x, \ x \in R^n, \quad (1.4.18)$$

$$\text{s.t.} \quad Ax - b = 0, \quad (1.4.19)$$

$$x \succeq_K 0, \quad (1.4.20)$$

*where $c \in R^n, A \in R^{p \times n}, b \in R^p$, $K$ is a proper cone in $R^n$.*

**Proof** The Lagrangian function of the problem is

$$L(x, \lambda, \nu) = c^{\mathrm{T}}x - \lambda^{\mathrm{T}}x + \nu^{\mathrm{T}}(Ax - b), \tag{1.4.21}$$

hence

$$g(\lambda, \nu) = \inf_{x \in R^n} L(x, \lambda, \nu) = \begin{cases} -b^{\mathrm{T}}\nu, & \text{if } c + A^{\mathrm{T}}\nu - \lambda = 0; \\ -\infty, & \text{otherwise.} \end{cases} \tag{1.4.22}$$

Therefore, the dual problem is

$$\max \quad -b^{\mathrm{T}}\nu, \tag{1.4.23}$$
$$\text{s.t.} \quad c + A^{\mathrm{T}}\nu - \lambda = 0, \tag{1.4.24}$$
$$\lambda \succeq_{K^*} 0. \tag{1.4.25}$$

∎

### 1.4.2.3 Duality theory

#### (1) Weak duality theorem
According to the inequality (1.4.15), we have the following theorem.

**Theorem 1.4.14** *(Weak duality theorem) Let $p^*$ be the optimal value of the primal problem (1.4.4)~(1.4.6) and $d^*$ be the optimal value of the dual problem (1.4.16)~(1.4.17). Then*

$$p^* = \inf\{f_0(x) | f_i(x) \preceq_{K_i} 0, i = 1, \cdots, m; a_i^{\mathrm{T}}x - b_i = 0, i = 1, \cdots, p; \ x \in R^n\}$$
$$\geqslant \sup\{g(\lambda, \nu) | \lambda_i \succeq_{K_i^*} 0, i = 1, \cdots, m; \nu \in R^p\}$$
$$= d^*. \tag{1.4.26}$$

**Corollary 1.4.15** *Let $\tilde{x}$ be the feasible point of the primal problem (1.4.4)~(1.4.6) and $(\tilde{\lambda}, \tilde{\nu})$ be the feasible point of the dual problem (1.4.16)~(1.4.17). If $f_0(\tilde{x}) = g(\tilde{\lambda}, \tilde{\nu})$, then $\tilde{x}$ and $(\tilde{\lambda}, \tilde{\nu})$ are their solutions respectively.*

#### (2) Strong duality theorem
Here strong duality is related with the following Slater's condition.

**Definition 1.4.16** *(Slater's condition) Problem (1.4.4)~(1.4.6) is said to satisfy Slater's condition if there exists a feasible point $x$ such that*

$$f_i(x) \prec_{K_i} 0, i = 1, \cdots, m; \quad a_i^{\mathrm{T}}x - b_i = 0, i = 1, \cdots, p. \tag{1.4.27}$$

**Theorem 1.4.17** *(Strong duality theorem) Consider the problem* $(1.4.4)\sim$
$(1.4.6)$ *satisfying Slater's condition. Let* $p^*$ *be the optimal value of the primal problem* $(1.4.4)\sim(1.4.6)$ *and* $d^*$ *be the optimal value of the dual problem* $(1.4.16)\sim(1.4.17)$. *Then*

$$
\begin{aligned}
p^* &= \inf\{f_0(x)|f_i(x) \preceq_{K_i} 0, i = 1, \cdots, m; a_i^{\mathrm{T}} x - b_i = 0, i = 1, \cdots, p; \ x \in R^n\} \\
&= \sup\{g(\lambda, \nu)|\lambda_i \succeq_{K_i^*} 0, i = 1, \cdots, m; \nu \in R^p\} \\
&= d^*.
\end{aligned}
\tag{1.4.28}
$$

*Furthermore, if* $p^*$ *is attained, i.e. there exists a solution* $x^*$ *to the primal problem, then* $d^*$ *is also attained, i.e. there exists a global solution* $(\lambda^*, \nu^*)$ *to the dual problem such that*

$$
p^* = f_0(x^*) = g(\lambda^*, \nu^*) = d^* < \infty.
\tag{1.4.29}
$$

### 1.4.3   Optimality conditions

In order to describe the optimality conditions we need to generalize the gradient of a scalar valued function.

**Definition 1.4.18** *(Jacobian matrix) Let* $F : R^n \to R^m$ *be a continuously differentiable map:* $F(x) = (f_1(x), \cdots, f_m(x))^{\mathrm{T}}$, $x = ([x]_1, \cdots, [x]_n)^{\mathrm{T}}$. *The Jacobian matrix of* $F$ *at* $x$ *is an* $m$ *by* $n$ *matrix and its element in the* $i$-*th row and* $j$-*th column is defined by*

$$
Jf(x)_{ij} = \frac{\partial f_i(x)}{\partial [x]_j}, \quad i = 1, \cdots, m, \ j = 1, \cdots, n.
\tag{1.4.30}
$$

**Definition 1.4.19** *(KKT conditions) Consider the problem* $(1.4.4)\sim(1.4.6)$. *The point* $x^*$ *is said to satisfy the KKT conditions if there exist the multiplier vectors* $\lambda^* = (\lambda_1^{*\mathrm{T}}, \cdots, \lambda_m^{*\mathrm{T}})^{\mathrm{T}}$ *and* $\nu^* = (\nu_1^*, \cdots, \nu_p^*)^{\mathrm{T}}$, *such that the Lagrangian function*

$$
L(x, \lambda, \nu) = f_0(x) + \sum_{i=1}^{m} \lambda_i^{\mathrm{T}} f_i(x) + \sum_{i=1}^{p} \nu_i(a_i^{\mathrm{T}} x - b_i)
\tag{1.4.31}
$$

*satisfies*

$$
a_i^{\mathrm{T}} x^* - b_i = 0, \quad i = 1, \cdots, p,
\tag{1.4.32}
$$

$$
f_i(x^*) \preceq_{K_i} 0, \quad i = 1, \cdots, m,
\tag{1.4.33}
$$

$$
\lambda_i^* \succeq_{K_i^*} 0, \quad i = 1, \cdots, m,
\tag{1.4.34}
$$

$$
\lambda_i^{*\mathrm{T}} f_i(x^*) = 0, \quad i = 1, \cdots, m,
\tag{1.4.35}
$$

$$
\nabla_x L(x^*, \lambda^*, \nu^*) = \nabla f_0(x^*) + \sum_{i=1}^{m} Jf_i(x^*)^{\mathrm{T}} \lambda_i^* + \sum_{i=1}^{p} \nu_i^* a_i = 0,
$$
$$
\tag{1.4.36}
$$

*where* $Jf_i(x^*)$ *is the Jacobian matrix of* $f_i(x)$ *at* $x^*$.

Corresponding to Theorem 1.2.23~Theorem 1.2.25, we have the following theorems:

**Theorem 1.4.20** *Consider the problem* (1.4.4)~(1.4.6) *satisfying Slater's condition. If $x^*$ is its solution, then $x^*$ satisfies the KKT conditions given by Definition 1.4.19.*

**Theorem 1.4.21** *Consider the problem* (1.4.4)~(1.4.6). *If $x^*$ satisfies the KKT conditions given by Definition 1.4.19, then $x^*$ is its solution.*

**Theorem 1.4.22** *Consider the problem* (1.4.4)~(1.4.6) *satisfying Slater's condition. Then for its solution $x^*$, it is necessary and sufficient condition that $x^*$ satisfies the KKT conditions given by Definition 1.4.19.*

The cone programming is one of the simplest convex programmings with generalized inequalities given by Definition 1.4.7.

**Definition 1.4.23** *The cone programming is a convex programming with generalized inequalities in the form*

$$\min \quad c^T x, \ x \in R^n, \tag{1.4.37}$$
$$s.t. \quad f_i(x) = F_i x + g_i \preceq_{K_i} 0, i = 1, \cdots, m, \tag{1.4.38}$$
$$Ax = b, \tag{1.4.39}$$

*where $c \in R^n$, $A \in R^{\times n}$, $b \in R^p$, $F_i \in R^{m_i \times n}$, $g_i \in R^{m_i}$, and $K_i, i = 1, \cdots, m$ is a proper cone.*

When $K$ is the nonnegative orthant, the cone programming reduces to the linear programming. The other two special cases, second-order cone programming and semidefinite programming obtained by replacing $K$ with other cones, will be investigated in the following two subsections.

### 1.4.4 Second-order cone programming

Second-order cone programming is a special case of the cone programming given by Definition 1.4.23. It is addressed here briefly, see [1] for a detailed discussion.

#### 1.4.4.1 Second-order cone programming and its dual problem

#### (1) Second-order cone programming

**Definition 1.4.24** *(Second-order cone) The cone $K$ is called a second-order cone in $R^m$ if*

$$K = \begin{cases} \{u = u_1 \in R | u_1 \geqslant 0\}, & m = 1; \\ \left\{u = (u_1, u_2, \cdots, u_m)^T \in R^m | u_1 \geqslant \sqrt{u_2^2 + \cdots + u_m^2}\right\}, & m \geqslant 2. \end{cases}$$

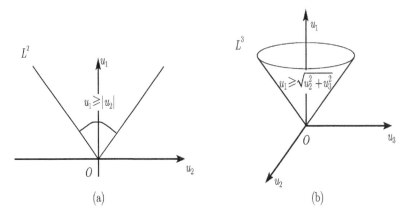

**FIGURE 1.9**: Boundary of a second-order cone: (a) in $R^2$; (b) in $R^3$.

Figure 1.9(a) and (b) show the second-order cone in $R^2$ and $R^3$ respectively.

Obviously, the second-order cone is a proper cone. Therefore, in the cone programming (Definition 1.4.23), the proper cones can be specified as the second-order cones. This leads to the following definition.

**Definition 1.4.25** *(Second-order cone programming) The second-order cone programming is a cone programming given by Definition 1.4.23 in the form*

$$\min \quad c^T x, \tag{1.4.40}$$
$$\text{s.t.} \quad \bar{A}_i x - \bar{b}_i \preceq_{L^{m_i}} 0, i = 1, 2, \cdots, m, \tag{1.4.41}$$
$$Ax - b = 0, \tag{1.4.42}$$

*where* $c \in R^n, A \in R^{p \times n}, b \in R^p, \bar{A}_i \in R^{m_i \times n}, \bar{b}_i \in R^{m_i}, i = 1, \cdots, m,$ *and* $L^{m_i}$ *is a second-order cone in* $R^{m_i}, m_i$ *is a positive integer,* $i = 1, \cdots, m.$

**(2) Dual problem**

In order to derive the dual problem of the second order cone programming (1.4.40)~(1.4.42), we need the following theorem.

**Theorem 1.4.26** *The second-order cone given by Definition 1.4.24 is self-dual, i.e.* $L^m = L^{m*}$.

**Proof** For the case $m = 1$, the conclusion is obvious. So we need only to show $L^m = L^{m*}$ when $m \geqslant 2$. In fact, on one hand, taking any $u = (u_1, \bar{u}^T)^T \in L^m$, for any $v = (v_1, \bar{v}^T)^T \in L^m$, we have

$$(u \cdot v) = u_1 v_1 + (\bar{u} \cdot \bar{v}) \geqslant u_1 v_1 - \|\bar{u}\| \|\bar{v}\| \geqslant 0 \tag{1.4.43}$$

by Cauchy-Schwarz inquality. Therefore $u \in L^{m*}$, hence

$$L^m \subseteq L^{m*}. \tag{1.4.44}$$

On the other hand, taking any $u = (u_1, \bar{u}^{\mathrm{T}})^{\mathrm{T}} \in L^{m*}$, for any $v = (v_1, \bar{v}^{\mathrm{T}})^{\mathrm{T}}$, we have $(u \cdot v) \geqslant 0$. Next we show that this leads to

$$u_1 \geqslant \|\bar{u}\| \tag{1.4.45}$$

by examining two different cases. If $\bar{u} = 0$, we have

$$(v \cdot u) = u_1 v_1 \geqslant 0, \tag{1.4.46}$$

thus $v_1 \geqslant 0$ since $v \in L^m$. Therefore $u_1 \geqslant 0 = \|\bar{u}\|$, i.e. inequality (1.4.45) is true. If $\bar{u} \neq 0$, selecting $v = (\|\bar{u}\|, -\bar{u}^{\mathrm{T}})^{\mathrm{T}} \in L^m$, we have

$$0 \leqslant (v \cdot u) = -\|\bar{u}\|^2 + u_1 \|\bar{u}\|, \tag{1.4.47}$$

which results in the inequality (1.4.45) and so $L^m \supseteq L^{m*}$. Therefore, noting inequality (1.4.44), the conclusion $L^m = L^{m*}$ is proved. ∎

According to (1.4.11), the Lagrangian function should be

$$L(x, \lambda, \nu) = c^{\mathrm{T}} x + \sum_{i=1}^{m} \lambda_i^{\mathrm{T}} (\bar{A}_i x - \bar{b}_i) + \nu^{\mathrm{T}} (Ax - b), \tag{1.4.48}$$

where $\lambda = (\lambda_1^{\mathrm{T}}, \cdots, \lambda_m^{\mathrm{T}})^{\mathrm{T}}$ and $\nu = (\nu_1, \cdots, \nu_p)^{\mathrm{T}}$ are the multiplier vectors. Thus we have the following theorem:

**Theorem 1.4.27** *Second-order cone programming*

$$\max \quad -\sum_{i=1}^{m} \bar{b}_i^{\mathrm{T}} \lambda_i - b^{\mathrm{T}} \nu, \tag{1.4.49}$$

$$\text{s.t.} \quad \sum_{i=1}^{m} \bar{A}_i^{\mathrm{T}} \lambda_i + A^{\mathrm{T}} \nu + c = 0, \tag{1.4.50}$$

$$\lambda_i \succeq_{L^{m_i}} 0, \ i = 1, \cdots, m \tag{1.4.51}$$

*is the dual problem of the problem* (1.4.40)∼(1.4.42).

**Proof** According to Definition 1.4.11, in order to get the dual problem of the problem (1.4.40)∼(1.4.42), we need to compute $g(\lambda, \nu)$

$$g(\lambda, \nu) = \begin{cases} -\sum\limits_{i=1}^{m} \bar{b}_i^{\mathrm{T}} \lambda_i - b^{\mathrm{T}} \nu, & \text{if } c + \sum_{i=1}^{m} \bar{A}_i^{\mathrm{T}} \lambda_i + A^{\mathrm{T}} \nu = 0; \\ -\infty, & \text{otherwise,} \end{cases} \tag{1.4.52}$$

where $\lambda_i \succeq_{L^{m_i}} 0$. This leads to the dual problem (1.4.49)∼(1.4.51), which is a second-order cone programming in the form (1.4.40)∼(1.4.42). ∎

### 1.4.4.2   Software for second-order cone programming

#### (1) Software SeDuMi

Self-Dual-Minimization (SeDuMi) is a tool for solving optimization problems. It can be used to solve linear programming, second-order cone programming and semidefinite programming introduced later, and is available at the website http://sedumi.mcmaster.ca.

Both the solution to the general second-order cone programming (1.4.40)~(1.4.42) and the solution to the dual problem (1.4.49)~(1.4.51) can be found by calling the main function of SeDuMi

$$[y, x] = \text{sedumi}(p_1, p_2, p_3, p_4), \tag{1.4.53}$$

where $p_i, i = 1, \cdots, 4$ are the input parameters given by

$$p_1 = (A^{\mathrm{T}}, \bar{A}_1^{\mathrm{T}}, \cdots, \bar{A}_m^{\mathrm{T}})^{\mathrm{T}}, \tag{1.4.54}$$

$$p_2 = -c^{\mathrm{T}}, \tag{1.4.55}$$

$$p_3 = (b^{\mathrm{T}}, b_1^{\mathrm{T}}, \cdots, b_m^{\mathrm{T}})^{\mathrm{T}}, \tag{1.4.56}$$

$$p_4 = [p_4.f, p_4.q], \tag{1.4.57}$$

where $p_4$ is the structural variable: $p_4.f = p$, $p_4.q = (m_1, m_2, \cdots, m_m)$. The outputs $x$ and $y$ are the solutions to the primal problem (1.4.40)~(1.4.42) and the dual problem (1.4.49)~(1.4.51) respectively.

#### (2) An application

**Example 1.4.28** *Solve the problem*

$$\min \quad c^{\mathrm{T}}x, \ x \in R^3, \tag{1.4.58}$$

$$\text{s.t.} \quad Ax - b = 0, \tag{1.4.59}$$

$$-\bar{a}_i^{\mathrm{T}}x + b_i \geqslant \varepsilon\|x\|, \ i = 1, \cdots, 3, \tag{1.4.60}$$

*where $c = (1, 1, 1)^{\mathrm{T}}$, $A = diag(0, 0, 1)$, $b = (0, 0, 0)^{\mathrm{T}}$, $\bar{a}_1 = (-1, 0, 1)^{\mathrm{T}}, b_1 = 0, \bar{a}_2 = (0, -1, 1)^{\mathrm{T}}, b_2 = 0, \bar{a}_3 = (1, 1, 1)^{\mathrm{T}}, b_3 = 1, \varepsilon = \dfrac{1}{2}.$*

*Select input parameters $p_i, i = 1, \cdots, 4$ as*

$$p_1 = (A, A_1, A_2, A_3)^{\mathrm{T}}, \tag{1.4.61}$$

$$p_2 = -c^{\mathrm{T}}, \tag{1.4.62}$$

$$p_3 = (b^{\mathrm{T}}, \hat{b}_1^{\mathrm{T}}, \hat{b}_2^{\mathrm{T}}, \hat{b}_3^{\mathrm{T}})^{\mathrm{T}}, \tag{1.4.63}$$

$$p_4.f = 3, p_4.q = (4, 4, 4), \tag{1.4.64}$$

*where $A_i = \left(\dfrac{1}{\varepsilon}\bar{a}_i, -I_{3\times3}\right)$, $\hat{b}_i = \left(\dfrac{1}{\varepsilon}b_i, 0, 0, 0\right)^{\mathrm{T}}, i = 1, 2, 3$. $I_{3\times3}$ is the $3 \times 3$*

*identity matrix. Call the main function (1.4.53) and get the solution*

$$x = 10^{-10} \begin{pmatrix} 0.3233 \\ 0.3233 \\ -0.0027 \end{pmatrix}. \tag{1.4.65}$$

### 1.4.5 Semidefinite programming

Semidefinite programming is another special case of cone programming given by Definition 1.4.23, see [89] for a detailed discussion.

#### 1.4.5.1 Semidefinite programming and its dual problem

#### (1) Semidefinite programming

As the name implies, semidefinite programming is a programming problem concerning the positive semidefinite matrices. However, the cone programming involves only the vectors, instead of the matrices. So we construct the map of a matrix $B = (b_{ij}) \in R^{m \times m}$ to an $m^2$-dimensional vector $\mathrm{vec}(\cdot)$:

$$\mathrm{vec}(B) = (b_{11}, b_{21}, \cdots, b_{m1}, b_{12}, b_{22}, \cdots, b_{m2}, b_{1m}, b_{2m}, \cdots, b_{mm})^{\mathrm{T}} \in R^{m^2}, \tag{1.4.66}$$

which forms a vector by stacking the matrix and the corresponding inverse map is the map of a $m^2$-dimensional vector $b = (b_{11}, b_{21}, \cdots, b_{m1}, b_{12}, b_{22}, \cdots, b_{m2}, b_{13}, b_{23}, \cdots, b_{mm})^{\mathrm{T}} \in R^{m^2}$ to an $m \times m$ matrix $\mathrm{mat}(\cdot)$:

$$\mathrm{mat}(b) = B = (b_{ij}) \in R^{m \times m}. \tag{1.4.67}$$

Some properties of the above map are given below:

**Theorem 1.4.29** *Suppose that $A = (a_{ij}) \in R^{m \times m}$, $B = (b_{ij}) \in R^{m \times m}$, then*

$$(\mathrm{vec}(A) \cdot \mathrm{vec}(B)) = \mathrm{vec}(A)^{\mathrm{T}} \mathrm{vec}(B) = \sum_{i,j=1}^{m} a_{ij} b_{ij} = \mathrm{tr}(AB^{\mathrm{T}}), \tag{1.4.68}$$

*where $(\cdot)$ is the inner product of two vectors and $\mathrm{tr}(\cdot)$ is the trace of a matrix.*

**Definition 1.4.30** *The Frobenius norm of the matrix $A = (a_{ij}) \in R^{m \times m}$ is defined as*

$$\|A\|_F = \left( \sum_{i,j=1}^{m} a_{ij}^2 \right)^{\frac{1}{2}}. \tag{1.4.69}$$

The above theorem and definition lead to the following theorem:

**Theorem 1.4.31** *Suppose that $A$, $B \in R^{m \times m}$, then*

$$\|\mathrm{vec}(A) - \mathrm{vec}(B)\| = \|\mathrm{vec}(A - B)\| = \|A - B\|_F, \tag{1.4.70}$$

*where $\|\cdot\|$ is the 2-norm of a vector and $\|\cdot\|_F$ the Frobenius norm of a matrix.*

**Theorem 1.4.32** *Suppose that*

$$S_+^m = \{A | A \text{ is an } m \times m \text{ symmetric positive semidefinite matrix}\}. \quad (1.4.71)$$

*Then $K(S_+^m)$ is a proper cone, where $K(S_+^m) = \{y | y = \mathrm{vec}(A), A \in S_+^m\}$ is the set obtained by the map of $S_+^m$ into the vector space $R^{m^2}$ via the relationship (1.4.66).*

**Proof** It is not difficult to show the conclusion by the following steps: (i) $K(S_+^m)$ is a close set; (ii) $K(S_+^m)$ is pointed; (iii) $int(K(S_+^m)) \neq \varnothing$. The detail is omitted.                                                                    ■

Now we are in a position to introduce the semidefinite programming problem from the cone programming given by Definition 1.4.23 by the following way:

(i) Change the value representation of the constraint function $f_i$ in the inequality constraints with $n = m_i^2$ from a $m_i^2$-dimensional vector into a $m_i \times m_i$ matrix via the corresponding relationship, i.e. $f_i : R^n \to R^{m_i \times m_i}$ is written as

$$f_i(x) = \sum_{j=1}^{n} [x]_j A_j^i - B^i, \quad (1.4.72)$$

where $x = ([x]_1, \cdots, [x]_n)^{\mathrm{T}}$, $A_j^i, B^i \in S^{m_i}$, $S^{m_i}$ is the set of symmetric $m_i \times m_i$ matrices. Here the $m_i \times m_i$ matrices should be understood as the $m_i^2$-dimensional vectors in our mind.

(ii) Specify the cones $K_i, i = 1, \cdots, m$. Corresponding to the value of the constraint $f_i$, $K_i$ is specified as a matrix in the form $K(s_+^{m_i})$ defined in the above theorem, i.e. its inequality constraint can be represented as

$$\mathrm{vec}\left(\sum_{j=1}^{n} [x]_j A_j^i - B^i\right) \preceq_{K(S_+^{m_i})} 0. \quad (1.4.73)$$

Next, we write these constraints in a more convenient form.

**Definition 1.4.33** *Suppose that the sets $S_+^m$ and $S_{++}^m$ are comprised of symmetric positive semidefinite matrices and positive definite matrices respectively. The matrix inequality $A \preceq_{S_+^m} B$ or $B \succeq_{S_+^m} A$ is said to be valid if $B - A \in S_+^m$; the matrix strict inequality $A \prec_{S_+^m} B$ or $B \succ_{S_+^m} A$ is said to be valid if $B - A \in S_{++}^m$.*

Therefore the vector inequality (1.4.73) can be written as the matrix inequality

$$\sum_{j=1}^{n} [x]_j A_j^i - B^i \preceq_{S_+^{m_i}} 0. \quad (1.4.74)$$

Thus semidefinite programming can be defined as follows:

**Definition 1.4.34** *(Semidefinite programming) A semidefinite programming is an optimization problem in the form*

$$\min \quad c^T x, \; x \in R^n, \tag{1.4.75}$$

$$\text{s.t.} \quad \sum_{j=1}^{n} [x]_j A_j^i - B^i \preceq_{S_+^{m_i}} 0, \; i = 1, \cdots, m, \tag{1.4.76}$$

$$Ax - b = 0, \tag{1.4.77}$$

*where $c \in R^n$, $A_j^i, B^i \in S^{m_i}$, $j = 1, \cdots, n, i = 1, \cdots, m$, $A \in R^{p \times n}$, $b \in R^p$, $S^{m_i}$ and $S_+^{m_i}$ are the sets comprised of $m_i \times m_i$ symmetric and symmetric positive semidefinite matrices respectively. Here the notation "$\preceq_{S_+^{m_i}}$" is usually simplified as "$\preceq$".*

It is obvious that the problem (1.4.75)~(1.4.77) can also be transformed equivalently to a problem with only a single linear matrix inequality constraint shown by the following theorem.

**Theorem 1.4.35** *Semidefinite programming (1.4.75)~(1.4.77) is equivalent to the problem*

$$\min \quad c^T x, \tag{1.4.78}$$

$$\text{s.t.} \quad \sum_{j=1}^{n} [x]_j \bar{A}_j - \bar{B} \preceq 0, \tag{1.4.79}$$

$$Ax - b = 0, \tag{1.4.80}$$

*where $c \in R^n$, $\bar{A}_j = \text{Diag}(A_j^1, \cdots, A_j^m), j = 1, \cdots, n$ and $\bar{B} = \text{Diag}(B^1, \cdots, B^m)$, $A \in R^{p \times n}, b \in R^p$.*

The following theorem shows that semidefinite programming is wider than second-order cone programming.

**Theorem 1.4.36** *A second-order cone programming problem can be written as a semidefinite programming problem.*

**Proof** See [17]. ∎

### (2) Dual problem

In order to derive the dual problem of the semidefinite programming (1.4.78)~(1.4.80), we need the following theorem.

**Theorem 1.4.37** *The cone $K(S_+^m)$ given by Theorem 1.4.32 is self-dual, i.e.*

$$K(S_+^m)^* = K(S_+^m). \tag{1.4.81}$$

**Proof** On one hand, suppose $\text{vec}(A) \in K(S_+^m)$, $\text{vec}(B) \in K(S_+^m)$. According to Theorem 1.4.29 we have

$$(\text{vec}(A) \cdot \text{vec}(B)) = \text{tr}(A^{\frac{1}{2}} A^{\frac{1}{2}} B^{\frac{1}{2}} B^{\frac{1}{2}}) = \text{tr}(A^{\frac{1}{2}} B^{\frac{1}{2}} B^{\frac{1}{2}} A^{\frac{1}{2}})$$

$$= \| A^{\frac{1}{2}} B^{\frac{1}{2}} \|^2 \geqslant 0. \tag{1.4.82}$$

This implies

$$K(S_+^m)^* \supset K(S_+^m). \tag{1.4.83}$$

On the other hand, suppose $\text{vec}(A) \in K(S_+^m)^*$. For any $\text{vec}(B) \in K(S_+^m)$, we have $(\text{vec}(A) \cdot \text{vec}(B)) \geqslant 0$. Therefore, for any $x \in R^m$ and the corresponding $B = xx^\mathrm{T}$, we have $\text{vec}(B) = \text{vec}(xx^\mathrm{T}) \in K(S_+^m)$ and

$$0 \leqslant (\text{vec}(A) \cdot \text{vec}(B)) = \text{tr}(Axx^\mathrm{T}) = \sum_{i,j} A_{ij}[x]_i[x]_j = x^\mathrm{T} A x. \tag{1.4.84}$$

This implies that

$$\text{vec}(A) \in K(S_+^m), \tag{1.4.85}$$

and hence $K(S_+^m)^* \subset K(S_+^m)$. The conclusion follows from (1.4.83) and (1.4.85). ∎

Now let us derive the dual problem of the problem (1.4.78)~(1.4.80). Introduce the Lagrangian function

$$L(x, \Lambda, \nu) = c^\mathrm{T} x + \text{tr}\left(\left(\sum_{i=1}^{n}[x]_i \bar{A}_i - \bar{B}\right)\Lambda\right) + \nu^\mathrm{T}(Ax - b),$$

$$= [x]_1(c_1 + \nu^\mathrm{T} a_{\cdot 1} + \text{tr}(\bar{A}_1 \Lambda)) + \cdots + [x]_n(c_n + \nu^\mathrm{T} a_{\cdot n} + \text{tr}(\bar{A}_n \Lambda))$$

$$- \text{tr}(\bar{B}\Lambda) - \nu^\mathrm{T} b, \tag{1.4.86}$$

where $a_{\cdot i}$ is the $i$-th column of the matrix $A$, $\nu \in R^p$ is the multiplier vector corresponding to the vector equality constraint (1.4.80), and $\Lambda \in R^{q \times q}$ is the multiplier matrix corresponding to the matrix inequality constraint (1.4.79). This leads to the following theorem.

**Theorem 1.4.38** *Denoting the $i$-th column of the matrix $A$ as $a_{\cdot i}$, semidefinite programming*

$$\max_{\Lambda, \nu} \quad -\text{tr}(\bar{B}\Lambda) - b^\mathrm{T}\nu, \tag{1.4.87}$$

$$\text{s.t.} \quad \text{tr}(\bar{A}_i \Lambda) + a_{\cdot i}^\mathrm{T}\nu + c_i = 0, i = 1, \cdots, n, \tag{1.4.88}$$

$$\Lambda \succeq 0 \tag{1.4.89}$$

*is the dual problem of the problem (1.4.78)~(1.4.80).*

**Proof** Remember Definition 1.4.11, equality (1.4.86) where $\Lambda \succeq_{S_+^q} 0$ due to Theorem 1.4.37. It is easy to see that

$$g(\Lambda, \nu) = \inf_x L(x, \Lambda, \nu)$$

$$= \begin{cases} -\text{tr}(\bar{B}\Lambda) - b^{\text{T}}\nu, & \text{if } c_i + a_{\cdot i}^{\text{T}}\nu + \text{tr}(\bar{A}_i\Lambda) = 0, \forall i = 1, \cdots, n; \\ -\infty, & \text{otherwise.} \end{cases} \quad (1.4.90)$$

Therefore, problem (1.4.87)~(1.4.89) is the dual problem of the problem (1.4.78)~(1.4.80). In addition, it can also be seen that the problem (1.4.87)~(1.4.89) is a semidefinite programming problem. ∎

### 1.4.5.2 Software for semidefinite programming

#### (1) Software SeDuMi for semidefinite programming
Semidefinite programming (1.4.78)~(1.4.80) and its dual problem (1.4.87)~(1.4.89) can be solved by SeDuMi at the same time. Now we only need to call the main function

$$[y, x] = \text{sedumi}(p_1, p_2, p_3, p_4), \quad (1.4.91)$$

of SeDuMi, in which the parameters $p_i, i = 1, \cdots, 4$ are given by

$$p_1 = (A; \text{vec}(\bar{A}_1), \cdots, \text{vec}(\bar{A}_n)), \quad (1.4.92)$$

$$p_2 = -c^{\text{T}}, \quad (1.4.93)$$

$$p_3 = (b^{\text{T}}, \text{vec}(\bar{B})^{\text{T}})^{\text{T}}, \quad (1.4.94)$$

$$p_4 = [p_4 \cdot f, p_4 \cdot s] = [p, q], \quad (1.4.95)$$

where $p_4$ is the structural variable: $p_4 \cdot f = p$ is the number of the linear constraints, $p_4 \cdot s = q$ is the order of the matrices in constraint (1.4.79). The outputs $x$ and $y$ are the solutions to the problems (1.4.78)~(1.4.80) and (1.4.87)~(1.4.89) respectively.
#### (2) An application

**Example 1.4.39** *Find the largest eigenvalue of the symmetric matrix*

$$M = \begin{pmatrix} 2 & -2 & 0 \\ -2 & 1 & -2 \\ 0 & -2 & 0 \end{pmatrix}. \quad (1.4.96)$$

*The problem can be written as a semidefinite problem*

$$\min \quad \lambda, \quad (1.4.97)$$

$$\text{s.t.} \quad -\lambda I + M \preceq 0, \quad (1.4.98)$$

*which can be solved by SeDuMi as follows:*

*Select input parameters $p_i, i = 1, \cdots, 4$ as*

$$p_1 = -\text{vec}(I_{3\times3}), \tag{1.4.99}$$
$$p_2 = -1, \tag{1.4.100}$$
$$p_3 = -\text{vec}(M), \tag{1.4.101}$$
$$p_4 \cdot s = 3, \tag{1.4.102}$$

*where $I_{3\times3}$ is the $3 \times 3$ identity matrix. Call the main function (1.4.91) and get the solution*

$$\lambda = 4.0000. \tag{1.4.103}$$

---

## *1.5  Convex Programming with Generalized Inequality Constraints in Hilbert Space

The usual convex programming in Euclidian space discussed in Section 1.2 has been extended in Section 1.3 and Section 1.4 respectively. Combining these extensions, we study the convex programming with generalized inequality constraints in Hilbert space in this section.

### 1.5.1  $K$-convex function and Fréchet derivative

In order to study the corresponding dual theory and the optimality conditions, we need to define the proper cone and $K$-convex map in Hilbert space. First we need the definitions of which can be given from Definitions 1.4.2 and 1.4.6 by replacing Euclidian space by Hilbert space. In addition, we need to extend Definition 1.3.1 as follows:

**Definition 1.5.1** *(Fréchet derivative and differentiability) Let both $\mathcal{H}_1$ and $\mathcal{H}_2$ be Hilbert spaces. A map $f : \mathcal{H}_1 \to \mathcal{H}_2$ is called Fréchet differentiable at $\bar{x} \in \mathcal{H}_1$ if there exists a bounded linear map $\mathcal{A}$ such that*

$$\|f(\bar{x} + h) - f(\bar{x}) - \mathcal{A}(h)\| = o(\|h\|). \tag{1.5.1}$$

*In this case, we call $\mathcal{A}$ the Fréchet derivative of $f$ at $\bar{x}$ and denote $\nabla f(\bar{x}) = \mathcal{A}$. In addition, a map $f$ which is Fréchet differentiable at any point of $\mathcal{H}_1$, and whose derivative is continuous, is said to be Fréchet continuously differentiable.*

### 1.5.2  Convex programming

Now we are able to represent the problem with which we are concerned.

**Definition 1.5.2** *(Convex programming problem with generalized inequality constraints in Hilbert space) Let $\mathcal{H}, \mathcal{H}_1, \cdots, \mathcal{H}_m$ be Hilbert spaces. A convex programming problem with generalized inequality constraints in Hilbert space is an optimization problem in the form*

$$\min \quad f_0(x), \tag{1.5.2}$$

$$\text{s.t.} \quad h_i(x) = (a_i \cdot x) - b_i = 0 , \quad i = 1, \cdots, p , \tag{1.5.3}$$

$$f_i(x) \preceq_{K_i} 0 , \quad i = 1, \cdots, m , \tag{1.5.4}$$

*where $f_0(x) : \mathcal{H} \to R$ are Fréchet continuously differentiable convex function, $K_i$ is a proper cone in $\mathcal{H}_i$, $f_i(x) : \mathcal{H} \to \mathcal{H}_i$ is a Fréchet continuously differentiable convex mapping, $i = 1, \cdots, m$, and $h_i(x) : \mathcal{H} \to R$ is a bounded linear mapping shown in (1.5.3), $i = 1, \cdots, p$.*

## 1.5.3 Duality theory

**Definition 1.5.3** *(Dual problem) Introduce the Lagrangian of the problem* (1.5.2)~(1.5.4)

$$L(x, \lambda_1, \cdots, \lambda_m, \nu) = f_0(x) + \sum_{i=1}^{m} (\lambda_i \cdot f_i(x)) + \sum_{i=1}^{p} \nu_i h_i(x), \tag{1.5.5}$$

*where $\lambda_i, i = 1, \cdots, m$, and $\nu = (\nu_1, \cdots, \nu_p)^{\mathrm{T}}$ are the Lagrangian multipliers. Problem*

$$\max \quad g(\lambda_1, \cdots, \lambda_m, \nu) = \inf_{x \in \mathcal{H}} L(x, \lambda_1, \cdots, \lambda_m, \nu), \tag{1.5.6}$$

$$\text{s.t.} \quad \lambda_i \in K_i^* , \quad i = 1, \cdots, m \tag{1.5.7}$$

*is called the dual problem of the problem* (1.5.2)~(1.5.4). *Correspondingly, problem* (1.5.2)~(1.5.4) *is called the primal problem.*

Here we also have the corresponding duality theory:

**Theorem 1.5.4** *(Weak duality theorem) Let $p^*$ be the optimal value of the primal problem* (1.5.2)~(1.5.4) *and $d^*$ be the optimal value of the dual problem* (1.5.6)~(1.5.7). *Then*

$$p^* = \inf\{f_0(x) | f_i(x) \preceq_{K_i} 0, i = 1, \cdots, m; h_i(x) = 0, i = 1, \cdots, p; \; x \in \mathcal{H}\}$$

$$\geqslant \sup\{g(\lambda_1, \cdots, \lambda_m, \nu) | \lambda_i \succeq_{K_i^*} 0, i = 1, \cdots, m; \nu \in R^p\}$$

$$= d^*. \tag{1.5.8}$$

**Corollary 1.5.5** *Let $\tilde{x}$ be the feasible point of the primal problem* (1.5.2)~(1.5.4) *and $(\tilde{\lambda}_1, \cdots, \tilde{\lambda}_m, \tilde{\nu})$ be the feasible point of the dual problem* (1.5.6)~(1.5.7). *If $f_0(\tilde{x}) = g(\tilde{\lambda}_1, \cdots, \tilde{\lambda}_m, \tilde{\nu})$, then $\tilde{x}$ and $(\tilde{\lambda}_1, \cdots, \tilde{\lambda}_m, \tilde{\nu})$ are their solutions respectively.*

**Definition 1.5.6** *(Slater's condition) Problem* (1.5.2)~(1.5.4) *is said to sat-isfy Slater's condition if there exists a feasible point* $x$ *such that*

$$f_i(x) \prec_{K_i} 0, i = 1, \cdots, m; \quad a_i^T x = b_i, i = 1, \cdots, p. \tag{1.5.9}$$

**Theorem 1.5.7** *(Strong duality theorem) Consider the problem* (1.5.2)~(1.5.4) *satisfying Slater's condition given by Definition 1.5.6. Let* $p^*$ *be the optimal value of the primal problem* (1.5.2)~(1.5.4) *and* $d^*$ *be the optimal value of the dual problem* (1.5.6)~(1.5.7). *Then*

$$\begin{aligned} p^* &= \inf\{f_0(x) | f_i(x) \preceq_{K_i} 0, i = 1, \cdots, m; h_i(x) = 0, i = 1, \cdots, p; \ x \in \mathcal{H}\} \\ &= \sup\{g(\lambda_1, \cdots, \lambda_m, \nu) | \lambda_i \succeq_{K_i^*} 0, i = 1, \cdots, m; \nu \in R^p\} \\ &= d^*. \end{aligned} \tag{1.5.10}$$

*Furthermore, if* $p^*$ *is attained, i.e. there exists a solution* $x^*$ *to the primal problem, then* $d^*$ *is also attained, i.e. there exists a solution* $(\lambda_1^*, \cdots, \lambda_m^*, \nu^*)$ *to the dual problem such that*

$$p^* = f_0(x^*) = g(\lambda_1^*, \cdots, \lambda_m^*, \nu^*) = d^* < \infty. \tag{1.5.11}$$

### 1.5.4 Optimality conditions

**Theorem 1.5.8** *Consider the problem* (1.5.2)~(1.5.4) *satisfying Slater's con-dition given by Definition 1.5.6. If* $x^*$ *is its solution, then* $x^*$ *satisfies the KKT conditions*

$$h_i(x^*) = 0, \quad i = 1, \cdots, p, \tag{1.5.12}$$

$$f_i(x^*) \preceq_{K_i} 0, \quad i = 1, \cdots, m, \tag{1.5.13}$$

$$\lambda_i^* \succeq_{K_i^*} 0, \quad i = 1, \cdots, m, \tag{1.5.14}$$

$$(\lambda_i^* \cdot f_i(x^*)) = 0, \quad i = 1, \cdots, m, \tag{1.5.15}$$

$$\nabla_x L(x^*, \lambda_1^*, \cdots, \lambda_m^*, \nu^*) = \nabla f_0(x^*) + \sum_{i=1}^m \nabla f_i(x^*)^{(*)} \lambda_i^* \tag{1.5.16}$$

$$+ \sum_{i=1}^p \nu_i^* \nabla h_i(x^*) = 0, \tag{1.5.17}$$

*where* $\nabla f_0(x^*)$ *and* $\nabla h_i(x^*)$ *are respectively the Fréchet derivatives of* $f_0(x)$ *and* $h_i(x), i = 1, \cdots, p$ *at* $x^*$, $\nabla f_i(x^*)^{(*)}$ *is the Fréchet derivative adjoint operator of* $f_i(x)$ *at* $x^*, i = 1, \cdots, m$[162].

**Theorem 1.5.9** *Consider the problem* (1.5.2)~(1.5.4). *If* $x^*$ *satisfies the KKT conditions* (1.5.12)~(1.5.17), *then* $x^*$ *is its solution.*

**Theorem 1.5.10** *Consider the problem (1.5.2)∼(1.5.4) satisfying Slater's condition given by Definition 1.5.6. Then for its solution, it is necessary and sufficient condition that $x^*$ satisfies the KKT conditions (1.5.12)∼(1.5.17).*

# Chapter 2

## Linear Classification

We are now beginning to study support vector machines starting from the linear classification problems. First, by investigating an example, we derive the maximal margin principle intuitively. Then, using this principle, the linear support vector classification is established.

## 2.1 Presentation of Classification Problems

### 2.1.1 A sample (diagnosis of heart disease)

Many researchers have done studies to develop intelligent medical decision support systems using existing data sets for cardiac disease diagnosis. For example, the data set provided by Cleveland Heart Disease Database (see [200]), recorded 13 relevant features of heart disease in 303 patients: blood pressure, cholesterol level, etc., and the 14th record having values 1,2,3,4 or not having heart disease with degree value 0. These records help the researchers to distinguish presence from absence of heart disease for new patients according to their recorded features. This kind of problem is referred to as classification or pattern recognition. In Probability and Statistics this is called discrimination analysis. Throughout this book, we use the terminology classification.

To make the classification problem easier to understand, we reduce the above problem to the following toy example, where only 2 features and 2 cases in the 14th record (value nonzero and value 0) are considered.

**Example 2.1.1** *Assume that diastolic (blood) pressure and the level of cholesterol are strong determinants of heart disease. Ten patients' clinical records are listed in Table 2.1. Here, $y_i = 1$ indicates that the $i$-th patient belongs to positive class having cardiac disease; $y_j = -1$ (not 0) indicates that the $j$-th patient belongs to negative class having no cardiac disease. The clinic record for the first patient is a two-dimensional vector $x_1 = ([x_1]_1, [x_1]_2)^\mathrm{T} = (73, 150)^\mathrm{T}$, and $y_1 = -1$, for the second patient is $x_2 = ([x_2]_1, [x_2]_2)^\mathrm{T} = (85, 165)^\mathrm{T}$, $y_2 = -1$, $\cdots$ and for the 10th patient is $x_{10} = ([x_{10}]_1, [x_{10}]_2)^\mathrm{T} = (110, 190)^\mathrm{T}$, $y_{10} = 1$. The $i$-th patient corresponds to $(x_i, y_i)$, which is called a training point; the*

**TABLE 2.1:** Clinical records of 10 patients.

| Patient number | Diastolic pressure ($[x]_1$ mmHg) | Cholesterol level ($[x]_2$ mg/dL) | Having heart disease ($y$) |
|---|---|---|---|
| 1 | $[x_1]_1 = 73$ | $[x_1]_2 = 150$ | $y_1 = -1$ |
| 2 | $[x_2]_1 = 85$ | $[x_2]_2 = 165$ | $y_2 = -1$ |
| $\vdots$ | $\vdots$ | $\vdots$ | $\vdots$ |
| 10 | $[x_{10}]_1 = 110$ | $[x_{10}]_2 = 190$ | $y_{10} = 1$ |

*ten training points consists of a training set $T$*

$$T = \{(x_1, y_1), \cdots, (x_{10}, y_{10})\}. \tag{2.1.1}$$

*The problem is, given the diastolic pressure and the level of cholesterol for a new patient (a two-dimensional vector $x = ([x]_1, [x]_2)^T$), how to deduce whether the patient has heart disease or not (to deduce whether the corresponding $y$ is 1 or $-1$), based on the training set $T$.*

This is a classification problem in two-dimensional space which can be shown by Figure 2.1. Each patient is represented by a training point in the coordinate plane. The $i$-th training point's location corresponds to the $i$-th two-dimensional vector $x_i$, and if $y_i = 1$, i.e. the patient has heart disease, the point is represented as "+", otherwise "○". The new patient corresponds

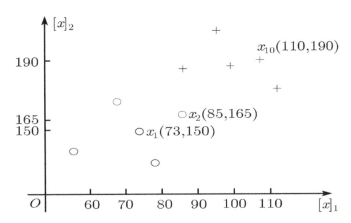

**FIGURE 2.1**: Data for heart disease.

to a new point in the plane and the problem is to deduce whether this point belongs to the positive or negative class. In other words, we need to separate the plane into two regions: region A and region B; if the point falls into region A, it belongs to the positive class, otherwise to the negative class. The key is how to separate the plane into two regions.

We know that any straight line $(w \cdot x) + b = 0$ (where $(w \cdot x)$ is the dot product between $w = ([w]_1, [w]_2)^T$ and $x = (x_1, x_2)^T$) will separate the plane into two regions: $(w \cdot x) + b \geqslant 0$ and $(w \cdot x) + b < 0$. That is, we can determine the value of the corresponding $y$ of any point $x$ by

$$y = f(x) = \text{sgn}((w \cdot x) + b), \tag{2.1.2}$$

where $\text{sgn}(\cdot)$ is a sign function defined by:

$$\text{sgn}(a) = \left\{ \begin{array}{ll} 1, & a \geqslant 0; \\ -1, & a < 0. \end{array} \right. \tag{2.1.3}$$

A value of 1 indicates the positive class, and a value of $-1$ the negative class.

Instead of the linear function $(w \cdot x) + b$, however, we can use nonlinear functions with much flexibility.

## 2.1.2   Classification problems and classification machines

Example 2.1.1 is a two-dimensional classification problem which contains two features, or $x \in R^2$, and 10 training points. Generally, we can consider the classification problem in $n$-dimensional space which contains $n$ features, i.e. $x \in R^n$, and $l$ training points. Denote the collection of training points as training set

$$T = \{(x_1, y_1), \cdots, (x_l, y_l)\}, \tag{2.1.4}$$

a general classification problem is that given a new input $x$, determine whether its corresponding $y$ is 1 or $-1$ according to the training set.

Let us formalize a classification problem mathematically as follows.

**Classification problem**: Given a training set

$$T = \{(x_1, y_1), \cdots, (x_l, y_l)\}, \tag{2.1.5}$$

where $x_i \in R^n, y_i \in \mathcal{Y} = \{1, -1\}, i = 1, \cdots, l$, find a real function $g(x)$ in $R^n$, to derive the value of $y$ for any $x$ by the decision function

$$f(x) = \text{sgn}(g(x)). \tag{2.1.6}$$

Thus it can be seen that solving a classification problem is to find a criterion to separate the $R^n$ space into two regions according to the training set $T$.

The above problem is a binary (or two-class) classification problem. Analogously, there are multiclass classification problems (see Chapter 8). In what follows it will be assumed, unless mentioned specifically, that all classification problems are two-class problems.

Note that in the training set $T$, $(x_i, y_i) \in R^n \times \mathcal{Y}$ is called training point or positive (negative) training point if the corresponding $y_i = 1$ ($y_i = -1$). The vector $x_i \in R^n$ is called input or positive (negative) input if the corresponding $y_i = 1$ ($y_i = -1$), its components are called features, $y_i \in \mathcal{Y} = \{1, -1\}$ is label or output.

According to the terminologies in the field of machine learning, we refer to the method for solving the above classification problems as classification machine or classification. Particularly, when $g(x)$ is restricted to be a linear function: $g(x) = (w \cdot x) + b$, the corresponding method is referred to as a linear classification machine or   linear classification, where the hyperplane $(w \cdot x) + b = 0$ separates $R^n$ space into two regions.

Intuitively speaking, simple linear classification machines can be used to solve such problems as shown in Figure 2.2 and Figure 2.3. On the other hand, for some other problems such as the one shown in Figure 2.4, general classification machines must be used, where $g(x)$ is allowed to be as a nonlinear function; otherwise a big error will be produced. The aim in this chapter is to establish linear classification machines.

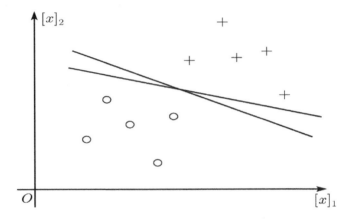

**FIGURE 2.2**: Linearly separable problem.

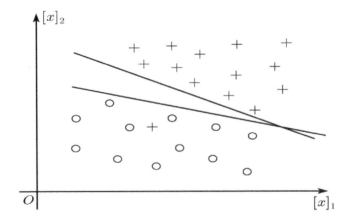

**FIGURE 2.3**: Approximately linearly separable problem.

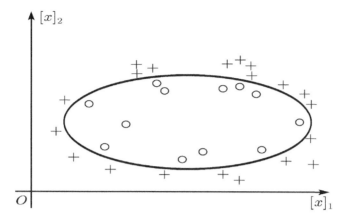

**FIGURE 2.4**: Linearly nonseparable problem.

## 2.2 Support Vector Classification (SVC) for Linearly Separable Problems

To construct linear classification machines, we consider linearly separable problems first. Roughly speaking, a linearly separable problem is a problem that the training set can be separated by a hyperplane correctly, such as the problem shown in Figure 2.1. The definition is as follows.

**Definition 2.2.1** *(Linearly separable problem) Consider the training set $T = \{(x_1, y_1), \cdots, (x_l, y_l)\} \in (R^n \times \mathcal{Y})^l$, where $x_i \in R^n, y_i \in \mathcal{Y} = \{1, -1\}, i = 1, \cdots, l$. If there exist $w \in R^n, b \in R$ and a positive number $\varepsilon$ such that for any subscripts $i$ with $y_i = 1$, we have $(w \cdot x_i) + b \geqslant \varepsilon$, and for any subscripts $i$ with $y_i = -1$, we have $(w \cdot x_i) + b \leqslant -\varepsilon$, we say the training set and its corresponding classification problem are linearly separable.*

### 2.2.1 Maximal margin method

#### 2.2.1.1 Derivation of the maximal margin method

Consider the separable problem in $R^2$ shown in Figure 2.1 and try to find a suitable straight line to separate the $R^2$ space into two regions. Obviously, it is natural to select the best separating straight line among the straight lines which are able to separate all of the positive inputs "+" and the negative inputs "○" correctly.

First let us investigate the case where the normal vector $w$ of the separating straight line is given. In Figure 2.5 $l_1$ is one of the straight lines with the given $w$, separating all of the positive and negative inputs correctly. But such a line is not unique; any line obtained parallel moving $l_1$ before approaching any input is a candidate. The two lines $l_2$ and $l_3$ in the extreme cases are called support lines. Among all the candidates the "middle one" between $l_2$ and $l_3$ should be the best. The above observation gives a method to construct the best separating straight line when the normal vector is given.

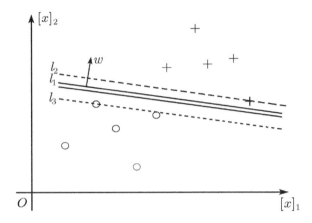

**FIGURE 2.5**: Optimal separating line with fixed normal direction.

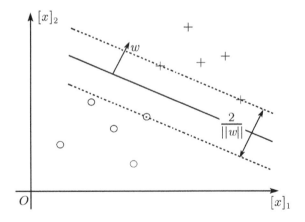

**FIGURE 2.6**: Separating line with maximal margin.

How to select the best normal direction $w$? It can be seen from the above analysis that there are two support lines for a given normal direction. The distance between the two support lines is called "margin". It is reasonable to select the normal direction which makes the margin maximal as shown in Figure 2.6.

Now let us formulate the problem to find the separating line $(w \cdot x) + b = 0$ as an optimization problem for the variables of $w$ and $b$. Suppose the separating line can be represented as $(\tilde{w} \cdot x) + \tilde{b} = 0$. Note that the separating line should be the middle line between two support lines; therefore the two support lines can be expressed as $(\tilde{w} \cdot x) + \tilde{b} = k$ and $(\tilde{w} \cdot x) + \tilde{b} = -k$ respectively. Let $w = \dfrac{\tilde{w}}{k}$, $b = \dfrac{\tilde{b}}{k}$, then the two support lines can equivalently be expressed as

$$(w \cdot x) + b = 1 \quad \text{and} \quad (w \cdot x) + b = -1. \tag{2.2.1}$$

Accordingly, the expression of the separating line becomes

$$(w \cdot x) + b = 0. \tag{2.2.2}$$

It yields from direct calculation that the margin, or the distance between the two support lines, is $\dfrac{2}{\|w\|}$. So the idea of maximal margin leads to the following optimization problem for $w$ and $b$:

$$\max_{w,b} \quad \frac{2}{\|w\|}, \tag{2.2.3}$$

$$\text{s.t.} \quad (w \cdot x) + b \geqslant 1, \quad \forall i : y_i = 1, \tag{2.2.4}$$

$$(w \cdot x) + b \leqslant -1, \quad \forall i : y_i = -1, \tag{2.2.5}$$

or

$$\min_{w,b} \quad \frac{1}{2}\|w\|^2, \tag{2.2.6}$$

$$\text{s.t.} \quad y_i((w \cdot x_i) + b) \geqslant 1, \quad i = 1, \cdots, 10. \tag{2.2.7}$$

The above optimization problem is derived from maximizing the margin between the two support lines in two-dimensional space $R^2$. It is not difficult to see that for solving classification problems in $n$-dimensional space $R^n$ we should maximize the margin between the two support hyperplanes. It is called the principle of maximal margin. The optimization problem obtained from this principle has the same form of the problem $(2.2.6)\sim(2.2.7)$. So we can establish the following algorithm:

**Algorithm 2.2.2** *(Maximal margin method for linearly separable problems)*

*(1) Input the training set* $T = \{(x_1, y_1), \cdots, (x_l, y_l)\}$, *where* $x_i \in R^n$, $y_i \in \mathcal{Y} = \{1, -1\}, i = 1, \cdots, l$;

*(2) Construct and solve the optimization problem*

$$\min_{w,b} \quad \frac{1}{2}\|w\|^2, \tag{2.2.8}$$

$$s.\,t. \quad y_i((w \cdot x_i) + b) \geqslant 1, i = 1, \cdots, l, \tag{2.2.9}$$

*obtaining the solution* $(w^*, b^*)$;

*(3) Construct the separating hyperplane* $(w^* \cdot x) + b^* = 0$, *and the decision function* $f(x) = \text{sgn}((w^* \cdot x) + b^*)$.

The above algorithm is sometimes called linear hard margin support vector classification since the constraint (2.2.9) implies that all inputs in the training set are required to be classified completely correctly and not in the margin tube $-1 < (\text{w} \cdot \text{x}) + b < 1$.

### 2.2.1.2   Properties of the maximal margin method

**Theorem 2.2.3** *For a linearly separable problem, there exists a solution* $(w^*, b^*)$ *to the optimization problem (2.2.8)~(2.2.9) and the solution satisfies:*

*(i)* $w^* \neq 0$;

*(ii) there exists a* $j \in \{i | y_i = 1\}$ *such that*

$$(w^* \cdot x_j) + b^* = 1; \tag{2.2.10}$$

*(iii) there exists a* $k \in \{i | y_i = -1\}$ *such that*

$$(w^* \cdot x_k) + b^* = -1. \tag{2.2.11}$$

**Proof**  We prove the existence of solution first. Since the training set is linearly separable, there is a feasible point $(\tilde{w}, \tilde{b})$ of the optimization problem (2.2.8) ~(2.2.9). Therefore the problem is equivalent to

$$\min_{w,b} \quad \frac{1}{2}\|w\|^2 \, , \tag{2.2.12}$$

$$\text{s.t.} \quad y_i((w \cdot x_i) + b) \geqslant 1 \, , i = 1, \cdots, l \, , \tag{2.2.13}$$

$$\frac{1}{2}\|w\|^2 \leqslant \frac{1}{2}\|\tilde{w}\|^2. \tag{2.2.14}$$

It is not difficult to see that the feasible region of the above problem is a non-empty bounded close set. According to the fact that the minimal value of a continuous function $(\frac{1}{2}\|w\|^2)$ is achieved in a non-empty bounded close set, the solution to the optimization problem (2.2.8)~(2.2.9) exits.

Now we turn to prove the properties (i)-(iii).

(i) We only need to prove $(w^*, b^*) = (0, b^*)$ is not a solution by contradiction. If $(w^*, b^*) = (0, b^*)$ is a solution, it should satisfy the constraints (2.2.9), which leads to $b^* \geqslant -1$ and $b^* \leqslant 1$ for positive and negative inputs respectively. This contradiction proves the conclusion.

(ii) We also use the proof by contradiction. Assume that the conclusion (ii) is not true, that is

$$(w^* \cdot x_i) + b^* > 1, \quad \forall i \in \{i | y_i = 1\}. \tag{2.2.15}$$

But since the solution $(w^*, b^*)$ should satisfy the constraints, we have

$$(w^* \cdot x_i) + b^* \leqslant -1, \quad \forall i \in \{i | y_i = -1\}. \tag{2.2.16}$$

Now it is sufficient to show that $(w^*, b^*)$ is not a solution from (2.2.15) and (2.2.16), then we have a contradiction. Let

$$\tilde{w} = \alpha w^*, \quad \tilde{b} = (b^* + 1)\alpha - 1. \tag{2.2.17}$$

If $\alpha \in (0, 1)$, then (2.2.16) is equivalent to

$$(\tilde{w} \cdot x_i) + \tilde{b} \leqslant -1, \quad \forall i \in \{i | y_i = -1\}. \tag{2.2.18}$$

On the other hand, for $i \in \{i | y_i = 1\}$ and from (2.2.15), we have

$$\lim_{\alpha \to 1-0} [(\tilde{w} \cdot x_i) + \tilde{b}] = \lim_{\alpha \to 1-0} [(\alpha w^* \cdot x_i) + (b^* + 1)\alpha - 1] = (w^* \cdot x_i) + b^* > 1. \tag{2.2.19}$$

Hence there exists an $\alpha \in (0, 1)$ such that

$$(\tilde{w} \cdot x_i) + \tilde{b} > 1, \quad \forall i \in \{i | y_i = 1\}. \tag{2.2.20}$$

Inequalities (2.2.18) and (2.2.20) indicate that $(\tilde{w}, \tilde{b})$ is a feasible point of the optimization problem and the corresponding value of the objective function is $\frac{1}{2} \|\tilde{w}\| = \alpha^2 \frac{1}{2} \|w^*\| < \frac{1}{2} \|w^*\|^2$, implying that $(w^*, b^*)$ is not a solution. This contradiction proves the conclusion.

(iii) Conclusion (iii) can be proved in a way similar to (ii). ∎

It should be noticed that the conclusion (i) shows that Algorithm 2.2.2 can always construct a hyperplane which is able to separate the inputs of two classes in the training set correctly, and conclusions (ii) and (iii) indicate that the two hyperplanes, $(w^* \cdot x) + b = \pm 1$, obtained using Algorithm 2.2.2 are the two support hyperplanes.

The following theorem shows the uniqueness of the separating hyperplane constructed by Algorithm 2.2.2.

**Theorem 2.2.4** *For a linearly separable problem, the solution to the optimization problem (2.2.8)$\sim$(2.2.9) is unique.*

**Proof** Suppose the problem has two solutions $(w_1^*, b_1^*)$ and $(w_2^*, b_2^*)$. From Theorem 1.2.15 in Chapter 1, the solution to the problem w.r.t. (with respect to) $w$ is unique, i.e.

$$w_1^* = w_2^*. \tag{2.2.21}$$

Hence the two solutions $(w_1^*, b_1^*)$ and $(w_2^*, b_2^*)$ can respectively be rewritten as $(w^*, b_1^*)$ and $(w^*, b_2^*)$. It yields from the conclusion (ii) of Theorem 2.2.3 that there are $j, j' \in \{1, \cdots, l\}$ such that $y_i = y_{j'} = 1$, and

$$(w^* \cdot x_j) + b_1^* = 1, \tag{2.2.22}$$
$$(w^* \cdot x_{j'}) + b_1^* \geq 1, \tag{2.2.23}$$
$$(w^* \cdot x_{j'}) + b_2^* = 1, \tag{2.2.24}$$
$$(w^* \cdot x_j) + b_2^* \geq 1. \tag{2.2.25}$$

Hence we have $b_1^* \geqslant b_2^*$ and $b_2^* \geqslant b_1^*$ from the above four expressions, then $b_1^* = b_2^*$. ∎

**Remark 2.2.5** *(Robustness of the maximal margin method) The margin is maximized for the separating hyperplane obtained from the maximal margin principle. This makes the corresponding decision function maintaining a good performance under certain perturbations. It is not sensitive for certain perturbations to the input $x_i$ of the training point $(x_i, y_i)$; it will still be classified correctly. Also the decision function $f(x) = \text{sgn}((w^* \cdot x) + b^*)$ itself is tolerant toward certain perturbations to $w^*$ and $b^*$; the decision function can still classify both the positive and negative inputs correctly.*

### 2.2.2 Linearly separable support vector classification

We now give another way to find the maximal margin hyperplane. That is, rather than directly solve the optimization problem $(2.2.8)\sim(2.2.9)$, we solve its dual problem.

#### 2.2.2.1 Relationship between the primal and dual problems

To derive the dual problem of the primal problem $(2.2.8)\sim(2.2.9)$, we introduce the Lagrange function:

$$L(w, b, \alpha) = \frac{1}{2}\|w\|^2 - \sum_{i=1}^{l} \alpha_i(y_i((w \cdot x_i) + b) - 1), \qquad (2.2.26)$$

where $\alpha = (\alpha_1, \cdots, \alpha_l)^{\mathrm{T}}$ is the Lagrange multiplier vector. We have the following theorems.

**Theorem 2.2.6** *Optimization problem*

$$\max_{\alpha} \quad -\frac{1}{2}\sum_{i=1}^{l}\sum_{j=1}^{l} y_i y_j (x_i \cdot x_j)\alpha_i \alpha_j + \sum_{j=1}^{l} \alpha_j, \qquad (2.2.27)$$

$$s.\,t. \quad \sum_{i=1}^{l} y_i \alpha_i = 0, \qquad (2.2.28)$$

$$\alpha_i \geqslant 0, \quad i = 1, \cdots, l \qquad (2.2.29)$$

*is the dual problem of the primal problem $(2.2.8)\sim(2.2.9)$.*

**Proof** According to Definition 1.2.16 in Chapter 1, the dual problem should have a form of

$$\max \quad g(\alpha) = \inf_{w,b} L(w, b, \alpha), \qquad (2.2.30)$$

$$s.\,t. \quad \alpha \geqslant 0. \qquad (2.2.31)$$

As $L(w, b, \alpha)$ is a strictly convex quadratic function of $w$, its minimal value is achieved at $w$ satisfying

$$\nabla_w L(w, b, \alpha) = w - \sum_{i=1}^{l} y_i x_i \alpha_i = 0, \qquad (2.2.32)$$

that is

$$w = \sum_{i=1}^{l} \alpha_i y_i x_i. \qquad (2.2.33)$$

Substituting the above in (2.2.26) yields

$$\inf_{w} L(w, b, \alpha) = -\frac{1}{2} \sum_{i=1}^{l} \sum_{j=1}^{l} y_i y_j (x_i \cdot x_j) \alpha_i \alpha_j + \sum_{j=1}^{l} \alpha_j - b \left( \sum_{i=1}^{l} y_i \alpha_i \right). \qquad (2.2.34)$$

Therefore,

$$\inf_{w,b} L(w, b, \alpha) = \begin{cases} -\dfrac{1}{2} \displaystyle\sum_{i=1}^{l} \sum_{j=1}^{l} y_i y_j \alpha_i \alpha_j (x_i \cdot x_j) + \sum_{j=1}^{l} \alpha_j, & if \ \displaystyle\sum_{i=1}^{l} y_i \alpha_i = 0; \\ -\infty, & \text{otherwise.} \end{cases}$$
$$(2.2.35)$$

Hence the problem (2.2.30)~(2.2.31) can be written as (2.2.27)~(2.2.29). ∎

**Theorem 2.2.7** *For linear separable problems, the dual problem (2.2.27)~(2.2.29) has a solution.*

**Proof** We use Theorem 1.2.21 in Chapter 1 (*Strong duality theorem*) to prove the conclusion. In fact, the primal problem (2.2.8)~(2.2.9) is a convex programming and Theorem 2.2.3 has already proved the existence of its solution. Furthermore, it satisfies the *Slater's condition* since its constraints contain linear inequalities only. Hence its dual problem (2.2.27)~(2.2.29) has a solution according to Theorem 1.2.21. ∎

The dual problem (2.2.27)~(2.2.29) is a maximization problem. In the optimization, a maximization problem is often replaced by its equivalent minimization problem. For the maximization problem (2.2.27)~(2.2.29), its equivalent minimization problem is:

$$\min_{\alpha} \quad \frac{1}{2} \sum_{i=1}^{l} \sum_{j=1}^{l} y_i y_j (x_i \cdot x_j) \alpha_i \alpha_j - \sum_{j=1}^{l} \alpha_j, \qquad (2.2.36)$$

$$\text{s.t.} \quad \sum_{i=1}^{l} y_i \alpha_i = 0, \qquad (2.2.37)$$

$$\alpha_i \geqslant 0, \quad i = 1, \cdots, l. \qquad (2.2.38)$$

Note that the minimization problem (2.2.36)~(2.2.38) has the same solution set as that to the maximization dual problem (2.2.27)~(2.2.29) and is often also called the dual problem of the problem (2.2.8)~(2.2.9).

**Theorem 2.2.8** *Optimization problem (2.2.36)~(2.2.38) is a convex quadratic programming.*

**Proof** Let

$$H = (y_i y_j (x_i \cdot x_j))_{l \times l}, \quad e = (1, \cdots, 1)^{\mathrm{T}},$$
$$\alpha = (\alpha_1, \cdots, \alpha_l)^{\mathrm{T}}, \quad y = (y_1, \cdots, y_l)^{\mathrm{T}}, \qquad (2.2.39)$$

then the problem (2.2.36)~(2.2.38) can be rewritten as

$$\min_{\alpha} \quad W(\alpha) = \frac{1}{2}\alpha^{\mathrm{T}}H\alpha - e^{\mathrm{T}}\alpha, \qquad (2.2.40)$$

$$\text{s.t.} \quad \alpha^{\mathrm{T}}y = 0, \qquad (2.2.41)$$

$$\alpha \geq 0. \qquad (2.2.42)$$

Let $Q = (y_1 x_1, \cdots, y_l x_l)$. It is clear that $H = Q^{\mathrm{T}}Q$ and so $H$ is positive semidefinite. Hence the above problem is a convex programming by Theorem 1.2.7 in Chapter 1. ∎

**Theorem 2.2.9** *Consider the linearly separable problem. For any solution to the dual problem (2.2.36)~(2.2.38), $\alpha^* = (\alpha_1^*, \cdots, \alpha_l^*)^{\mathrm{T}}$, there must be a nonzero component $\alpha_j^*$. Furthermore, for any nonzero component $\alpha_j^*$ of $\alpha^*$, the unique solution to the primal problem (2.2.8)~(2.2.9) can be obtained in the following way:*

$$w^* = \sum_{i=1}^{l} \alpha_i^* y_i x_i, \qquad (2.2.43)$$

$$b^* = y_j - \sum_{i=1}^{l} \alpha_i^* y_i (x_i \cdot x_j). \qquad (2.2.44)$$

**Proof** Firstly we show that, for $w^*$ given by (2.2.43), there exists a $\tilde{b}^*$ such that $(w^*, \tilde{b}^*)$ is the solution to the problem (2.2.8)~(2.2.9). Theorem 2.2.8 shows that problem (2.2.36)~(2.2.38) can be rewritten as the problem (2.2.40)~(2.2.42). So it is easy to see that problem (2.2.40)~(2.2.42) satisfies the Slater condition. Accordingly, if $\alpha^*$ is a solution to the problem (2.2.40)~(2.2.42), it yields from Theorem 1.2.23 (in Chapter 1) that there exists a multiplier $\tilde{b}^*$ and a multiplier vector $s^*$ such that

$$\alpha^{*\mathrm{T}}y = 0, \quad \alpha^* \geqslant 0, \qquad (2.2.45)$$

$$s^* \geqslant 0, \quad s^{*\mathrm{T}}\alpha^* = 0, \qquad (2.2.46)$$

$$H\alpha^* - e + \tilde{b}^* y - s^* = 0. \qquad (2.2.47)$$

Therefore, from (2.2.46) and (2.2.47), we have

$$H\alpha^* - e + \tilde{b}^* y \geqslant 0. \qquad (2.2.48)$$

From (2.2.43), that is equivalent to the following:

$$y_i((w^* \cdot x_i) + \tilde{b}^*) \geqslant 1, \qquad i = 1, \cdots, l, \qquad (2.2.49)$$

which implies that $(w^*, \tilde{b}^*)$ is a feasible solution to the primal problem (2.2.8)~(2.2.9).

Furthermore, from (2.2.45)~(2.2.47) we have

$$\frac{1}{2}\|w^*\|^2 = \frac{1}{2}\alpha^{*T}H\alpha^*$$

$$= \frac{1}{2}\alpha^{*T}H\alpha^* - \alpha^{*T}(H\alpha^* + \tilde{b}^*y - e - s^*)$$

$$= -\frac{1}{2}\alpha^{*T}H\alpha^* - \tilde{b}^*\alpha^{*T}y + e^T\alpha^* + s^{*T}\alpha^*$$

$$= -\frac{1}{2}\alpha^{*T}H\alpha^* + e^T\alpha^* . \qquad (2.2.50)$$

This shows that the objective function's value of the primal problem at the point $(w^*, \tilde{b}^*)$ is equal to the optimum value of its dual problem and therefore $(w^*, \tilde{b}^*)$ is the solution to the primal problem (2.2.8)~(2.2.9) according to Corollary 1.2.19 in Chapter 1.

Secondly, we show that $\alpha^*$ is nonzero. If it is not true, i.e. $\alpha^* = 0$, then the $w^*$ defined by (2.2.43) is a zero vector, which contradicts the conclusion (i) of Theorem 2.2.3, and so $\alpha^* \neq 0$.

Finally, we show that $(w^*, b^*)$ obtained from (2.2.43)~(2.2.44) is the unique solution to the primal problem (2.2.8)~(2.2.9). In fact, for the problem (2.2.8)~(2.2.9), the uniqueness of its solution can be derived immediately from Theorem 2.2.4 and so it is sufficient to show that the multiplier $\tilde{b}^*$ has the expression (2.2.44). Actually, note that $\alpha_j^* \neq 0$ implies $s_j^* = 0$ from (2.2.46). It yields from (2.2.47) that the $j$th entry of $H\alpha^* - e + \tilde{b}^*y$ is zero. Solving the equation w.r.t. $\tilde{b}^*$ results in expression (2.2.44). ∎

### 2.2.2.2 Linearly separable support vector classification

Theorem 2.2.9 gives a way to construct the classification decision function: starting from an arbitrary solution $\alpha^* = (\alpha_1^*, \cdots, \alpha_l^*)^T$ to the problem (2.2.36)~(2.2.38), we can find the solution $(w^*, b^*)$ to the primal problem according to (2.2.43)~(2.2.44). Thus, the following algorithm is established.

**Algorithm 2.2.10** *(Linearly separable support vector classification)*

*(1) Input the training set $T = \{(x_1, y_1), \cdots, (x_l, y_l)\}$, where $x_i \in R^n, y_i \in \mathcal{Y} = \{1, -1\}, i = 1, \cdots, l;$*

*(2) Construct and solve the convex quadratic programming*

$$\min_{\alpha} \quad \frac{1}{2}\sum_{i=1}^{l}\sum_{j=1}^{l} y_i y_j (x_i \cdot x_j)\alpha_i \alpha_j - \sum_{j=1}^{l}\alpha_j , \qquad (2.2.51)$$

$$s.\,t. \quad \sum_{i=1}^{l} y_i \alpha_i = 0 , \qquad (2.2.52)$$

$$\alpha_i \geqslant 0, \quad i = 1, \cdots, l , \qquad (2.2.53)$$

*obtaining a solution* $\alpha^* = (\alpha_1^*, \cdots, \alpha_l^*)^{\mathrm{T}};$

*(3) Compute* $w^* = \sum_{i=1}^{l} \alpha_i^* y_i x_i.$ *Choose a positive component of* $\alpha^*$, $\alpha_j^*$, *then compute* $b^*$

$$b^* = y_j - \sum_{i=1}^{l} \alpha_i^* y_i (x_i \cdot x_j); \qquad (2.2.54)$$

*(4) Construct the separating hyperplane* $(w^* \cdot x) + b^* = 0$, *and its associated decision function*

$$f(x) = sgn(g(x)), \qquad (2.2.55)$$

*where*

$$g(x) = (w^* \cdot x) + b^* = \sum_{i=1}^{l} y_i \alpha_i^* (x_i \cdot x) + b^* . \qquad (2.2.56)$$

## 2.2.3    Support vector

It is clear from step (3) and (4) of Algorithm 2.2.10 that the decision function is fully specified by a subset of the training set; the subset consists of the training points corresponding to the nonzero (positive) components of $\alpha^*$. Other training points play no part in determining the separating hyperplane that is chosen. To pay more attention to these determinant training points, we give the following definition.

**Definition 2.2.11** *(Support vector) Suppose that* $\alpha^* = (\alpha_1^*, \cdots, \alpha_l^*)^{\mathrm{T}}$ *is a solution to the dual problem obtained using Algorithm 2.2.10. The input* $x_i$, *associated with the training point* $(x_i, y_i)$, *is said to be a support vector if the corresponding component* $\alpha_i^*$ *of* $\alpha^*$ *is nonzero and otherwise it is a nonsupport vector.*

It should be pointed out that the problem (2.2.51)~(2.2.53) is convex but not strictly convex. Hence its solutions may not be unique. Therefore, support vectors are determined not fully by the training set, but also depend on which solution is obtained from Algorithm 2.2.10.

Obviously, in Algorithm 2.2.10, the decision function is decided only by the training points corresponding to support vectors. This is the reason why

Algorithm 2.2.10 is referred to as support vector classification. The following theorem characterizes the support vectors:

**Theorem 2.2.12** *Suppose that the linearly separable problems are solved using Algorithm 2.2.10 and that the $g(x)$ is defined by (2.2.56). Then*

*(i) support vector $x_i$ satisfies $y_i g(x_i) = y_i((w^* \cdot x_i) + b^*) = 1$, i.e. all support vectors are on the two support hyperplanes.*

*(ii) nonsupport vector $x_i$ satisfies $y_i g(x_i) = y_i((w^* \cdot x_i) + b^*) \geqslant 1$.*

    **Proof** Now observe (2.2.45)~(2.2.47) again. From the fact that $\alpha^* \geqslant 0$ in (2.2.45) and (2.2.46), we have $s_i^* \alpha_i^* = 0, i = 1, \cdots, l$. Then from (2.2.47), we obtain

$$s_i^* = y_i((w_i^* \cdot x_i) + b^*) - 1, \quad i = 1, \cdots, l. \tag{2.2.57}$$

Hence

$$s_i^* \alpha_i^* = \alpha_i^* (y_i((w_i^* \cdot x_i) + b^*) - 1) = 0, \quad i = 1, \cdots, l. \tag{2.2.58}$$

The conclusion (i) is valid from (2.2.58) and the fact that $\alpha_i^* \neq 0$ associated with the support vector $x_i$. The validity of the conclusion (ii) is derived from (2.2.57) and (2.2.46). ∎

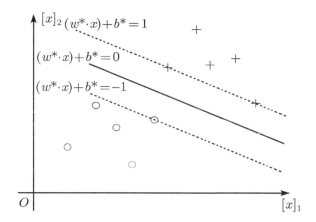

**FIGURE 2.7**: Geometric interpretation of Theorem 2.2.12.

    The geometric interpretation of the above theorem is shown in Figure 2.7 where $(w^* \cdot x) + b^* = 0$ is the separating straight line, $(w^* \cdot x) + b^* = 1$ and $(w^* \cdot x) + b^* = -1$ are the two support lines. A nonsupport vector belonging to the positive inputs lies on, or the aside of, the former support line and nonsupport vector belonging to the negative inputs lies on, or the aside of, the later. Moreover, support vectors are on either of the two support lines. That is what the name "support vector" comes from.

## 2.3　Linear $C$-Support Vector Classification

We discuss the linear separators for general classification problems. Suppose the training set is

$$T = \{(x_1, y_1), \cdots, (x_l, y_l)\}, \tag{2.3.1}$$

where $x_i \in R^n, y_i \in \mathcal{Y} = \{1, -1\}, i = 1, \cdots, l$. It is still of form (2.1.5) but now we do not restrict corresponding problems to be linearly separable ones.

### 2.3.1　Maximal margin method

#### 2.3.1.1　Derivation of the maximal margin method

For a general classification problem, which may be a linearly nonseparable problem, it is possible that any hyperplane is unable to separate all of the positive and negative inputs correctly. If we still want to use a hyperplane as a separator, we need to adopt the following two strategies: On one hand, in order to relax the requirement to separate all of the inputs correctly, allow the existence of training points that violate the constraints $y_i((w \cdot x_i) + b) \geqslant 1$ by introducing slack variables

$$\xi_i \geqslant 0, \quad i = 1, \cdots, l, \tag{2.3.2}$$

then yielding loose constraints

$$y_i((w \cdot x_i) + b) \geqslant 1 - \xi_i, \quad i = 1, \cdots, l. \tag{2.3.3}$$

On the other hand, in order to make the above violation as little as possible, avoid making $\xi_i$ too large by superimposing a penalty upon them in the objective function. For instance, we can add a term $\sum_i \xi_i$ to the objective function resulting in changing the primal problem (2.2.8)~(2.2.9) into

$$\min_{w, b, \xi} \quad \frac{1}{2}\|w\|^2 + C\sum_{i=1}^{l} \xi_i, \tag{2.3.4}$$

$$\text{s.t.} \quad y_i((w \cdot x_i) + b) \geqslant 1 - \xi_i, \ i = 1, \cdots, l, \tag{2.3.5}$$

$$\xi_i \geqslant 0, \ i = 1, \cdots, l, \tag{2.3.6}$$

where $\xi = (\xi_1, \cdots, \xi_l)^{\mathrm{T}}$, and $C > 0$ is a penalty parameter. The two terms in the objective function (2.3.4) indicate that we not only minimize $\|w\|^2$ (maximize the margin), but also minimize $\sum_{i=1}^{l} \xi_i$, which is a measurement of violation of the constraints $y_i((w \cdot x_i) + b) \geqslant 1, i = 1, \cdots, l$. The parameter $C$ determines the weighting between the two terms.

Thus we obtain an algorithm with soft margin which is an improved version of Algorithm 2.2.2 and can be described briefly as follows.

**Algorithm 2.3.1** *(Linear maximal margin method) Solve the primal problem (2.3.4)~(2.3.6), obtaining a solution $(w^*, b^*, \xi^*)$. Then construct the separating hyperplane and the corresponding decision function $f(x) = \text{sgn}(g(x))$, where $g(x) = (w^* \cdot x) + b^*$.*

#### 2.3.1.2 Properties of the maximal margin method

As the decision function is determined by the part $(w^*, b^*)$ of the solution $(w^*, b^*, \xi^*)$ to the primal problem (2.3.4)~(2.3.6), the main issue that concerns us is this part. According to Definition 1.2.13 (in Chapter 1), consider the solutions to the primal problem w.r.t. $(w, b)$ and w.r.t. $w$ and $b$.

**Theorem 2.3.2** *There exist solutions to the primal problem (2.3.4)~(2.3.6) w.r.t. $(w, b)$.*

**Proof** Similar to the proof of Theorem 2.2.3, take arbitrary $\tilde{w}, \tilde{b}$, and construct $\tilde{\xi} = (\tilde{\xi}_1, \cdots, \tilde{\xi}_l)^{\text{T}}$ by

$$\tilde{\xi}_i = \max\{1 - y_i((\tilde{w} \cdot x_i) + \tilde{b}), 0\}. \tag{2.3.7}$$

It is easy to see that $(\tilde{w}, \tilde{b}, \tilde{\xi})$ is a feasible point of the primal problem. Furthermore we can construct an optimization problem which is equivalent to the primal problem (2.3.4)~(2.3.6):

$$\min_{w,b,\xi} \quad \frac{1}{2}\|w\|^2 + C\sum_{i=1}^{l}\xi_i, \tag{2.3.8}$$

$$\text{s.t.} \quad y_i((w \cdot x_i) + b) \geqslant 1 - \xi_i, \ i = 1, \cdots, l, \tag{2.3.9}$$

$$\xi_i \geqslant 0, \ i = 1, \cdots, l, \tag{2.3.10}$$

$$\frac{1}{2}\|w\|^2 + C\sum_{i=1}^{l}\xi_i \leqslant \frac{1}{2}\|\tilde{w}\|^2 + C\sum_{i=1}^{l}\tilde{\xi}_i, \tag{2.3.11}$$

and now it is easy to show the existence of its solutions. The details are omitted here. ∎

**Theorem 2.3.3** *The solution $w^*$ of the primal problem (2.3.4)~(2.3.6) w.r.t. $w$ is unique.*

**Proof** The conclusion is true immediately from Theorem 1.2.15 in Chapter 1. ∎

**Remark 2.3.4** *It is different from the situation for linearly separable problems and possible that the solution $w^*$ to the primal problem w.r.t. $w$ may be zero. So we may be unable to construct the separating hyperplane and decision function in this way theoretically. However, in practical applications this possibility is nearly zero, which is why we would not go further. Readers who are interested in the details can refer to [121].*

The following counterexample shows that the solution to primal problem w.r.t. $b$ may not be unique which is different from that of primal problem for linearly separable problems.

**Example 2.3.5** *Consider a classification problem in $R$ (one dimensional space). Suppose the training set is*

$$T = \{(x_1, y_1), (x_2, y_2)\} = \{(-1, -1), (1, 1)\} . \qquad (2.3.12)$$

*Choose a penalty parameter $C < \dfrac{1}{2}$ and the primal problem is*

$$\min_{w,b,\xi} \quad \frac{1}{2}\|w\|^2 + C(\xi_1 + \xi_2), \qquad (2.3.13)$$

$$s.\, t. \qquad w - b \geqslant 1 - \xi_1, \qquad (2.3.14)$$

$$w + b \geqslant 1 - \xi_2, \qquad (2.3.15)$$

$$\xi_1, \xi_2 \geqslant 0. \qquad (2.3.16)$$

*Find the solutions of the above problem w.r.t. $b$.*

Introduce the corresponding Lagrange function:

$$L(w, b, \xi, \alpha, \eta) = \frac{1}{2}\|w\|^2 + C(\xi_1 + \xi_2) + \alpha_1(1 - \xi_1 - w + b)$$
$$+ \alpha_2(1 - \xi_2 - w - b) - \eta_1\xi_1 - \eta_2\xi_2. \qquad (2.3.17)$$

Then we find $w$, $b$, $\xi = (\xi_1, \xi_2)^{\mathrm{T}}$ and $\alpha = (\alpha_1, \alpha_2)^{\mathrm{T}}, \eta = (\eta_1, \eta_2)^{\mathrm{T}}$ satisfying KKT conditions. The KKT conditions are as follows:

$$1 - \xi_1 - w + b \leqslant 0, \quad 1 - \xi_2 - w - b \leqslant 0, \quad -\xi_1 \leqslant 0, \quad -\xi_2 \leqslant 0, \qquad (2.3.18)$$

$$\alpha_1 \geqslant 0, \quad \alpha_2 \geqslant 0, \quad \eta_1 \geqslant 0, \quad \eta_2 \geqslant 0, \qquad (2.3.19)$$

$$\alpha_1(1 - \xi_1 - w + b) = 0, \quad \alpha_2(1 - \xi_2 - w - b) = 0, \quad \eta_1\xi_1 = 0,$$

$$\eta_2\xi_2 = 0, \qquad (2.3.20)$$

$$\nabla_w L = w - \alpha_1 - \alpha_2 = 0, \quad \nabla_b L = \alpha_1 - \alpha_2 = 0, \qquad (2.3.21)$$

$$\nabla_{\xi_1} L = C - \alpha_1 - \eta_1 = 0, \quad \nabla_{\xi_2} L = C - \alpha_2 - \eta_2 = 0, \qquad (2.3.22)$$

Obviously, these conditions imply that

$$\alpha_1 = \alpha_2, \quad \eta_1 = \eta_2. \qquad (2.3.23)$$

Hence what we need now is to find all the solutions that satisfy conditions (2.3.18)~(2.3.22) according to three different cases:

(i) Case of $\eta_1 = \eta_2 \neq 0, \alpha_1 = \alpha_2 \neq 0$. In this case, we immediately have $\xi_1 = \xi_2 = 0$, $b = 0$, $w = 1, \alpha_1 = \alpha_2 = \dfrac{1}{2}, \eta_1 = C - \dfrac{1}{2} < 0$. But the solution dose not exist since the last expression contradicts (2.3.19).

(ii) Case of $\eta_1 = \eta_2 \neq 0$, $\alpha_1 = \alpha_2 = 0$. In this case, we have $w = 0$, $\eta_1 = \eta_2 = C$, $\xi_1 = \xi_2 = 0$, $1 + b \leqslant 0$, $1 - b \leqslant 0$. The last two expressions are in contradiction with each other and so we have still no solutions.

(iii) Case of $\eta_1 = \eta_2 = 0$. In this case, we have

$$w = 2C, \quad \alpha_1 = \alpha_2 = C, \quad \eta_1 = \eta_2 = 0, \quad b \in [\,\underline{b}, \overline{b}\,],$$
$$\xi_1 = 1 - 2C + b, \quad \xi_2 = 1 - 2C - b, \tag{2.3.24}$$

where $\underline{b} = -1 + 2C$, $\overline{b} = 1 - 2C$. According to Theorem 1.2.9 in Chapter 1 we know that the set of solutions w.r.t. $b$ is the close interval $[\underline{b}, \overline{b}] = [-1 + 2C, 1 - 2C]$.

**Theorem 2.3.6** *The solution set to the primal problem (2.3.4)~(2.3.6) w.r.t. $b$ is a bounded close interval $[\,\underline{b}, \overline{b}\,]$, where $\underline{b} \leqslant \overline{b}$.*

**Proof** According to Theorem 2.3.2, we know that the solution set to the problem (2.3.4)~(2.3.6) w.r.t. $b$ is not empty. And Theorem 1.2.9 shows that the solution set forms a convex set. This leads to the solution set being bounded at close interval since the solutions w.r.t. $b$ are bounded. ∎

### 2.3.2 Linear $C$-support vector classification

The basic idea of linear support vector classification is finding the solution to the primal problem (2.3.4)~(2.3.6) by means of solving its dual problem.

#### 2.3.2.1 Relationship between the primal and dual problems

Firstly we introduce the dual problem. The Lagrange function corresponding to the primal problem (2.3.4)~(2.3.6) is:

$$L(w, b, \xi, \alpha, \beta) = \frac{1}{2}\|w\|^2 + C\sum_{i=1}^{l}\xi_i - \sum_{i=1}^{l}\alpha_i(y_i((w \cdot x_i) + b) - 1 + \xi_i) - \sum_{i=1}^{l}\beta_i\xi_i,$$
$$\tag{2.3.25}$$

where $\alpha = (\alpha_1, \cdots, \alpha_l)^{\mathrm{T}}$ and $\beta = (\beta_1, \cdots, \beta_l)^{\mathrm{T}}$ are Lagrange multiplier vectors. Then we have the following theorem.

**Theorem 2.3.7** *Optimization problem*

$$\max_{\alpha,\beta} \quad -\frac{1}{2}\sum_{i=1}^{l}\sum_{j=1}^{l}y_iy_j\alpha_i\alpha_j(x_i \cdot x_j) + \sum_{j=1}^{l}\alpha_j, \tag{2.3.26}$$

$$\text{s. t.} \quad \sum_{i=1}^{l}y_i\alpha_i = 0, \tag{2.3.27}$$

$$C - \alpha_i - \beta_i = 0, \quad i = 1, \cdots, l, \tag{2.3.28}$$

$$\alpha_i \geqslant 0, \quad i = 1, \cdots, l, \tag{2.3.29}$$

$$\beta_i \geqslant 0, \quad i = 1, \cdots, l \tag{2.3.30}$$

*is the dual problem of the primal problem (2.3.4)~(2.3.6).*

**Proof** It is similar to the proof of Theorem 2.2.6. Also it is a special case of Theorem 4.1.1 in Chapter 4. The details are omitted here.                    ■

**Theorem 2.3.8** *Dual problem* (2.3.26)~(2.3.30) *has solutions.*

**Proof** It is similar to the proof of Theorem 2.2.7 and the details are omitted here.                                                                         ■

Dual problem (2.3.26)~(2.3.30) can be simplified to a problem only for a single variable $\alpha$ by eliminating the variable $\beta$ and then rewritten as a minimization problem:

$$\min_{\alpha} \quad \frac{1}{2}\sum_{i=1}^{l}\sum_{j=1}^{l}y_iy_j(x_i \cdot x_j)\alpha_i\alpha_j - \sum_{j=1}^{l}\alpha_j \,, \tag{2.3.31}$$

$$\text{s.t.} \quad \sum_{i=1}^{l}y_i\alpha_i = 0 \,, \tag{2.3.32}$$

$$0 \leqslant \alpha_i \leqslant C, \quad i = 1,\cdots,l \,. \tag{2.3.33}$$

**Theorem 2.3.9** *Suppose that* $\alpha^* = (\alpha_1^*,\cdots,\alpha_l^*)^{\mathrm{T}}$ *is any solution to the convex quadratic program* (2.3.31)~(2.3.33). *If there exists a component of* $\alpha^*$, $\alpha_j^*$, *such that* $\alpha_j^* \in (0,C)$, *then a solution* $(w^*,b^*)$ *to the primal problem* (2.3.4)~(2.3.6) *w.r.t.* $(w,b)$ *can be obtained by*

$$w^* = \sum_{i=1}^{l}\alpha_i^*y_ix_i \,, \tag{2.3.34}$$

$$b^* = y_j - \sum_{i=1}^{l}\alpha_i^*y_i(x_i \cdot x_j). \tag{2.3.35}$$

**Proof** We omit the details as there is a special case of Theorem 4.1.3 later.
                                                                              ■

#### 2.3.2.2   Linear $C$-support vector classification

Now we can establish an algorithm according to Theorem 2.3.9 as follows:

**Algorithm 2.3.10** *(Linear C-support vector classification, Linear C-SVC)*

*(1) Input the training set* $T = \{(x_1,y_1),\cdots,(x_l,y_l)\}$, *where* $x_i \in R^n, y_i \in \mathcal{Y} = \{1,-1\}, i = 1,\cdots,l$;

*(2) Choose an appropriate penalty parameter* $C > 0$;

*(3) Construct and solve the convex quadratic program*

$$\min_{\alpha} \quad \frac{1}{2}\sum_{i=1}^{l}\sum_{j=1}^{l} y_i y_j (x_i \cdot x_j)\alpha_i \alpha_j - \sum_{j=1}^{l} \alpha_j \,, \tag{2.3.36}$$

$$s.\,t. \quad \sum_{i=1}^{l} y_i \alpha_i = 0 \,, \tag{2.3.37}$$

$$0 \leqslant \alpha_i \leqslant C, \quad i = 1,\cdots,l \,, \tag{2.3.38}$$

*obtaining a solution* $\alpha^* = (\alpha_1^*,\cdots,\alpha_l^*)^{\mathrm{T}};$

*(4) Compute* $b^*$: *choose a component of* $\alpha^*$, $\alpha_j^* \in (0,C)$ *and compute*

$$b^* = y_j - \sum_{i=1}^{l} y_i \alpha_i^* (x_i \cdot x_j); \tag{2.3.39}$$

*(5) Construct the decision function*

$$f(x) = sgn(g(x)), \tag{2.3.40}$$

*where*

$$g(x) = \sum_{i=1}^{l} y_i \alpha_i^* (x_i \cdot x) + b^*. \tag{2.3.41}$$

Algorithm 2.3.10 can be used for general classification problems including linearly separable problems. So both Algorithm 2.3.10 and Algorithm 2.2.10 (linear separable support vector classification) are able to deal with linear separable problems. Now for these kinds of problems, we compare their performance. Theoretically, it is not difficult to see that when the parameter $C \to \infty$, the primal problem $(2.3.4)\sim(2.3.6)$ will be reduced to the primal problem $(2.2.8)\sim(2.2.9)$ for linearly separable problems. In fact the advantage of Algorithm 2.3.10 will be given from theoretical point of view in Section 5.6.3 in Chapter 5. In this case, the two algorithms can be deemed the same. However, the primal problems associated with the two algorithms, problems $(2.3.4)\sim(2.3.6)$ and $(2.2.8)\sim(2.2.9)$, are not usually the same. So that, generally speaking, the decision functions obtained from the two algorithms would be different. The decision functions resulting in using Algorithm 2.2.10 are not necessarily better although it is designed particularly for these kinds of problems. One of the reasons is due to the case when the training set contains a few "wild points" which may be marked wrongly and will affect the resulting hyperplane seriously. But Algorithm 2.3.10 can overcome this shortcoming to a certain extent.

# Chapter 3

## Linear Regression

Now we turn to the linear regression problems. The linear support vector regression is established by converting the linear regression problems to the linear classification problems.

---

### 3.1 Regression Problems and Linear Regression Problems

Similar to classification problems, regression problems consist of finding a real function, for a given training set T: $T = \{(x_1, y_1), \cdots, (x_l, y_l)\}$, where $x_i \in R^n$ is an input, and $y_i \in \mathcal{Y} = \mathcal{R}$ is an output, $i = 1, \cdots, l$. Rather than just $\mathcal{Y} = \{-1, 1\}$ in classification problems, $\mathcal{Y}$ is generalized to the real set in regression problems. Correspondingly, the goal of regression problems is to derive the real value of an output $y$ for any input $x$, based on a training set T.

A regression problem can be formalized as follows.

**Regression problem**: Given a training set

$$T = \{(x_1, y_1), \cdots, (x_l, y_l)\}, \tag{3.1.1}$$

where $x_i \in R^n, y_i \in \mathcal{Y} = R, i = 1, \cdots, l$, find a real function $g(x)$ in $R^n$, to derive the value of $y$ for any $x$ by the function $y = g(x)$.

The above problem is defined in the $n$-dimensional space. In order to explain it graphically, Figure 3.1 shows an example in one-dimensional space, where the training points are represented by "×". Geometrically, our goal is to find a curve $y = g(x)$ that fits the given points.

Particularly, when the function $g(x)$ is restricted to be a linear function

$$y = g(x) = (w \cdot x) + b, \tag{3.1.2}$$

the corresponding problem is defined as the linear regression problem.

**Linear regression problem**: Given a training set

$$T = \{(x_1, y_1), \cdots, (x_l, y_l)\}, \tag{3.1.3}$$

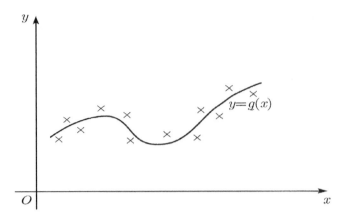

**FIGURE 3.1**: A regression problem in $R$.

where $x_i \in R^n, y_i \in \mathcal{Y} = R, i = 1, \cdots, l$, find a real function $g(x) = (w \cdot x) + b$ in $R^n$, to derive the value of $y$ for any $x$ by the function $y = g(x)$.

Geometrically, a linear regression problem in $n$-dimensional space corresponds to find a hyperplane in $(n+1)$-dimensional space for a given set (3.1.3), since a linear function defined in $n$-dimensional space is equivalent to a hyperplane in the $R^n \times R$. Figure 3.2 shows a simple case in one-dimensional space. Roughly speaking, for the given points ("×"), our goal is to find a straight line with a small "deviation" from these points. This leads to the following definition of hard $\bar{\varepsilon}$-band hyperplane.

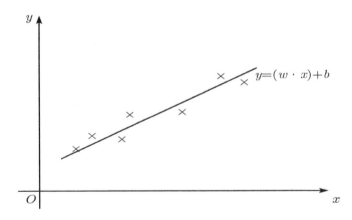

**FIGURE 3.2**: A linear regression problem in $R$.

## 3.2 Hard $\bar{\varepsilon}$-Band Hyperplane

### 3.2.1 Linear regression problem and hard $\bar{\varepsilon}$-band hyperplane

In order to solve regression problems, firstly we introduce the definitions of $\bar{\varepsilon}$-band and hard $\bar{\varepsilon}$-band hyperplane.

**Definition 3.2.1** *($\bar{\varepsilon}$-band of a hyperplane) For a given $\bar{\varepsilon} > 0$, the $\bar{\varepsilon}$-band of a hyperplane $y = (w \cdot x) + b$ is the set $\{(x, y)|(w \cdot x) + b - \bar{\varepsilon} < y < (w \cdot x) + b + \bar{\varepsilon}\}$, i.e. the region between two parallel hyperplanes: $y = (w \cdot x) + b - \bar{\varepsilon}$ and $y = (w \cdot x) + b + \bar{\varepsilon}$.*

Notice that the region in the above definition is open, i.e. it does not contain the points $(x, y)$ satisfying

$$(w \cdot x) + b - \bar{\varepsilon} = y \text{ and } (w \cdot x) + b + \bar{\varepsilon} = y. \tag{3.2.1}$$

**Definition 3.2.2** *(Hard $\bar{\varepsilon}$-band hyperplane) For a given $\bar{\varepsilon} > 0$ and a training set $T$ defined by (3.1.3), we say that a hyperplane $y = (w \cdot x) + b$ is the hard $\bar{\varepsilon}$-band hyperplane for the training set $T$, if all the training points are inside its $\bar{\varepsilon}$-band, i.e. the hyperplane $y = (w \cdot x) + b$ satisfies that*

$$-\bar{\varepsilon} < y_i - ((w \cdot x_i) + b) < \bar{\varepsilon}, \quad i = 1, \cdots, l. \tag{3.2.2}$$

Figure 3.3 shows an example of a hard $\bar{\varepsilon}$-band hyperplane in a linear regression problem. "×" represents the training points, and the solid line represents the hyperplane (straight line) $y = (w \cdot x) + b$. The region between two dashed lines is the $\bar{\varepsilon}$-band of the hyperplane $y = (w \cdot x) + b$. Obviously, all of training points are inside this tube, so the hyperplane is so-called a hard $\bar{\varepsilon}$-band hyperplane.

Now we consider the hard $\bar{\varepsilon}$-band hyperplane for any training set (3.1.3). When $\bar{\varepsilon}$ is large enough, there always exists a hard $\bar{\varepsilon}$-band hyperplane, since the number of the training points is limited. And the value of $\bar{\varepsilon}$ corresponding to a hard $\bar{\varepsilon}$-band hyperplane should not be so small, it should be larger than the optimal value $\varepsilon_{\inf}$ of the following optimization problem:

$$\min_{w,b,\bar{\varepsilon}} \quad \bar{\varepsilon}, \tag{3.2.3}$$

$$\text{s.t.} \quad -\bar{\varepsilon} \leqslant y_i - ((w \cdot x_i) + b) \leqslant \bar{\varepsilon}, \, i = 1, \cdots, l. \tag{3.2.4}$$

Obviously, there are two possibilities for a given $\bar{\varepsilon} > 0$: (i) if $\bar{\varepsilon} > \varepsilon_{\inf}$, then the hard $\bar{\varepsilon}$-band hyperplanes exist, and not uniquely; (ii) if $\bar{\varepsilon} \leq \varepsilon_{\inf}$, then there does not exist any hard $\bar{\varepsilon}$-band hyperplane.

Roughly speaking, for a given training set $T$, when there exists a hard $\bar{\varepsilon}$-band hyperplane for a small $\bar{\varepsilon}$, it is reasonable to choose this hyperplane as the solution to the linear regression problem. Therefore our following work is to construct a hard $\bar{\varepsilon}$-band hyperplane.

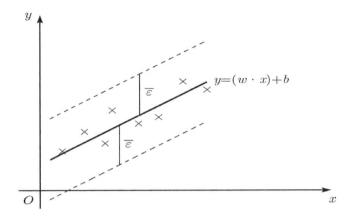

**FIGURE 3.3**: A hard $\bar{\varepsilon}$-band hyperplane (line) in $R$.

### 3.2.2  Hard $\bar{\varepsilon}$-band hyperplane and linear classification

In this section, we try to construct a hard $\bar{\varepsilon}$-tube hyperplane using the classification method. Figure 3.4 shows the idea of converting the construction of a hard $\bar{\varepsilon}$-band hyperplane to a classification problem. Consider a linear regression problem in $R$. Suppose that the training set is $\{A_1, A_2, \cdots, A_7\}$ represented by "×". For a given $\bar{\varepsilon} > 0$ and $i = 1, \cdots, 7$, the following steps can help us find a hard $\bar{\varepsilon}$-band hyperplane. Firstly, we move the points $A_i$ up and down with the distance of $\bar{\varepsilon}$, and obtain the points $A_i^+$ and $A_i^-$. Secondly, we join $A_i^+$ to $A_i^-$, and obtain line segments $A_i^+ A_i^-$ just as shown by the dashed lines in Figure 3.4. These line segments are open. Lastly, any line that passes through these open line segments is a hard $\bar{\varepsilon}$-band hyperplane. This implies that the line separating the two class points $\{A_1^+, A_2^+, \cdots, A_7^+\}$ and $\{A_1^-, A_2^-, \cdots, A_7^-\}$ correctly is just what we want. So, we find the relationship between constructing a hard $\bar{\varepsilon}$-band hyperplane and linear classification.

According to the above discussion, we construct two classes based on the training set (3.1.3) by adding and subtracting $\bar{\varepsilon}$ to $y$ of every training points, and obtain two sets of the positive and negative points respectively:

$$D^+ = \{(x_i^T, y_i + \bar{\varepsilon})^T, i = 1, \cdots, l\}\,, \tag{3.2.5}$$
$$D^- = \{(x_i^T, y_i - \bar{\varepsilon})^T, i = 1, \cdots, l\}\,. \tag{3.2.6}$$

Then, the training set for classification is

$$\{((x_1^T, y_1 + \bar{\varepsilon})^T, 1), \cdots, ((x_l^T, y_l + \bar{\varepsilon})^T, 1), ((x_1^T, y_1 - \bar{\varepsilon})^T, -1), \cdots,$$
$$((x_l^T, y_l - \bar{\varepsilon})^T, -1)\}, \tag{3.2.7}$$

where $(x_i^T, y_i + \bar{\varepsilon})^T$ or $(x_i^T, y_i - \bar{\varepsilon})^T$ represents the input, and the last component, 1 or $-1$, represents the output. The problem of constructing a hard $\bar{\varepsilon}$-band hyperplane is equivalent to linearly separating the above training sets

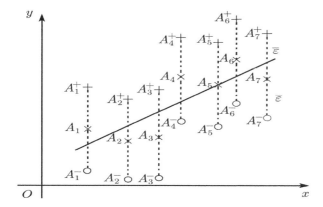

**FIGURE 3.4**: Demonstration of constructing a hard $\bar{\varepsilon}$-band hyperplane (line) in $R$.

(3.2.7). In fact, the following theorem depicts the relationship between these two problems.

**Theorem 3.2.3** *For a given training set (3.1.3) and $\bar{\varepsilon} > 0$, a hyperplane $y = (w \cdot x) + b$ is a hard $\bar{\varepsilon}$-band hyperplane if and only if the sets $D^+$ and $D^-$ defined by (3.2.5)$\sim$(3.2.6) locate on both sides of this hyperplane respectively, and all of the points in $D^+$ and $D^-$ do not touch this hyperplane.*

**Proof** For a given $\bar{\varepsilon} > 0$, if a hyperplane $y = (w \cdot x) + b$ is a hard $\bar{\varepsilon}$-band hyperplane, then by Definition 3.2.2, we have

$$-\bar{\varepsilon} < y_i - ((w \cdot x_i) + b) < \bar{\varepsilon}, \quad i = 1, \cdots, l. \tag{3.2.8}$$

This implies

$$y_i + \bar{\varepsilon} > (w \cdot x_i) + b > y_i - \bar{\varepsilon}, \quad i = 1, \cdots, l, \tag{3.2.9}$$

so the sets $D^+$ and $D^-$ locate on both sides of this hyperplane respectively, and all of the points do not touch this hyperplane.

Conversely, if the sets $D^+$ and $D^-$ locate on both sides of this hyperplane, and all of the points do not touch it, then (3.2.9) holds. Furthermore, (3.2.9) is equivalent to (3.2.8). So the hyperplane $y = (w \cdot x) + b$ is a hard $\bar{\varepsilon}$-band hyperplane. $\blacksquare$

As discussed before, in order to solve a regression problem with the training set (3.1.3), it is reasonable to find a hard $\bar{\varepsilon}$-band hyperplane. According to Theorem 3.2.3, we know that constructing a hard $\bar{\varepsilon}$-tube hyperplane is equivalent to constructing a separating hyperplane for the training set (3.2.7). This provides us a way of transforming a regression problem to a classification problem.

### 3.2.3 Optimization problem of constructing a hard $\bar{\varepsilon}$-band hyperplane

In this section, we consider how to construct a hard $\bar{\varepsilon}$-band hyperplane. It is easy to see that there exist a lot of hard $\bar{\varepsilon}$-tube hyperplanes for the case of $\bar{\varepsilon} > \varepsilon_{\inf}$, where $\varepsilon_{\inf}$ is the optimal value of the problem $(3.2.3)\sim(3.2.4)$. However, which one is the best? Theorem 3.2.3 shows that the better the hard $\bar{\varepsilon}$-band hyperplane, the better the separating hyperplane with the training set $(3.2.7)$. So, we can construct a hard $\bar{\varepsilon}$-band hyperplane using the classification method. Specifically, when $\bar{\varepsilon} > \varepsilon_{\inf}$, we can derive the optimization problem of constructing a hard $\bar{\varepsilon}$-band hyperplane, according to the maximal margin method for a linearly separable problem.

Note that the classification problem is in $R^{n+1}$. Assume that the hyperplane is $(w \cdot x) + \eta y + b = 0$, where the normal vector is $(w^T, \eta)^T$, $w \in R^n$ corresponds to $x$, and $\eta \in R$ corresponds to $y$. Similar to the problem $(2.2.3)\sim(2.2.5)$, we get the following quadratic programming problem w.r.t. $(w, \eta, b)$

$$\min_{w,\eta,b} \quad \frac{1}{2}\|w\|^2 + \frac{1}{2}\eta^2 \,, \tag{3.2.10}$$

$$\text{s.t.} \quad (w \cdot x_i) + \eta(y_i + \bar{\varepsilon}) + b \geqslant 1 \,, \quad i = 1, \cdots, l \,, \tag{3.2.11}$$

$$(w \cdot x_i) + \eta(y_i - \bar{\varepsilon}) + b \leqslant -1 \,, \quad i = 1, \cdots, l \,. \tag{3.2.12}$$

Then the separating hyperplane is

$$(\bar{w} \cdot x) + \bar{\eta}y + \bar{b} = 0, \tag{3.2.13}$$

where $(\bar{w}, \bar{\eta}, \bar{b})$ is the solution to the problem $(3.2.10)\sim(3.2.12)$. At last, the regression function is

$$y = (w^* \cdot x) + b^*, \tag{3.2.14}$$

where

$$w^* = -\frac{\bar{w}}{\bar{\eta}}, b^* = -\frac{\bar{b}}{\bar{\eta}}. \tag{3.2.15}$$

The above discussion provides a way to find a linear regression function. Firstly, we construct the problem $(3.2.10)\sim(3.2.12)$ and get its solution $(\bar{w}, \bar{\eta}, \bar{b})$; Next, we compute $(w^*, b^*)$ using $(3.2.15)$. However, the following way is more direct: construct an optimization problem that $(w^*, b^*)$ should satisfy and get its solution. The following theorem will tell us what this problem is, when $\bar{\eta}$ of the solution $(\bar{w}, \bar{\eta}, \bar{b})$ to the problem $(3.2.10)\sim(3.2.12)$ is given.

**Theorem 3.2.4** *Suppose that $(\bar{w}, \bar{b}, \bar{\eta})$ is the solution to the problem $(3.2.10)\sim(3.2.12)$, then $\bar{\eta} \neq 0$. Furthermore, let*

$$\varepsilon = \bar{\varepsilon} - \frac{1}{\bar{\eta}}, \tag{3.2.16}$$

*then*

*(i) $\varepsilon$ satisfies*

$$\varepsilon_{\inf} \leqslant \varepsilon < \bar{\varepsilon}, \tag{3.2.17}$$

*where $\varepsilon_{\inf}$ is the optimal value of the problem $(3.2.3)\sim(3.2.4)$;*

*(ii) $(w^*, b^*) = \left(-\dfrac{\bar{w}}{\bar{\eta}}, -\dfrac{\bar{b}}{\bar{\eta}}\right)$ is the solution to the following problem:*

$$\min_{w,b} \quad \frac{1}{2}\|w\|^2, \tag{3.2.18}$$

$$\text{s.t.} \quad (w \cdot x_i) + b - y_i \leqslant \varepsilon, \ i = 1, \cdots, l, \tag{3.2.19}$$

$$\quad y_i - (w \cdot x_i) - b \leqslant \varepsilon, \ i = 1, \cdots, l \tag{3.2.20}$$

**Proof** Firstly, we prove $\bar{\eta} \neq 0$. In fact, if $\bar{\eta} = 0$, there does not exist $(\bar{w}, \bar{b})$ such that $(\bar{w}, \bar{b}, 0)$ satisfies the constraints of the problem $(3.2.10)\sim(3.2.12)$.

Secondly, we prove the conclusion (i). On one hand, since the solution $(\bar{w}, \bar{b}, \bar{\eta})$ satisfies the constraints $(3.2.11)$ and $(3.2.12)$, we have

$$(\bar{w} \cdot x_i) + \bar{\eta}(y_i + \bar{\varepsilon}) + \bar{b} \geqslant 1, \tag{3.2.21}$$

$$(\bar{w} \cdot x_i) + \bar{\eta}(y_i - \bar{\varepsilon}) + \bar{b} \leqslant -1. \tag{3.2.22}$$

From the above two equations, we have $\bar{\eta} \geqslant \dfrac{1}{\bar{\varepsilon}} > 0$. So, $\varepsilon = \bar{\varepsilon} - \dfrac{1}{\bar{\eta}} < \bar{\varepsilon}$. On the other hand, if $\varepsilon < \varepsilon_{\inf}$, then $(w^*, b^*) = \left(-\dfrac{\bar{w}}{\bar{\eta}}, -\dfrac{\bar{b}}{\bar{\eta}}\right)$ satisfies the constraints $(3.2.19)\sim(3.2.20)$, which contradicts the definition of $\varepsilon_{\inf}$.

Lastly, we prove the conclusion (ii). Let the variable $\eta$ in the problem $(3.2.10)\sim(3.2.12)$ be $\bar{\eta}$, then the problem with the variable $(\tilde{w}, \tilde{b})$ is derived

$$\min_{\tilde{w},\tilde{b}} \quad \frac{1}{2}\|\tilde{w}\|^2 + \frac{1}{2}\bar{\eta}^2, \tag{3.2.23}$$

$$\text{s.t.} \quad (\tilde{w} \cdot x_i) + \bar{\eta}(y_i + \bar{\varepsilon}) + \tilde{b} \geqslant 1, \ i = 1, \cdots, l, \tag{3.2.24}$$

$$\quad (\tilde{w} \cdot x_i) + \bar{\eta}(y_i - \bar{\varepsilon}) + \tilde{b} \leqslant -1, \ i = 1, \cdots, l. \tag{3.2.25}$$

Obviously, $(\bar{w}, \bar{b})$ is the solution to this problem. Introducing the variables $w = -\dfrac{\tilde{w}}{\bar{\eta}}, b = -\dfrac{\tilde{b}}{\bar{\eta}}$, the problem $(3.2.23)\sim(3.2.25)$ can be rewritten as $(3.2.18)\sim(3.2.20)$. So, $(w^*, b^*) = \left(-\dfrac{\bar{w}}{\bar{\eta}}, -\dfrac{\bar{b}}{\bar{\eta}}\right)$ is the solution to the problem $(3.2.18)\sim(3.2.20)$. ∎

According to the above theorem, in order to get a linear regression function, we only need to solve the problem $(3.2.18)\sim(3.2.20)$ and do not need to solve the problem $(3.2.10)\sim(3.2.12)$, where $\varepsilon > 0$ is a pre-selected parameter less than $\bar{\varepsilon}$. So, one reasonable way is: (i) choose the parameter $\varepsilon$, construct the problem $(3.2.18)\sim(3.2.20)$; (ii) solve the problem $(3.2.18)\sim(3.2.20)$; (iii) find the linear regression function: $y = (w^* \cdot x) + b^*$, where $(w^*, b^*)$ is the solution to the problem $(3.2.18)\sim(3.2.20)$.

## 3.3   Linear Hard $\varepsilon$-band Support Vector Regression

The goal of this section is to find the linear hard $\varepsilon$-band support vector regression machine for the training set (3.1.3).

### 3.3.1   Primal problem

The primal problem is the problem (3.2.18)~(3.2.20) introduced in Section 3.2:

$$\min_{w,b} \quad \frac{1}{2}\|w\|^2 \, , \tag{3.3.1}$$

$$\text{s.t.} \quad (w \cdot x_i) + b - y_i \leqslant \varepsilon \, , \ i = 1, \cdots, l \, , \tag{3.3.2}$$

$$y_i - (w \cdot x_i) - b \leqslant \varepsilon \, , \ i = 1, \cdots, l \, . \tag{3.3.3}$$

For the problem (3.3.1)~(3.3.3), we have the following theorem:

**Theorem 3.3.1** *Suppose that $\varepsilon_{\inf}$ is the optimal value of the following problem:*

$$\min_{w,b,\varepsilon} \quad \varepsilon \, , \tag{3.3.4}$$

$$\text{s.t.} \quad -\varepsilon \leqslant y_i - ((w \cdot x_i) + b) \leqslant \varepsilon \, , \ i = 1, \cdots, l, \tag{3.3.5}$$

*if $\varepsilon > \varepsilon_{\inf}$, then the primal problem (3.3.1)~(3.3.3) has solutions, and the solution w.r.t. $w$ is unique.*

**Proof** If $\varepsilon > \varepsilon_{\inf}$, then the feasible set of the problem (3.3.1)~(3.3.3) is nonempty, bounded and closed. This problem has solutions since a continuous function can attain its minimum in a nonempty, bounded and closed set. And Theorem 1.2.15 shows that the solution w.r.t. $w$ is unique. ∎

It is not necessarily true that the solution to the primal problem (3.3.1)~(3.3.3) w.r.t. $b$ is unique. In fact, when $\varepsilon$ is large enough, there exist many $b^*$ with different values, such that $(w^*, b^*) = (0, b^*)$ are the solutions. This shows that the solution to the primal problem w.r.t. $b$ is not unique.

### 3.3.2   Dual problem and relationship between the primal and dual problems

In this section, we start by a derivation of the dual problem of the primal problem (3.3.1)~(3.3.3), followed by developing the relationship between these two problems.

In order to derive the dual problem, we introduce the Lagrange function

$$L(w, b, \alpha^{(*)}) = \frac{1}{2}\|w\|^2 - \sum_{i=1}^{l} \alpha_i(\varepsilon + y_i - (w \cdot x_i) - b) - \sum_{i=1}^{l} \alpha_i^*(\varepsilon - y_i + (w \cdot x_i) + b) ,$$

$$(3.3.6)$$

where $\alpha^{(*)} = (\alpha_1, \alpha_1^*, \cdots, \alpha_l, \alpha_l^*)^T \in R^{2l}$ is the Lagrange multipliers vector, and $(*)$ is a shorthand implying both the vector with and without asterisks. We have the following theorems.

**Theorem 3.3.2** *Optimization problem*

$$\max_{\alpha^{(*)} \in R^{2l}} \quad -\frac{1}{2} \sum_{i,j=1}^{l} (\alpha_i^* - \alpha_i)(\alpha_j^* - \alpha_j)(x_i \cdot x_j) - \varepsilon \sum_{i=1}^{l} (\alpha_i^* + \alpha_i)$$

$$+ \sum_{i=1}^{l} y_i(\alpha_i^* - \alpha_i) , \qquad (3.3.7)$$

$$s.t. \quad \sum_{i=1}^{l} (\alpha_i^* - \alpha_i) = 0 , \qquad (3.3.8)$$

$$\alpha_i^{(*)} \geqslant 0, \ i = 1, \cdots, l \qquad (3.3.9)$$

*is the dual problem of the primal problem (3.3.1)~(3.3.3)*

**Proof** According to Definition 1.2.16 in Chapter 1, the dual problem should have a form of

$$\max \quad g(\alpha^{(*)}) = \inf_{w,b} L(w, b, \alpha^{(*)}), \qquad (3.3.10)$$

$$s.t. \quad \alpha^{(*)} \geqslant 0. \qquad (3.3.11)$$

As $L(w, b, \alpha^{(*)})$ is a strictly convex quadratic function of $w$, its minimal value is achieved at $w$ satisfying

$$\nabla_w L(w, b, \alpha^{(*)}) = w - \sum_{i=1}^{l} (\alpha_i^* - \alpha_i)x_i = 0, \qquad (3.3.12)$$

that is

$$w = \sum_{i=1}^{l} (\alpha_i^* - \alpha_i)x_i. \qquad (3.3.13)$$

Substituting the above in (3.3.6) yields

$$\inf_{w} L(w, b, \alpha^{(*)}) = -\frac{1}{2} \sum_{i=1}^{l} \sum_{j=1}^{l} (\alpha_i^* - \alpha_i)(\alpha_j^* - \alpha_j)(x_i \cdot x_j) - \varepsilon \sum_{i=1}^{l} (\alpha_i^* + \alpha_i)$$

$$+ \sum_{i=1}^{l} y_i(\alpha_i^* - \alpha_i) - b\left(\sum_{i=1}^{l} (\alpha_i^* - \alpha_i)\right). \qquad (3.3.14)$$

Therefore,

$$
\inf_{w,b} L(w,b,\alpha^{(*)}) =
\begin{cases}
-\dfrac{1}{2}\displaystyle\sum_{i=1}^{l}\sum_{j=1}^{l}(\alpha_i^* - \alpha_i)(\alpha_j^* - \alpha_j)(x_i \cdot x_j) \\[3mm]
\quad -\varepsilon\displaystyle\sum_{i=1}^{l}(\alpha_i^*+\alpha_i)+\sum_{i=1}^{l} y_i(\alpha_i^*-\alpha_i) \\[3mm]
\qquad\quad \text{if } \displaystyle\sum_{i=1}^{l}(\alpha_i^* - \alpha_i) = 0; \\[3mm]
-\infty, \qquad\qquad\qquad\qquad\qquad \text{otherwise.}
\end{cases}
$$

$$(3.3.15)$$

Hence the problem $(3.3.10)\sim(3.3.11)$ can be written as $(3.3.7)\sim(3.3.9)$. ∎

**Theorem 3.3.3** *If $\varepsilon > \varepsilon_{\text{inf}}$, then the dual problem $(3.3.7)\sim(3.3.9)$ has a solution, where $\varepsilon_{\text{inf}}$ is the optimal value of the problem $(3.3.4)\sim(3.3.5)$.*

**Proof** If $\varepsilon > \varepsilon_{\text{inf}}$, then the primal problem $(3.3.1)\sim(3.3.3)$ has a solution by Theorem 3.3.1. Furthermore, note that the primal problem is a convex programming and its constraints contain linear inequalities only, so it satisfies the Slater's condition. Hence its dual problem $(3.3.7)\sim(3.3.9)$ has a solution according to Theorem 1.2.21 in Chapter 1. ∎

In this book, the problem $(3.3.7)\sim(3.3.9)$ is replaced by its equivalent minimization problem:

$$
\min_{\alpha^{(*)}\in R^{2l}} \quad \frac{1}{2}\sum_{i,j=1}^{l}(\alpha_i^* - \alpha_i)(\alpha_j^* - \alpha_j)(x_i \cdot x_j) + \varepsilon\sum_{i=1}^{l}(\alpha_i^* + \alpha_i)
$$

$$
- \sum_{i=1}^{l} y_i(\alpha_i^* - \alpha_i) , \tag{3.3.16}
$$

$$
\text{s.t.} \quad \sum_{i=1}^{l}(\alpha_i^* - \alpha_i) = 0 , \tag{3.3.17}
$$

$$
\alpha_i^{(*)} \geqslant 0, \ i = 1,\cdots,l. \tag{3.3.18}
$$

Note that the minimization problem $(3.3.16)\sim(3.3.18)$ has the same solution set as that to the maximization dual problem $(3.3.7)\sim(3.3.9)$ and is often also called the dual problem of the problem $(3.3.1)\sim(3.3.3)$.

**Theorem 3.3.4** *Optimization problem $(3.3.16)\sim(3.3.18)$ is a convex quadratic programming.*

**Proof** It is similar to the proof of Theorem 2.2.8 in Chapter 2; the details are omitted here. ∎

**Theorem 3.3.5** *For any solution to the problem (3.3.16)~(3.3.18), $\bar{\alpha}^{(*)} = (\bar{\alpha}_1, \bar{\alpha}_1^*, \cdots, \bar{\alpha}_l, \bar{\alpha}_l^*)^T$, if $\bar{\alpha}^{(*)} \neq 0$, the solution to the primal problem (3.3.1)~(3.3.3), $(\bar{w}, \bar{b})$, can be obtained in the following way*

$$\bar{w} = \sum_{i=1}^{l}(\bar{\alpha}_i^* - \bar{\alpha}_i)x_i, \qquad (3.3.19)$$

*and for any nonzero component $\bar{\alpha}_j > 0$ of $\bar{\alpha}^{(*)}$,*

$$\bar{b} = y_j - (\bar{w} \cdot x_j) + \varepsilon, \qquad (3.3.20)$$

*or for any nonzero component $\bar{\alpha}_k^* > 0$ of $\bar{\alpha}^{(*)}$,*

$$\bar{b} = y_k - (\bar{w} \cdot x_k) - \varepsilon. \qquad (3.3.21)$$

**Proof** Firstly we show that, for $\bar{w}$ given by (3.3.19), there exists a $\tilde{b}$ such that $(\bar{w}, \tilde{b})$ is the solution to the problem (3.3.1)~(3.3.3). Let $H = ((x_i \cdot x_j))_{l \times l}, y = (y_1, \cdots, y_l)^T, e = (1, \cdots, 1)^T \in R^l$, the problem (3.3.16)~(3.3.18) can be rewritten as

$$\min_{\alpha^{(*)} \in R^{2l}} \quad \frac{1}{2}(\alpha^* - \alpha)^T H(\alpha^* - \alpha) + \varepsilon e^T(\alpha^* + \alpha) - y^T(\alpha^* - \alpha), \quad (3.3.22)$$

$$\text{s.t.} \quad e^T(\alpha^* - \alpha) = 0, \qquad (3.3.23)$$

$$\alpha^{(*)} \geqslant 0. \qquad (3.3.24)$$

Using the above theorem, this problem is a convex programming. In addition, it satisfies the Slater's condition. Accordingly, if $\bar{\alpha}^{(*)}$ is a solution to the problem (3.3.16)~(3.3.18), it yields from Theorem 1.2.23 (in Chapter 1) that there exists a multiplier $\tilde{b}$ and a multiplier vector $\bar{s}^{(*)}$ such that

$$e^T(\bar{\alpha}^* - \bar{\alpha}) = 0, \quad \bar{\alpha}^{(*)} \geqslant 0, \qquad (3.3.25)$$

$$H(\bar{\alpha}^* - \bar{\alpha}) + \varepsilon e - y + \tilde{b}e - \bar{s}^* = 0, \qquad (3.3.26)$$

$$-H(\bar{\alpha}^* - \bar{\alpha}) + \varepsilon e + y - \tilde{b}e - \bar{s} = 0, \qquad (3.3.27)$$

$$\bar{s}^{(*)} \geqslant 0, \quad \bar{s}^{(*)T}\bar{\alpha}^{(*)} = 0. \qquad (3.3.28)$$

Therefore, from (3.3.26)~(3.3.28), we have

$$H(\bar{\alpha}^* - \bar{\alpha}) - y + \tilde{b}e \geqslant -\varepsilon e, \qquad (3.3.29)$$

$$-H(\bar{\alpha}^* - \bar{\alpha}) + y - \tilde{b}e \geqslant -\varepsilon e. \qquad (3.3.30)$$

From (3.3.19), that is equivalent to the following:

$$((\bar{w} \cdot x_i) + \tilde{b}) - y_i \leqslant \varepsilon, \quad i = 1, \cdots, l, \qquad (3.3.31)$$

$$y_i - ((\bar{w} \cdot x_i) + \tilde{b}) \leqslant \varepsilon, \quad i = 1, \cdots, l \qquad (3.3.32)$$

which implies that $(\bar{w}, \tilde{b})$ is a feasible solution to the primal problem (3.3.1)~(3.3.3).

Furthermore, from $(3.3.26)\sim(3.3.28)$, we have

$$-\frac{1}{2}\|\bar{w}\|^2 = -\frac{1}{2}\|\bar{w}\|^2 + \bar{\alpha}^{*\mathrm{T}}(H(\bar{\alpha}^* - \bar{\alpha}) + \varepsilon e - y + \tilde{b}e - \bar{s}^*)$$
$$+ \bar{\alpha}^{\mathrm{T}}(-H(\bar{\alpha}^* - \bar{\alpha}) + \varepsilon e + y - \tilde{b}e - \bar{s}) \tag{3.3.33}$$
$$= \frac{1}{2}(\bar{\alpha}^* - \bar{\alpha})^{\mathrm{T}} H(\bar{\alpha}^* - \bar{\alpha}) + \varepsilon e^{\mathrm{T}}(\bar{\alpha}^* + \bar{\alpha}) - y^{\mathrm{T}}(\bar{\alpha}^* - \bar{\alpha}) \tag{3.3.34}$$

This shows that the objective function's value of the primal problem at the point $(\bar{w}, \tilde{b})$ is equal to the optimal value of its dual problem and therefore $(\bar{w}, \tilde{b})$ is the optimal solution to the primal problem $(3.3.1)\sim(3.3.3)$, according to Corollary 1.2.19 in Chapter 1.

Finally, we show that $(\bar{w}, \bar{b})$ obtained by $(3.3.19)$ and $(3.3.20)$ or $(3.3.21)$ is the solution to the primal problem. It is sufficient to show $\bar{b} = \tilde{b}$. Actually, $\bar{\alpha}^{(*)} \neq 0$ implies that there exists nonzero component $\bar{\alpha}_j > 0$ or $\bar{\alpha}_k^* > 0$. It yields from $(3.3.26)\sim(3.3.28)$ that

$$\tilde{b} = y_j - (\bar{w} \cdot x_j) + \varepsilon \; ; \tag{3.3.35}$$

or

$$\tilde{b} = y_k - (\bar{w} \cdot x_k) - \varepsilon \; . \tag{3.3.36}$$

So $\bar{b} = \tilde{b}$. ∎

### 3.3.3 Linear hard $\varepsilon$-band support vector regression

Based on Theorem 3.3.5, the following algorithm is established.

**Algorithm 3.3.6** *(Linear hard $\varepsilon$-band support vector regression)*

*(1) Input the training set $T = \{(x_1, y_1), \cdots, (x_l, y_l)\}$, where $x_i \in R^n, y_i \in \mathcal{Y} = R, i = 1, \cdots, l$;*

*(2) Choose the parameter $\varepsilon > 0$;*

*(3) Construct and solve the convex quadratic programming*

$$\min_{\alpha^{(*)} \in R^{2l}} \quad \frac{1}{2} \sum_{i,j=1}^{l} (\alpha_i^* - \alpha_i)(\alpha_j^* - \alpha_j)(x_i \cdot x_j) + \varepsilon \sum_{i=1}^{l} (\alpha_i^* + \alpha_i)$$
$$- \sum_{i=1}^{l} y_i (\alpha_i^* - \alpha_i) \; , \tag{3.3.37}$$

$$\text{s.t.} \quad \sum_{i=1}^{l} (\alpha_i^* - \alpha_i) = 0 \; , \tag{3.3.38}$$

$$\alpha_i^{(*)} \geqslant 0, \; i = 1, \cdots, l \; , \tag{3.3.39}$$

*obtaining a solution $\bar{\alpha}^{(*)} = (\bar{\alpha}_1, \bar{\alpha}_1^*, \cdots, \bar{\alpha}_l, \bar{\alpha}_l^*)^{\mathrm{T}}$;*

*(4) Compute* $\bar{w} = \sum_{i=1}^{l} (\bar{\alpha}_i^* - \bar{\alpha}_i) x_i$. *Choose a positive component of* $\bar{\alpha}^{(*)}$, $\bar{\alpha}_j > 0$, *then compute*

$$\bar{b} = y_j - (\bar{w} \cdot x_j) + \varepsilon \; ; \tag{3.3.40}$$

*Or choose a positive component of* $\bar{\alpha}^{(*)}$, $\bar{\alpha}_k^* > 0$, *then compute*

$$\bar{b} = y_k - (\bar{w} \cdot x_k) - \varepsilon \; ; \tag{3.3.41}$$

*(5) Construct the regression function* $y = g(x) = (\bar{w} \cdot x) + \bar{b} = \sum_{i=1}^{l} (\bar{\alpha}_i^* - \bar{\alpha}_i)(x_i \cdot x) + \bar{b}$ .

The above algorithm is called linear hard $\varepsilon$-band support vector regression, which corresponds to linear hard margin support vector classification (Algorithm 2.2.2) in Chapter 2.

**Definition 3.3.7** *(Support vector) Suppose that* $\bar{\alpha}^{(*)} = (\bar{\alpha}_1, \bar{\alpha}_1^*, \cdots, \bar{\alpha}_l, \bar{\alpha}_l^*)^{\mathrm{T}}$ *is a solution to the dual problem* (3.3.37)$\sim$(3.3.39) *obtained by Algorithm 3.3.6. The input* $(x_i, y_i)$ *is said to be a support vector if the corresponding component* $\bar{\alpha}_i$ *or* $\bar{\alpha}_i^*$ *is nonzero, otherwise it is a nonsupport vector.*

Support vectors are determined by the solutions to problem (3.3.37)$\sim$(3.3.39). The following theorem deals with the case where some components of the solution are zero.

**Theorem 3.3.8** *Suppose that* $\bar{\alpha}^{(*)} = (\bar{\alpha}_1, \bar{\alpha}_1^*, \cdots, \bar{\alpha}_l, \bar{\alpha}_l^*)^{\mathrm{T}}$ *is the solution to problem* (3.3.37)$\sim$(3.3.39), *for* $i = 1, \cdots, l$, *there exists only one nonzero component between* $\bar{\alpha}_i$ *and* $\bar{\alpha}_i^*$.

**Proof** By the KKT condition of the problem (3.3.37)$\sim$(3.3.39), there exist the Lagrange multipliers $\bar{b}$ and $\bar{s}^{(*)}$ such that

$$\left( \sum_{j=1}^{l} (\bar{\alpha}_j^* - \bar{\alpha}_j) x_j \cdot x_i \right) + \varepsilon - y_i + \bar{b} - \bar{s}_i^* = 0, \quad i = 1, \cdots, l, \tag{3.3.42}$$

$$- \left( \sum_{j=1}^{l} (\bar{\alpha}_j^* - \bar{\alpha}_j) x_j \cdot x_i \right) + \varepsilon + y_i - \bar{b} - \bar{s}_i = 0, \quad i = 1, \cdots, l, \tag{3.3.43}$$

$$\bar{s}_i^{(*)} \geqslant 0, \quad \bar{s}_i^{(*)} \bar{\alpha}_i^{(*)} = 0, \quad i = 1, \cdots, l. \tag{3.3.44}$$

Consider the case $\bar{\alpha}_i > 0$, let $\bar{w} = \sum_{j=1}^{l} (\bar{\alpha}_j^* - \bar{\alpha}_j) x_j$, then by (3.3.43)$\sim$(3.3.44), we have

$$\bar{\alpha}_i (\varepsilon + y_i - (\bar{w} \cdot x_i) - \bar{b}) = 0, \tag{3.3.45}$$

so $y_i - (\bar{w} \cdot x_i) - \bar{b} = -\varepsilon$. Furthermore, (3.3.42) and (3.3.44) yields that

$$\bar{\alpha}_i^*(\varepsilon - y_i + (\bar{w} \cdot x_i) + \bar{b}) = 2\bar{\alpha}_i^*\varepsilon = 0. \tag{3.3.46}$$

Therefore $\bar{\alpha}_i^* = 0$. Similarly, we can obtain that $\bar{\alpha}_i = 0$, when $\bar{\alpha}_i^* > 0$. ∎

The following theorem provides the new interpretation of support vectors geometrically.

**Theorem 3.3.9** *Suppose that $\bar{\alpha}^{(*)} = (\bar{\alpha}_1, \bar{\alpha}_1^*, \cdots, \bar{\alpha}_l, \bar{\alpha}_l^*)^{\mathrm{T}}$ is a solution to the problem (3.3.37)$\sim$ (3.3.39) solved by Algorithm 3.3.6, and $y = (\bar{w} \cdot x) + \bar{b}$ is the regression function obtained by Algorithm 3.3.6. If $\varepsilon > \varepsilon_{\inf}$, where $\varepsilon_{\inf}$ is the optimal value of the problem (3.3.4)$\sim$(3.3.5), then*

*(i) All support vectors are on the boundary of the $\varepsilon$-band of hyperplane $y = (\bar{w} \cdot x) + \bar{b}$;*

*(ii) All nonsupport vectors are inside or on the boundary of the $\varepsilon$-band of hyperplane $y = (\bar{w} \cdot x) + \bar{b}$.*

**Proof** To prove our conclusion, we only need to prove:

(i) If $\bar{\alpha}_i > 0, \bar{\alpha}_i^* = 0$ or $\bar{\alpha}_i = 0, \bar{\alpha}_i^* > 0$, then the corresponding point $(x_i, y_i)$ is on the boundary of the $\varepsilon$-band of hyperplane $y = (\bar{w} \cdot x) + \bar{b}$;

(ii) If $\bar{\alpha}_i = \bar{\alpha}_i^* = 0$, then the corresponding point $(x_i, y_i)$ is inside or on the boundary of the $\varepsilon$-band of hyperplane $y = (\bar{w} \cdot x) + \bar{b}$.

In fact, by the KKT condition of the problem (3.3.37)$\sim$(3.3.39), there exist the Lagrange multipliers $\bar{b}, \bar{s}^{(*)}$ such that

$$(\bar{w} \cdot x_i) + \varepsilon - y_i + \bar{b} - \bar{s}_i^* = 0, \quad i = 1, \cdots, l, \tag{3.3.47}$$

$$-(\bar{w} \cdot x_i) + \varepsilon + y_i - \bar{b} - \bar{s}_i = 0, \quad i = 1, \cdots, l, \tag{3.3.48}$$

$$\bar{s}_i^{(*)} \geqslant 0, \quad \bar{s}_i^{(*)}\alpha_i^{(*)} = 0, \quad i = 1, \cdots, l, \tag{3.3.49}$$

where $\bar{w} = \sum_{j=1}^{l}(\bar{\alpha}_j^* - \bar{\alpha}_j)x_j$. Hence,

$$\bar{\alpha}_i(\varepsilon + y_i - (\bar{w} \cdot x_i) - \bar{b}) = 0, \quad i = 1, \cdots, l, \tag{3.3.50}$$

$$\bar{\alpha}_i^*(\varepsilon - y_i + (\bar{w} \cdot x_i) + \bar{b}) = 0, \quad i = 1, \cdots, l. \tag{3.3.51}$$

Then the conclusions (i) and (ii) are derived from (3.3.50) and (3.3.51). ∎

## 3.4    Linear $\varepsilon$-Support Vector Regression

### 3.4.1    Primal problem

Similar to support vector classification, by introducing the slack variable $\xi^{(*)} = (\xi_1, \xi_1^*, \cdots, \xi_l, \xi_l^*)^{\mathrm{T}}$ and penalty parameter $C$, the primal problem of linear $\varepsilon$-support vector regression machine can be written as:

$$\min_{w,b,\xi^{(*)}} \quad \frac{1}{2}\|w\|^2 + C\sum_{i=1}^{l}(\xi_i + \xi_i^*), \tag{3.4.1}$$

$$\text{s.t.} \quad ((w \cdot x_i) + b) - y_i \leqslant \varepsilon + \xi_i \, , \, i = 1, \cdots, l, \tag{3.4.2}$$

$$y_i - ((w \cdot x_i) + b) \leqslant \varepsilon + \xi_i^* \, , \, i = 1, \cdots, l, \tag{3.4.3}$$

$$\xi_i^{(*)} \geqslant 0 \, , \, i = 1, \cdots, l, \tag{3.4.4}$$

where $(*)$ is a shorthand implying both the vector with and without asterisks. This problem is a convex quadratic programming.

After obtaining the solution to the primal problem $(3.4.1)\sim(3.4.4)$, $(\bar{w}, \bar{b}, \bar{\xi}^{(*)})$, we construct the regression function:

$$y = g(x) = (\bar{w} \cdot x) + \bar{b}. \tag{3.4.5}$$

Note that $\bar{\xi}^{(*)}$ in the solution $(\bar{w}, \bar{b}, \bar{\xi}^{(*)})$ does not exist in the regression function. So the main issues are the solutions to the primal problem $(3.4.1)\sim(3.4.4)$ w.r.t. $(w, b)$.

**Theorem 3.4.1** *There exist solutions to the primal problem $(3.4.1)\sim(3.4.4)$ w.r.t. $(w, b)$, and the solution w.r.t. $w$ is unique.*

**Proof** It is similar to the proof of Theorem 3.3.1. The details are omitted here. ∎

**Remark 3.4.2** *The solutions to the primal problem $(3.4.1)\sim(3.4.4)$ w.r.t. $(w, b)$ are not unique. In fact, when $\varepsilon$ is large enough, $(\bar{w}, \bar{b}, \bar{\xi}^{(*)}) = (0, \bar{b}, 0)$ are solutions, where $\bar{b}$ can take different values. Therefore, $(\bar{w}, \bar{b}) = (0, \bar{b})$ are solutions w.r.t. $(w, b)$.*

## 3.4.2 Dual problem and relationship between the primal and dual problems

In order to derive the dual problem of the primal problem $(3.4.1)\sim(3.4.4)$, we introduce Lagrange function

$$L(w, b, \xi^{(*)}, \alpha^{(*)}, \eta^{(*)}) = \frac{1}{2}\|w\|^2 + C\sum_{i=1}^{l}(\xi_i + \xi_i^*) - \sum_{i=1}^{l}(\eta_i \xi_i + \eta_i^* \xi_i^*)$$

$$- \sum_{i=1}^{l} \alpha_i(\varepsilon + \xi_i + y_i - (w \cdot x_i) - b)$$

$$- \sum_{i=1}^{l} \alpha_i^*(\varepsilon + \xi_i^* - y_i + (w \cdot x_i) + b) \, , \tag{3.4.6}$$

where $\alpha^{(*)} = (\alpha_1, \alpha_1^*, \cdots, \alpha_l, \alpha_l^*)^{\mathrm{T}}, \eta^{(*)} = (\eta_1, \eta_1^*, \cdots, \eta_l, \eta_l^*)^{\mathrm{T}}$ are Lagrange multiplier vectors.

The proof of the following Theorem 3.4.3 and Theorem 3.4.4 are omitted here as they are the special cases of Theorem 4.1.5 and Theorem 4.1.6 later.

**Theorem 3.4.3** *Optimization problem*

$$\max_{\alpha^{(*)}, \eta^{(*)} \in R^{2l}} \quad -\frac{1}{2} \sum_{i,j=1}^{l} (\alpha_i^* - \alpha_i)(\alpha_j^* - \alpha_j)(x_i \cdot x_j) - \varepsilon \sum_{i=1}^{l} (\alpha_i^* + \alpha_i)$$

$$+ \sum_{i=1}^{l} y_i (\alpha_i^* - \alpha_i) , \tag{3.4.7}$$

$$\text{s.t.} \quad \sum_{i=1}^{l} (\alpha_i^* - \alpha_i) = 0 , \tag{3.4.8}$$

$$C - \alpha_i^{(*)} - \eta_i^{(*)} = 0, \ i = 1, \cdots, l, \tag{3.4.9}$$

$$\alpha_i^{(*)} \geqslant 0, \ \eta_i^{(*)} \geqslant 0 , \ i = 1, \cdots, l \tag{3.4.10}$$

*is the dual problem of the primal problem (3.4.1)~(3.4.4).*

**Theorem 3.4.4** *Dual problem (3.4.7)~(3.4.10) has solutions.*

Dual problem (3.4.7)~(3.4.10) can be simplified to a problem only for a single variable $\alpha^{(*)}$ by eliminating the variable $\eta^{(*)}$ and then rewritten as a minimization problem:

$$\min_{\alpha^{(*)} \in R^{2l}} \quad \frac{1}{2} \sum_{i,j=1}^{l} (\alpha_i^* - \alpha_i)(\alpha_j^* - \alpha_j)(x_i \cdot x_j) + \varepsilon \sum_{i=1}^{l} (\alpha_i^* + \alpha_i)$$

$$- \sum_{i=1}^{l} y_i (\alpha_i^* - \alpha_i) , \tag{3.4.11}$$

$$\text{s.t.} \quad \sum_{i=1}^{l} (\alpha_i^* - \alpha_i) = 0 , \tag{3.4.12}$$

$$0 \leqslant \alpha_i^{(*)} \leqslant C , \ i = 1, \cdots, l. \tag{3.4.13}$$

This problem is called the dual problem of the problem (3.4.1)~(3.4.4) in the later. We have following two theorems. Their proofs are omitted here, since the former is obvious, and the latter is a special case of Theorem 4.1.7.

**Theorem 3.4.5** *Optimization problem (3.4.11)~(3.4.13) is a convex quadratic programming problem.*

**Theorem 3.4.6** *Suppose that $\bar{\alpha}^{(*)} = (\bar{\alpha}_1, \bar{\alpha}_1^*, \cdots, \bar{\alpha}_l, \bar{\alpha}_l^*)^{\mathrm{T}}$ is any solution to the problem (3.4.11)~(3.4.13). If there exists a component of $\bar{\alpha}^{(*)}$, $\bar{\alpha}_j \in (0, C)$ or $\bar{\alpha}_k^* \in (0, C)$, then a solution $(\bar{w}, \bar{b})$ to the primal problem (3.4.1)~ (3.4.4) w.r.t. $(w, b)$ can be obtained by*

$$\bar{w} = \sum_{i=1}^{l} (\bar{\alpha}_i^* - \bar{\alpha}_i) x_i, \tag{3.4.14}$$

$$\bar{b} = y_j - \sum_{i=1}^{l} (\bar{\alpha}_i^* - \bar{\alpha}_i)(x_i \cdot x_j) + \varepsilon, \tag{3.4.15}$$

*or*

$$\bar{b} = y_k - \sum_{i=1}^{l} (\bar{\alpha}_i^* - \bar{\alpha}_i)(x_i \cdot x_k) - \varepsilon. \tag{3.4.16}$$

### 3.4.3 Linear $\varepsilon$-support vector regression

Now we can establish an algorithm according to Theorem 3.4.6 as follows:

**Algorithm 3.4.7** *(Linear $\varepsilon$-support vector regression, Linear $\varepsilon$-SVR)*

*(1) Input the training set $T = \{(x_1, y_1), \cdots, (x_l, y_l)\}$, where $x_i \in R^n, y_i \in \mathcal{Y} = R, i = 1, \cdots, l$;*

*(2) Choose an appropriate parameter $\varepsilon$ and the penalty parameter $C > 0$;*

*(3) Construct and solve the convex quadratic program:*

$$\min_{\alpha^{(*)} \in R^{2l}} \quad \frac{1}{2} \sum_{i,j=1}^{l} (\alpha_i^* - \alpha_i)(\alpha_j^* - \alpha_j)(x_i \cdot x_j) + \varepsilon \sum_{i=1}^{l} (\alpha_i^* + \alpha_i)$$

$$- \sum_{i=1}^{l} y_i (\alpha_i^* - \alpha_i), \tag{3.4.17}$$

$$\text{s.t.} \quad \sum_{i=1}^{l} (\alpha_i - \alpha_i^*) = 0, \tag{3.4.18}$$

$$0 \leqslant \alpha_i^{(*)} \leqslant C, \ i = 1, \cdots, l, \tag{3.4.19}$$

*obtaining a solution $\bar{\alpha}^{(*)} = (\bar{\alpha}_1, \bar{\alpha}_1^*, \cdots, \bar{\alpha}_l, \bar{\alpha}_l^*)^{\mathrm{T}}$;*

*(4) Compute $\bar{b}$: choose a component of $\bar{\alpha}^{(*)}$ in the internal $(0, C)$. If the component is $\bar{\alpha}_j \in (0, C)$, compute*

$$\bar{b} = y_j - \sum_{i=1}^{l} (\bar{\alpha}_i^* - \bar{\alpha}_i)(x_i \cdot x_j) + \varepsilon; \tag{3.4.20}$$

*If the component is $\bar{\alpha}_k^* \in (0, C)$, compute*

$$\bar{b} = y_k - \sum_{i=1}^{l} (\bar{\alpha}_i^* - \bar{\alpha}_i)(x_i \cdot x_k) - \varepsilon \; ; \tag{3.4.21}$$

*(5) Construct the decision function*

$$y = g(x) = \sum_{i=1}^{l} (\bar{\alpha}_i^* - \bar{\alpha}_i)(x_i \cdot x) + \bar{b} \; . \tag{3.4.22}$$

# Chapter 4

## Kernels and Support Vector Machines

In this chapter, we generalize the linear support vector machine described in Chapter 2 and Chapter 3 to nonlinear support vector machines, in which the key step is introducing kernels.

## 4.1 From Linear Classification to Nonlinear Classification

Linear support vector classification described in Chapter 2 is based on linear classification, and linear support vector regression in Chapter 3 is also derived from linear classification; therefore the first step from linear support vector machine to nonlinear support vector machine is to generalize the linear classification to nonlinear classification.

### 4.1.1 An example of nonlinear classification

Linear classification is obviously not suitable for some classification problems at hand, such as the classification problem containing 20 training points in $R^2$ shown in Figure 4.1. In this figure, "+" and "∘" represent the positive inputs corresponding to label $y_i = +1$ and the negative inputs corresponding to $y_i = -1$ respectively. We can see that the appropriate separating line for this problem seems a curve like an ellipse centered on the origin in the $([x]_1, O[x]_2)$ plane, i.e, a nonlinear classification instead of the linear classification. However, how to obtain the separating ellipse? Because we have already had the method searching for separating straight line, it is natural to try to apply it to get the separating ellipse. Here the sticking point is whether the "curve (ellipse)" can be transformed to a "straight line". Obviously, the answer is positive. In fact, considering the map $x = \Phi(x)$ from the points in the plane $[x]_1 O[x]_2$ to the points $([x]_1, [x]_2)$ in the plane $[x]_1 O[x]_2$:

$$\Phi : \begin{aligned} [x]_1 &= [x]_1^2 \,, \\ [x]_2 &= [x]_2^2 \,, \end{aligned} \qquad (4.1.1)$$

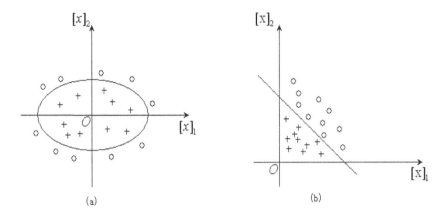

**FIGURE** 4.1: A nonlinear classification problem (a) In $x$-space; (b) In x-space.

which maps the ellipse $\alpha[x]_1^2 + \beta[x]_2^2 - r^2 = 0$ in the plane $[x]_1 O [x]_2$ to the straight line $\alpha[\mathrm{x}]_1 + \beta[\mathrm{x}]_2 - r^2 = 0$ in the plane $[\mathrm{x}]_1 O [\mathrm{x}]_2$, see Figure 4.1(a), (b). Therefore, we only need to apply (4.1.1) to map the inputs of the training points in the plane $[x]_1 O [x]_2$ into the plane $[\mathrm{x}]_1 O [\mathrm{x}]_2$ separately, then perform the linear support vector classification to get the separating straight line in the plane $[\mathrm{x}]_1 O [\mathrm{x}]_2$, at last transform the separating line back into the plane $[x]_1 O [x]_2$, so the separating curve (ellipse) and the decision function we are searching for can be obtained.

### 4.1.2   Classification machine based on nonlinear separation

The above example shows that in order to generalize the "linear separation" to "nonlinear separation", only an appropriate map $\Phi$ is needed. Note that for the above two-dimensional problem, the map $\Phi$ transforms a two-dimensional vector $x$ into another two-dimensional vector x. For a general $n$-dimensional problem, a map $\Phi$ is allowed to transform an $n$-dimensional vector $x$ into another $m$-dimensional vector x in Euclidian space $R^m$, or even an infinite dimensional vector x in Hilbert space discussed in Chapter 1, Section 1.3. Thus the map can be expressed as

$$\Phi: \quad \begin{array}{l} R^n \to \mathcal{H}\,, \\ x = ([x]_1, \cdots, [x]_n)^\mathrm{T} \to \mathrm{x} = ([\mathrm{x}]_1, [\mathrm{x}]_2, \cdots)^\mathrm{T} = \Phi(x)\,. \end{array} \qquad (4.1.2)$$

Suppose the original training set is given by

$$T = \{(x_1, y_1), \cdots, (x_l, y_l)\}, \qquad (4.1.3)$$

where $x_i \in R^n, y_i \in \mathcal{Y} = \{-1, 1\}\,, i = 1, \cdots, l$. Under the map (4.1.2), the training set $T$ is transformed to

$$T_\Phi = \{(\mathrm{x}_1, y_1), \cdots, (\mathrm{x}_l, y_l)\}, \qquad (4.1.4)$$

where $x_i = \Phi(x_i) \in \mathcal{H}$, $y_i \in \mathcal{Y} = \{-1, 1\}$, $i = 1, \cdots, l$. Next step is to compute the linear separating hyperplane $(w^* \cdot x) + b^* = 0$ in this space, thus deduce the separating hypersurface $(w^* \cdot \Phi(x)) + b^* = 0$ and the decision function $f(x) = \text{sgn}((w^* \cdot x) + b^*) = \text{sgn}((w^* \cdot \Phi(x)) + b^*)$ in the original space $R^n$.

Note that in the Hilbert space the distance between the two hyperplanes

$$(w \cdot x) + b = 1 \text{ and } (w \cdot x) + b = -1 \tag{4.1.5}$$

can still be represented by $\dfrac{2}{\|w\|}$, so we can construct the primal problem corresponding to the problem $(2.3.4) \sim (2.3.6)$ in Chapter 2

$$\min_{w,b,\xi} \quad \frac{1}{2}\|w\|^2 + C\sum_{i=1}^{l} \xi_i , \tag{4.1.6}$$

$$\text{s.t.} \quad y_i((w \cdot \Phi(x_i)) + b) \geqslant 1 - \xi_i , \ i = 1, \cdots, l , \tag{4.1.7}$$

$$\xi_i \geqslant 0 , \ i = 1, \cdots, l. \tag{4.1.8}$$

According to Theorem 1.3.3 in Chapter 1, this primal problem is a convex quadratic programming defined as Definition 1.3.2. The further discussion is based on the content in Section 1.3. In fact, introduce the Lagrange function

$$L(w, b, \xi, \alpha, \beta) = \frac{1}{2}\|w\|^2 + C\sum_{i=1}^{l} \xi_i - \sum_{i=1}^{l} \alpha_i(y_i((w \cdot \Phi(x_i)) + b) - 1 + \xi_i) - \sum_{i=1}^{l} \beta_i \xi_i , \tag{4.1.9}$$

where $\alpha = (\alpha_1, \cdots, \alpha_l)^{\text{T}}$ and $\beta = (\beta_1, \cdots, \beta_l)^{\text{T}}$ are the Lagrange multiplier vectors. We have the following theorems.

**Theorem 4.1.1** *Optimization problem*

$$\max_{\alpha,\beta} \quad -\frac{1}{2}\sum_{i=1}^{l}\sum_{j=1}^{l} y_i y_j \alpha_i \alpha_j (\Phi(x_i) \cdot \Phi(x_j)) + \sum_{j=1}^{l} \alpha_j , \tag{4.1.10}$$

$$\text{s.t.} \quad \sum_{i=1}^{l} y_i \alpha_i = 0 , \tag{4.1.11}$$

$$C - \alpha_i - \beta_i = 0, \quad i = 1, \cdots, l , \tag{4.1.12}$$

$$\alpha_i \geqslant 0, \quad i = 1, \cdots, l , \tag{4.1.13}$$

$$\beta_i \geqslant 0, \quad i = 1, \cdots, l \tag{4.1.14}$$

*is the dual problem of the primal problem $(4.1.6) \sim (4.1.8)$.*

**Proof** According to Definition 1.3.6 in Chapter 1, the dual problem of the primal problem $(4.1.6) \sim (4.1.8)$ should be

$$\max \quad \inf_{w,b,\xi} L(w, b, \xi, \alpha, \beta) \tag{4.1.15}$$

$$\text{s.t.} \quad \alpha \geqslant 0, \ \beta \geqslant 0, \tag{4.1.16}$$

where $L(\mathrm{w}, b, \xi, \alpha, \beta)$ is given by (4.1.9), of which minimal value w.r.t. $w$ is achieved by

$$\nabla_{\mathrm{w}} L(\mathrm{w}, b, \xi, \alpha, \beta) = 0, \tag{4.1.17}$$

that is

$$\mathrm{w} = \sum_{i=1}^{l} \alpha_i y_i \Phi(x_i). \tag{4.1.18}$$

So

$$\inf_{\mathrm{w}} L(\mathrm{w}, b, \xi, \alpha, \beta) = -\frac{1}{2} \sum_{i=1}^{l} \sum_{j=1}^{l} y_i y_j \alpha_i \alpha_j (\Phi(x_i) \cdot \Phi(x_j)) + \sum_{j=1}^{l} \alpha_j$$
$$+ \left( \sum_{i=1}^{l} y_i \alpha_i \right) b + \sum_{i=1}^{l} (C - \alpha_i - \beta_i)\xi_i. \tag{4.1.19}$$

Note that, when $\displaystyle\sum_{i=1}^{l} y_i \alpha_i = 0$ and $C - \alpha_i - \beta_i = 0,\ i = 1, \cdots, l$ are not valid at the same time, we always have $\displaystyle\inf_{\mathrm{w}, b, \xi} L\ (\mathrm{w}, b, \xi, \alpha, \beta) = -\infty$. Therefore, the problem (4.1.15)$\sim$(4.1.16) can be written as (4.1.10)$\sim$(4.1.14). ∎

**Theorem 4.1.2** *Dual problem* (4.1.10)$\sim$(4.1.14) *has a solution* $\alpha^* = (\alpha_1^*, \cdots, \alpha_l^*)^{\mathrm{T}}, \beta^* = (\beta_1^*, \cdots, \beta_l^*)^{\mathrm{T}}$.

**Proof** Dual problem (4.1.10)$\sim$(4.1.14) is an optimization problem in the Euclidean space $R^{2l}$, its objective function is continuous and the feasible domain is a nonempty bounded close set, so it must have a solution. ∎

Note that the dual problem (4.1.10)$\sim$(4.1.14) has the same solution set w.r.t.$\alpha$ as that to the following convex quadratic programming problem in the Euclidean space $R^l$

$$\min_{\alpha} \quad \frac{1}{2} \sum_{i=1}^{l} \sum_{j=1}^{l} y_i y_j \alpha_i \alpha_j (\Phi(x_i) \cdot \Phi(x_j)) - \sum_{j=1}^{l} \alpha_j, \tag{4.1.20}$$

$$\text{s.t.} \quad \sum_{i=1}^{l} y_i \alpha_i = 0, \tag{4.1.21}$$

$$0 \leqslant \alpha_i \leqslant C, \quad i = 1, \cdots, l. \tag{4.1.22}$$

**Theorem 4.1.3** *Suppose* $\alpha^* = (\alpha_1^*, \cdots, \alpha_l^*)^{\mathrm{T}}$ *is a solution to the problem* (4.1.20)$\sim$(4.1.22). *If there exists a component of* $\alpha^*$, $\alpha_j^* \in (0, C)$, *then the solution* $(\mathrm{w}^*, b^*)$ *to the primal problem* (4.1.6)$\sim$(4.1.8) *w.r.t.* $(\mathrm{w}, b)$ *can be obtained in the following way:*

$$\mathrm{w}^* = \sum_{i=1}^{l} \alpha_i^* y_i \mathrm{x}_i \tag{4.1.23}$$

*and*

$$b^* = y_j - \sum_{i=1}^{l} y_i \alpha_i^* (\mathbf{x}_i \cdot \mathbf{x}_j). \tag{4.1.24}$$

**Proof** Firstly we show that, for $w^*$ given by (4.1.23), there exists a $\tilde{b}^*$ such that $(w^*, \tilde{b}^*)$ is the solution to the primal problem (4.1.6)~(4.1.8). In fact, Let $H = (y_i y_j (\mathbf{x}_i \cdot \mathbf{x}_j))_{l \times l}$, $e = (1, \cdots, 1)^T$, $y = (y_1, \cdots, y_l)^T$, problem (4.1.20)~(4.1.22) can be rewritten as

$$\min_{\alpha} \quad W(\alpha) = \frac{1}{2} \alpha^T H \alpha - e^T \alpha , \tag{4.1.25}$$

$$\text{s.t.} \quad \alpha^T y = 0 , \tag{4.1.26}$$

$$0 \leqslant \alpha \leqslant Ce. \tag{4.1.27}$$

If $\alpha^* = (\alpha_1^*, \cdots, \alpha_l^*)^T$ is a solution to the problem (4.1.25)~(4.1.27), it yields from Theorem 1.2.23 (in Chapter 1) that there exist a multiplier $\tilde{b}^*$, multiplier vectors $s^*$ and $\xi^*$ such that

$$0 \leqslant \alpha^* \leqslant Ce, \quad \alpha^{*T} y = 0, \tag{4.1.28}$$

$$H\alpha^* - e + \tilde{b}^* y - s^* + \xi^* = 0, \quad s^* \geqslant 0, \quad \xi^* \geqslant 0, \tag{4.1.29}$$

$$\xi^{*T} (\alpha^* - Ce) = 0, \quad s^{*T} \alpha^* = 0. \tag{4.1.30}$$

Equation (4.1.29) means that

$$H\alpha^* - e + \tilde{b}^* y + \xi^* \geqslant 0. \tag{4.1.31}$$

Let $w^* = \sum_{i=1}^{l} \alpha_i^* y_i \mathbf{x}_i$, equation (4.1.31) is equivalent to

$$y_i ((w^* \cdot \mathbf{x}_i) + \tilde{b}^*) \geqslant 1 - \xi_i^*, \quad i = 1, \cdots, l. \tag{4.1.32}$$

Therefore, above equation and the third part of equation (4.1.29) imply that $(w^*, \tilde{b}^*, \xi^*)$ is a feasible solution to the primal problem (4.1.6)~(4.1.8).

Furthermore, from (4.1.28)~(4.1.30) we have

$$-\frac{1}{2} \|w^*\|^2 - C \sum_{i=1}^{l} \xi_i^* = -\frac{1}{2} \alpha^{*T} H \alpha^* - Ce^T \xi^*$$

$$= -\frac{1}{2} \alpha^{*T} H \alpha^* - Ce^T \xi^* + \alpha^{*T} (H\alpha^* + \tilde{b}^* y - e - s^* + \xi^*)$$

$$= \frac{1}{2} \alpha^{*T} H \alpha^* - \xi^{*T} (Ce - \alpha^*) + \tilde{b}^* \alpha^{*T} y - e^T \alpha^* - s^{*T} \alpha^*$$

$$= \frac{1}{2} \alpha^{*T} H \alpha^* - e^T \alpha^* . \tag{4.1.33}$$

This shows that the objective function's value of the primal problem (4.1.6)~(4.1.8) is equal to the optimum value of its dual problem

$(4.1.10) \sim (4.1.14)$, and therefore $(w^*, \tilde{b}^*, \xi^*)$ is the optimal solution to the primal problem according to the results corresponding to Corollary 1.2.19 mentioned in Section 1.3 in Chapter 1.

Therefore, in order to show that $(w^*, b^*)$ obtained from $(4.1.23) \sim (4.1.24)$ is the solution to the primal problem, we only need to show $b^* = \tilde{b}^*$. In fact, from KKT conditions $(4.1.29) \sim (4.1.30)$ we have

$$y_i((w^* \cdot x_i) + \tilde{b}^*) - 1 - s_i^* + \xi_i^* = 0 , \quad i = 1, \cdots, l , \quad (4.1.34)$$
$$\xi_i^*(\alpha_i^* - C) = 0 , \quad i = 1, \cdots, l , \quad (4.1.35)$$
$$s_i^* \alpha_i^* = 0 , \quad i = 1, \cdots, l . \quad (4.1.36)$$

If there exists $\alpha_j^* \in (0, C)$, then $s_j^* = 0, \xi_j^* = 0$, and we have $b^* = \tilde{b}^*$. ∎

Based on the above theorem, when the solution $\alpha^* = (\alpha_1^*, \cdots, \alpha_l^*)^{\mathrm{T}}$ to the problem $(4.1.20) \sim (4.1.22)$ is derived, the separating hyperplane in the space $\mathcal{H}$ where x lies in can be constructed as

$$(w^* \cdot x) + b^* = 0, \quad (4.1.37)$$

where $w^*$ and $b^*$ are given by $(4.1.23)$ and $(4.1.24)$ respectively. Obviously the hyperplane $(4.1.37)$ corresponds to the following hypersurface in the space $R^n$ where $x$ lies in

$$\sum_{i=1}^{l} \alpha_i^* y_i (\Phi(x_i) \cdot \Phi(x)) + b^* = 0,$$

where $b^*$ is given by $(4.1.24)$. That is just the surface realizing nonlinear separation we are searching for. So, the following algorithm is established:

**Algorithm 4.1.4** *(Classification machine based on nonlinear separation)*

*(1) Input the training set $T = \{(x_1, y_1), \cdots, (x_l, y_l)\}$, where $x_i \in R^n, y_i \in \mathcal{Y} = \{1, -1\}, i = 1, \cdots, l$;*

*(2) Choose an appropriate map $\Phi : x = \Phi(x)$ from the space $R^n$ to the Hilbert space and a penalty parameter $C > 0$;*

*(3) Construct and solve the convex quadratic programming problem*

$$\min_{\alpha} \quad \frac{1}{2} \sum_{i=1}^{l} \sum_{j=1}^{l} y_i y_j \alpha_i \alpha_j (\Phi(x_i) \cdot \Phi(x_j)) - \sum_{j=1}^{l} \alpha_j , \quad (4.1.38)$$

$$\text{s.t.} \quad \sum_{i=1}^{l} y_i \alpha_i = 0 , \quad (4.1.39)$$

$$0 \leqslant \alpha_i \leqslant C , \quad i = 1, \cdots, l , \quad (4.1.40)$$

*obtaining a solution $\alpha^* = (\alpha_1^*, \cdots, \alpha_l^*)^{\mathrm{T}}$;*

*(4) Compute $b^*$: choose a component of $\alpha^*$, $\alpha_j^* \in (0, C)$, and compute*

$$b^* = y_j - \sum_{i=1}^{l} y_i \alpha_i^* (\Phi(x_i) \cdot \Phi(x_j)); \qquad (4.1.41)$$

*(5) Construct the decision function*

$$f(x) = sgn(g(x)), \qquad (4.1.42)$$

*where*

$$g(x) = \sum_{i=1}^{l} y_i \alpha_i^* (\Phi(x_i) \cdot \Phi(x)) + b^*. \qquad (4.1.43)$$

It is easy to see that the only difference between the above algorithm and Algorithm 2.3.10 is that: the former uses the inner product $(\Phi(x_i) \cdot \Phi(x_j))$ and inner product $(\Phi(x_i) \cdot \Phi(x))$ to replace the inner product $(x_i \cdot x_j)$ and $(x_i \cdot x)$ of the latter respectively.

### 4.1.3 Regression machine based on nonlinear separation

Similar to the generalization of Algorithm 2.3.10 (Linear support vector classification) to Algorithm 4.1.4 (Classification machine based on nonlinear separation), we now generalize Algorithm 3.4.7 (Linear $\varepsilon$- support vector regression). Remember that Algorithm 3.4.7 searches for the linear regression function based on the linear separation since the regression problem is transformed to a classification problem. So in order to get the nonlinear regression function, we only need to use the nonlinear separation instead of the linear separation. In other words, for the purpose of generalizing Algorithm 3.4.7, we only need to introduce the map as (4.1.2):

$$\Phi : \quad \begin{array}{l} R^n \to \mathcal{H} , \\ x \to \mathrm{x} = \Phi(x) , \end{array} \qquad (4.1.44)$$

and solve the primal problem corresponding to the problem (3.4.1)~(3.4.4)

$$\min_{\mathrm{w}, b, \xi^{(*)}} \quad \frac{1}{2}\|\mathrm{w}\|^2 + C \sum_{i=1}^{l} (\xi_i + \xi_i^*), \qquad (4.1.45)$$

$$\text{s.t.} \quad ((\mathrm{w} \cdot \Phi(x_i)) + b) - y_i \leqslant \varepsilon + \xi_i , \ i = 1, \cdots, l, \qquad (4.1.46)$$

$$y_i - ((\mathrm{w} \cdot \Phi(x_i)) + b) \leqslant \varepsilon + \xi_i^* , \ i = 1, \cdots, l, \qquad (4.1.47)$$

$$\xi_i^{(*)} \geqslant 0 , \ i = 1, \cdots, l, \qquad (4.1.48)$$

where $(*)$ denotes two cases of a vector with $*$ and without $*$.

According to Theorem 1.3.3, primal problem (4.1.45)~(4.1.48) is a convex quadratic programming problem defined by Definition 1.3.2. Further discussion should be based on the content in Section 1.3. In order to deduce its dual problem, introduce the Lagrange function

$$L(\mathbf{w}, b, \xi^{(*)}, \alpha^{(*)}, \eta^{(*)}) = \frac{1}{2}\|\mathbf{w}\|^2 + C\sum_{i=1}^{l}(\xi_i + \xi_i^*) - \sum_{i=1}^{l}(\eta_i\xi_i + \eta_i^*\xi_i^*)$$

$$- \sum_{i=1}^{l}\alpha_i(\varepsilon + \xi_i + y_i - (\mathbf{w}\cdot\Phi(x_i)) - b)$$

$$- \sum_{i=1}^{l}\alpha_i^*(\varepsilon + \xi_i^* - y_i + (\mathbf{w}\cdot\Phi(x_i)) + b) , \quad (4.1.49)$$

where $\alpha^{(*)} = (\alpha_1, \alpha_1^*, \cdots, \alpha_l, \alpha_l^*)^{\mathrm{T}}, \eta^{(*)} = (\eta_1, \eta_1^*, \cdots, \eta_l, \eta_l^*)^{\mathrm{T}}$ are the Lagrange multiplier vectors. We have the following theorems:

**Theorem 4.1.5** *Optimization problem*

$$\max_{\alpha^{(*)}, \eta^{(*)}\in R^{2l}} \quad -\frac{1}{2}\sum_{i,j=1}^{l}(\alpha_i^* - \alpha_i)(\alpha_j^* - \alpha_j)(\Phi(x_i)\cdot\Phi(x_j)) - \varepsilon\sum_{i=1}^{l}(\alpha_i^* + \alpha_i)$$

$$+ \sum_{i=1}^{l}y_i(\alpha_i^* - \alpha_i) , \quad (4.1.50)$$

$$\text{s.t.} \quad \sum_{i=1}^{l}(\alpha_i^* - \alpha_i) = 0 , \quad (4.1.51)$$

$$C - \alpha_i^{(*)} - \eta_i^{(*)} = 0, \ i = 1, \cdots, l, \quad (4.1.52)$$

$$\alpha_i^{(*)} \geqslant 0, \ \eta_i^{(*)} \geqslant 0 , \ i = 1, \cdots, l \quad (4.1.53)$$

*is the dual problem of the primal problem (4.1.45)~(4.1.48).*

**Proof** According to Definition 1.3.6 in Chapter 1, the dual problem of the primal problem should be

$$\max \quad \inf_{\mathbf{w}, b, \xi^{(*)}} L(\mathbf{w}, b, \xi^{(*)}, \alpha^{(*)}, \eta^{(*)}), \quad (4.1.54)$$

$$\text{s.t.} \quad \alpha^{(*)} \geqslant 0, \ \eta^{(*)} \geqslant 0. \quad (4.1.55)$$

Note that $L(\mathbf{w}, b, \xi^{(*)}, \alpha^{(*)}, \eta^{(*)})$ is a quadratic function of w, of which minimal value w.r.t. w satisfying

$$\nabla_{\mathbf{w}} L(\mathbf{w}, b, \xi^{(*)}, \alpha^{(*)}, \eta^{(*)}) = \mathbf{w} - \sum_{i=1}^{l}(\alpha_i^* - \alpha_i)\Phi(x_i) = 0, \quad (4.1.56)$$

that is

$$\mathbf{w} = \sum_{i=1}^{l}(\alpha_i^* - \alpha_i)\Phi(x_i). \quad (4.1.57)$$

So substituting the above equation to (4.1.49), we have

$$
\inf_{\mathbf{w}} L(\mathbf{w}, b, \xi^{(*)}, \alpha^{(*)}, \eta^{(*)}) = -\frac{1}{2} \sum_{i=1}^{l} \sum_{j=1}^{l} (\alpha_i^* - \alpha_i)(\alpha_j^* - \alpha_j)(\Phi(x_i) \cdot \Phi(x_j))
$$

$$
- \varepsilon \sum_{i=1}^{l} (\alpha_i^* + \alpha_i) + \sum_{i=1}^{l} y_i(\alpha_i^* - \alpha_i)
$$

$$
- b \left( \sum_{i=1}^{l} (\alpha_i^* - \alpha_i) \right) + \sum_{i=1}^{l} (C - \alpha_i - \eta_i)\xi_i
$$

$$
+ \sum_{i=1}^{l} (C - \alpha_i^* - \eta_i^*)\xi_i^*, \tag{4.1.58}
$$

Note that when $\sum_{i=1}^{l}(\alpha_i^* - \alpha_i) = 0$, $C - \alpha_i - \eta_i = 0$, $i = 1, \cdots, l$ and $C - \alpha_i^* - \eta_i^* = 0$, $i = 1, \cdots, l$ are not valid at the same time, we always have $\inf_{\mathbf{w}, b, \xi^{(*)}} L(\mathbf{w}, b, \xi^{(*)}, \alpha^{(*)}, \eta^{(*)}) = -\infty$. Therefore, the problem (4.1.54)~(4.1.55) can be written as (4.1.50)~(4.1.53). ∎

**Theorem 4.1.6** *Dual problem (4.1.50)~(4.1.53) has a solution* $\bar{\alpha}^{(*)} = (\bar{\alpha}_1, \bar{\alpha}_1^*, \cdots, \bar{\alpha}_l, \bar{\alpha}_l^*)^{\mathrm{T}}$, $\bar{\eta}^{(*)} = (\bar{\eta}_1, \bar{\eta}_1^*, \cdots, \bar{\eta}_l, \bar{\eta}_l^*)^{\mathrm{T}}$.

**Proof** This is an optimization problem in the Euclidean space $R^{2l}$. It is easy to show that it has a solution. ∎

To simplify the dual problem (4.1.50)~(4.1.53), we eliminate the variable $\eta^{(*)}$ by the equality constraint (4.1.52) to make it be a problem only with variable $\alpha^{(*)}$, then rewrite this maximization problem to a convex quadratic programming problem in the space $R^{2l}$

$$
\min_{\alpha^{(*)} \in R^{2l}} \quad \frac{1}{2} \sum_{i,j=1}^{l} (\alpha_i^* - \alpha_i)(\alpha_j^* - \alpha_j)(\Phi(x_i) \cdot \Phi(x_j)) + \varepsilon \sum_{i=1}^{l} (\alpha_i^* + \alpha_i)
$$

$$
- \sum_{i=1}^{l} y_i(\alpha_i^* - \alpha_i), \tag{4.1.59}
$$

$$
\text{s.t.} \quad \sum_{i=1}^{l} (\alpha_i^* - \alpha_i) = 0, \tag{4.1.60}
$$

$$
0 \leqslant \alpha_i^{(*)} \leqslant C, \quad i = 1, \cdots, l. \tag{4.1.61}
$$

In the later sections, we replace the problem (4.1.50)~(4.1.53) by the problem (4.1.59)~(4.1.61).

**Theorem 4.1.7** *Suppose $\bar{\alpha}^{(*)} = (\bar{\alpha}_1, \bar{\alpha}_1^*, \cdots, \bar{\alpha}_l, \bar{\alpha}_l^*)^T$ is a solution to the convex quadratic programming problem (4.1.59)~(4.1.61). If there exist components of $\bar{\alpha}^{(*)}$ of which value is in the interval $(0, C)$, then the solution $(\bar{w}, \bar{b})$ to the primal problem (4.1.45)~(4.1.48) w.r.t. (w, b) can be obtained in the following way: Let*

$$\bar{w} = \sum_{i=1}^{l} (\bar{\alpha}_i^* - \bar{\alpha}_i) \Phi(x_i), \tag{4.1.62}$$

*and choose a component of $\bar{\alpha}^{(*)}$, $\bar{\alpha}_j \in (0, C)$, compute*

$$\bar{b} = y_j - \sum_{i=1}^{l} (\bar{\alpha}_i^* - \bar{\alpha}_i)(\Phi(x_i) \cdot \Phi(x_j)) + \varepsilon, \tag{4.1.63}$$

*or choose a component of $\bar{\alpha}^{(*)}$, $\bar{\alpha}_k^* \in (0, C)$, compute*

$$\bar{b} = y_k - \sum_{i=1}^{l} (\bar{\alpha}_i^* - \bar{\alpha}_i)(\Phi(x_i) \cdot \Phi(x_k)) - \varepsilon. \tag{4.1.64}$$

**Proof** Firstly we show that, for $\bar{w}$ given by (4.1.62), there exists a $\tilde{b}$ such that $(\bar{w}, \tilde{b})$ is the solution to the primal problem (4.1.45)~(4.1.48) w.r.t. (w, b). In fact, let $H = (\Phi(x_i) \cdot \Phi(x_j))_{l \times l}, y = (y_1, \cdots, y_l)^T, e = (1, \cdots, 1)^T \in R^l$, problem (4.1.59)~(4.1.61) can be rewritten as

$$\min_{\alpha^{(*)} \in R^{2l}} \quad W(\alpha^{(*)}) = \frac{1}{2}(\alpha^* - \alpha)^T H(\alpha^* - \alpha)$$
$$+ \varepsilon e^T(\alpha^* + \alpha) - y^T(\alpha^* - \alpha), \tag{4.1.65}$$
$$\text{s.t.} \quad e^T(\alpha^* - \alpha) = 0, \tag{4.1.66}$$
$$0 \leqslant \alpha^{(*)} \leqslant Ce. \tag{4.1.67}$$

It is easy to show that problem (4.1.65)~(4.1.67) is a convex programming. Furthermore, it also satisfies Slater condition, so if $\bar{\alpha}^{(*)}$ is the solution to the problem (4.1.65)~(4.1.67), it yields from Theorem 1.2.23 in Chapter 1 that there exist a multiplier $\tilde{b}$, multiplier vectors $\bar{s}^{(*)}$ and $\bar{\xi}^{(*)}$ such that

$$e^T(\bar{\alpha}^* - \bar{\alpha}) = 0, \quad 0 \leqslant \bar{\alpha}^{(*)} \leqslant Ce, \tag{4.1.68}$$
$$H(\bar{\alpha}^* - \bar{\alpha}) + \varepsilon e - y + \tilde{b}e - \bar{s}^* + \bar{\xi}^* = 0, \tag{4.1.69}$$
$$-H(\bar{\alpha}^* - \bar{\alpha}) + \varepsilon e + y - \tilde{b}e - \bar{s} + \bar{\xi} = 0, \tag{4.1.70}$$
$$\bar{s}^{(*)} \geqslant 0, \quad \bar{\xi}^{(*)} \geqslant 0, \tag{4.1.71}$$
$$\bar{s}^{(*)^T} \bar{\alpha}^{(*)} = 0, \quad \bar{\xi}^{(*)^T}(Ce - \bar{\alpha}^{(*)}) = 0. \tag{4.1.72}$$

Equations (4.1.69)~(4.1.71) mean that

$$H(\bar{\alpha}^* - \bar{\alpha}) - y + \tilde{b}e \geqslant -\varepsilon e - \bar{\xi}^*, \tag{4.1.73}$$
$$-H(\bar{\alpha}^* - \bar{\alpha}) + y - \tilde{b}e \geqslant -\varepsilon e - \bar{\xi}. \tag{4.1.74}$$

From (4.1.62), the above inequalities are equivalent to

$$((\bar{w} \cdot \Phi(x_i)) + \tilde{b}) - y_i \leqslant \varepsilon + \bar{\xi}_i, \quad i = 1, \cdots, l, \tag{4.1.75}$$

$$y_i - ((\bar{w} \cdot \Phi(x_i)) + \tilde{b}) \leqslant \varepsilon + \bar{\xi}_i^*, \quad i = 1, \cdots, l. \tag{4.1.76}$$

which imply that $(\bar{w}, \tilde{b}, \bar{\xi}^{(*)})$ is a feasible solution to the problem (4.1.45)~(4.1.48).

Furthermore, from (4.1.69)~(4.1.72) we have

$$-\frac{1}{2}\|\bar{w}\|^2 - C\sum_{i=1}^{l}(\bar{\xi}_i + \bar{\xi}_i^*) = -\frac{1}{2}\|\bar{w}\|^2 - C\sum_{i=1}^{l}(\bar{\xi}_i + \bar{\xi}_i^*)$$

$$+\bar{\alpha}^{*T}(H(\bar{\alpha}^* - \bar{\alpha}) + \varepsilon e - y + \tilde{b}e - \bar{s}^* + \bar{\xi}^*)$$

$$+\bar{\alpha}^{T}(-H(\bar{\alpha}^* - \bar{\alpha}) + \varepsilon e + y - \tilde{b}e - \bar{s} + \bar{\xi})$$

$$= \frac{1}{2}(\bar{\alpha}^* - \bar{\alpha})^T H(\bar{\alpha}^* - \bar{\alpha}) + \varepsilon e^T(\bar{\alpha}^* + \bar{\alpha})$$

$$-y^T(\bar{\alpha}^* - \bar{\alpha}). \tag{4.1.77}$$

This shows that the objective function value of the primal problem (4.1.45)~(4.1.48) is equal to the optimal value of its dual problem (4.1.50)~(4.1.53), therefore $(\bar{w}, \tilde{b}, \bar{\xi}^{(*)})$ is the optimal solution to the primal problem (4.1.45)~(4.1.48) according to the results corresponding to Corollary 1.2.19 mentioned in Section 1.3 in Chapter 1.

Therefore, in order to show that $(w, \bar{b})$ obtained from (4.1.62) and (4.1.63) or (4.1.64) is the solution to the primal problem w.r.t. $(w, b)$, we only need to show $\bar{b} = \tilde{b}$. In fact, suppose that there exists a component of $\bar{\alpha}^{(*)}$, $\bar{\alpha}_j \in (0, C)$, KKT conditions (4.1.68)~(4.1.72) imply that $\bar{\xi}_j = \bar{s}_j = 0$ and

$$(\bar{w} \cdot \Phi(x_j)) + \tilde{b} - y_j = \varepsilon, \tag{4.1.78}$$

i.e. $\tilde{b}$ equals to the $\bar{b}$ given by (4.1.63).

Similarly, suppose that there exists a component of $\bar{\alpha}^{(*)}$, $\bar{\alpha}_k^* \in (0, C)$, we can also prove that $\tilde{b}$ equals to the $\bar{b}$ given by (4.1.64). ∎

Based on the above theorem, when the solution $\bar{\alpha}^{(*)} = (\bar{\alpha}_1, \bar{\alpha}_1^*, \cdots, \bar{\alpha}_l, \bar{\alpha}_l^*)^T$ to the problem (4.1.59)~(4.1.61) is derived, the decision function in the space $\mathcal{H}$ can be constructed as

$$y = (\bar{w} \cdot x) + \bar{b}, \tag{4.1.79}$$

where $\bar{w}$ and $\bar{b}$ are given by (4.1.62)~(4.1.64). Obviously, the decision function in the space $R^n$ can be written as

$$y = g(x) = \sum_{i=1}^{l}(\bar{\alpha}_i^* - \bar{\alpha}_i)(\Phi(x_i) \cdot \Phi(x)) + \bar{b}. \tag{4.1.80}$$

So, the following algorithm for nonlinear regression function is established:

**Algorithm 4.1.8** *(Regression machine based on nonlinear separation)*

*(1) Input the training set* $T = \{(x_1, y_1), \cdots, (x_l, y_l)\}$, *where* $x_i \in R^n, y_i \in \mathcal{Y} = R, i = 1, \cdots, l$;

*(2) Choose an appropriate map* $\Phi : x = \Phi(x)$ *from the space* $R^n$ *to the Hilbert space, and accuracy* $\varepsilon > 0$ *and a penalty parameter* $C > 0$;

*(3) Construct and solve the convex quadratic programming problem*

$$
\min_{\alpha^{(*)} \in R^{2l}} \quad \frac{1}{2} \sum_{i,j=1}^{l} (\alpha_i^* - \alpha_i)(\alpha_j^* - \alpha_j)(\Phi(x_i) \cdot \Phi(x_j)) + \varepsilon \sum_{i=1}^{l} (\alpha_i^* + \alpha_i)
$$

$$
- \sum_{i=1}^{l} y_i(\alpha_i^* - \alpha_i) , \tag{4.1.81}
$$

$$
s.t. \quad \sum_{i=1}^{l} (\alpha_i - \alpha_i^*) = 0 , \tag{4.1.82}
$$

$$
0 \leqslant \alpha_i^{(*)} \leqslant C , \quad i = 1, \cdots, l, \tag{4.1.83}
$$

*obtaining a solution* $\bar{\alpha}^{(*)} = (\bar{\alpha}_1, \bar{\alpha}_1^*, \cdots, \bar{\alpha}_l, \bar{\alpha}_l^*)^{\mathrm{T}}$;

*(4) Compute* $\bar{b}$: *choose a component of* $\bar{\alpha}^{(*)}$ *of which value is in the interval* $(0, C)$, $\bar{\alpha}_j$ *or* $\bar{\alpha}_k^*$. *If* $\bar{\alpha}_j$ *is chosen, then*

$$
\bar{b} = y_j - \sum_{i=1}^{l} (\bar{\alpha}_i^* - \bar{\alpha}_i)(\Phi(x_i) \cdot \Phi(x_j)) + \varepsilon ; \tag{4.1.84}
$$

*else if* $\bar{\alpha}_k^*$ *is chosen, then*

$$
\bar{b} = y_k - \sum_{i=1}^{l} (\bar{\alpha}_i^* - \bar{\alpha}_i)(\Phi(x_i) \cdot \Phi(x_k)) - \varepsilon ; \tag{4.1.85}
$$

*(5) Construct the decision function*

$$
y = g(x) = \sum_{i=1}^{l} (\bar{\alpha}_i^* - \bar{\alpha}_i)(\Phi(x_i) \cdot \Phi(x)) + \bar{b}. \tag{4.1.86}
$$

---

## 4.2    Kernels

Reviewing Algorithm 4.1.4 and Algorithm 4.1.8, we can see that the map $\Phi$ implements its role totally through the inner products $(\Phi(x_i) \cdot \Phi(x_j))$ and $(\Phi(x_i) \cdot \Phi(x))$. In other words, the map $\Phi$ always appears in the form of the inner product $(\Phi(x_i) \cdot \Phi(x_j))$ or $(\Phi(x_i) \cdot \Phi(x))$; it never appears independent. This shows that the function

$$K(x, x') = (\Phi(x) \cdot \Phi(x')) \tag{4.2.1}$$

is very important. In fact, for Algorithms 4.1.4 and 4.1.8, if we choose the function $K$ instead of the $\Phi$, and substitute the corresponding inner product $(\Phi(\cdot) \cdot \Phi(\cdot))$ by $K(\cdot, \cdot)$, we can still get the same decision function. The function defined by (4.2.1) is called kernel function, or kernel briefly. In this section we will analyze the function introduced by the inner product, and then deduce the commonly used standard support vector machines.

### 4.2.1 Properties

Firstly we formalize the definition of the kernel.

**Definition 4.2.1** *(Kernel) A function $K(x, x')$ defined on $R^n \times R^n$ is called a kernel on $R^n \times R^n$ or kernel briefly if there exists a map $\Phi$ from the space $R^n$ to the Hilbert space*

$$\Phi: \quad \begin{array}{l} R^n \to \mathcal{H}, \\ x \mapsto \Phi(x), \end{array} \tag{4.2.2}$$

*such that*

$$K(x, x') = (\Phi(x) \cdot \Phi(x')), \tag{4.2.3}$$

*where $(\cdot)$ denotes the inner product of space $\mathcal{H}$.*

The next theorem describes the characteristic of the kernels by Gram matrix defined as follows.

**Definition 4.2.2** *(Gram matrix) For a function $K(x, x') : R^n \times R^n \to R$ and $l$ points $x_1, \cdots, x_l \in R^n$, the $l \times l$ matrix $K$, of which the $i$-th row $j$-th column element is $K_{ij} = K(x_i, x_j)$, is called the Gram matrix of the function $K(x, x')$ w.r.t. $x_1, \cdots, x_l$.*

**Theorem 4.2.3** *(Property of a kernel) A symmetric function $K(x, x')$ defined on $R^n \times R^n$ is a kernel if and only if the Gram matrix of $K(x, x')$ w.r.t. $x_1, \cdots, x_l$ is positive semidefinite for any $l$ and any $x_1, \cdots, x_l \in R^n$.*

**Proof** See [42] or [124]. ∎

### 4.2.2 Construction of kernels

A natural question at this point is what kind of functions are kernels, i.e., what is the coverage of the kernels. In accordance with the mathematical approach dealing with such problem, we shall take the following three steps to give an answer:

(1) Find out the basic kernels;

(2) Find out the operations keeping kernels;

(3) From the basic kernels, construct the commonly used kernels by applying the operations keeping kernels.

### 4.2.2.1  Basic kernels

**Theorem 4.2.4** *The function $K(x, x') = (x \cdot x')$ defined on $R^n \times R^n$ is a kernel.*

**Proof** Let $\Phi(x) = x$, then $K(x, x')$ can be expressed as

$$K(x, x') = (x \cdot x') = (\Phi(x) \cdot \Phi(x')). \qquad (4.2.4)$$

According to Definition 4.2.1, we know that $K(x, x') = (x \cdot x')$ is a kernel. ∎

**Theorem 4.2.5** *If $f(\cdot)$ is a real-valued function defined on $R^n$, then $K(x, x') = f(x)f(x')$ is a kernel. Particularly, the function $K(x, x') \equiv a$ where $a$ is a nonnegative scalar, is a kernel.*

**Proof** For any $x_1, \cdots, x_l \in R^n$, consider the Gram matrix $(K(x_i, x_j))_{l \times l}$ of the function $K(x, x') = f(x)f(x')$. For any vector $\alpha = (\alpha_1, \cdots, \alpha_l)^T \in R^l$, we have

$$\alpha^T (K(x_i, x_j))_{l \times l} \alpha = \sum_{i=1}^{l} \sum_{j=1}^{l} \alpha_i \alpha_j K(x_i, x_j) = \sum_{i=1}^{l} \sum_{j=1}^{l} \alpha_i \alpha_j f(x_i) f(x_j)$$

$$= \sum_{i=1}^{l} \alpha_i f(x_i) \sum_{j=1}^{l} \alpha_j f(x_j) = \left( \sum_{i=1}^{l} \alpha_i f(x_i) \right)^2 \geq 0 .$$

$$(4.2.5)$$

So this Gram matrix is positive semidefinite. Therefore according to Theorem 4.2.3 we know that $K(x, x')$ is a kernel. Particularly, this conclusion is also valid for $f(x) \equiv \sqrt{a}$. ∎

### 4.2.2.2  Operations keeping kernels

**Theorem 4.2.6** *Suppose $K_1(x, x')$ and $K_2(x, x')$ are all kernels on $R^n \times R^n$, then their sum*

$$K(x, x') = K_1(x, x') + K_2(x, x') \qquad (4.2.6)$$

*and product*

$$K(x, x') = K_1(x, x') K_2(x, x') \qquad (4.2.7)$$

*are also kernels.*

**Proof** According to Theorem 4.2.3, we only need to show that, for any set of $l$ points $\{x_1, \cdots, x_l\}$ in $R^n$, the Gram matrices of both $K_1(x, x') + K_2(x, x')$ and $K_1(x, x') K_2(x, x')$ w.r.t. $\{x_1, \cdots, x_l\}$ are positive semidefinite.

Firstly consider the function $K_1(x, x') + K_2(x, x')$. Let $K_1$ and $K_2$ be the corresponding Gram matrices of $K_1(x, x')$ and $K_2(x, x')$ w.r.t. to $\{x_1, \cdots, x_l\}$ respectively. For any $\alpha \in R^l$, we have

$$\alpha^{\mathrm{T}}(K_1 + K_2)\alpha = \alpha^{\mathrm{T}} K_1 \alpha + \alpha^{\mathrm{T}} K_2 \alpha \geqslant 0 , \tag{4.2.8}$$

and so $K_1 + K_2$ is positive semidefinite.

Furthermore, suppose $K$ is the Gram matrix of $K(x, x') = K_1(x, x') \cdot K_2(x, x')$ w.r.t.$\{x_1, \cdots, x_l\}$, it is easy to see that $K$ is known as the Schur product of the Gram matrix $K_1$ of $K_1(x, x')$ and the Gram matrix $K_2$ of $K_2(x, x')$, i.e. the element of $K$ is the product of the corresponding elements of $K_1$ and $K_2$

$$K = K_1 \circ K_2 . \tag{4.2.9}$$

Now prove $K$ is positive semidefinite. Let $K_1 = C^{\mathrm{T}} C$ , $K_2 = D^{\mathrm{T}} D$, hence for any $\alpha \in R^l$, we have

$$\begin{aligned}
\alpha^{\mathrm{T}}(K_1 \circ K_2)\alpha &= \mathrm{tr}[(\mathrm{diag}\ \alpha)K_1(\mathrm{diag}\ \alpha)K_2^{\mathrm{T}}] \\
&= \mathrm{tr}[(\mathrm{diag}\ \alpha)C^{\mathrm{T}}C(\mathrm{diag}\ \alpha)D^{\mathrm{T}}D] \\
&= \mathrm{tr}[D(\mathrm{diag}\ \alpha)C^{\mathrm{T}}C(\mathrm{diag}\ \alpha)D^{\mathrm{T}}] \\
\\
&= \mathrm{tr}[[C(\mathrm{diag}\ \alpha)D^{\mathrm{T}}]^{\mathrm{T}}C(\mathrm{diag}\ \alpha)D^{\mathrm{T}}] \geqslant 0 . \tag{4.2.10}
\end{aligned}$$

The third equal sign of the above equation is based on the equality $\mathrm{tr}AB = \mathrm{tr}BA$. For any two matrices $A$ and $B$, so (4.2.10) demonstrates that $K$ is positive semidefinite. ∎

**Theorem 4.2.7** *Suppose $K_3(\theta, \theta')$ is a kernel on $R^m \times R^m$. If $\theta(x)$ is a map from $R^n$ to $R^m$, then $K(x, x') = K_3(\theta(x), \theta(x'))$ is a kernel on $R^n \times R^n$. Particularly, if a $n \times n$ matrix $B$ is positive semidefinite, then $K(x, x') = x^{\mathrm{T}} B x'$ is a kernel on $R^n \times R^n$.*

**Proof** For any given $x_1, \cdots, x_l \in R^n$, the corresponding Gram matrix of $K(x, x') = K_3(\theta(x), \theta(x'))$ is

$$(K(x_i, x_j))_{i,j=1}^l = (K_3(\theta(x_i), \theta(x_j)))_{i,j=1}^l . \tag{4.2.11}$$

Let $\theta(x_t) = \theta_t, t = 1, \cdots, l$, we have

$$(K(x_i, x_j))_{i,j=1}^l = (K_3(\theta_i, \theta_j))_{i,j=1}^l . \tag{4.2.12}$$

That $K_3(\theta, \theta')$ is a kernel indicates that the right matrix in the above equation is positive semidefinite, so the left matrix is positive semidefinite, hence $K(x, x')$ is a kernel according to Theorem 4.2.3.

In particular, consider the positive semidefinite matrix $B$. Obviously it can be decomposed into the form

$$B = V^{\mathrm{T}} \Lambda V , \tag{4.2.13}$$

where $V$ is an orthogonal matrix, $\Lambda$ is a diagonal matrix containing the non-negative eigenvalues of $B$. Defining a kernel $K_3(\theta, \theta') = (\theta \cdot \theta')$ on $R^n \times R^n$, and letting $\theta(x) = \sqrt{\Lambda} V x$, we have by the just-proved conclusion

$$K(x, x') = K_3(\theta(x), \theta(x')) = \theta(x)^T \theta(x') = x^T V^T \sqrt{\Lambda} \sqrt{\Lambda} V x' = x^T B x' \tag{4.2.14}$$

is a kernel. ∎

**Theorem 4.2.8** *If a sequence of kernels $K_1(x, x'), K_2(x, x'), \cdots$ on $R^n \times R^n$ has a limit, i.e.*

$$\lim_{i \to \infty} K_i(x, x') = K(x, x'), \tag{4.2.15}$$

*then the limit $K(x, x')$ is also a kernel.*

**Proof** Theorem 4.2.3 can be directly used to prove this conclusion. ∎

### 4.2.2.3  Commonly used kernels

Now we are in a position to construct two commonly used kernels based on the basic kernels proposed above by the operations keeping kernels.

**(1) Polynomial kernel**

**Theorem 4.2.9** *Suppose $d$ is a positive integer, then $d$-order homogeneous polynomial function*

$$K(x, x') = (x \cdot x')^d \tag{4.2.16}$$

*and $d$-order non-homogeneous polynomial function*

$$K(x, x') = ((x \cdot x') + 1)^d \tag{4.2.17}$$

*are all kernels.*

**Proof** We can draw this conclusion directly from Theorems 4.2.4~4.2.6. ∎

**(2) Gaussian radial basis function kernel**

**Theorem 4.2.10** *Gaussian radial basis function with a parameter $\sigma$*

$$K(x, x') = \exp(-\|x - x'\|^2 / \sigma^2) \tag{4.2.18}$$

*is a kernel.*

**Proof** (i) Firstly, we prove that if $K_1(x, x')$ is a kernel on $R^n \times R^n$, $p(x)$ is a polynomial with positive coefficients, then the function

$$p(K_1(x, x')) \tag{4.2.19}$$

is a kernel. In fact, let the polynomial with positive coefficients be $p(x) = a_q x^q + \cdots + a_1 x + a_0$, then

$$p(K_1(x, x')) = a_q [K_1(x, x')]^q + \cdots + a_1 K_1(x, x') + a_0 . \qquad (4.2.20)$$

According to the conclusion about the particular case of Theorem 4.2.5 and Theorem 4.2.6, all the terms $a_i [K_1(x, x')]^i, i = 0, 1, \cdots, q$ are kernels. Therefore the function described by (4.2.19) is a kernel according to Theorem 4.2.6.

(ii) Secondly, we prove that if $K_1(x, x')$ is a kernel on $R^n \times R^n$, then the function

$$\exp\left(K_1(x, x')\right) \qquad (4.2.21)$$

is a kernel. In fact, the exponential function $\exp(\cdot)$ can be arbitrarily closely approximated by polynomials with positive coefficients, and hence $\exp(K_1(x, x'))$ is a limit of kernels. Therefore, the function described by (4.2.21) is a kernel according to Theorem 4.2.8 and conclusion (i).

(iii) At last, we prove that the Gaussian function (4.2.18) is a kernel. In fact, it can be obviously decomposed into the form

$$\exp(-\|x - x'\|^2 / \sigma^2) = \exp(-\|x\|^2 / \sigma^2) \cdot \exp(-\|x'\|^2 / \sigma^2) \cdot \exp(2(x \cdot x') / \sigma^2) . \qquad (4.2.22)$$

The first two factors together form a kernel by Theorem 4.2.5, while the third factor is a kernel by conclusion (ii). Therefore, the function described by (4.2.18) is a kernel according to Theorem 4.2.6. ∎

In addition to the polynomial kernel given by Theorem 4.2.9 and the Gaussian radial basis function kernel given by Theorem 4.2.10, there exist $B$-Spline kernel, Fourier kernel, etc., the interested reader can refer to the literature [35, 73, 137].

### 4.2.2.4 Graph kernel

At first glance, Algorithms 4.1.4 and 4.1.8 need a training set $T$ where the $n$-dimensional vectors $x_1, \cdots, x_l$ stand for objects, and a kernel, i.e. for any two $n$-dimensional vectors $x$ and $x'$, an appropriate real value $K(x, x')$ is given. However, on closer examination, we can see that it is not necessary to represent objects by vectors in $R^n$. Instead, what it needs is only the classes the objects $x_1, \cdots, x_l$ belong to, and a kernel, that is for any two objects $x$ and $x'$, an appropriate real value $K(x, x')$ is given.

In this case, the key point is to construct a suitable kernel for a concrete problem. As an example, the simple graph classification problem is considered here. Simple graph classification has been applied successfully to the protein function prediction in the field of bio-informatics; see the literature [16]. Next we intuitively introduce the method constructing kernels for it. Firstly we introduce several basic concepts[46].

**Definition 4.2.11** *(Undirected graph) An undirected graph consists of two parts: a nonempty finite set $V$ and a set $E$ of disordered pairs composed of* several elements in $V$. Denote $G = (V, E)$, where $V$ is called the set of vertices of the undirected graph $G$, each element of $V$ is called a vertex; $E$ is called the set of edges of the undirected graph $G$, each element of $E$ is called an edge, denoted as $\{v_i, v_j\}$ or $\{v_j, v_i\}$, where $v_i, v_j \in V$.

**Definition 4.2.12** *(Simple graph)* *If* $\{v_i, v_j\} \in E$, *then the edge* $\{v_i, v_j\}$ *is named connecting* $v_i$ *and* $v_j$, *and the vertices* $v_i$ *and* $v_j$ *are called the endpoints of the edge* $\{v_i, v_j\}$. *An edge is called a loop if its two endpoints coincide into a vertex. An undirected graph is called a simple graph if there is neither a loop nor two edges connecting the same pair of vertices in it.*

**Example 4.2.13** $G$ *in Figure 4.2 is a simple graph; it can be represented by* $G = (V, E)$, *where*

$$V = \{v_1, v_2, v_3\}, \quad E = \{\{v_1, v_2\}, \{v_2, v_3\}, \{v_3, v_1\}\},$$

*or*

$$E = \{\{v_2, v_1\}, \{v_1, v_3\}, \{v_3, v_2\}\}. \tag{4.2.23}$$

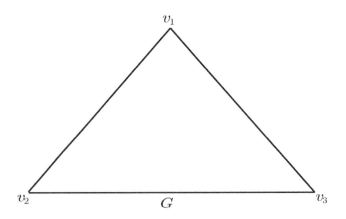

**FIGURE 4.2**: Simple graph.

**Definition 4.2.14** *(Path) In the simple graph* $G$, *an alternate sequence of vertices and edges*

$$(v_i, \{v_i, v_j\}, v_j, \cdots, v_p, \{v_p, v_q\}, v_q) \tag{4.2.24}$$

*is called a path from* $v_i$ *to* $v_q$ *in the graph* $G$. *The number of the edges included in the path is called its length.*

Now consider the quantification problem of a simple graph. We describe a simple graph using the numbers of the path. Specifically, for a simple graph $G$, denote the numbers of all the paths with length $k$ in $G$ as $\phi^k(G)$. In order to describe $G$, we adopt the infinitely dimensional vector

$$\phi(G) = (\phi^0(G), \phi^1(G), \cdots, \phi^n(G), \cdots)^{\mathrm{T}}, \tag{4.2.25}$$

or

$$\Phi(G) = (\Phi^0(G), \Phi^1(G), \cdots, \Phi^n(G), \cdots)^{\mathrm{T}}, \tag{4.2.26}$$

where

$$\Phi^k(G) = \sqrt{\lambda^k} \phi^k(G), \quad k = 0, 1, 2, \cdots, \tag{4.2.27}$$

here $\lambda$ is a weight factor between 0 and 1. Now we can define the kernel of the simple graph.

**Definition 4.2.15** *(Graph kernel based on the path) Consider two simple graphs $G = (V, E), G' = (V', E')$, and the weight factor $0 < \lambda < 1$ is given, then the value of the graph kernel based on the path at $G, G'$ is*

$$K(G, G') = (\Phi(G) \cdot \Phi(G')) = \sum_{k=0}^{\infty} \lambda^k \phi^k(G) \phi^k(G'), \tag{4.2.28}$$

*where $\Phi(\cdot)$ is given by (4.2.26).*

Now the issue that remains is to compute the value of the above equation practically. To this end, introduce the concept of adjacent matrix.

**Definition 4.2.16** *(Adjacent matrix of the graph) A simple graph $G = (V, E)$ corresponds to a $|V| \times |V|$ matrix $A = (a_{ij})$, where $|V|$ denotes the numbers of the elements in the set $V$, while*

$$a_{ij} = \begin{cases} 1, & if\{v_i, v_j\} \in E; \\ 0, & otherwise. \end{cases} \tag{4.2.29}$$

*The matrix $A$ is called the adjacent matrix of the graph $G$.*

**Theorem 4.2.17** *Suppose the adjacent matrix of the simple graph $G = (V, E)$ is $A = (a_{ij})$, and note the $k$-th power of $A$ as $A^k = (a_{ij}^k)$. Then the value of the element $a_{ij}^k$ at the $i$-th row $j$-th column is exactly the numbers of the paths with length $k$ from the vertex $v_i$ to $v_j$. Therefore the numbers $\phi^k(G)$ of the paths with length $k$ in $G$ can be expressed as*

$$\phi^k(G) = \sum_{i,j=1}^{|V|} a_{ij}^k, \tag{4.2.30}$$

**Example 4.2.18** *For the simple graph in Figure 4.2, its adjacent matrix $A$ and its second power $A^2$ are*

$$A = \begin{pmatrix} 0 & 1 & 1 \\ 1 & 0 & 1 \\ 1 & 1 & 0 \end{pmatrix}, \quad A^2 = \begin{pmatrix} 2 & 1 & 1 \\ 1 & 2 & 1 \\ 1 & 1 & 2 \end{pmatrix}. \tag{4.2.31}$$

*respectively. The element 2 at the first row first column means that there are two paths with length 2 from the vertex $v_1$ to $v_1$; the element 2 at the second row the third column means that there is one path with length 2 from the vertex $v_2$ to $v_3$. Furthermore, the numbers of all the paths with length 2 in $G$ is the sum of all the elements in $A^2$, i.e. $\phi^2(G) = 12$.*

In order to compute $K(G, G')$ defined as (4.2.28), we first give the definition of Kronecker product of the matrix.

**Definition 4.2.19** *The Kronecker product of matrix $A = (a_{ij}) \in R^{m \times m}$ and matrix $A' = (a'_{ij}) \in R^{n \times n}$ is*

$$A \otimes A' = \begin{pmatrix} a_{11} A' & \cdots & a_{1m} A' \\ \vdots & & \vdots \\ a_{m1} A' & \cdots & a_{mm} A' \end{pmatrix} \in R^{mn \times mn}. \tag{4.2.32}$$

It is easy to verify that the Kronecker product of matrix $A = (a_{ij}) \in R^{m \times m}$ and matrix $A' = (a'_{ij}) \in R^{n \times n}$ has the following property:

**Theorem 4.2.20** *The Kronecker product of matrix $A$ and matrix $A'$ satisfies*

$$\sum_{i,j=1}^{mn} (A \otimes A')_{ij} = \left( \sum_{i,j=1}^{m} a_{ij} \right) \cdot \left( \sum_{i,j=1}^{n} a'_{ij} \right) \tag{4.2.33}$$

$$(A \otimes A')^k = A^k \otimes A'^k, \tag{4.2.34}$$

*where $(\cdot)^k$ and $\cdot^k$ are the k-order powers of the matrix.*

**Theorem 4.2.21** *Consider the k-order powers $A^k = (a_{ij}^k)$ and $A'^k = a_{ij}'^k$ of matrices, $A$ and $A'$, and the k-order power $A_\times^k = (a_{\times ij}^k)$ of $A_\times = A \otimes A' = (a_{\times ij})$, where $\otimes$ is the Kronecker product of the matrices; then*

$$\sum_{i,j=1}^{mn} a_{\times ij}^k = \sum_{i,j=1}^{m} a_{ij}^k \sum_{i,j=1}^{n} a_{ij}'^k. \tag{4.2.35}$$

Now we can give one kind of quantitative representation of the graph kernel based on the path.

**Theorem 4.2.22** *Suppose the graphs $G = (V, E), G' = (V', E')$ are given, of which adjacent matrices are $A$ and $A'$ respectively. Suppose the $k$-order power of $A_\times = A \otimes A' = (a_{\times ij})$ is $A_\times^k = (a_{\times ij}^k)$, and the weight factor $0 < \lambda < 1$ is given, then the above defined kernel about the graphs $G, G'$ can be expressed as*

$$K(G, G') = \sum_{k=0}^{\infty} \lambda^k \sum_{i,j=1}^{|V||V'|} a_{\times ij}^k, \qquad (4.2.36)$$

*where $\otimes$ is the Kronecker product of the matrices, $|V|$ and $|V'|$ are the number of the elements in the sets $V$ and $V'$. Furthermore, when $\lambda$ is small enough, the right term of (4.2.36) converges, and can be expressed as*

$$K(G, G') = \sum_{k=0}^{\infty} (e^{\mathrm{T}} A_{\times e}^k) = e^{\mathrm{T}} \left( \sum_{k=0}^{\infty} \lambda^k A_\times^k \right) e = e^{\mathrm{T}} (I - \lambda A_\times)^{-1} e, \quad (4.2.37)$$

*where $e$ is a $|V||V'|$-dimensional vector of ones, $I$ is a $|V||V'| \times |V||V'|$ identity matrix.*

The kernel given by the last equation (4.2.37) of the above theorem and some simple graphs with class label 1 or $-1$ can be used in Algorithm 4.1.4, and solve the classification problem [103].

---

## 4.3 Support Vector Machines and Their Properties

In this section we introduce the most commonly used standard support vector machines.

### 4.3.1 Support vector classification

#### 4.3.1.1 Algorithm

As we pointed out in the former section, in Algorithm 4.1.4 (Classification machine based on nonlinear separation), we can choose a kernel $K$ instead of the map $\Phi$, and replace the inner product $(\Phi(\cdot) \cdot \Phi(\cdot))$ by the value of the kernel $K(\cdot, \cdot)$. Hence the commonly used standard $C$-support vector classification is established as follows.

**Algorithm 4.3.1** *(C-support vector classification, C-SVC)*

*(1) Input the training set $T = \{(x_1, y_1), \cdots, (x_l, y_l)\}$, where $x_i \in R^n, y_i \in \mathcal{Y} = \{1, -1\}, i = 1, \cdots, l;$*

*(2) Choose an appropriate kernel $K(x, x')$ and a penalty parameter $C > 0;$*

*(3) Construct and solve the convex quadratic programming problem*

$$\min_{\alpha} \quad \frac{1}{2}\sum_{i=1}^{l}\sum_{j=1}^{l} y_i y_j K(x_i, x_j)\alpha_i\alpha_j - \sum_{j=1}^{l}\alpha_j \,, \tag{4.3.1}$$

$$s.t. \quad \sum_{i=1}^{l} y_i\alpha_i = 0 \,, \tag{4.3.2}$$

$$0 \leqslant \alpha_i \leqslant C \,, \ i = 1, \cdots, l \,, \tag{4.3.3}$$

*obtaining a solution* $\alpha^* = (\alpha_1^*, \cdots, \alpha_l^*)^{\mathrm{T}};$

*(4) Compute* $b^*$: *Choose a component of* $\alpha^*$, $\alpha_j^* \in (0, C)$, *and compute*

$$b^* = y_j - \sum_{i=1}^{l} y_i\alpha_i^* K(x_i, x_j); \tag{4.3.4}$$

*(5) Construct the decision function*

$$f(x) = sgn(g(x)), \tag{4.3.5}$$

*where*

$$g(x) = \sum_{i=1}^{l} y_i\alpha_i^* K(x_i, x) + b^*. \tag{4.3.6}$$

The above algorithm only considers the case where there exists a component of $\alpha^*$, $\alpha_j^* \in (0, C)$. Although almost all practical problems belong to this case, theoretically there still exists the case that all the components of $\alpha^*$ are zero. It is not difficult to imagine that in this case the values of threshold $b^*$ compose a closed interval according to Theorem 2.3.6. Detailed discussion is omitted here.

**Remark 4.3.2** *The decision function in the above algorithm can be rewritten as:*

$$f(x) = \left\{ \begin{array}{ll} 1, & g(x) \geq 0; \\ -1, & g(x) < 0; \end{array} \right.$$

*This means that 0 is a cutoff value for distinguishing the positive and negative classes. However, in some practical problems, a lower or higher cutoff value may be more appropriate than 0. For example, in Example 2.1.1 (Diagnosis of heart disease), we usually pay more attention to the positive class than the negative class; in other words, we hope that no patients having heart disease are misclassified. To deal with this case, a lower cutoff value is used. Hence the decision function with a cutoff level is introduced:*

$$f(x, cutoff) = \left\{ \begin{array}{ll} 1, & \text{when } g(x) \geqslant \text{cutoff}; \\ -1, & \end{array} \right. \tag{4.3.7}$$

*otherwise, where cutoff is a real number.*

### 4.3.1.2 Support vector

Now we introduce the concept of support vector for the above algorithm ($C$-support vector classification) and discuss its properties.

**Definition 4.3.3** *(Support vector) Suppose $\alpha^* = (\alpha_1^*, \cdots, \alpha_l^*)^\mathrm{T}$ is a solution to the problem (4.3.1) ~(4.3.3) obtained using Algorithm 4.3.1. The input $x_i$, associated with the training point $(x_i, y_i)$, is said to be a support vector if the corresponding component $\alpha_i^*$ of $\alpha^*$ is nonzero and otherwise it is a nonsupport vector.*

The following theorem characterizes the support vectors:

**Theorem 4.3.4** *Suppose $\alpha^* = (\alpha_1^*, \cdots, \alpha_l^*)^\mathrm{T}$ is a solution to the problem (4.3.1) ~(4.3.3) obtained using Algorithm 4.3.1. If $g(x)$ is defined by (4.3.6), then*

*(i) support vector $x_i$ corresponding to $\alpha_i^* \in (0, C)$ satisfies $y_i g(x_i) = 1$;*

*(ii) support vector $x_i$ corresponding to $\alpha_i^* = C$ satisfies $y_i g(x_i) \leqslant 1$;*

*(iii) nonsupport vector $x_i$ satisfies $y_i g(x_i) \geqslant 1$.*

**Proof** Because $\alpha^* = (\alpha_1^*, \cdots, \alpha_l^*)^\mathrm{T}$ is a solution to the problem (4.3.1) ~(4.3.3) in Algorithm 4.3.1 and problem (4.3.1)~(4.3.3) satisfies Slater condition, according to Theorem 1.2.23 in Chapter 1, $\alpha^*$ satisfies the KKT conditions, i.e. there exist multipliers $b^*, \xi_i^*,\ s_i^*, i = 1, \cdots, l$ such that

$$y_i \left( \sum_{j=1}^{l} y_j \alpha_j^* K(x_j, x_i) + b^* \right) + \xi_i^* - 1 = s_i^* \geqslant 0, \quad i = 1, \cdots, l,$$

$$(4.3.8)$$

$$\alpha_i^* s_i^* = \alpha_i^* (y_i g(x_i) + \xi_i^* - 1) = 0, \quad i = 1, \cdots, l, \quad (4.3.9)$$

$$\xi_i^* (C - \alpha_i^*) = 0, \quad i = 1, \cdots, l, \quad (4.3.10)$$

$$\xi_i^* \geqslant 0, \quad i = 1, \cdots, l, \quad (4.3.11)$$

$$\sum_{i=1}^{l} \alpha_i^* y_i = 0, \quad 0 \leqslant \alpha_i^* \leqslant C, \quad i = 1, \cdots, l. \quad (4.3.12)$$

Now we prove the conclusions respectively:

(i) For support vector $x_i$ corresponding to $\alpha_i^* \in (0, C)$, we have $\xi_i^* = 0$ from (4.3.10), furthermore from (4.3.9) we have

$$y_i g(x_i) = 1. \quad (4.3.13)$$

(ii) For support vector $x_i$ corresponding to $\alpha_i^* = C$, we have $y_i g(x_i) = 1 - \xi_i^*$ from (4.3.9) because $\alpha_i^* = C > 0$. And because $\xi_i^* \geqslant 0$, hence

$$y_i g(x_i) \leqslant 1. \quad (4.3.14)$$

(iii) For nonsupport vector $x_i$, we have $\xi_i^* = 0$ from (4.3.10) because $\alpha_i^* = 0$. Furthermore from (4.3.8), we have

$$y_i g(x_i) \geqslant 1. \qquad (4.3.15)$$

∎

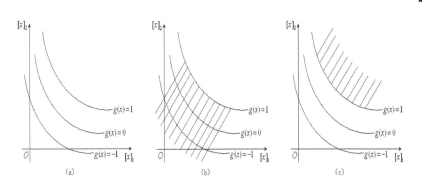

**FIGURE 4.3**: Geometric interpretation of Theorem 4.3.4.

The geometric interpretation of the above theorem with $x \in R^2$ is shown in Figure 4.3 where only the positive training points are considered and the curve $g(x) = 0$ is the separating line, (a) shows that the positive support vector corresponding to $\alpha_i^* \in (0, C)$ must lie on the curve $g(x) = 1$, i.e. it is sufficiently classified correctly. (b) shows that the positive support vector corresponding to $\alpha_i^* = C$ must lie in the shadow including $g(x) = 1$, i.e. it is classified wrongly, or barely classified correctly. (c) shows that a non-support vector belonging to the positive class must lie in the shadow including the boundary $g(x) = 1$, i.e. it must be classified not only correctly but also sufficiently classified correctly.

#### 4.3.1.3 Properties

Algorithm 4.3.1 ($C$-support vector classification) reflects three characters which support vector machines usually have.

(1) **Conversion of the problem scale.** Our goal is to find the decision function $f(x)$ from the training set (4.1.3), where $x$ is an $n$-dimension vector. The direct way is to solve the primal problem (4.1.6)~(4.1.8) with the scale depending on $n$. When $n$ increases, computation cost will increase rapidly, which is just the "curse of dimensionality" encountered to common methods. However, the problem solved in support vector machines is the dual problem. Note that the number of the variables of this dual problem is $l$ (number of the training points); in other words, the scale of the dual problem needed to be solved has barely anything to do with the dimension of the input space. That provides a way of conquering the curse of dimensionality.

(2) **Employment of the kernel.** Applying the kernel $K(\cdot, \cdot)$ instead of the map $\Phi(\cdot)$ realizes the transition elegantly from linear classification to nonlinear

classification, i.e. we only need to choose a kernel $K$ rather than a map $\Phi$. This can be not only more convenient but also simplify the computation, because computing inner products in high-dimensional spaces costs much, while computing kernels is very cheap.

(3) **Sparsity**. We can see from the decision function (4.3.6) that not all the training points, but the training points corresponding to the nonzero components $\alpha_i^*$ of the solution $\alpha^*$ to the dual problem (4.3.1)~(4.3.3) make sense. In other words, only the training points corresponding to the support vectors contribute to the decision function, while the remaining training points corresponding to the non-support vectors contribute nothing. Generally speaking, when the training set is very large, the proportion of support vectors is small, and most coefficients $\alpha_i^*$ is zero. This fact reflects the sparsity of support vector classification, which is important to the computation of large scale problems.

### 4.3.1.4   Soft margin loss function

In establishing Algorithm 4.3.1 ($C$-support vector classification), we hope that the decision function generates smaller deviations for each training point $(x_i, y_i)$ in the training set $T = \{(x_1, y_1), \cdots, (x_l, y_l)\}$. Now consider how it measures this deviation. Generally speaking, in order to measure the deviation, a triplet function $c(x, y, f(x))$ is often introduced, where $x$ is an input, $y$ is an observation corresponding to $x$, and $f(x)$ is the value of the decision function $f$ at $x$, thus the value $c(x, y, f(x))$ denotes the deviation of the decision function $f$ at the input $x$. This triplet function is called a loss function. Now analyze what the loss function used in $C$-support vector machine is. Reviewing the primal problem (4.1.6)~(4.1.8), it is obvious that minimizing $\sum_{i=1}^{l} \xi_i$ of the objective function aims at keeping the decision rule consistent with all training points as much as possible, where $\xi_i$ is used to measure the deviation of the decision function at the training point $(x_i, y_i)$

$$\xi_i = \begin{cases} 0, & y_i((w \cdot \Phi(x_i)) + b) \geqslant 1; \\ 1 - y_i((w \cdot \Phi(x_i)) + b), & y_i((w \cdot \Phi(x_i)) + b) < 1, \end{cases} \qquad (4.3.16)$$

while the corresponding decision function is

$$f(x) = \text{sgn}(g(x)), \quad \text{where } g(x) = (w \cdot \Phi(x)) + b. \qquad (4.3.17)$$

Hence from (4.3.16), for the decision function $f(x)$ with the form (4.3.17), the deviation is measured by the function

$$c(x, y, f(x)) = \max\{0, 1 - yg(x)\}. \qquad (4.3.18)$$

Figure 4.4 shows the function (4.3.18) evaluating deviation, which is often named the soft margin loss function or the hinge loss function. Though strictly speaking it does not satisfy the condition $c(x, y, y) = 0$ which the usual loss function should have (refer to Chapter 5, Definition 5.1.5).

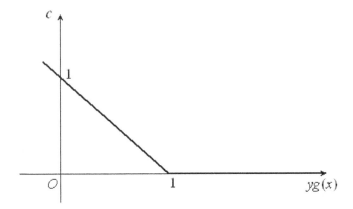

**FIGURE 4.4**: Soft margin loss function.

It should be pointed out that the sparsity of Algorithm 4.3.1 ($C$-support vector machine) is closely related to the soft margin loss function used. From the intuitive explanation of the non-support vectors in Figure 4.2(c), we may find that the positive training points in the shadow (excluding the boundary) give no contribution to the decision function due to employing the soft margin loss function.

### 4.3.1.5    Probabilistic outputs

Suppose the training set is $T = \{(x_1, y_1), \cdots, (x_l, y_l)\}$, where $x_i \in R^n$, $y_i \in \{1, -1\}$. Consider the decision function (4.3.5) obtained from Algorithm 4.3.1 ($C$-support vector machine)

$$f(x) = \text{sgn}(g(x)), \qquad (4.3.19)$$

where $g(x)$ is given by (4.3.6), an input $x$ is classified to the positive class if $g(x) \geq 0$. However we cannot guarantee that the deduction is absolutely correct. So sometimes we hope to know how much confidence we have, i.e. the probability of the input $x$ belonging to the positive class. To answer this question, investigate the information contained in $g(x)$. It is not difficult to imagine that the larger $g(x)$ is, the larger the probability is. So the value of $g(x)$ can be used to estimate the probability $P(y = 1|g(x))$ of the input $x$ belonging to the positive class. In fact, we only need to establish an appropriate monotonic function from $(-\infty, +\infty)$ where $g(x)$ takes value to the probability values interval $[0, 1]$, such as the S-type function

$$p(g) = \frac{1}{1 + \exp(c_1 g + c_2)}, \qquad (4.3.20)$$

where $c_1 < 0$ and $c_2$ are two parameters to be found. This function $p(g)$ maps $g \in (-\infty, +\infty)$ monotonously to the interval $p \in [0, 1]$, see Figure 4.5. Now how to choose the optimal values $c_1^*$ and $c_2^*$ is under our consideration.

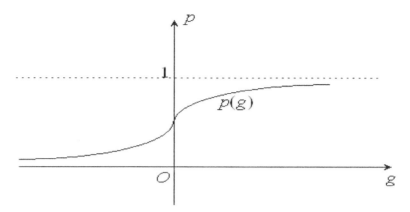

**FIGURE 4.5**: S-type function.

To this end we construct an optimization problem of $c_1^*$ and $c_2^*$ following the idea of maximum likelihood estimation. In fact, for each input $x_i$ of the training set, $g_i = g(x_i)$ can be computed by the $g(x)$, then the probability $p_i = p_i(c_1, c_2)$ of it belonging to the positive class is computed from (4.3.20)

$$p_i = p_i(c_1, c_2) = \frac{1}{1 + \exp(c_1 g_i + c_2)}, \quad i = 1, \cdots, l. \tag{4.3.21}$$

Obviously we hope that the corresponding $p_i$ is as large as possible for all positive inputs $x_i$, while the corresponding $p_i$ is as small as possible for all negative inputs $x_i$, i.e. $1 - p_i$ is as large as possible. Therefore we get the unconstrained optimization problem with variables $c_1$ and $c_2$

$$\max \prod_{y_i=1} p_i \prod_{y_i=-1} (1 - p_i). \tag{4.3.22}$$

The equivalent problem can be constructed by taking the negative log of the objective function in the above problem

$$\min -\left\{ \sum_{y_i=1} \log p_i + \sum_{y_i=-1} \log(1 - p_i) \right\}. \tag{4.3.23}$$

Introduce the variable

$$t_i = \frac{y_i + 1}{2} = \begin{cases} 1, & y_i = 1; \\ 0, & y_i = -1, \end{cases} \tag{4.3.24}$$

we have

$$\sum_{y_i=1} \log p_i = \sum_{i=1}^{l} t_i \log p_i, \tag{4.3.25}$$

$$\sum_{y_i=-1} \log(1 - p_i) = \sum_{i=1}^{l} (1 - t_i) \log(1 - p_i). \tag{4.3.26}$$

Hence the problem (4.3.23) can be written as

$$\min - \sum_{i=1}^{l} [t_i \log p_i + (1 - t_i) \log(1 - p_i)], \tag{4.3.27}$$

where $p_i = p_i(c_1, c_2)$ is given by (4.3.21).

However the numerical experiments results are not ideal if we directly solve the above problem because it tends to make the resulted S-type function $p(g)$ overly steep. So the optimization problem (4.3.22) is modified as

$$\max \prod_{y_i=1} (p_i)^{1-\varepsilon_+} (1 - p_i)^{\varepsilon_+} \prod_{y_i=-1} (1 - p_i)^{1-\varepsilon_-} (p_i)^{\varepsilon_-}, \tag{4.3.28}$$

where $\varepsilon_+$ and $\varepsilon_-$ are small positive numbers. One interpretation of this modification is that in (4.3.22) the output of the positive input $x_i$ is believed as 1, i.e. the probabilities of taking $-1$ and 1 is 1 and 0 respectively while in (4.3.28) the probabilities are changed to $1 - \varepsilon_+$ and $\varepsilon_+$ respectively, and corresponding change with $\varepsilon_-$ is similar. The values of $\varepsilon_+$ and $\varepsilon_-$ are recommended to be

$$\varepsilon_+ = \frac{1}{N_+ + 2}, \quad \varepsilon_- = \frac{1}{N_- + 2}, \tag{4.3.29}$$

where $N_+$ and $N_-$ are the numbers of the positive and negative points respectively. Therefore the final optimization problem is obtained as

$$\min - \sum_{i=1}^{l} \{t_i \log p_i(c_1, c_2) + (1 - t_i) \log(1 - p_i(c_1, c_2))\}, \tag{4.3.30}$$

where

$$t_i = \begin{cases} \frac{N_+ + 1}{N_+ + 2}, & y_i = 1; \\ \frac{1}{N_- + 2}, & y_i = -1, \end{cases} \tag{4.3.31}$$

here $N_+$ and $N_-$ are the numbers of the positive and negative points respectively.

Thus the classification algorithm with probabilistic output can be described as follows:

**Algorithm 4.3.5** *(Support vector classification with probabilistic output)*

*(1) Input the training set $T = \{(x_1, y_1), \cdots, (x_l, y_l)\}$, where $x_i \in R^n, y_i \in \mathcal{Y} = \{1, -1\}, i = 1, \cdots, l$;*

*(2) Perform Algorithm 4.3.1, obtaining the $g(x)$ given by (4.3.6);*

*(3) Solve the unconstrained optimization problem (4.3.30) with variables $c_1, c_2$, where for $i = 1, \cdots, l$, $p_i(c_1, c_2)$ is given by (4.3.21), in which $g_i = g(x_i)$, $t_i$ is given by (4.3.31), obtaining a solution $(c_1^*, c_2^*)$;*

*(4) Construct the decision function with probabilistic output*

$$\tilde{p}(x) = \frac{1}{1 + \exp(c_1^* g(x) + c_2^*)},\tag{4.3.32}$$

*this value is just the probability of the output being 1 corresponding to the input $x$.*

## 4.3.2 Support vector regression

### 4.3.2.1 Algorithm

Using kernel Algorithm 4.1.8 (Regression machine based on nonlinear separation) can be rewritten as the following commonly used $\varepsilon$-support vector regression. It can be regarded as the extension of Algorithm 3.4.7 (Linear $\varepsilon$-support vector regression) from linear regression to nonlinear regression.

**Algorithm 4.3.6** *($\varepsilon$-support vector regression, $\varepsilon$-SVR)*

*(1) Input the training set $T = \{(x_1, y_1), \cdots, (x_l, y_l)\}$, where $x_i \in R^n, y_i \in \mathcal{Y} = R, i = 1, \cdots, l$;*

*(2) Choose an appropriate kernel $K(x, x')$, an appropriate accuracy $\varepsilon > 0$ and the penalty parameter $C > 0$;*

*(3) Construct and solve the convex quadratic programming problem*

$$\min_{\alpha^{(*)} \in R^{2l}} \quad \frac{1}{2} \sum_{i,j=1}^{l} (\alpha_i^* - \alpha_i)(\alpha_j^* - \alpha_j) K(x_i, x_j)$$

$$+ \varepsilon \sum_{i=1}^{l} (\alpha_i^* + \alpha_i) - \sum_{i=1}^{l} y_i (\alpha_i^* - \alpha_i),\tag{4.3.33}$$

$$s.t. \quad \sum_{i=1}^{l} (\alpha_i - \alpha_i^*) = 0,\tag{4.3.34}$$

$$0 \leqslant \alpha_i^{(*)} \leqslant C, \quad i = 1, \cdots, l,\tag{4.3.35}$$

*obtaining a solution $\bar{\alpha}^{(*)} = (\bar{\alpha}_1, \bar{\alpha}_1^*, \cdots, \bar{\alpha}_l, \bar{\alpha}_l^*)^T$;*

*(4) Compute $\bar{b}$: Choose a component of $\bar{\alpha}^{(*)}$, $\bar{\alpha}_j \in (0, C)$, or $\bar{\alpha}_k^* \in (0, C)$. If $\bar{\alpha}_j$ is chosen, compute*

$$\bar{b} = y_j - \sum_{i=1}^{l} (\bar{\alpha}_i^* - \bar{\alpha}_i) K(x_i, x_j) + \varepsilon;\tag{4.3.36}$$

*if $\bar{\alpha}_k^*$ is chosen, compute*

$$\bar{b} = y_k - \sum_{i=1}^{l} (\bar{\alpha}_i^* - \bar{\alpha}_i) K(x_i, x_k) - \varepsilon;\tag{4.3.37}$$

*(5) Construct the decision function*

$$y = g(x) = \sum_{i=1}^{l} (\bar{\alpha}_i^* - \bar{\alpha}_i)K(x_i, x) + \bar{b}. \tag{4.3.38}$$

### 4.3.2.2 Support vector

Now we introduce the concept of support vector for the above algorithm 4.3.6 ($\varepsilon$-support vector regression) and discuss its properties.

**Definition 4.3.7** *(Support vector) Suppose* $\bar{\alpha}^{(*)} = (\bar{\alpha}_1, \bar{\alpha}_1^*, \cdots, \bar{\alpha}_l, \bar{\alpha}_l^*)^{\mathrm{T}}$ *is a solution to the problem* (4.1.81)~(4.3.35) *obtained using Algorithm 4.3.6. The training point* $(x_i, y_i)$ *is said to be a support vector if the corresponding component* $\bar{\alpha}_i$ *or* $\bar{\alpha}_i^*$ *of* $\bar{\alpha}^{(*)}$ *is nonzero, and otherwise it is a nonsupport vector.*

**Theorem 4.3.8** *Suppose* $\bar{\alpha}^{(*)} = (\bar{\alpha}_1, \bar{\alpha}_1^*, \cdots, \bar{\alpha}_l, \bar{\alpha}_l^*)^{\mathrm{T}}$ *is a solution to the convex quadratic programming problem* (4.1.81)~(4.3.35), *then for* $i = 1, \cdots, l$, *each pair of* $\bar{\alpha}_i$ *and* $\bar{\alpha}_i^*$ *cannot be both simultaneously nonzero.*

**Theorem 4.3.9** *Suppose* $\bar{\alpha}^{(*)} = (\bar{\alpha}_1, \bar{\alpha}_1^*, \cdots, \bar{\alpha}_l, \bar{\alpha}_l^*)^{\mathrm{T}}$ *is a solution to the problem* (4.1.81) ~(4.3.35) *obtained using Algorithm 4.3.6. If* $g(x)$ *is defined by* (4.3.38), *then*

*(i) support vector* $(x_i, y_i)$ *corresponding to* $\bar{\alpha}_i \in (0, C), \bar{\alpha}_i^* = 0$ *or* $\bar{\alpha}_i^* \in (0, C), \bar{\alpha}_i = 0$ *satisfies* $y_i = g(x_i) - \varepsilon$ *or* $y_i = g(x_i) + \varepsilon$;

*(ii) support vector* $(x_i, y_i)$ *corresponding to* $\bar{\alpha}_i = C, \bar{\alpha}_i^* = 0$ *or* $\bar{\alpha}_i^* = C, \bar{\alpha}_i = 0$ *satisfies* $y_i \leqslant g(x_i) - \varepsilon$ *or* $y_i \geqslant g(x_i) + \varepsilon$;

*(iii) nonsupport vector* $(x_i, y_i)$ *satisfies* $g(x_i) - \varepsilon \leqslant y_i \leqslant g(x_i) + \varepsilon$.

**Proof** If $\bar{\alpha}^{(*)} = (\bar{\alpha}_1, \bar{\alpha}_1^*, \cdots, \bar{\alpha}_l, \bar{\alpha}_l^*)^{\mathrm{T}}$ is a solution to the problem (4.1.81)~(4.3.35), then $\bar{\alpha}^{(*)}$ satisfies the KKT conditions, i.e. there exist multipliers $\bar{b}, \bar{s}_i^{(*)}, \bar{\xi}_i^{(*)}, i = 1, \cdots, l$ such that

$$\sum_{j=1}^{l} (\bar{\alpha}_j^* - \bar{\alpha}_j)K(x_i, x_j) + \bar{b} - y_i - \varepsilon - \bar{\xi}_i = -\bar{s}_i \leqslant 0, i = 1, \cdots, l, \tag{4.3.39}$$

$$\bar{\alpha}_i \bar{s}_i = 0, i = 1, \cdots, l, \tag{4.3.40}$$

$$y_i - \sum_{j=1}^{l} (\bar{\alpha}_j^* - \bar{\alpha}_j)K(x_i, x_j) - \bar{b} - \varepsilon - \bar{\xi}_i^* = -\bar{s}_i^* \leqslant 0, i = 1, \cdots, l, \tag{4.3.41}$$

$$\bar{\alpha}_i^* \bar{s}_i^* = 0, i = 1, \cdots, l, \tag{4.3.42}$$

$$\bar{\xi}_i(C - \bar{\alpha}_i) = 0, i = 1, \cdots, l, \tag{4.3.43}$$

$$\bar{\xi}_i^*(C - \bar{\alpha}_i^*) = 0, i = 1, \cdots, l, \tag{4.3.44}$$

$$\sum_{i=1}^{l} (\bar{\alpha}_i - \bar{\alpha}_i^*) = 0, \quad 0 \leqslant \bar{\alpha}_i, \bar{\alpha}_i^* \leqslant C, \quad i = 1, \cdots, l. \tag{4.3.45}$$

Now we prove the conclusions separately:

(i) For support vector $(x_i, y_i)$ corresponding to $\bar{\alpha}_i \in (0, C), \bar{\alpha}_i^* = 0$, we have $\bar{\xi}_i = 0$ from (4.3.43), furthermore from (4.3.39)~(4.3.40) we have

$$y_i = g(x_i) - \varepsilon - \bar{\xi}_i = g(x_i) - \varepsilon. \qquad (4.3.46)$$

For support vector $(x_i, y_i)$ corresponding to $\bar{\alpha}_i^* \in (0, C), \bar{\alpha}_i = 0$, we can draw the conclusion from (4.3.39), (4.3.42), and (4.3.44).

(ii) For support vector $(x_i, y_i)$ corresponding to $\bar{\alpha}_i = C, \bar{\alpha}_i^* = 0$, from (4.3.39)~(4.3.40) we have $g(x_i) - y_i = \varepsilon + \bar{\xi}_i$. And because $\xi_i \geqslant 0$, so

$$y_i \leqslant g(x_i) - \varepsilon. \qquad (4.3.47)$$

For support vector $(x_i, y_i)$ corresponding to $\bar{\alpha}_i^* = C, \bar{\alpha}_i = 0$, the conclusion can be obtained by (4.3.41)~(4.3.42).

(iii) For non-support vector $(x_i, y_i)$, because $\bar{\alpha}_i = \bar{\alpha}_i^* = 0$; hence from (4.3.43)~(4.3.44) we have $\bar{\xi}_i^{(*)} = 0$. Furthermore, (4.3.39) and (4.3.41) lead to

$$g(x_i) - \varepsilon \leqslant y_i \leqslant g(x_i) + \varepsilon. \qquad (4.3.48)$$

∎

The geometric interpretation of the above theorem with $x \in R^2$ is shown in Figure 4.6, where the curve $y = g(x)$ is the decision function. (a) shows that support vector corresponding to $\bar{\alpha}_i \in (0, C), \bar{\alpha}_i^* = 0$ or $\bar{\alpha}_i^* \in (0, C), \bar{\alpha}_i = 0$ must lie on the curve $y = g(x) - \varepsilon$ or $y = g(x) + \varepsilon$, i.e. its deviation to the decision function is not large. (b) shows that support vector corresponding to $\bar{\alpha}_i = C, \bar{\alpha}_i^* = 0$ or $\bar{\alpha}_i^* = C, \bar{\alpha}_i = 0$ must lie in the shadow region including the boundaries $y = g(x) + \varepsilon$ and $y = g(x) - \varepsilon$, i.e. its deviation to the decision function may be larger. (c) shows that non-support vector must lie in the shadow region including the boundaries $y = g(x) + \varepsilon$ and $y = g(x) - \varepsilon$, i.e. its deviation to the decision function is very small.

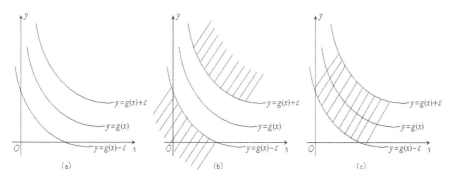

**FIGURE 4.6**: Geometric interpretation of Theorem 4.3.9.

### 4.3.2.3    Properties

Algorithm 4.3.6 ($\varepsilon$-support vector regression) also possesses the 3 properties in Algorithm 4.3.1 ($C$-support vector classification) described in Section
4.3.1: Conversion of the problem scale, employment of the kernel and sparsity.
We will not repeat them here.

### 4.3.2.4    $\varepsilon$-Insensitive loss function

Consider the primal problem (4.1.45) $\sim$(4.1.48). Suppose its solution is
$(\bar{w}, \bar{b}, \bar{\xi}^{(*)})$, and the corresponding function is $g(x) = (\bar{w} \cdot \Phi(x)) + \bar{b}$, then the
sum of two components $\bar{\xi}_i + \bar{\xi}_i^*$ reflects the "deviation" or "loss" of the decision
function on the training point $(\Phi(x_i), y_i)$. It is easy to see that

$$\xi_i + \xi_i^* = \begin{cases} 0, & |y_i - ((\bar{w} \cdot \Phi(x_i)) + \bar{b})| < \varepsilon; \\ |y_i - ((\bar{w} \cdot \Phi(x_i)) + \bar{b})| - \varepsilon, & \text{otherwise.} \end{cases}$$

$$(4.3.49)$$

$\sum\limits_{i=1}^{l}(\xi_i + \xi_i^*)$ contained in the objective function (4.1.45) of the primal problem
implies minimizing the sum of the loss at all the training points. This shows
the loss function used here is

$$c(x, y, g(x)) = \begin{cases} 0, & |y - g(x)| < \varepsilon; \\ |y - g(x)| - \varepsilon, & \text{otherwise,} \end{cases} \qquad (4.3.50)$$

where $\varepsilon$ is a predetermined positive number. The loss function with the form
(4.3.50) is called the $\varepsilon$-insensitive loss function. The $\varepsilon$-insensitive loss function
is shown in Figure 4.7 and often written as

$$c(x, y, g(x)) = |y - g(x)|_\varepsilon , \qquad (4.3.51)$$

where

$$|y - g(x)|_\varepsilon = \max\{0, |y - g(x)| - \varepsilon\} . \qquad (4.3.52)$$

The idea behind the $\varepsilon$-insensitive loss function is: when the deviation between
the observation $y$ of $x$ and the prediction $g(x)$ does not exceed the given $\varepsilon$,
there is no loss of the prediction $g(x)$ at this point, though the prediction $g(x)$
and the observation $y$ may not be exactly equal.

It is easy to see that the $\varepsilon$-insensitive loss function has the following characteristic: it does not always bring the loss when the value $g(x)$ of the decision
function is different with $y$ corresponding to $x$; instead it has a certain tolerance, i.e. the loss is regarded as zero when the difference between the two
above values is in a certain range. This characteristic is not available in many
other loss functions, e.g. the loss function

$$c(x, y, g(x)) = (y - g(x))^2, \qquad (4.3.53)$$

traditionally used in the least square method in the curve fitting problem,

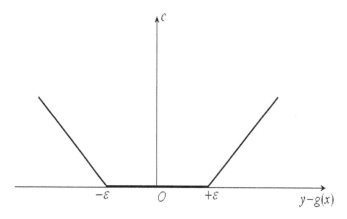

**FIGURE 4.7**: $\varepsilon$-insensitive loss function with $\varepsilon > 0$.

which does not have such characteristic. Precisely because of adopting the $\varepsilon$-insensitive loss function in Algorithm 4.3.6 both $\bar{\alpha}_i$ and $\bar{\alpha}_i^*$ corresponding to the training points $(\Phi(x_i), y_i)$ in the $\varepsilon$-band of the hyperplane $y = (\bar{w} \cdot \Phi(x)) + \bar{b}$ is made to be zero, resulting in the valuable sparsity.

### 4.3.3 Flatness of support vector machines

For the support vector machines derived from the maximal margin princi-ple, we give another intuitive interpretation in this section. For example, for a regression problem with the training set (3.1.1)

$$T = \{(x_1, y_1), \cdots, (x_l, y_l)\} \in (R^n \times \mathcal{Y})^l, \tag{4.3.54}$$

where $x_i \in R^n, y_i \in \mathcal{Y} = R, i = 1, \cdots, l$, the primal problem in $\varepsilon$-SVR is

$$\min_{w,b,\xi^{(*)}} \quad \frac{1}{2}\|w\|^2 + C\sum_{i=1}^{l}(\xi_i + \xi_i^*), \tag{4.3.55}$$

$$\text{s.t.} \quad ((w \cdot \Phi(x_i)) + b) - y_i \leqslant \varepsilon + \xi_i, \ i = 1, \cdots, l, \tag{4.3.56}$$

$$y_i - ((w \cdot \Phi(x_i)) + b) \leqslant \varepsilon + \xi_i^*, \ i = 1, \cdots, l, \tag{4.3.57}$$

$$\xi_i^{(*)} \geqslant 0, \ i = 1, \cdots, l, \tag{4.3.58}$$

where two objectives are concerned:
(i) Minimize $\|w\|$;
(ii) Minimize the "deviation" or "loss" of the decision function $(w \cdot \Phi(x)) + b$ at all the training points $(\Phi(x_i), y_i), \ i = 1, \cdots, l$.

Intuitively speaking, the objective (ii) is natural. How to understand the objective (i)?

#### 4.3.3.1 Runge phenomenon

The above question leads to an old problem: can we take minimizing the deviation as the unique objective in regression?

Consider a simple one-dimensional regression problem. Suppose that there is a function $h(x)$ defined in the interval $[-1, 1]$. Let us find a regression function $g(x)$, taking the smallest deviation as the unique objective and using the training set $\{(x_1, y_1), \cdots, (x_1, y_1)\}$, where $y_i = h(x_i), i = 1, \cdots, l$, and examine if the regression function $g(x)$ is able to approximate the original function $h(x)$. The following example will give some enlightenment.

**Example 4.3.10** *(Runge phenomenon)   Consider the one-dimensional regression problem in the interval $[-1, 1]$ with the training set $\{(x_1, y_1), \cdots, (x_l, y_l)\}$, where the inputs are equally-spaced points*

$$x_i = -1 + (i-1)\frac{2}{l-1}, \quad i = 1, 2, \cdots, l, \tag{4.3.59}$$

*and $y_i = h(x_i), i = 1, \cdots, l$, defined by the Runge function*

$$h(x) = \frac{1}{1 + 25x^2}. \tag{4.3.60}$$

*In order to achieve the zero deviation, a natural way is to select the $(l-1)$th order polynomial $g(x) = P_{(l-1)}(x)$ as our regression function, where $g(x_i) = h(x_i) = P_{(l-1)}(x_i), i = 1, \cdots, l$. It may be expected that larger $l$ yields better regression function. However, it is not the case, as shown in Figure 4.8, where the Runge function and the polynomials with $l = 5$ and $9$ are depicted. The red curve is the Runge function. The blue curve is a 4th order polynomial. The green curve is a 8th order polynomial. Note that at all of the input points, the deviation between the Runge function and the regression polynomial is zero. Between the input points (especially in the region close to the endpoints $1$ and $-1$), the deviation between the Runge function and the regression polynomial gets worse for higher-order polynomials particularly at the edges of the interval $[-1, 1]$. The problem of oscillation at the edges of the interval that occurs when the regression functions are polynomials of high degree is called Runge's phenomenon. This is important because it shows that going to higher degrees does not always improve accuracy. Even worse, it can even be proved that the deviation tends toward infinity when $l$ increases.*

$$\lim_{l \to \infty} ( \max_{-1 \leqslant x \leqslant 1} |h(x) - P_{l-1}(x)|) = \infty \tag{4.3.61}$$

One approach to mitigate this problem is to relax the deviation requirement and suppress the oscillation. More precisely, keep minimizing deviation as one of the objectives and introduce the second objective: maximizing flatness of the decision function.

Next we show in detail that this is just what support vector machines do.

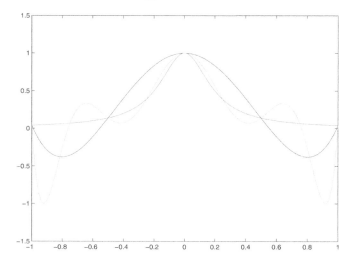

**FIGURE 4.8**: Runge phenomenon.

#### 4.3.3.2 Flatness of $\varepsilon$-support vector regression

Now we show that $\varepsilon$-SVR can be considered to solve a problem with the above two objectives. First it should be pointed out that the deviation of a decision function w.r.t. the training set (3.1.1) is measured by the $\varepsilon$-insensitive loss function. On the other hand, for a linear decision function $g(x) = (w{\cdot}x)+b$, its flatness is measured by the norm $\|w\|$ of its gradient $w$, which is its greatest rate of change; the smaller this term, the flatter the decision function.

**(1) Linear hard $\varepsilon$-band support vector regression**

For the training set (3.1.1), the linear decision function $g(x) = (w \cdot x) + b$ is obtained from a solution of the primal problem

$$\min_{w,b} \quad \frac{1}{2}\|w\|^2 , \tag{4.3.62}$$

$$\text{s.t.} \quad (w \cdot x_i) + b - y_i \leqslant \varepsilon , \; i = 1, \cdots , l , \tag{4.3.63}$$

$$y_i - (w \cdot x_i) - b \leqslant \varepsilon , \; i = 1, \cdots , l . \tag{4.3.64}$$

It is easy to see that, on one hand, for the decision function $g(x) = (w{\cdot}x)+b$, the constraints $(4.3.63){\sim}(4.3.64)$ are equivalent to the zero deviation of the decision function w.r.t. the training set (3.1.1) measured by the $\varepsilon$-insensitive loss function. On the other hand, the flatness is measured by the quantity $\|w\|$. Therefore the primal problem implies finding the flattest linear function among the linear functions with zero deviation.

The geometric meaning of the flatness is very clear when we consider a linear regression problem in the one-dimensional space $R$. In fact, suppose that the training points are represented by "$\times$" in Figure 4.9. Constraints

$(4.3.63)\sim(4.3.64)$ require that all of the training points should be inside the
$\varepsilon$-band of the regression line, and the objective function means that this line
is the one with the smallest slope satisfying the above constraints. So, we can
find a regression line by the following way: (i) select a band that is closest to
the horizontal band from the bands with the length $2\varepsilon$ that contain all of the
training points; (ii) select the central line in the band as the regression line,
shown by Figure 4.9(a). Obviously, when $\varepsilon$ is very large, the regression line
we choose is horizontal, shown by Figure 4.9(b).

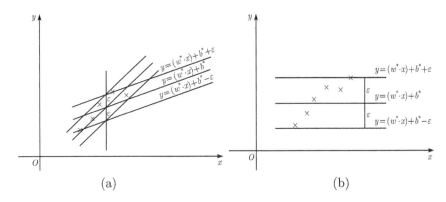

**FIGURE 4.9**: Geometric interpretation of the flatness in $R$: (a) sloping regression line; (b) horizontal regression line.

It is interesting to see that for the case when all of the training points lie
in a line as shown in Figure 4.10, the regression line obtained is not this line,
but the central line among three parallel lines in the figure.

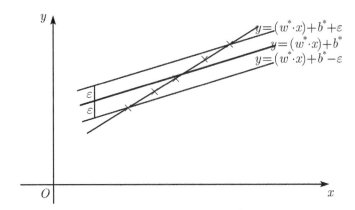

**FIGURE 4.10**: Flat regression line for the case where all of the training
points lie in a line.

**(2) Linear $\varepsilon$-support vector regression**

Now for the training set (3.1.1), the linear decision function $g(x) = (w \cdot x) + b$ is obtained from a solution of the primal problem

$$\min_{w,b,\xi^{(*)}} \quad \frac{1}{2}\|w\|^2 + C\sum_{i=1}^{l}(\xi_i + \xi_i^*), \tag{4.3.65}$$

$$\text{s.t.} \quad ((w \cdot x_i) + b) - y_i \leqslant \varepsilon + \xi_i , \; i = 1, \cdots, l, \tag{4.3.66}$$

$$y_i - ((w \cdot x_i) + b) \leqslant \varepsilon + \xi_i^* , \; i = 1, \cdots, l, \tag{4.3.67}$$

$$\xi_i^{(*)} \geqslant 0 , \; i = 1, \cdots, l, \tag{4.3.68}$$

The two terms in the objective function (4.3.65) indicate that we not only maximize the flatness, but also minimize the deviation. The parameter $C$ determines the weighting between the two of them, smaller $C$ will lead to more flatter decision function. In other words, the final decision function should be the flattest one among the linear functions whose deviations do not exceed a certain level.

**(3) $\varepsilon$-support vector regression**

For the training set (3.1.1), introducing a transformation $x = \Phi(x)$ and the kernel $K(x, x') = (\Phi(x) \cdot \Phi(x'))$, the linear decision function $(w \cdot x) + b$ in x-space is obtained from a solution of the primal problem

$$\min_{w,b,\xi^{(*)}} \quad \frac{1}{2}\|w\|^2 + C\sum_{i=1}^{l}(\xi_i + \xi_i^*), \tag{4.3.69}$$

$$\text{s.t.} \quad ((w \cdot \Phi(x_i)) + b) - y_i \leqslant \varepsilon + \xi_i , \; i = 1, \cdots, l, \tag{4.3.70}$$

$$y_i - ((w \cdot \Phi(x_i)) + b) \leqslant \varepsilon + \xi_i^* , \; i = 1, \cdots, l, \tag{4.3.71}$$

$$\xi_i^{(*)} \geqslant 0 , \; i = 1, \cdots, l, \tag{4.3.72}$$

This is similar to the above linear $\varepsilon$-SVR and has two objectives: maximize the flatness and minimize the deviation. The final decision function $g(x)$ in the input $x$-space is the counterpart of the above linear decision function in x-space. It can be expected that the smaller $C$ yields flatter decision function.

**Example 4.3.11** *Consider the one-dimensional regression problem in the interval $[-10, 10]$ with the training set $\{(x_1, y_1), \cdots, (x_{100}, y_{100})\}$ $r = 1, \cdots 100$, where the inputs are drawn uniformly from $[-10, 10]$, and*

$$y_i = \frac{\sin x_i}{x_i} + v_i, \; i = 1, \cdots, 100, \tag{4.3.73}$$

*the noise $v_i$ were drawn from a Normal distribution with zero mean and variance $\sigma^2$, here $\sigma = 0.1$. In other words, the training set is produced based on a noisy sinc $= \dfrac{\sin x}{x}$ function. The training points are shown by "+" and the sinc function is displayed by the red curve in Figure 4.11.*

*We apply ε-SVR to solve this regression problem, in which the RBF kernel is used, and the parameter ε is fixed to be 0.0625. If the parameter C varies, we will get decision functions with different flatness; smaller C, more flat the function, see Figure 4.11. We can see that the black curve corresponding to the smallest C = 0.01 is the most flat curve among four curves.*

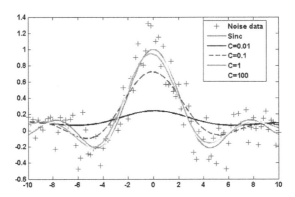

**FIGURE** 4.11: Flat functions in the input space for a regression problem.

#### 4.3.3.3   Flatness of *C*-support vector classification

Let us turn to *C*-SVC and show that it can also be considered to solve a problem with the above two objectives: deviation and flatness, where the deviation of a decision function w.r.t the training set (2.1.5) is measured by the soft margin loss function. Here for a linear decision function $f(x) = \text{sgn}(g(x)) = \text{sgn}((w \cdot x) + b)$, we consider the function $g(x) = (w \cdot x) + b$ and its flatness is also measured by the norm $\|w\|$.

**(1) Linear hard margin support vector classification**

For the training set (2.1.5), the linear function $g(x) = (w \cdot x) + b$ is obtained from a solution of the primal problem

$$\min_{w,b} \quad \frac{1}{2}\|w\|^2 , \tag{4.3.74}$$

$$\text{s.t.} \quad y_i((w \cdot x_i) + b) \geqslant 1 , i = 1, \cdots, l . \tag{4.3.75}$$

On one hand, for the function $f(x) = (w \cdot x) + b$, the constraints (4.3.74)~(4.3.75) are equivalent to the zero deviation of the decision function w.r.t. the training set (2.1.5) measured by the soft margin loss function. On the other hand, the flatness is measured by the quantity $\|w\|$. Therefore the primal problem implies finding the flattest linear function among the linear functions with zero deviation. Remember that the above primal problem is derived by maximizing margin. Now it is interpreted by maximizing flatness. So it is interesting to show that "maximizing margin" and "maximizing flatness" are equivalent. Consider a two-dimensional classification from geometric point of view. A function $g(x) = (w \cdot x) + b$ has zero deviation w.r.t. the training set (2.1.5) if and only if the straight line $(w \cdot x) + b = 0$ is able to separate all inputs correctly and there is no any input between the straight lines $(w \cdot x) + b = -1$ and $(w \cdot x) + b = 1$. Denoting the distance between the straight lines $(w \cdot x) + b = -1$ and $(w \cdot x) + b = 1$ as $d$, moving the distance $d$ from a point in the straight line $(w \cdot x) + b = -1$ to a point in the line $(w \cdot x) + b = 1$ yields the fixed increase 2 from $-1$ to 1. Obviously, maximizing flatness requires finding the straight line $(w \cdot x) + b = 0$ with the largest $d$, which is just what maximizing margin required. So their equivalence is observed.

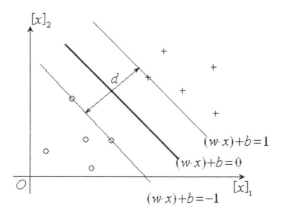

**FIGURE 4.12**: Flat separating straight line in $R^2$.

**(2) Linear support vector classification**

Now for the training set (2.1.5), the linear function $g(x) = (w \cdot x) + b$ is obtained from a solution of the primal problem

$$\min_{w,b,\xi} \quad \frac{1}{2}\|w\|^2 + C\sum_{i=1}^{l} \xi_i ,  \tag{4.3.76}$$

$$\text{s.t.} \quad y_i((w \cdot x_i) + b) \geqslant 1 - \xi_i , i = 1, \cdots, l ,  \tag{4.3.77}$$

$$\xi_i \geqslant 0 , i = 1, \cdots, l .  \tag{4.3.78}$$

The two terms in the objective function (4.3.76) indicate that we not only maximize the flatness, but also minimize the deviation. The parameter $C$ determines the weighting between them. The smaller $C$ yields the larger distance between the line $g(x) = (w \cdot x) + b = 1$ and the line $g(x) = (w \cdot x) + b = -1$, and therefore makes the function $g(x) = (w \cdot x) + b$ more flat.

**(3) $C$-support vector classification**

For the training set (2.1.5), introducing a transformation $x = \Phi(x)$ and the kernel $K(x, x') = (\Phi(x) \cdot \Phi(x'))$, the linear function $(w \cdot x) + b$ in x-space is obtained from a solution of the primal problem

$$\min_{w,b,\xi} \quad \frac{1}{2}\|w\|^2 + C\sum_{i=1}^{l}\xi_i , \tag{4.3.79}$$

$$\text{s.t.} \quad y_i((w \cdot x_i) + b) \geqslant 1 - \xi_i , i = 1, \cdots, l , \tag{4.3.80}$$

$$\xi_i \geqslant 0 , i = 1, \cdots, l , \tag{4.3.81}$$

This is similar to the above linear $C$-SVC and has two objectives: maximize flatness and minimize the deviation. The final decision function $g(x)$ in the input space is the counterpart of the above linear function. It can be imagined that, if a function $(w \cdot x) + b$ is flat in x-space, its counterpart $g(x)$ in the input $x$-space is also flat to some extent. So, roughly speaking, $C$-SVC also has two objectives: maximize flatness in the input space and minimize the deviation. The following example illustrates the flatness in the input space geometrically.

**Example 4.3.12** *The iris data set is an established data set used for demonstrating the performance of classification algorithms which contains three classes (Setosa, Versilcolor, Viginica) and four attributes for an iris [201], and the goal is to classify the class of iris based on these four attributes. In order to visualize the flatness discussed above, here we restrict ourselves to the two classes (Versilcolor, Viginica), and the two features that contain the most information about the class, namely the petal length and the petal width. The distribution of the data is illustrated in Figure 4.13, where "o"s and "+"s represent classes Versilcolor and Viginica respectively.*

*We apply $C$-SVC to solve this classification problem, in which the RBF kernel is used, and the parameter $\sigma$ of RBF kernel is fixed to be 1.0. Suppose that the decision function obtained is $f(x) = \text{sgn}(g(x))$, if the parameter $C$ varies, we will get different $g(x)$; see Figure 4.13(a) with $C = 100$, Figure 4.13(b) with $C = 10$, Figure 4.13(c) with $C = 1$ and Figure 4.13(d) with $C = 0.1$, where the separating curves $g(x) = 0$ are illustrated in various colors, and the dotted curves are the corresponding curves $g(x) = \pm 1$. The situation is somewhat similar to the case Linear support vector classification: the smaller $C$ yields the larger distance between the line $g(x) = 1$ and the line $g(x) = -1$, and therefore makes the function $g(x) = (w \cdot x) + b$ more flat.*

---

## 4.4   Meaning of Kernels

Remembering the classification problem, suppose the training set is

$$T = \{(x_1, y_1), \cdots, (x_l, y_l)\} \tag{4.4.1}$$

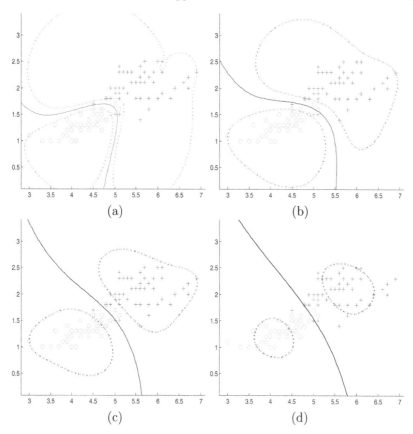

**FIGURE 4.13**: Flat functions in the input space for a classification problem.

where $x_i \in R^n, y_i \in \mathcal{Y} = \{1, -1\}, i = 1, \cdots, l$. Our task is to find out a decision function, and deduce the corresponding output $y$ of any new input $x$, i.e. whether it belongs to the positive class or negative class. The starting point of solving this problem is that similar inputs should have the same outputs. So what we need to do is to measure whether the new input $x$ is more similar to those positive inputs or those negative inputs. If the new input $x$ is more similar to the positive inputs, its output $y$ should be 1; otherwise, its output should be $-1$. This involves the concept of "similarity". The similarity between two inputs is measured by their distance; the smaller the distance, the more similar. It should be pointed out that there are many kinds of distances and the distance used in Algorithm 4.3.1 and Algorithm 4.3.6 is directly decided by the selected kernel

$$K(x, x') = (\Phi(x) \cdot \Phi(x')). \tag{4.4.2}$$

More precisely, the distance between two inputs $x$ and $x'$ is defined by the 2-norm distance between the two vectors x and x' in x-space, where x $= \Phi(x)$

and $\mathbf{x}' = \Phi(x')$. Next we show by a toy problem that selecting different kernels reflect different distances and similarity measures in detail.

**Problem 4.4.1** *Suppose the training set is given as*

$$T = \{(x_1, y_1), (x_2, y_2)\} = \{(x_+, 1), (x_-, -1)\}, \qquad (4.4.3)$$

*where $x_+$ and $x_-$ are positive and negative inputs in $R^2$ respectively, $\mathcal{Y} = \{-1, 1\}$, find the decision function deducing the ownership of any input $x$.*

(i) Firstly, the similarity between two inputs is measured by their Euclidian distance, i.e., the nearer the more similar. Solve Problem 4.4.1 using kernel

$$K(x, x') = (x \cdot x'). \qquad (4.4.4)$$

After selecting this kernel, Algorithm 4.3.1 ($C$-support vector machine) constructs and solves the dual problem

$$\min \quad \frac{1}{2}(\alpha_1\alpha_1(x_+ \cdot x_+) - 2\alpha_1\alpha_2(x_+ \cdot x_-) + \alpha_2\alpha_2(x_- \cdot x_-))$$
$$-\alpha_1 - \alpha_2, \qquad (4.4.5)$$
$$\text{s.t.} \quad 0 \leqslant \alpha_1 = \alpha_2 \leqslant C. \qquad (4.4.6)$$

When the penalty parameter $C$ is greater than $2/\|x_+ - x_-\|^2$, this problem has a unique solution $\alpha_1 = \alpha_2 = \alpha^* = 2/\|x_+ - x_-\|^2$. Noticing $\alpha^* \in (0, C)$, we have

$$\mathbf{w}^* = \alpha^*(x_+ - x_-) = 2(x_+ - x_-)/\|x_+ - x_-\|^2, \qquad (4.4.7)$$
$$b^* = 1 - \alpha^*((x_+ - x_-) \cdot x_+) = (\|x_-\|^2 - \|x_+\|^2)/\|x_+ - x_-\|^2, \qquad (4.4.8)$$

and the corresponding decision function is

$$\begin{aligned} y &= \text{sgn}((\mathbf{w}^* \cdot \mathbf{x}) + b^*) \\ &= \text{sgn}\left((2(x_+ \cdot x) - 2(x_- \cdot x) + \|x_-\|^2 - \|x_+\|^2)/\|x_+ - x_-\|^2\right). \end{aligned}$$
$$(4.4.9)$$

Now the separating line determined by the decision function is the vertical bisector of the segment $x_+x_-$ as shown in Figure 4.14. Note that kernel (4.4.4) corresponds to the transformation $\mathbf{x} = \Phi(x) = x$, which implies that the similarity between two inputs $x'$ and $x''$ is measured by the Euclidian distance between $\mathbf{x}' = \Phi(x')$ and $\mathbf{x}'' = \Phi(x'')$ in x-space; returning to the $x$-space, the similarity is measured by the usual distance $\|x' - x''\|$; the smaller, the more similar. So the obtained decision function is: if $x$ is nearer to $x_+$, i.e. $\|x - x_+\| < \|x - x_-\|$, $x$ is deemed more similar to $x_+$ and is decided to the positive class; otherwise $x$ is deemed more similar to $x_-$ and is decided to the negative class, the separating line consists of the points.

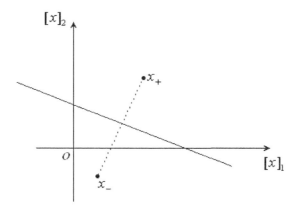

**FIGURE 4.14**: Case (i). The separating line when the similarity measure between two inputs is defined by their Euclidian distance.

(ii) Secondly, the similarity between two inputs is measured by the difference between their length, i.e., the smaller, the more similar. Solve Problem 4.4.1 using kernel

$$K(x, x') = \|x\|\|x'\|. \tag{4.4.10}$$

After selecting this kernel, Algorithm 4.3.1 ($C$-support vector machine) constructs and solves the dual problem

$$\min \quad \frac{1}{2}(\alpha_1\alpha_1 \|x_+\| \|x_+\| - 2\alpha_1\alpha_2 \|x_+\| \|x_-\| + \alpha_2\alpha_2 \|x_-\| \|x_-\|)$$
$$- \alpha_1 - \alpha_2, \tag{4.4.11}$$
$$\text{s.t.} \quad 0 \leqslant \alpha_1 = \alpha_2 \leqslant C. \tag{4.4.12}$$

When the suitable penalty parameter $C$ is greater than $2/(\|x_+\| - \|x_-\|)^2$, this problem has a unique solution $\alpha_1 = \alpha_2 = \alpha^* = 2/(\|x_+\| - \|x_-\|)^2$. Noticing $\alpha^* \in (0, C)$, we have

$$w^* = \alpha^*(\|x_+\| - \|x_-\|) = 2/(\|x_+\| - \|x_-\|), \tag{4.4.13}$$
$$b^* = 1 - \alpha^*\|x_+\|(\|x_+\| - \|x_-\|) = 1 - 2\|x_+\|/(\|x_+\| - \|x_-\|). \tag{4.4.14}$$

and the corresponding decision function is

$$y = \text{sgn}(w^*\|x\| + b^*) = \text{sgn}\left((\|x\| - (\|x_+\| + \|x_-\|)/2)/(\|x_+\| - \|x_-\|)\right). \tag{4.4.15}$$

Now the separating line determined by the decision function is the circle with the center at the origin and the radius $(\|x_+\| + \|x_-\|)/2$ as shown in Figure 4.15. Note that kernel (4.4.10) corresponds to the transformation $x = \Phi(x) = \|x\|$, which implies that the similarity between two inputs $x'$ and

$x''$ is measured by the Euclidian distance between x$'$ = $\|x'\|$ and x$''$ = $\|x''\|$ in x-space; returning to the $x$-space, the similarity is measured by the difference $\|\|x'\| - \|x''\|\|$ between their lengths; the smaller, the more similar. So the obtained decision function is: if $\|\|x\| - \|x_+\|\| < \|\|x\| - \|x_-\|\|$, $x$ is deemed more similar to $x_+$ and is decided to the positive class; otherwise $x$ is deemed more similar to $x_-$ and is decided to the negative class, the separating circle consists of the points.

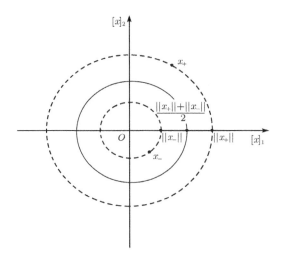

**FIGURE 4.15**: Case (ii). The separating line when the similarity measure between two inputs is defined by the difference between their lengths.

(iii) Lastly, the similarity between the two inputs is measured by the difference between their arguments, i.e., the smaller, the more similar. Solve Problem 4.4.1 using kernel

$$K(x, x') = \frac{(x \cdot x')}{\|x\| \|x'\|}. \tag{4.4.16}$$

After selecting this kernel, Algorithm 4.3.1 (*C*-support vector machine) constructs and solves the dual problem

$$\min_{\alpha_1, \alpha_2} \quad \frac{1}{2}\left(\alpha_1\alpha_1 \frac{(x_+ \cdot x_+)}{\|x_+\| \|x_+\|} - 2\alpha_1\alpha_2 \frac{(x_+ \cdot x_-)}{\|x_+\| \|x_-\|} + \alpha_2\alpha_2 \frac{(x_- \cdot x_-)}{\|x_-\| \|x_-\|}\right)$$
$$-\alpha_1 - \alpha_2, \tag{4.4.17}$$
$$\text{s.t.} \quad 0 \leqslant \alpha_1 = \alpha_2 \leqslant C. \tag{4.4.18}$$

when the suitable penalty parameter $C$ is greater than $2\Big/\left(\left\|\frac{x_+}{\|x_+\|} - \frac{x_-}{\|x_-\|}\right\|^2\right)$,

this problem has a unique solution $\alpha_1 = \alpha_2 = \alpha^* = 2\Big/\left(\left\|\frac{x_+}{\|x_+\|} - \frac{x_-}{\|x_-\|}\right\|^2\right)$.

Noticing $\alpha^* \in (0, C)$, according to Algorithm 4.3.1 ($C$-support vector machine), we have

$$\mathbf{w}^* = \alpha^* \left( \frac{x_+}{\|x_+\|} - \frac{x_-}{\|x_-\|} \right) = 2 \left( \frac{x_+}{\|x_+\|} - \frac{x_-}{\|x_-\|} \right) \bigg/ \left( \| \frac{x_+}{\|x_+\|} - \frac{x_-}{\|x_-\|} \|^2 \right),$$
(4.4.19)

$$b^* = 1 - 2 \left( \left( \frac{x_+}{\|x_+\|} - \frac{x_-}{\|x_-\|} \right) \cdot \frac{x_+}{\|x_+\|} \right) \bigg/ \left( \| \frac{x_+}{\|x_+\|} - \frac{x_-}{\|x_-\|} \|^2 \right).$$
(4.4.20)

The corresponding decision function is

$$y = \mathrm{sgn}\left( \left( \mathbf{w}^* \cdot \frac{x}{\|x\|} \right) + b^* \right) = \mathrm{sgn}\left( \left( x \cdot \left( \frac{x_+}{\|x_+\|} - \frac{x_-}{\|x_-\|} \right) \right) \right).$$
(4.4.21)

The separating line determined by the decision function is now the vertical

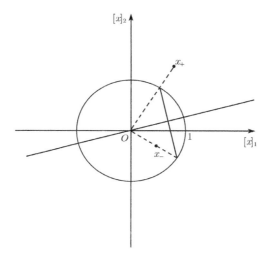

**FIGURE 4.16**: Case (iii). The separating line when the similarity measure between two inputs is defined by the difference between their arguments.

bisector of the segment $\left[ \frac{x_-}{\|x_-\|}, \frac{x_+}{\|x_+\|} \right]$, i.e. the bisector of the angle $x_+ O x_-$ as shown in Figure 4.16. Note that kernel (4.4.16) corresponds to the transformation $\mathbf{x} = \Phi(x) = x/\|x\|$, which implies that the similarity between two inputs $x'$ and $x''$ is measured by the Euclidian distance between $\mathbf{x}' = x'/\|x'\|$ and $\mathbf{x}'' = x''/\|x''\|$ in x-space; returning to the $x$-space, the similarity is measured by the difference $|x'/\|x'\| - x''/\|x''\||$ or the difference between their arguments, angle $x' O x''$, the smaller, the more similar. So the obtained decision function is: if the angle between $x$ and $x_+$ is less than the angle between $x$ and $x_-$, $x$ is deemed more similar to $x_+$ and is decided to the positive class; otherwise $x$ is deemed more similar to $x_-$ and is decided to the negative class, the separating line consists of the points.

# Chapter 5

## Basic Statistical Learning Theory of C-Support Vector Classification

The main purpose of this chapter is to show the theoretical foundation of C-support vector classification (C-SVC) by developing a relationship between C-SVC and the statistical learning theory (SLT). We start by an overview of SLT, followed by a description of the structural risk minimization (SRM) principle. Lastly, we show a conclusion given by our paper [186] that the decision function obtained by C-SVC is just one of the decision functions obtained by solving the optimization problem derived directly from the SRM principle.

---

### 5.1 Classification Problems on Statistical Learning Theory

In this section, we introduce some basic concepts that describe classification problems in the framework of SLT.

#### 5.1.1 Probability distribution

Consider a discrete random variable $(x, y)$, where $x \in R^n$ can take values of $x_1, x_2, \cdots$, or $x_m$, and $y \in \mathcal{Y} = \{-1, 1\}$ can take values of $y_1 = -1$ or $y_2 = 1$. Its probability distribution is described in Table 5.1, where $p_{ij}$ is the probability of $(x, y) = (x_i, y_i)$, $p_{i\cdot}$ and $p_{\cdot j}$ are the marginal distribution of $(x, y)$ on $x$ and $y$ respectively, i.e.,

$$p_{i\cdot} = \sum_{j=1}^{2} p_{ij} = P(x = x_i), i = 1, \cdots, m \tag{5.1.1}$$

and

$$p_{\cdot j} = \sum_{i=1}^{m} p_{ij} = P(y = y_j), j = 1, 2. \tag{5.1.2}$$

Obviously, the probability $p_{ij}, i = 1, \cdots, m, j = 1, 2$ in Table 5.1 should

**TABLE 5.1:** Probability distribution of a discrete random variable.

| $y\backslash x$ | $x_1$ | $x_2$ | $\cdots$ | $x_m$ | $p._j$ |
|---|---|---|---|---|---|
| $y_1 = -1$ | $p_{11}$ | $p_{21}$ | $\cdots$ | $p_{m1}$ | $p._1$ |
| $y_2 = 1$ | $p_{12}$ | $p_{22}$ | $\cdots$ | $p_{m2}$ | $p._2$ |
| $p_{i\cdot}$ | $p_{1\cdot}$ | $p_{2\cdot}$ | $\cdots$ | $p_{m\cdot}$ | 1 |

**TABLE 5.2:** Probability distribution of a mixed random variable.

| $y\backslash x$ | $x$ | |
|---|---|---|
| $y_1 = -1$ | $p(x, y_1)$ | $p._1$ |
| $y_2 = 1$ | $p(x, y_2)$ | $p._2$ |
| | $p_x(x)$ | 1 |

satisfy

$$p_{ij} \geq 0, i = 1, \cdots, m, j = 1, 2, \tag{5.1.3}$$

$$\sum_{i=1}^{m} \sum_{j=1}^{2} p_{ij} = 1, \tag{5.1.4}$$

which implies that

$$\sum_{i=1}^{m} p_{i\cdot} = 1, \quad \sum_{j=1}^{2} p._j = 1. \tag{5.1.5}$$

Based on Table 5.1, we can calculate the conditional probabilities. For example, the conditional probability of $y = y_j$ under the condition $x = x_i$ is:

$$P(y = y_j | x = x_i) = \frac{p_{ij}}{p_{i1} + p_{i2}} = \frac{p_{ij}}{p_{i\cdot}}, \quad i = 1, \cdots, m, j = 1, 2. \tag{5.1.6}$$

Corresponding to the above discrete random variable, we turn to describe a mixed random variable. Consider a random variable $(x, y)$, where $y$ can take values of $y_1 = -1$ or $y_2 = 1$ like a discrete random variable, but the values of $x$ spread out over an interval in $R^n$ like a continuous variable. Table 5.2 shows this situation, where $p(x, y_j)$ is the probability density function when $y = y_j$ $(j = 1, 2)$, $p_x(x)$ and $p._j$ are the marginal density function and marginal distribution of $(x, y)$ on $x$ and $y$ respectively, i.e.

$$p_x(x) = p(x, y_1) + p(x, y_2) \tag{5.1.7}$$

and

$$p._j = \int_{-\infty}^{+\infty} p(x, y_i) dx, \quad j = 1, 2. \tag{5.1.8}$$

For $j = 1, 2$, $p(x, y_j)$ should satisfy that

$$p(x, y_j) \geq 0, j = 1, 2, \tag{5.1.9}$$

$$\int_{-\infty}^{+\infty} [p(x, y_1) + p(x, y_2)] dx = 1. \tag{5.1.10}$$

**TABLE 5.3:**   An example of a mixed random variable.

| $y \backslash x$ | $x \in (-\infty, 0)$ | $x \in (0, \frac{1}{2})$ | $x \in (\frac{1}{2}, 1)$ | $x \in (1, +\infty)$ | $P_{\cdot j}$ |
|---|---|---|---|---|---|
| $y_1 = -1$ | $p(x, y_1) = 0$ | $p(x, y_1) = \frac{1}{3}$ | $p(x, y_1) = \frac{3}{4}$ | $p(x, y_1) = 0$ | $p_{\cdot 1} = \frac{13}{24}$ |
| $y_2 = 1$ | $p(x, y_2) = 0$ | $p(x, y_2) = \frac{2}{3}$ | $p(x, y_2) = \frac{1}{4}$ | $p(x, y_2) = 0$ | $p_{\cdot 2} = \frac{11}{24}$ |
| $P_x(x)$ | $0$ | $1$ | $1$ | $0$ | $1$ |

This implies

$$\int_{-\infty}^{+\infty} p_x(x) = 1, \quad \sum_{j=1}^{2} p_{\cdot j} = 1. \tag{5.1.11}$$

Based on Table 5.2, we can calculate the conditional probabilities. For example, the conditional probability of $y = y_j$ under the condition $x = \bar{x}$ is

$$P(y = y_j | x = \bar{x}) = \frac{p(\bar{x}, y_j)}{p(\bar{x}, y_1) + p(\bar{x}, y_2)}, \quad j = 1, 2. \tag{5.1.12}$$

**Example 5.1.1** *Find the marginal density function, marginal distribution, and conditional probability of the mixed random variable given by Table 5.3.*

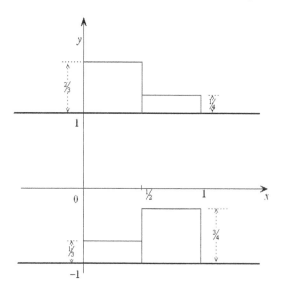

**FIGURE 5.1**: Probability distribution given by Table 5.3.

The probability distribution in Table 5.3 can be described graphically by Figure 5.1. The random variable $(x, y)$ can only take values in the straight lines $y = -1$ or $y = 1$, and its corresponding density function can take values *in the size of the vertical direction. So the marginal density function on x is*

$$p_x(x) = \begin{cases} 0, & x \in (-\infty, 0); \\ 1, & x \in (0, 1); \\ 0, & x \in (1, +\infty). \end{cases} \tag{5.1.13}$$

*And the marginal distributions on y are respectively*

$$p_{.1} = \int_{-\infty}^{+\infty} p(x, y_1)dx = \frac{13}{24}, \tag{5.1.14}$$

$$p_{.2} = \int_{-\infty}^{+\infty} p(x, y_2)dx = \frac{11}{24}. \tag{5.1.15}$$

*The conditional probability of y = −1 under the condition x = x̄ is*

$$p(y = -1 | x = \bar{x}) = \begin{cases} 0, & \bar{x} \in (-\infty, 0); \\ \frac{1}{3}, & \bar{x} \in (0, \frac{1}{2}); \\ \frac{3}{4}, & \bar{x} \in (\frac{1}{2}, 1); \\ 0, & \bar{x} \in (1, +\infty). \end{cases} \tag{5.1.16}$$

In order to describe the above discrete and mixed random variables in a unified form, the following probability distribution function is introduced.

**Definition 5.1.2** *(Probability distribution function) Suppose that $(x, y)$ is a random variable, where $x = ([x]_1, \cdots, [x]_n)^{\mathrm{T}} \in R^n, y \in \mathcal{Y} = \{-1, 1\}$. The function $P(\bar{x}, \bar{y}) = P(x \leqslant \bar{x}, y \leqslant \bar{y})$ defined in $R^n \times \mathcal{Y}$ is called the probability distribution function of $(x, y)$, where $P(x \leqslant \bar{x}, y \leqslant \bar{y})$ is the probability of the event "$x \leqslant \bar{x}$" and the event "$y \leqslant \bar{y}$" occurring together, and "$x \leqslant \bar{x}$" means that "$[x]_1 \leqslant [\bar{x}]_1, \cdots, [x]_n \leqslant [\bar{x}]_n$". For simplicity, the probability distribution function is sometimes called the probability distribution.*

Based on the probability distribution given by Tables 5.1 and 5.2, the corresponding probability distribution function $P(\bar{x}, \bar{y})$ can be calculated. For example, for the case in Table 5.2, we have

$$P(\bar{x}, \bar{y}) = \begin{cases} 0, & \text{if } \bar{y} < -1; \\ \int_{-\infty}^{\bar{x}} p(x, y_1)dx, & \text{if } -1 \leq \bar{y} < 1; \\ \int_{-\infty}^{\bar{x}} [p(x, y_1) + p(x, y_2)]dx, & \text{if } \bar{y} \geq 1. \end{cases} \tag{5.1.17}$$

**Example 5.1.3** *Find the probability distribution function of $(\bar{x}, \bar{y})$ given in Example 5.1.1.*

The probability distribution function $P(\bar{x}, \bar{y})$ is

$$P(\bar{x}, \bar{y}) = \begin{cases} 0, & \text{if } \bar{y} < -1; \\ p(x, -1), & \text{if } -1 \leq \bar{y} < 1; \\ p(x, 1), & \text{if } \bar{y} \geq 1, \end{cases} \tag{5.1.18}$$

where

$$P(\bar{x}, -1) = \begin{cases} 0, & \text{if } \bar{x} \in (-\infty, 0); \\ \frac{1}{3}\bar{x}, & \text{if } \bar{x} \in (0, \frac{1}{2}); \\ \frac{3}{4}\bar{x} - \frac{5}{24}, & \text{if } \bar{x} \in (\frac{1}{2}, 1); \\ \frac{13}{24}, & \text{if } \bar{x} \in (1, +\infty), \end{cases} \tag{5.1.19}$$

and

$$P(\bar{x}, 1) = \begin{cases} 0, & \text{if } \bar{x} \in (-\infty, 0); \\ \bar{x}, & \text{if } \bar{x} \in (0, 1); \\ 1, & \text{if } \bar{x} \in (1, +\infty). \end{cases} \tag{5.1.20}$$

## 5.1.2 Description of classification problems

In Section 2.1.2 of Chapter 2, the definition of the classification problem is given as follows: Given a training set

$$T = \{(x_1, y_1), \cdots, (x_l, y_l)\}, \tag{5.1.21}$$

where $x_i \in R^n, y_i \in \mathcal{Y} = \{-1, 1\}, i = 1, \cdots, l$, find the possible output $y$ for any unseen input $x$. In other words, classification problem is to find a function $f : R^n \to \mathcal{Y}$ such that $f(x)$ is a good approximation of the output $y$ to an arbitrary $x$. Obviously, in order to find such a function, it is necessary that the already collected training points $(x_i, y_i)(i = 1, \cdots, l)$ have something in common with the pair $(x, y)$ of the unseen input and corresponding output. In the framework of SLT, this is guaranteed by the following assumption.

**Assumption 5.1.4** *Assume that the training points $(x_i, y_i), i = 1, \cdots, l$ in the training set and future point $(x, y)$ are independent and identically distributed (i.i.d.), i.e., generated independently and identically (i.i.d.) according to an unknown but fixed probability distribution $P(x, y)$ on $R^n \times \mathcal{Y}$.*

This is a standard assumption in SLT. Every pair $(\hat{x}, \hat{y})$ can be considered to be generated in two steps. First, the input $\hat{x}$ is generated according to the marginal distribution $P_x(x)$. Second, the output $\hat{y}$ is generated according to the conditional probability $P(\cdot|\hat{x})$ on $\mathcal{Y}$ given the input $\hat{x}$. Note that assuming the output $y$ to a given input $x$ is stochastically generated by $P(\cdot|x)$ accommodated the fact that in general the information contained in $x$ may not be sufficient to determine a single output response in a deterministic manner. So, the goal of classification is to estimate the value of the random variable $y$.

We conclude that in SLT, classification problem can be described as follows: Given a training set generated i.i.d, its goal is to find a decision function $f : R^n \to \mathcal{Y}$ such that $f(x)$ is a good approximation of the output $y$ to an arbitrary $x$. In order to find such a function, we need to propose a quantity index to evaluate it; therefore the concept of loss function is introduced at first.

**Definition 5.1.5** *(Loss function) Denote by $(x, y, f(x)) \in R^n \times \mathcal{Y} \times \mathcal{Y}$ the triplet consisting of an input(observation) $x$, an output $y$ and a prediction $f(x)$. Then the map $c : R^n \times \mathcal{Y} \times \mathcal{Y} \to [0, \infty)$ with the property $c(x, y, y) = 0$ for all $x \in R^n$ and $y \in \mathcal{Y}$ is called a loss function.*

The most simple and natural loss function is the $0 - 1$ loss function.

**Example 5.1.6** *The $0 - 1$ loss function is defined by*

$$c(x, y, f(x)) = \hat{c}(y - f(x)), \tag{5.1.22}$$

*where*

$$\hat{c}(\xi) = \begin{cases} 0, & \text{if } \xi = 0; \\ 1, & \text{otherwise.} \end{cases} \tag{5.1.23}$$

Clearly, the value of a loss function $c(x, y, f(x))$ indicates the quality of the decision function $f(x)$ for a particular $(x, y)$. In order to evaluate the quality of the decision function $f(x)$ itself, suppose that the pair $(x, y)$ is generated by a distribution on $R^n \times \mathcal{Y}$ with the probability density functions $p(x, -1)$ and $p(x, 1)$, then the average loss for unseen pairs is

$$\int_{R^n} c(x, -1, f(x))p(x, -1)\mathrm{d}x + \int_{R^n} c(x, 1, f(x))p(x, 1)\mathrm{d}x. \tag{5.1.24}$$

Generally the following expected risk is used to assess the quality of a decision function.

**Definition 5.1.7** *(Expected risk) Suppose that the training set (5.1.21) is generated by $P(x, y)$ on $R^n \times \mathcal{Y}$. Let $f : R^n \to \mathcal{Y} = \{-1, 1\}$ be a decision function and $c(x, y, f(x))$ be a loss function. The expected risk of $f(x)$ is defined by the Riemann-Stieltjes integration of $c(x, y, f(x))$ on $P(x, y)$, i.e.,*

$$R[f] \triangleq E[c(x, y, f(x))] = \int_{R^n \times \mathcal{Y}} c(x, y, f(x))\mathrm{d}P(x, y)$$

$$= \int_{R^n} c(x, -1, f(x))\mathrm{d}P(x, -1) + \int_{R^n} c(x, 1, f(x))\mathrm{d}P(x, 1). \tag{5.1.25}$$

Here, the integration is carried out with respect to the distribution $P(x, y)$ and the loss function $c(x, y, f(x))$. In general, $P(x, y)$ is unknown, but fixed, while the choice of $c(x, y, f(x))$ depends strongly on the specific application. The expected risk can be interpreted as the "average" loss of $f(x)$. For example, in the case of the $0 - 1$ loss function it reflects the "average" weights of predictive errors.

**Example 5.1.8** *Consider the probability distribution in Examples 5.1.1 and 5.1.3. Suppose that the decision function is*

$$f(x) = \begin{cases} 1, & x \in [0, 1/2]; \\ -1, & x \in (1/2, 1] \end{cases} \tag{5.1.26}$$

*Find its expected risk for the $0-1$ loss function.*

Noticing that the expected risk can be expressed by (5.1.25) and using Table 5.3, the expected risk for any decision function $\tilde{f}$ can be written as:

$$R[\tilde{f}] = \int_{-\infty}^{\infty} c(x, y_1, \tilde{f}(x)) p(x, y_1) dx + \int_{-\infty}^{\infty} c(x, y_2, \tilde{f}(x)) p(x, y_2) dx$$

$$= \frac{1}{3} \int_0^{1/2} c(x, -1, \tilde{f}(x)) dx + \frac{3}{4} \int_{1/2}^1 c(x, -1, \tilde{f}(x)) dx$$

$$+ \frac{2}{3} \int_0^{1/2} c(x, 1, \tilde{f}(x)) dx + \frac{1}{4} \int_{1/2}^1 c(x, 1, \tilde{f}(x)) dx. \tag{5.1.27}$$

The definition of $0-1$ loss function implies that $\hat{c}(-1 - \tilde{f}(\bar{x})) + \hat{c}(1 - \tilde{f}(\bar{x})) = 1$, so the above equation is equivalent to:

$$R[\tilde{f}] = \frac{1}{3} \times \frac{1}{2} + \frac{1}{3} \int_0^{1/2} \hat{c}(1 - \tilde{f}(\bar{x})) d\bar{x} + \frac{1}{4} \times \frac{1}{2} + \frac{1}{2} \int_{1/2}^1 \hat{c}(-1 - \tilde{f}(\bar{x})) d\bar{x}.$$

$$\tag{5.1.28}$$

Clearly, when the decision function $\tilde{f}(x) = f(x)$ defined by (5.1.26), the expected risk is $\frac{1}{3} \times \frac{1}{2} + \frac{1}{4} \times \frac{1}{2} = \frac{7}{24}$. In other words, the "average" error rate is $\frac{7}{24}$.

The definition of the expected risk helps us formalize a classification problem from the statistical learning theory as follows:

**Classification problem on SLT**: Given the training set

$$T = \{(x_1, y_1), \cdots, (x_l, y_l)\}, \tag{5.1.29}$$

where $x_i \in R^n, y_i \in \mathcal{Y} = \{-1, 1\}, i = 1, \cdots, l$. Suppose that the training points $(x_i, y_i), i = 1, \cdots, l$ and future point $(x, y)$ are generated i.i.d according to an unknown distribution $P(x, y)$ on $R^n \times \mathcal{Y}$. Let $c(x, y, f(x))$ be a loss function. Find a decision function $f(x)$ such that its expected risk $R[f]$ is minimized.

The above formulation can be explained clearly by a simple example, where the training set is generated from $P(x, y)$ in Examples 5.1.1 and 5.1.3. Solving the classification problem implies to find a function that minimizes the expected risk. By (5.1.28), it is easy to see that $f(x)$ given by (5.1.26) is what we need. Furthermore, we can see that, as a solution, the decision function (5.1.26) is only an estimation (prediction) for a random variable. For instance, when the input $x \in (0, 1/2)$, we are not able to conclude that the corresponding output $y$ must be the value $f(x) = 1$ given by the decision function because it may be either 1 (with probability 1/3) or $-1$ (with probability 2/3). So the value $f(x) = 1$ is just only a best estimation in some sense.

It should be pointed out that the above example only shows the implication of the classification problem; it does not give any practical method because in the classification problem, we do not know the distribution $P(x, y)$, what we do know is only the training set $T$. In other words, we only know that there exists a distribution such that on which the training points $(x_i, y_i), i = 1, \cdots, l$ and future point $(x, y)$ are independently and identically generated, but we do not know what this distribution is. So we can imagine that it is intractable to find an exact function, like (5.1.26), with the minimal expected risk only using the information in the training set. Therefore we are going to find an approximation function whose risk is close to the minimal expected risk below.

## 5.2 Empirical Risk Minimization

Let us now recall that the classification problem on SLT is to find a decision function that (approximately) achieves the smallest expected risk. Since the distribution generating the training set is unknown, the expected risk is not computable, and consequently it is impossible to find the decision function via the expected risk directly. So we should find some computable and approximate substitute to replace the expected risk. The following empirical risk seems to be one of them.

**Definition 5.2.1** *(Empirical risk) Given the training set $T = \{(x_1, y_1), \cdots, (x_l, y_l)\} \in (R^n \times \mathcal{Y})^l$, where $x_i \in R^n, y \in \mathcal{Y} = \{-1, 1\}, i = 1, \cdots, l$. Suppose that $c(x, y, f(x))$ is a loss function. Then the empirical risk of a decision function $f(x)$ is*

$$R_{\text{emp}}[f] = \frac{1}{l} \sum_{i=1}^{l} c(x_i, y_i, f(x_i)). \tag{5.2.1}$$

The empirical risk has the advantage that, given the training data, we can readily compute it. At the same time, it seems to be a reasonable quality measure for the decision function because the better decision function should result in smaller empirical risk. It may appear that all that remains to be done is to find the decision function by minimizing the empirical risk $R_{\text{emp}}[f]$. However, this strategy is not reliable as shown by the following example, where an absurd result is induced.

**Example 5.2.2** *Consider the training set* $T = \{(x_1, y_1), \cdots, (x_l, y_l)\}$, *where* $x_i \in R^n, y_i \in \mathcal{Y} = \{-1, 1\}, i = 1, \cdots, l$, *and all the inputs are different, i.e.* $x_i \neq x_j$, *for* $i \neq j$, $i, j = 1, \cdots, l$. *Suppose that the* $0 - 1$ *loss function is considered. Then the decision function*

$$f(x) = \begin{cases} y_i, & when \ x = x_i, i = 1, \cdots, l \ ; \\ 1, & otherwise \end{cases} \tag{5.2.2}$$

*is clearly a minimizer of* $R_{emp}[f]$ *with minimal value 0. Obviously this decision function is of no use at all. But according to the above strategy it is our final choice, whereas it is in general a very poor approximation of* $R[f]$.

This example is an extreme form of a phenomenon called overfitting, in which the learning method produces a function that models too closely the output values in the training set and as a result, has poor performance on future data. One common way to avoid overfitting is to choose a suitable class of functions $\mathcal{F}$ and minimize $R_{emp}[f]$ over $\mathcal{F}$, instead of over all functions. This leads to the following empirical risk minimization (ERM) principle.

**Definition 5.2.3** *(Empirical risk minimization principle) For the training set*

$$T = \{(x_1, y_1), \cdots, (x_l, y_l)\}, \tag{5.2.3}$$

*where* $x_i \in R^n, y_i \in \mathcal{Y} = \{-1, 1\}, i = 1, \cdots, l$, *select a loss function* $c(x, y, f(x))$ *and a decision function candidate set* $\mathcal{F}$ *where* $f \in \mathcal{F}, f : R^n \to \mathcal{Y} = \{-1, 1\}$. *The empirical risk minimization principle says that, finding a function which minimizes the empirical risk over* $\mathcal{F}$, *take the function as the decision function.*

The above ERM principle has already appeared in the traditional statistical learning theory. For example, the least square regression is an implementation of this idea. The law of large numbers shows that the empirical risk $R_{emp}[f]$ is a good approximation of the expected risk $R[f]$ for each single $f$ when the number of training points is very large. However, when the number is small, $R_{emp}[f]$ does not in general lead to an approximation of $R[f]$. How to get a reasonably good approximation of $R[f]$ in this case will be studied in the following section.

## 5.3 Vapnik Chervonenkis (VC) Dimension

The ERM principle tends to choose the decision function which minimizes the empirical risk $R_{emp}[f]$ over a decision function candidate set $\mathcal{F}$. This approach has a serious issue: how to select the set $\mathcal{F}$. To resolve this issue, we introduce the VC dimension to descibe the size of $\mathcal{F}$ (or the growth of $\mathcal{F}$).

**Definition 5.3.1** *($\mathcal{F}$ shatters a set $Z_l$) Suppose that $\mathcal{F}$ is a decision function candidate set, and $Z_l = \{x_1, \cdots, x_l\}$, where $x_i \in R^n, i = 1, \cdots, l$. We say that $\mathcal{F}$ shatters the set $Z_l$ or $Z_l$ is shattered by $\mathcal{F}$ if for any training set*

$$T = \{(x_1, y_1), \cdots, (x_l, y_l)\}, \tag{5.3.1}$$

*where $x_i \in Z_l, y_i = 1$ or $-1$, $i = 1, \cdots, l$, there exists a function $f$ in $\mathcal{F}$ which can separate the training set, i.e. $f$ satisfies that*

$$f(x_i) = y_i, \quad i = 1, \cdots, l. \tag{5.3.2}$$

**Example 5.3.2** *Consider a classification problem in $R^2$. Suppose that $\mathcal{F}$ is a set of the decision functions used in linear support vector classification, i.e.,*

$$\begin{aligned}
\mathcal{F} = \{f(x) &= \text{sgn}((w \cdot x) + b) \\
&= \text{sgn}(w_1[x]_1 + w_2[x]_2 + b) \mid w = (w_1, w_2)^T \in R^2, \ b \in R\}.
\end{aligned} \tag{5.3.3}$$

*If $Z_3 = \{x_1, x_2, x_3\} \subset R^2$, and $x_1, x_2, x_3$ are not in a straight line, then $Z_3$ can be shattered by $\mathcal{F}$.*

In fact, there exist $2^3 = 8$ modes for the points $x_1, x_2, x_3$ shown in Figure 5.2 where the points labeled 1 are represented by "+", and the points labeled $-1$ are represented by "○". It is easy to see that for every mode there exists a straight line such that all "+" lie in one side and all "○" in the other side of the line. This implies that there exists $f \in \mathcal{F}$ such that $f(x_i) = y_i$ for all $i = 1, 2, 3$. Therefore $Z_3$ is shattered by $\mathcal{F}$.

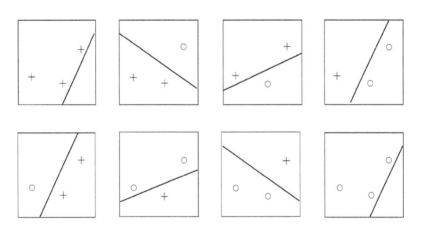

**FIGURE 5.2**: Eight labels for three fixed points in $R^2$ (a) four points are in a line; (b) only three points are in a line; (c) any three points are not in a line and these four points form a convex quadrilateral; (d) any three points are not in a line and one point is inside of the triangle of other three points.

It is easy to see that the larger the number of points that can be shattered by $\mathcal{F}$ is, the richer the set $\mathcal{F}$ is.

**Definition 5.3.3** *(VC dimension) Suppose that $\mathcal{F}$ is a decision function candidate set. The VC dimension of $\mathcal{F}$, denoted by $VCdim(\mathcal{F})$, is defined as the maximal number of points in $R^n$ which can be shattered by $\mathcal{F}$. More precisely, the VC dimension of $\mathcal{F}$ is $l$ if there exists a set with $l$ points which can be shattered by $\mathcal{F}$, but any sets with $l+1$ points cannot be shattered by $\mathcal{F}$. If the maximum does not exist, the VC dimension is said to be $\infty$.*

**Example 5.3.4** *For $\mathcal{F}$ defined in Example 5.3.2, compute its VC dimension $VCdim(\mathcal{F})$.*

Example 5.3.2 has shown that $VCdim(\mathcal{F}) \geqslant 3$. In order to prove $VCdim(\mathcal{F})=3$, we only need to show that for any four points $\{x_1, x_2, x_3, x_4\}$ in $R^2$, there is always a label mode such that they cannot be shattered by $\mathcal{F}$. In fact, there are four cases: (i) four points are in a line; (ii) only three points are in a line; (iii) any three points are not in a line and these four points form a convex quadrilateral; (iv) any three points are not in a line and one point is inside of the triangle of other three points. Figure 5.3 (a)$\sim$(d) correspond to these four cases. For every case with the label mode shown in this figure, there is no line such that all "+"s and all "o"s lie separately in its two sides. Therefore the corresponding 4 points cannot be shattered by $\mathcal{F}$. Thus we have $VCdim(\mathcal{F}) = 3$.

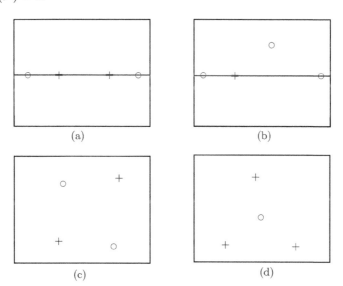

**FIGURE 5.3**: Four cases for four points in $R^2$.

The above conclusion in $R^2$ can be extended to the one in $R^n$ as shown by the following theorem.

**Theorem 5.3.5** *Consider classification problems in $R^n$. Suppose that $\mathcal{F}$ is the set of decision functions in linear support vector classofication, i.e.*

$$\mathcal{F} = \left\{ f(x) = sgn\left((w \cdot x) + b\right) \mid w = (w_1, \cdots, w_n)^{\mathrm{T}} \in R^n, \ b \in R \right\}, \quad (5.3.4)$$

*then the VC dimension of $\mathcal{F}$ is $n + 1$.*

**Proof** See the details in [158]. ∎

## 5.4 Structural Risk Minimization

The goal of this section is to derive the structural risk minimization (SRM) principle that is an improvement of the ERM principle.

Consider the training set

$$T = \{(x_1, y_1), \cdots, (x_l, y_l)\}, \quad (5.4.5)$$

where $x_i \in R^n, y_i \in \mathcal{Y} = \{+1, -1\}, i = 1, \cdots, l$, where $T$ is generated i.i.d. from an unknown distribution $P(x, y)$. Suppose that $\mathcal{F}$ is a decision function candidate set and $c(x, y, f(x))$ is a loss function. Let us derive an upper bound of the expected risk. Taking the empirical risk $R_{\text{emp}}[f]$ as an approximation, the problem is transferred to estimate the difference. We have described that our problem is to find a function which minimizes $R[f]$, then the ERM principle tends to replace $R[f]$ by $R_{\text{emp}}[f]$. So, it is crucial to ensure that $R_{\text{emp}}[f]$ is a good approximation of $R[f]$. In other words, we want to guarantee that the approximation error $R[f] - R_{\text{emp}}[f]$ is sufficiently small. The following theorem provides an upper bound of the probability of the event $\sup_{f \in \mathcal{F}}(R[f] - R_{\text{emp}}[f]) > \varepsilon$, where $\varepsilon$ is a positive number.

**Theorem 5.4.1** *Denote the VC dimension of $\mathcal{F}$ by $h$. If $l > h$ and $l\varepsilon^2 \geqslant 2$, then*

$$P\left\{ \sup_{f \in \mathcal{F}}(R[f] - R_{\text{emp}}[f]) > \varepsilon \right\} \leqslant 4\exp\left( h\left( \ln \frac{2l}{h} + 1 \right) - \frac{l\varepsilon^2}{8} \right). \quad (5.4.6)$$

**Proof** See the details in [42, 157, 158]. ∎

Set the right-hand side of (5.4.6) equal to some $\delta > 0$, i.e.

$$4\exp\left( h\left( \ln \frac{2l}{h} + 1 \right) - \frac{l\varepsilon^2}{8} \right) = \delta, \quad (5.4.7)$$

and then solve for $\varepsilon$

$$\varepsilon = \sqrt{ \frac{8}{l}\left( h\left( \ln \frac{2l}{h} + 1 \right) + \ln \frac{4}{\delta} \right) }. \quad (5.4.8)$$

By the above two equations, we get an upper bound of $R[f]$.

**Theorem 5.4.2** *Denote the VC dimension of $\mathcal{F}$ by $h$. If*

$$l > h, \tag{5.4.9}$$

*and*

$$h\left(\ln\frac{2l}{h} + 1\right) + \ln\frac{4}{\delta} \geqslant \frac{1}{4}, \tag{5.4.10}$$

*then for any distribution $P(x, y)$, $\delta \in (0, 1]$ and $f \in \mathcal{F}$, the following inequality holds with a probability at least $1 - \delta$*

$$R[f] \leqslant R_{\text{emp}}[f] + \varphi(h, l, \delta), \tag{5.4.11}$$

*where*

$$\varphi(h, l, \delta) = \sqrt{\frac{8}{l}\left(h\left(\ln\frac{2l}{h} + 1\right) + \ln\frac{4}{\delta}\right)}. \tag{5.4.12}$$

The right-hand side of (5.4.11) is called the structural risk, its first term is the empirical risk, and the second term is called the confidential interval. Theorem 5.4.2 shows that the structural risk is an upper bound of the expected risk $R[f]$. So we turn to minimize this bound. Its main contribution is, instead of simply being employed to find a decision function, being employed as a guideline to establish and justify some important conclusions.

It is interesting to estimate the impact of the size of $\mathcal{F}$ on the expected risk by investigating the impact of the size of $\mathcal{F}$ on the empirical risk. It is easy to see that the confidential interval (5.4.12) is a decreasing function about the size of training set $l$ and tends to 0 when $l \to \infty$. Therefore, the expected risk is close to the value of the empirical risk and the expected risk can be replaced by the empirical risk simply. However, in general, the confidential interval probably plays an important role and therefore the impact of the size of $\mathcal{F}$ on both the empirical risk and the confidential interval in the expected risk should be taken account.

Figure 5.4 shows the size $t$ of $\mathcal{F}$ on the horizontal axis and the value on the right-hand side of (5.4.11) on the vertical axis. On one hand, when the set $\mathcal{F}$ is increasing, the candidate decision functions increase, resulting in the decrease of the empirical risk; on the other hand, when the set $\mathcal{F}$ is increasing, the VC dimension $h$ increases, resulting in the increase of confidence interval (5.4.12) because it is an increasing function of $h$. It can be expected that the structural risk has a minimum at $\hat{t}$ which should be selected. This leads to the following structural risk minimization (SRM) principle.

**Definition 5.4.3** *(Structural risk minimization principle) For the training set*

$$T = \{(x_1, y_1), \cdots, (x_l, y_l)\}, \tag{5.4.13}$$

*where $x_i \in R^n, y_i \in \mathcal{Y} = \{-1, 1\}, i = 1, \cdots, l$, select a loss function $c(x, y, f(x))$ and a decision function candidate set $\mathcal{F}(t)$ depending on a real parameter $t$ with the following property:*

$$\mathcal{F}(t_1) \subset \mathcal{F}(t_2), \quad \forall t_1 < t_2, \tag{5.4.14}$$

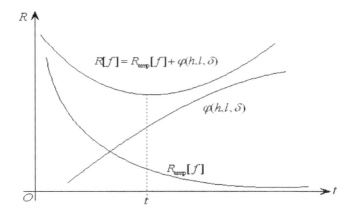

**FIGURE 5.4**: Structural risk minimization.

*For every $t$, find a function $f^t$ in $\mathcal{F}(t)$ which minimizes the empirical risk. Thus every pair $(t, f^t)$ corresponds to a value of the structural risk. The structural risk minimization principle says that, finding a $\hat{t}$ which minimizes the structural risk, take the function $f^{\hat{t}}$ as the decision function.*

---

## 5.5    An Implementation of Structural Risk Minimization

An implementation of structural risk minimization was proposed in [12] and improved from theoretical point of view in our paper [186].

### 5.5.1    Primal problem

Consider the classification problem with the training set

$$T = \{(x_1, y_1), \cdots, (x_1, y_l)\}, \tag{5.5.1}$$

where $x_i \in R^n, y_i \in \mathcal{Y} = \{-1, 1\}, i = 1, \cdots, l$. First consider the linear separation and select a decision function candidate set $\mathcal{F}(t)$ depending on a real parameter $t$:

$$\mathcal{F}(t) = \{f(x) = \text{sgn}((w \cdot x) + b) \mid \|w\| \leqslant t, \quad t \in [0, \infty)\}. \tag{5.5.2}$$

Then the set $\mathcal{F}(t)$ increases with $t$. Suppose that the loss function to be the soft margin loss function defined by (4.3.18)

$$c(x, y, f(x)) = \max\{0, 1 - yg(x)\}, \quad \text{where } g(x) = (w \cdot x) + b. \tag{5.5.3}$$

Thus its empirical risk is

$$R_{\text{emp}}[f] = \frac{1}{l}\sum_{i=1}^{l} c(x_i, y_i, f(x_i)) = \frac{1}{l}\sum_{i=1}^{l} \max\{0, 1 - y_i g(x_i)\}. \tag{5.5.4}$$

For different $t$, we need to find the minimizer of the empirical risk. This leads to the optimization problem with the parameter $t$:

$$\min \quad R_{\text{emp}}[f] = \frac{1}{l}\sum_{i=1}^{l} c(x_i, y_i, f(x_i)), \tag{5.5.5}$$

$$\text{s.t.} \quad f \in \mathcal{F}(t). \tag{5.5.6}$$

More specially, the following theorem provides us an equivalent form of the problem (5.5.5)~(5.5.6).

**Theorem 5.5.1** *Suppose that the loss function is the soft margin loss function, and the decision function candidate set is defined by (5.5.2), then the problem (5.5.5)~(5.5.6) is equivalent to the following convex programming:*

$$\min_{w,b,\xi} \quad \sum_{i=1}^{l} \xi_i, \tag{5.5.7}$$

$$\text{s.t.} \quad y_i((w \cdot x) + b) \geq 1 - \xi_i, \ i = 1, \cdots, l, \tag{5.5.8}$$

$$\xi_i \geq 0, \ i = 1, \cdots, l, \tag{5.5.9}$$

$$\|w\| \leq t. \tag{5.5.10}$$

**Proof** Obviously, problem (5.5.7)~(5.5.10) is a convex programming. Now we turn to prove the problem (5.5.5)~(5.5.6) is equivalent to the problem (5.5.7)~(5.5.10). By (5.5.3), the constraints (5.5.8)~(5.5.9) mean that for $i = 1, \cdots, l$,

$$\xi_i = \begin{cases} 0, & \text{if } y_i g(x_i) \geq 1; \\ 1 - y_i g(x_i), & \text{if } y_i g(x_i) < 1 \end{cases}$$
$$= \max\{0, 1 - y_i g(x_i)\}. \tag{5.5.11}$$

By (5.5.3), we have

$$\xi_i = c(x_i, y_i, f(x_i)). \tag{5.5.12}$$

Therefore, the problem (5.5.7)~(5.5.10) can be transformed to the problem (5.5.5)~(5.5.6). ∎

Here, problem (5.5.7)~(5.5.10) is the primal problem.

## 5.5.2   Quasi-dual problem and relationship between quasi-dual problem and primal problem

According to the standard approach, we need to establish the dual problem of the primal problem (5.5.7)~(5.5.10). It is declared in [12] that the following problem

$$\min_{\alpha} \quad t\sqrt{\sum_{i=1}^{l}\sum_{j=1}^{l} y_i y_j \alpha_i \alpha_j (x_i \cdot x_j)} - \sum_{i=1}^{l} \alpha_i , \tag{5.5.13}$$

$$\text{s.t.} \quad \sum_{i=1}^{l} y_i \alpha_i = 0 , \tag{5.5.14}$$

$$0 \leqslant \alpha_i \leqslant 1, \quad i = 1, \cdots, l . \tag{5.5.15}$$

is the dual problem. Unfortunately, the proof is not rigorous since their derivation is based on some hypotheses that may not be true. However, as pointed in our paper [186], there still exists a similar relationship between the primal problem and the problem (5.5.13)~(5.5.15). So, we call the problem (5.5.13)~(5.5.15) quasi-dual problem and have the following theorems.

**Theorem 5.5.2** *Quasi-dual problem* (5.5.13)~(5.5.15) *is a convex programming.*

**Proof** To prove the problem (5.5.13)~(5.5.15) is a convex programming, we only need to prove the objective function is convex. Let $H = (y_i y_j (x_i \cdot x_j))_{l \times l}$, $\alpha = (\alpha_1, \cdots, \alpha_l)^{\mathrm{T}}$, $e = (1, \cdots, 1)^{\mathrm{T}}$, then the objective function is rewritten as

$$f(\alpha) = t\sqrt{\alpha^{\mathrm{T}} H \alpha} - e^{\mathrm{T}} \alpha. \tag{5.5.16}$$

We only need to show that for any $\bar{\alpha}, \tilde{\alpha} \in R^l$ and $\lambda \in [0, 1]$,

$$f(\lambda\bar{\alpha} + (1 - \lambda)\tilde{\alpha}) \leqslant \lambda f(\bar{\alpha}) + (1 - \lambda)f(\tilde{\alpha}), \tag{5.5.17}$$

i.e.,

$$\sqrt{(\lambda\bar{\alpha} + (1 - \lambda)\tilde{\alpha})^{\mathrm{T}} H (\lambda\bar{\alpha} + (1 - \lambda)\tilde{\alpha})} \leqslant \lambda\sqrt{\bar{\alpha}^{\mathrm{T}} H \bar{\alpha}} + (1 - \lambda)\sqrt{\tilde{\alpha}^{\mathrm{T}} H \tilde{\alpha}}. \tag{5.5.18}$$

Based on the Cauchy-Schwarz inequality, we have

$$2\lambda(1 - \lambda)\bar{\alpha}^{\mathrm{T}} H \tilde{\alpha} \leqslant 2\lambda(1 - \lambda)\sqrt{\bar{\alpha}^{\mathrm{T}} H \bar{\alpha} \tilde{\alpha}^{\mathrm{T}} H \tilde{\alpha}}. \tag{5.5.19}$$

Furthermore,

$$\lambda^2\bar{\alpha}^{\mathrm{T}} H \bar{\alpha} + 2\lambda(1 - \lambda)\bar{\alpha}^{\mathrm{T}} H \tilde{\alpha} + (1 - \lambda)^2\tilde{\alpha}^{\mathrm{T}} H \tilde{\alpha}$$
$$\leqslant \lambda^2\bar{\alpha}^{\mathrm{T}} H \bar{\alpha} + 2\lambda(1 - \lambda)\sqrt{\bar{\alpha}^{\mathrm{T}} H \bar{\alpha} \tilde{\alpha}^{\mathrm{T}} H \tilde{\alpha}} + (1 - \lambda)^2\tilde{\alpha}^{\mathrm{T}} H \tilde{\alpha}, \tag{5.5.20}$$

i.e.,

$$(\lambda\bar{\alpha} + (1 - \lambda)\tilde{\alpha})^{\mathrm{T}} H (\lambda\bar{\alpha} + (1 - \lambda)\tilde{\alpha}) \leqslant (\lambda\sqrt{\bar{\alpha}^{\mathrm{T}} H \bar{\alpha}} + (1 - \lambda)\sqrt{\tilde{\alpha}^{\mathrm{T}} H \tilde{\alpha}})^2. \tag{5.5.21}$$

This implies (5.5.18). ∎

**Theorem 5.5.3** *Suppose* $\alpha^{t*} = (\alpha_1^{t*}, \cdots, \alpha_l^{t*})^T$ *is a solution to the quasi-dual problem* (5.5.13)~(5.5.15), *where* $t > 0$. *If there exists a component,* $\alpha_j^{t*}$ *such that* $\alpha_j^{t*} \in (0,1)$, *then a solution* $(w^{t*}, b^{t*})$ *to the primal problem* (5.5.7)~(5.5.10) *w.r.t.* $(w, b)$ *can be obtained by*

$$w^{t*} = \frac{1}{\gamma^*} \sum_{i=1}^{l} \alpha_i^{t*} y_i x_i, \tag{5.5.22}$$

$$b^{t*} = y_j - \frac{1}{\gamma^*} \sum_{i=1}^{l} y_i \alpha_i^{t*} (x_i \cdot x_j), \tag{5.5.23}$$

*where*

$$\gamma^* = \frac{\sqrt{\alpha^{t*T} H \alpha^{t*}}}{t}, \quad H = (y_i y_j (x_i \cdot x_j))_{l \times l}. \tag{5.5.24}$$

**Proof** Since $\alpha^{t*}$ is the solution to the problem (5.5.13)~(5.5.15), there exist Lagrange multiplier $\tilde{b}^{t*}$ and Lagrange multiplier vectors $\tilde{\xi}^* = (\tilde{\xi}_1^*, \cdots, \tilde{\xi}_l^*)^T, \tilde{s}^* = (\tilde{s}_1^*, \cdots, \tilde{s}_l^*)^T$ satisfying the following KKT conditions:

$$\frac{t}{\sqrt{\alpha^{t*T} H \alpha^{t*}}} y_i \left( x_i \cdot \sum_{j=1}^{l} y_j \alpha_j^{t*} x_j \right) - 1$$

$$+ y_i \tilde{b}^{t*} + \tilde{\xi}_i^* - \tilde{s}_i^* = 0, \quad i = 1, \cdots, l, \tag{5.5.25}$$

$$\tilde{\xi}_i^* (\alpha_i^{t*} - 1) = 0, \quad i = 1, \cdots, l, \tag{5.5.26}$$

$$\tilde{s}_i^* \alpha_i^{t*} = 0, \quad i = 1, \cdots, l, \tag{5.5.27}$$

$$\tilde{\xi}_i^* \geqslant 0, \quad i = 1, \cdots, l, \tag{5.5.28}$$

$$\tilde{s}_i^* \geqslant 0, \quad i = 1, \cdots, l, \tag{5.5.29}$$

$$\alpha_i^{t*} \leqslant 1, \quad i = 1, \cdots, l, \tag{5.5.30}$$

$$\alpha_i^{t*} \geqslant 0, \quad i = 1, \cdots, l, \tag{5.5.31}$$

$$\sum_{i=1}^{l} y_i \alpha_i^{t*} = 0. \tag{5.5.32}$$

First of all, let us prove that $w^{t*}$ given by (5.5.22) and Lagrange multiplier $\tilde{b}^{t*}$ are the solution to primal problem (5.5.7)~(5.5.10) with respect to $(w, b)$. In fact, by Theorem 1.2.24, we just need to show that there exist $\xi^{t*}$ and Lagrange multiplier vectors $\alpha^* = (\alpha_1^*, \cdots, \alpha_l^*)^T, s^* = (s_1^*, \cdots, s_l^*)^T, \gamma^*$ that satisfy KKT conditions. This just requires that when $\gamma^*$ is shown in (5.5.24), and

$$\xi^{t*} = \tilde{\xi}^*, \quad \alpha^* = \alpha^{t*}, \quad s^* = \tilde{s}^* = e - \alpha^{t*} \tag{5.5.33}$$

the following conditions hold:

$$-\sum_{i=1}^{l} \alpha_i^{t*} y_i x_i + \gamma^* w^{t*} = 0, \qquad (5.5.34)$$

$$\sum_{i=1}^{l} \alpha_i^{t*} y_i = 0, \qquad (5.5.35)$$

$$1 - \alpha_i^{t*} - \tilde{s}_i^* = 0, \quad i = 1, \cdots, l, \qquad (5.5.36)$$

$$\alpha_i^{t*} (y_i((w^{t*} \cdot x_i) + \tilde{b}^{t*}) - 1 + \tilde{\xi}_i^*) = 0, \quad i = 1, \cdots, l, \qquad (5.5.37)$$

$$\tilde{s}_i^* \tilde{\xi}_i^* = 0, \quad i = 1, \cdots, l, \qquad (5.5.38)$$

$$\gamma^* (t^2 - \|w^{t*}\|^2) = 0, \qquad (5.5.39)$$

$$\alpha_i^{t*} \geq 0, \quad i = 1, \cdots, l, \qquad (5.5.40)$$

$$\tilde{s}_i^* \geqslant 0, \quad i = 1, \cdots, l, \qquad (5.5.41)$$

$$\gamma^* \geqslant 0, \qquad (5.5.42)$$

$$y_i((w^{t*} \cdot x_i) + \tilde{b}^{t*}) - 1 + \tilde{\xi}_i^* \geqslant 0, \quad i = 1, \cdots, l, \qquad (5.5.43)$$

$$\tilde{\xi}_i^* \geqslant 0, \quad i = 1, \cdots, l, \qquad (5.5.44)$$

$$\|w^{t*}\|^2 \leqslant t^2. \qquad (5.5.45)$$

It is easy to get (5.5.34)~(5.5.45) by the above KKT conditions (5.5.25)~(5.5.32). Therefore, $(w^{t*}, \tilde{b}^{t*})$ is the solution to problem (5.5.7)~(5.5.10) with respect to $(w, b)$.

Furthermore, to prove $(w^{t*}, b^{t*})$ is the solution to primal problem (5.5.7)~(5.5.10) with respect to $(w, b)$, we only need to show $\tilde{b}^{t*} = b^{t*}$. If there exists a component $\alpha_j^{t*}$ of the solution $\alpha^{t*}$ such that $\alpha_j^{t*} \in (0, 1)$, then $\tilde{\xi}_j^* = 0$, by (5.5.26); on the other hand, by (5.5.37),

$$y_j((w^{t*} \cdot x_j) + \tilde{b}^{t*}) - 1 = 0. \qquad (5.5.46)$$

So, by comparing the above equation and (5.5.23), together with (5.5.24), we can get $\tilde{b}^{t*} = b^{t*}$, that is $(w^{t*}, b^{t*})$ is the solution to the primal problem (5.5.7)~(5.5.10) with respect to $(w, b)$. ∎

### 5.5.3 Structural risk minimization classification

As an implementation of the SRM principle, we can establish the classification algorithm based on Theorem 5.5.3. Only the linear classification is considered here. Please see references [12, 186] for the complete algorithm with kernels.

**Algorithm 5.5.4** *(Linear structural risk minimization classification)*

*(1) Input the training set $T = \{(x_1, y_1), \cdots, (x_l, y_l)\}$, where $x_i \in R^n, y_i \in \mathcal{Y} = \{-1, 1\}, i = 1, \cdots, l$;*

*(2) Choose an appropriate parameter $\hat{t} > 0$;*

*(3) Construct and solve the problem (5.5.13)~(5.5.15), obtaining a solution $\alpha^{t*} = (\alpha_1^{t*}, \cdots, \alpha_l^{t*})^{\mathrm{T}}$;*

*(4) Construct the decision function $f(x) = sgn((w^{t*} \cdot x) + b^{t*})$ based on Theorem 5.5.3.*

## 5.6 Theoretical Foundation of $C$-Support Vector Classification on Statistical Learning Theory

Now let us turn to our main purpose of this chapter to show that support vector machines are the implementation of the structural risk minimization principle by taking the standard $C$-support vector classification as a representative.

### 5.6.1 Linear $C$-support vector classification

We recall that in linear $C$-SVC, the primal problem is

$$\min_{w,b,\xi} \quad \frac{1}{2}\|w\|^2 + C\sum_{i=1}^{l}\xi_i \ , \tag{5.6.1}$$

$$\text{s.t.} \quad y_i((w \cdot x_i) + b) \geqslant 1 - \xi_i \ , \ i = 1, \cdots, l \ , \tag{5.6.2}$$

$$\xi_i \geqslant 0 \ , \ i = 1, \cdots, l \tag{5.6.3}$$

and the dual problem is

$$\min_{\alpha} \quad \frac{1}{2}\sum_{i=1}^{l}\sum_{j=1}^{l} y_i y_j \alpha_i \alpha_j (x_i \cdot x_j) - \sum_{j=1}^{l}\alpha_j \ , \tag{5.6.4}$$

$$\text{s.t.} \quad \sum_{i=1}^{l} y_i \alpha_i = 0 \ , \tag{5.6.5}$$

$$0 \leqslant \alpha_i \leqslant C, \quad i = 1, \cdots, l \ . \tag{5.6.6}$$

**Theorem 5.6.1** *Suppose that $w^{C*}$ is a solution to the problem (5.6.1)~(5.6.3) with respect to $w$. Then the function $\psi(C) = \|w^{C*}\|$, defined in the interval $(0, +\infty)$, is well-defined.*

**Proof** By Theorems 2.3.2 and 2.3.3 in Chapter 2, there exists a unique solution $w^{C*}$ to primal problem (5.6.1)~(5.6.3) with respect to $w$ for any $C > 0$. So, the function $\psi(C) = \|w^{C*}\|$, defined in the interval $(0, +\infty)$, is well-defined. ∎

**Theorem 5.6.2** *The function $\psi(C)$ introduced in Theorem 5.6.1 is nondecreasing in the interval $(0, +\infty)$.*

**Proof** Without loss of generality, suppose that $0 < \bar{C} < \tilde{C}$. To prove $\psi(C)$ is nondecreasing, it only needs to provide evidence that the solution $w^{\bar{C}*}$ and $w^{\tilde{C}*}$ to primal problem (5.6.1)~(5.6.3) for $\bar{C}$ and $\tilde{C}$ respectively satisfy

$$\|w^{\bar{C}*}\|^2 \leqslant \|w^{\tilde{C}*}\|^2. \tag{5.6.7}$$

In fact, suppose that $(w^{\bar{C}*}, b^{\bar{C}*}, \xi^{\bar{C}*})$ and $(w^{\tilde{C}*}, b^{\tilde{C}*}, \xi^{\tilde{C}*})$ are solutions to the primal problem (5.6.1)~(5.6.3). Then their objective function values satisfy:

$$\frac{1}{2}\|w^{\bar{C}*}\|^2 + \bar{C}\sum_{i=1}^{l}\xi_i^{\bar{C}*} \leqslant \frac{1}{2}\|w^{\tilde{C}*}\|^2 + \bar{C}\sum_{i=1}^{l}\xi_i^{\tilde{C}*}, \tag{5.6.8}$$

$$\frac{1}{2}\|w^{\bar{C}*}\|^2 + \tilde{C}\sum_{i=1}^{l}\xi_i^{\bar{C}*} \geqslant \frac{1}{2}\|w^{\tilde{C}*}\|^2 + \tilde{C}\sum_{i=1}^{l}\xi_i^{\tilde{C}*}. \tag{5.6.9}$$

The two equations listed above are equivalent to

$$\frac{1}{\bar{C}}\frac{1}{2}\|w^{\bar{C}*}\|^2 + \sum_{i=1}^{l}\xi_i^{\bar{C}*} \leqslant \frac{1}{\bar{C}}\frac{1}{2}\|w^{\tilde{C}*}\|^2 + \sum_{i=1}^{l}\xi_i^{\tilde{C}*}, \tag{5.6.10}$$

$$\frac{1}{\tilde{C}}\frac{1}{2}\|w^{\bar{C}*}\|^2 + \sum_{i=1}^{l}\xi_i^{\bar{C}*} \geqslant \frac{1}{\tilde{C}}\frac{1}{2}\|w^{\tilde{C}*}\|^2 + \sum_{i=1}^{l}\xi_i^{\tilde{C}*}. \tag{5.6.11}$$

Using (5.6.10) minus (5.6.11), then

$$\left(\frac{1}{\bar{C}} - \frac{1}{\tilde{C}}\right)\frac{1}{2}\|w^{\bar{C}*}\|^2 \leqslant \left(\frac{1}{\bar{C}} - \frac{1}{\tilde{C}}\right)\frac{1}{2}\|w^{\tilde{C}*}\|^2. \tag{5.6.12}$$

Therefore when $\bar{C} < \tilde{C}$, (5.6.7) stands. ∎

### 5.6.2 Relationship between dual problem and quasi-dual problem

In order to show the relationship between $C$-SVC and the structural risk minimization classification, we first consider the relationship between the dual problem (5.6.4)~(5.6.6) and the quasi-dual problem (5.5.13)~(5.5.15).

**Theorem 5.6.3** *The function $\psi(C)$ introduced in Theorem 5.6.1 satisfies that when $t = \psi(C) > 0$, $\alpha^{t*} = \dfrac{\alpha^{C*}}{C}$ is a solution to the quasi-dual problem (5.5.13)~(5.5.15), where $\alpha^{C*}$ is a solution to the dual problem (5.6.4)~(5.6.6).*

**Proof** The Lagrange function of quasi-dual problem (5.5.13)~(5.5.15) is

$$L(\alpha, \tilde{b}, \tilde{\xi}, \tilde{s}) = t\sqrt{\alpha^T H \alpha} - \sum_{i=1}^{l} \alpha_i + \tilde{b} \sum_{i=1}^{l} y_i \alpha_i + \sum_{i=1}^{l} \tilde{\xi}_i(\alpha_i - 1) - \sum_{i=1}^{l} \tilde{s}_i \alpha_i, \quad (5.6.13)$$

where $H = (y_i y_j (x_i \cdot x_j))_{l \times l}$. By Theorem 5.5.2, to prove our conclusion, it is necessary to verify that when $t = \psi(C)$, there exist Lagrange multiplier $\tilde{b}$ and Lagrange multiplier vectors $\tilde{\xi} = (\tilde{\xi}_1, \cdots, \tilde{\xi}_l)^T, \tilde{s} = (\tilde{s}_1, \cdots, \tilde{s}_l)^T$ such that $\alpha^{t*}, \tilde{b}, \tilde{\xi}, \tilde{s}$ satisfy the following KKT conditions

$$\frac{t}{\sqrt{\alpha^{t*T} H \alpha^{t*}}} H \alpha^{t*} - e + \tilde{b} y + \tilde{\xi} - \tilde{s} = 0, \quad (5.6.14)$$

$$\tilde{\xi}_i(\alpha_i^{t*} - 1) = 0, \quad i = 1, \cdots, l, \quad (5.6.15)$$

$$\tilde{s}_i \alpha_i^{t*} = 0, \quad i = 1, \cdots, l, \quad (5.6.16)$$

$$\tilde{\xi}_i \geqslant 0, \quad i = 1, \cdots, l, \quad (5.6.17)$$

$$\tilde{s}_i \geqslant 0, \quad i = 1, \cdots, l, \quad (5.6.18)$$

$$\alpha_i^{t*} \leqslant 1, \quad i = 1, \cdots, l, \quad (5.6.19)$$

$$\alpha_i^{t*} \geqslant 0, \quad i = 1, \cdots, l, \quad (5.6.20)$$

$$\sum_{i=1}^{l} y_i \alpha_i^{t*} = 0. \quad (5.6.21)$$

In fact, since $\alpha^{C*}$ is the solution to dual problem (5.6.4)~(5.6.6), there exist Lagrange multiplier $\tilde{b}^*$ and Lagrange multiplier vectors $\tilde{\xi}^* = (\tilde{\xi}_1^*, \cdots, \tilde{\xi}_l^*)^T, \tilde{s}^* = (\tilde{s}_1^*, \cdots, \tilde{s}_l^*)^T$ such that $\alpha^{C*}, \tilde{b}^*, \tilde{\xi}^*, \tilde{s}^*$ satisfy the following conditions

$$H \alpha^{C*} - e + \tilde{b}^* y + \tilde{\xi}^* - \tilde{s}^* = 0, \quad (5.6.22)$$

$$\tilde{\xi}_i^*(\alpha_i^{C*} - C) = 0, \quad i = 1, \cdots, l, \quad (5.6.23)$$

$$\tilde{s}_i^* \alpha_i^{C*} = 0, \quad i = 1, \cdots, l, \quad (5.6.24)$$

$$\tilde{\xi}_i^* \geqslant 0, \quad i = 1, \cdots, l, \quad (5.6.25)$$

$$\tilde{s}_i^* \geqslant 0, \quad i = 1, \cdots, l, \quad (5.6.26)$$

$$\alpha_i^{C*} \leqslant C, \quad i = 1, \cdots, l, \quad (5.6.27)$$

$$\alpha_i^{C*} \geqslant 0, \quad i = 1, \cdots, l, \quad (5.6.28)$$

$$\sum_{i=1}^{l} y_i \alpha_i^{C*} = 0. \quad (5.6.29)$$

To compare (5.6.14)~(5.6.21) and (5.6.22)~(5.6.29), it is suggested that when $t = \psi(C)$, which means $t = \sqrt{\alpha^{C*T} H \alpha^{C*}}$. Let $\tilde{b} = \tilde{b}^*, \tilde{\xi} = \tilde{\xi}^*, \tilde{s} = \tilde{s}^*$, then $\alpha^{t*}, \tilde{b}, \tilde{\xi}, \tilde{s}$ satisfy the KKT condition (5.6.14)~(5.6.21). Therefore, our conclusion is proved. ■

### 5.6.3   Interpretation of $C$-support vector classification

**Theorem 5.6.4** *The nondecreasing function $\psi(C)$ introduced in Theorem 5.6.1 and discussed in Theorem 5.6.2 has the following property: If for some $C > 0$, the solution $\alpha^{C*}$ to the dual problem (5.6.4)~(5.6.6) has a component $\alpha_j^{C*} \in (0, C)$, then when $t = \psi(C)$, $(w^{C*}, b^{C*})$ obtained by $C$-SVC is also a solution to the primal problem (5.5.7)~(5.5.10) with respect to $(w, b)$.*

**Proof** Let us prove the conclusion in two different situations.

(i) When $t = \psi(C) = 0$, $w^{C*} = 0$ by the definition of $\psi(C)$; on the other hand, if $t = 0$, from the constraint (5.5.10), it can be known that $w^{C*} = 0$ is the solution to the primal problem (5.5.7)~(5.5.10) with respect to $w$; furthermore, it is easy to verify that the solution $b^{C*}$ to linear $C$-SVC with respect to $b$ is the solution to the primal problem (5.5.7)~(5.5.10) with respect to $b$.

(ii) When $t = \psi(C) > 0$, if there exists a component $\alpha^{C*}$ of a solution $\alpha^{C*}$ to the dual problem (5.6.4)~(5.6.6), such that $\alpha_j^{C*} \in (0, C)$, then by Theorem 5.6.3, the solution to linear $C$-SVC with $(w, b)$ can be expressed as

$$w^{C*} = \sum_{i=1}^{l} \alpha_i^{C*} y_i x_i = C \sum_{i=1}^{l} \alpha_i^{t*} y_i x_i, \qquad (5.6.30)$$

$$b^{C*} = y_j - \sum_{i=1}^{l} y_i \alpha_i^{C*} (x_i \cdot x_j) = y_j - C \sum_{i=1}^{l} y_i \alpha_i^{t*} (x_i \cdot x_j), \qquad (5.6.31)$$

where $\alpha^{t*} = \dfrac{\alpha^{C*}}{C}$ is the solution to the quasi-dual problem (5.5.13)~(5.5.15).

So according to Theorem 5.5.3, to prove $(w^{C*}, b^{C*})$ is the solution to the primal problem (5.5.7)~(5.5.10), we only need to prove $C = \dfrac{1}{\gamma^*}$, where $\gamma^*$ is given by (5.5.24). In fact, it can be obtained by (5.5.24), together with the relationship between $\alpha^{t*}$ and $\alpha^{C*}$, that is

$$\gamma^* = \frac{\sqrt{\alpha^{t*\,\mathrm{T}} H \alpha^{t*}}}{t} = \frac{\sqrt{\alpha^{C*\,\mathrm{T}} H \alpha^{C*}}}{C\|w^{C*}\|} = \frac{1}{C}. \qquad (5.6.32)$$

Therefore, $(w^{C*}, b^{C*})$ is the solution to the primal problem (5.5.7)~(5.5.10) with respect to $(w, b)$. ∎

**Remark 5.6.5** Note that for the above theorem, the conclusion is proved under the extra condition that for some $C > 0$, the solution $\alpha^{C*}$ to the dual problem (5.6.4)~(5.6.6) has a component $\alpha_j^{C*} \in (0, C)$. It should be pointed out that the conclusion is also true when the above condition is not valid. In addition, the conclusion can be extended to the general $C$-SVC with kernels. Please see [186] for the details.

Theorems 5.6.4 and Remark 5.6.5 provide the theoretical foundation of $C$-SVC on SLT: the decision function obtained by $C$-SVC with suitable $C$ is just one of the decision functions obtained by Algorithm 5.5.4 (linear structural risk minimization classification). Therefore, $C$-SVC with a suitable parameter $C$ is a direct implementation of the SRM principle. In addition, a very interesting and important meaning of the parameter $C$ is given by showing that $C$ corresponds to the size of the decision function candidate set in the SRM principle: the larger the value of $C$, the larger the decision function candidate set.

Along with the discussion in Chapter 2 and Chapter 4, $C$-SVC can be summarized and understood from three points of view: (i) construct a decision function by selecting a proper size of the decision function candidate set via adjusting the parameter $C$; (ii) construct a decision function by selecting the weighting between the margin of the decision function and the deviation of the decision function measured by the soft-margin loss function via adjusting the parameter $C$; (iii) construct a decision function by selecting the weighting between flatness of the decision function and the deviation of the decision function measured by the soft-margin loss function via adjusting the parameter $C$.

# Chapter 6

## Model Construction

This chapter investigates how to solve practical problems by SVMs. Only the classification problems are considered here since the regression problems can be dealt with in a similar way.

Roughly speaking, a practical classification problem can be described as follows: Suppose that there is a kind of object that is divided into two classes, positive class and negative class, and we know some of them belong to the former and some to the latter. Our task is to establish a criterion and deduce whether a new object belongs to the positive or negative class.

In order to solve a practical classification problem by SVC, a complete model is usually constructed in the following steps:

(i) According to the objects with the known class labels, generate an initial training set;

(ii) Construct the training set by preprocessing the initial training set;

(iii) Select an appropriate kernel and parameters in SVC;

(iv) Find the decision function by SVC on the training set;

(v) For the decision function obtained, give an explanation that can be easily interpreted by humans.

This chapter will focus on the first three steps, and the last step in Sections 6.1, 6.2, 6.3 and Section 6.4, respectively.

## 6.1 Data Generation

When we apply SVC to solve practical classification problems, the first step is to generate an initial training set. For doing this, we first describe the objects to be classified in a vector form by extracting some features that are relevant to objects and their labels, and developing a quantitative indicator for every feature. So, an object is represented by an $n$-dimensional vector $x = ([x]_1, \cdots, [x]_n)^{\mathrm{T}}$, where $n$ is the number of features and $[x]_i$ is the value of the $i$-th feature, $i = 1, \cdots, n$. Thus, suppose that we know $l$ objects with the label 1 or $-1$ representing that they belong to positive class or negative class respectively, then an initial training set can be constructed as follows:

$$T = \{(x_1, y_1), \cdots, (x_l, y_l)\}, \tag{6.1.1}$$

where $(x_i, y_i)$ is a training point, $x_i = ([x_i]_1, \cdots, [x_i]_n)^{\mathrm{T}} \in R^n$ and $y_i \in \mathcal{Y} = \{-1, 1\}$ are the $i$-th input and label respectively, $i = 1, \cdots, l$.

In the above process, one of the key points is to represent the objects by vectors. This work is trivial sometimes, e.g. for the problem in Example 2.1.1 (Diagnosis of heart disease), where a patient (an object) is represented by a two-dimensional vector that consists of two features: diastolic pressure and cholesterol level. However, this is not always the case. In fact, for most practical problems, excellent skills and professional knowledge are needed as shown by the following classification problem concerned with post-translational modification sites in bioinformatics.

The prediction of post-translational modification sites can be formulated as a binary classification problem, where the objects to be classified are ordinal sequences formed from 20 amino acids and a dummy amino acid, i.e. character strings that are composed of 21 characters in the set:

$$U = \{A, C, \cdots, Z, O\} \tag{6.1.2}$$

with certain length, where $A, C, \cdots, Z$ represent 20 amino acids respectively and $O$ represents the dummy amino acid. In order to apply SVC, the first is to represent the above strings by vectors.

Instead of the above character string, let us consider the more general one

$$a = \alpha_{[1]} \alpha_{[2]} \cdots \alpha_{[m]} \tag{6.1.3}$$

with length $m$, where $\alpha_{[i]} (i = 1, \cdots, m)$ is the $i$-th character of the string and belongs to the set:

$$S = \{\alpha_1, \alpha_2, \cdots, \alpha_p\}. \tag{6.1.4}$$

The methods representing the string (6.1.3) by a vector are called encoding schemes. Some of them are introduced below[142].

## 6.1.1 Orthogonal encoding

The basic idea of this orthogonal encoding scheme is to transform $p$ characters in $S$ into $p$ orthonormal vectors[88]; all of characters in $S$ are ordered from 1 to $p$, and the $i$-th character is transformed to the binary vector of $p$ components with the $i$-th component set to "1" and all others to "0"s, for $i = 1, 2, \cdots, p$, i.e.,

$$
\begin{aligned}
\alpha_1 &\longrightarrow & e_1 &= (1, 0, 0, \cdots, 0)^{\mathrm{T}} \in R^p \\
\alpha_2 &\longrightarrow & e_2 &= (0, 1, 0, \cdots, 0)^{\mathrm{T}} \in R^p \\
& \cdots & & \\
\alpha_p &\longrightarrow & e_p &= (0, 0, 0, \cdots, 1)^{\mathrm{T}} \in R^p.
\end{aligned}
\tag{6.1.5}
$$

Replacing the characters by the corresponding orthonormal vectors, the character string $a$ with length $m$ given by (6.1.3) is encoded in a $p \times m$-dimensional vector. For example, for the character string

$$a = \alpha_1\alpha_3\alpha_2\alpha_1\alpha_3 \tag{6.1.6}$$

with

$$S = \{\alpha_1, \alpha_2, \alpha_3\}, \tag{6.1.7}$$

we have $e_1 = (1,0,0)^{\mathrm{T}}, e_2 = (0,1,0)^{\mathrm{T}}, e_3 = (0,0,1)^{\mathrm{T}}$. And this string can be transformed into the 15-dimensional vector: $(e_1^{\mathrm{T}}, e_3^{\mathrm{T}}, e_2^{\mathrm{T}}, e_1^{\mathrm{T}}, e_3^{\mathrm{T}})^{\mathrm{T}} = (1,0,0,0,0,1,0,1,0,1,0,0,0,0,1)^{\mathrm{T}}$.

## 6.1.2 Spectrum profile encoding[97, 103]

Let us first show the basic idea of spectrum profile encoding scheme by the character string $a$ defined by (6.1.6) and (6.1.7). Here we are interested in the distribution of two adjacent characters of the string $a$ such as $\alpha_1\alpha_2, \alpha_1\alpha_3$. Clearly, there are $3^2 = 9$ possible combinations of two contiguous characters in (6.1.6) shown in the set:

$$S^2 = \{\alpha_1\alpha_1, \alpha_1\alpha_2, \alpha_1\alpha_3, \alpha_2\alpha_1, \alpha_2\alpha_2, \alpha_2\alpha_3, \alpha_3\alpha_1, \alpha_3\alpha_2, \alpha_3\alpha_3\}. \tag{6.1.8}$$

Now calculate the number of times that each element in $S^2$ occurred in the string $a$ and consider this number as the score for each element of $S^2$. Then we can get the 9-dimensional vector:

$$(0,0,2,1,0,0,0,1,0)^{\mathrm{T}}, \tag{6.1.9}$$

where each component is the number of times the corresponding two contiguous subsequences of (6.1.8) occur in the string $a$. For example, the first and second 0 in (6.1.9) mean that both $\alpha_1\alpha_1$ and $\alpha_1\alpha_2$ never occur in $a$, while the third element 2 in (6.1.9) means that $\alpha_1\alpha_3$ occurs twice in $a$.

Now let us define a mapping based on the above idea to encode any string $a$ defined by (6.1.3). We consider the occurrence of $k$ contiguous subsequences as the extension of the two contiguous subsequences in the above example. Given the set $S$ defined by (6.1.4), there are $p^k$ possible combinations regarding $k$ contiguous subsequences, and we can get the following set indexed by all these $p^k$ possible combinations with a specific order:

$$S^k = \{a_1, a_2, \cdots, a_{p^k}\}. \tag{6.1.10}$$

Then we can encode the string $a$ into a vector in $R^{p^k}$ space:

$$\Phi_k(a) = (\phi_{a_1}(a), \phi_{a_2}(a), \cdots, \phi_{a_{p^k}}(a))^{\mathrm{T}}, \tag{6.1.11}$$

where $\phi_{a_i}(a), i = 1, 2, \cdots, p^k$ is the number of times the subsequence $a_i$ occurred in $a$.

The example in the beginning of this section is just a special case of the above mapping. That is, (6.1.10) and (6.1.11) are equivalent to (6.1.8) and (6.1.9) respectively when $k = 2$, the set $S$ and the character string $a$ are given by (6.1.7) and (6.1.6) respectively.

It may be interesting to extend the above encoding approach for any possible combinations rather than only consider the contiguous subsequences. For instance, given a sequence $a$ defined by (6.1.6), the subsequence $\alpha_1\alpha_3$ appears in $a$ as the contiguous subsequences of the first character and the second character, and the fourth and the fifth characters, as well as the non-contiguous combination of the first character and the fifth character if gaps allowed. For detailed discussion, we refer the reader to [97].

## 6.1.3 Positional weighted matrix encoding[23, 135, 175]

For a classification problem when the objects are strings, it is necessary to know several strings with class labels. This information can be represented by the set

$$T = \{(a_1, y_1), \cdots, (a_l, y_l)\}, \qquad (6.1.12)$$

where $a_i$ is a character string that is composed of $p$ characters in the set $S$ defined by (6.1.4) and $y_i \in \{1, -1\}$ $(i = 1, \cdots, l)$.

The positional weighted matrix encoding is based on the above set, and its process consists of two parts: (i) Construct the positional weighted matrix $P = (P_{ij})$, where $P_{ij}$ is the frequency of the $i$-th character in set $S$ appearing at the $j$-th position in all of the characters $a_t$ in $S$ with $y_t = 1(t = 1, \cdots, l)$, $i = 1, 2, \cdots, p, j = 1, 2, \cdots m$. (ii) Encode the character string $a$ defined by (6.1.3) in a $m$-dimensional vector, and its $j$-th $(j = 1, \cdots, m)$ component is the corresponding value of $P_{kj}$, where $k$ is defined in the following way: the character appearing at the $j$-th position in $a$ is the $k$-th character in set $S$.

Let us show this encoding method more clearly through the following example. Given the set

$$\{(a_1, y_1), (a_2, y_2), (a_3, y_3)\}, \qquad (6.1.13)$$

where $a_1 = \alpha_{10}\alpha_{10}\alpha_2\alpha_9\alpha_1, y_1 = 1, a_2 = \alpha_7\alpha_4\alpha_2\alpha_6\alpha_1, y_2 = 1, a_3 = \alpha_7\alpha_5\alpha_2\alpha_8\alpha_{10}, y_3 = -1, S = \{\alpha_1, \alpha_2, \cdots, \alpha_{10}\}$, represent the strings $\alpha_{10}\alpha_{10}\alpha_2\alpha_9\alpha_1$ and $\alpha_2\alpha_4\alpha_1\alpha_6\alpha_9$ by vectors.

The positional weighted matrix is shown in Table 6.1 and the strings required can be represented by 5-dimensional vectors.

$$\alpha_{10}\alpha_{10}\alpha_2\alpha_9\alpha_1 \longrightarrow (P_{10\ 1}, P_{10\ 2}, P_{2\ 3}, P_{9\ 4}, P_{1\ 5})^{\mathrm{T}} = (0.5, 0.5, 1, 0.5, 1)^{\mathrm{T}},$$
$$(6.1.14)$$

$$\alpha_2\alpha_4\alpha_1\alpha_6\alpha_9 \longrightarrow (P_{2\ 1}, P_{4\ 2}, P_{1\ 3}, P_{6\ 4}, P_{9\ 5})^{\mathrm{T}} = (0, 0.5, 0, 0.5, 0)^{\mathrm{T}}.$$
$$(6.1.15)$$

An improvement of this approach is proposed in [175].

**TABLE 6.1:** Positional weighted matrix.

|          | 1   | 2   | 3   | 4   | 5   |
|----------|-----|-----|-----|-----|-----|
| $\alpha_1$    | 0   | 0   | 0   | 0   | 1   |
| $\alpha_2$    | 0   | 0   | 1   | 0   | 0   |
| $\alpha_3$    | 0   | 0   | 0   | 0   | 0   |
| $\alpha_4$    | 0   | 0.5 | 0   | 0   | 0   |
| $\alpha_5$    | 0   | 0   | 0   | 0   | 0   |
| $\alpha_6$    | 0   | 0   | 0   | 0.5 | 0   |
| $\alpha_7$    | 0.5 | 0   | 0   | 0   | 0   |
| $\alpha_8$    | 0   | 0   | 0   | 0   | 0   |
| $\alpha_9$    | 0   | 0   | 0   | 0.5 | 0   |
| $\alpha_{10}$ | 0.5 | 0.5 | 0   | 0   | 0   |

## 6.2   Data Preprocessing

Applying $C$-SVC algorithm directly on the above initial training set (6.1.1) often results in poor performance. Therefore, the data should be preprocessed in order to improve the quality of the data. Some data preprocessing techniques are introduced below.

### 6.2.1   Representation of nominal features

Consider the classification problem of some foods. For simplicity, we describe a food by only one feature — its taste. Suppose that there are three different tastes: bitter, sweet, and salted, which can be represented by the symbolic integers: 1, 2, and 3 in one-dimensional Euclidian space, respectively. This feature is a nominal feature, whose feature values are completely unordered. So, the above representation is not suitable for classification. In order to describe the disorder, we embed the one-dimensional Euclidian space $R$ into three-dimensional Euclidian space $R^3$, and transform the symbolic integers 1, 2, and 3 in $R$ to the coordinate vectors: $p_1$, $p_2$, $p_3$ in $R^3$, see Figure 6.1. Thus the bitter, sweet, and salted foods can be represented as $(1,0,0)^{\mathrm{T}}$, $(0,1,0)^{\mathrm{T}}$, and $(0,0,1)^{\mathrm{T}}$, respectively.

In the above example, the nominal feature takes values in three states. It is easy to be extended to the case where the nominal feature takes values in $M$ states, which are represented by 1, 2, $\cdots$, $M$ in $R$. In fact, we only need to embed the one-dimensional Euclidian space $R$ into an $M$-dimensional Euclidian space $R^M$, and establish the transformation from 1, 2, $\cdots$, $M$ in $R$ to the coordinate vectors $e_1$, $\cdots$, $e_M$ in $R^M$. Thus the nominal feature that takes values in $M$ states can be represented as $(1,0,\cdots,0)^{\mathrm{T}}$, $(0,1,\cdots,0)^{\mathrm{T}}$ and $(0,\cdots,0,1)^{\mathrm{T}}$, respectively.

Please see references [147, 150] for further discussion of nominal features.

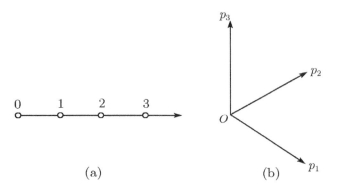

**FIGURE 6.1**: Representation of nominal features.

## 6.2.2    Feature selection

In the initial training sets, an object to be classified is represented by an input (vector $x = ([x]_1, \cdots, [x]_n)^{\mathrm{T}}$ with $n$ features). Some of these features may be irrelevant to the class. The goal of feature selection is to remove the irrelevant features and maintain the features that are as close as possible to the class. The benefit of feature selection is twofold. On one hand, feature selection is meaningful since it can identify the features that contribute most to classification. For example, in Example 2.1.1 (Diagnosis of heart disease), there are 13 features in the initial training set. Feature selection can provide us with the most important features that cause the heart disease. On the other hand, feature selection is helpful for solving the classification problem since it cannot only reduce the dimension of input space and speed up the computation procedure, but can also improve the classification accuracy. The problem of feature selection is described as follows.

**Feature selection**: Given an initial training set

$$T = \{(x_i, y_i), \cdots, (x_l, y_l)\}, \tag{6.2.1}$$

where $x_i = ([x_i]_1, \cdots, [x_i]_n)^{\mathrm{T}} \in R^n, y_i \in \mathcal{Y} = \{1, -1\}, i = 1, \cdots, l$, feature selection is to remove the irrelevant features, and construct an appropriate training set.

There exist numerous methods of feature selection in the literature [13, 110]. In the following, we introduce some of them.

### 6.2.2.1    *F-score method*

$F$-score is a simple and generally quite effective technique [27]. Given the initial training set (6.2.1), the $F$-score of $k$-th feature is defined as

$$F(k) = \frac{([\bar{x}]_k^+ - [\bar{x}]_k)^2 + ([\bar{x}]_k^- - [\bar{x}]_k)^2}{\dfrac{1}{l_+ - 1}\sum_{y_i=1}([x_i]_k - [\bar{x}]_k^+)^2 + \dfrac{1}{l_- - 1}\sum_{y_i=-1}([x_i]_k - [\bar{x}]_k^-)^2}, \quad k=1,\cdots,n,$$

$$\tag{6.2.2}$$

where $l_+$ and $l_-$ are the number of positive and negative points respectively, and

$$[\bar{x}]_k^+ = \frac{1}{l_+} \sum_{y_i=1} [x_i]_k, \quad k = 1, \cdots, n, \tag{6.2.3}$$

$$[\bar{x}]_k^- = \frac{1}{l_-} \sum_{y_i=-1} [x_i]_k, \quad k = 1, \cdots, n, \tag{6.2.4}$$

$$[\bar{x}]_k = \frac{1}{l} \sum_{i=1}^{l} [x_i]_k, \quad k = 1, \cdots, n. \tag{6.2.5}$$

The numerator of $F(k)$ indicates the discrimination of $k$-th feature between the positive and negative sets, and the denominator of $F(k)$ indicates the one within each of the two sets. The larger the $F$-score is, the more likely this feature is more discriminative. Therefore, this score can be used as a feature selection criterion. The algorithm is summarized below:

**Algorithm 6.2.1** *(F-score method)*

*(1) Input the training set $T$ defined by (6.2.1) and the number of selected features: $d$;*

*(2) According to (6.2.2), calculate the F-score of every feature: $F(1), F(2), \cdots,$ $F(n)$;*

*(3) Array the F-scores in ascending order: $F(k_1), F(k_2), \cdots, F(k_n)$, where*

$$F(k_1) \geqslant F(k_2) \geqslant \cdots \geqslant F(k_n). \tag{6.2.6}$$

*Select the features that correspond to the index $k_1, \cdots, k_d$.*

#### 6.2.2.2 Recursive feature elimination method

Linear $C$-SVC (Algorithm 2.3.10) can be applied directly to feature selection: Given the initial training set (6.2.1), conduct Algorithm 2.3.10 on the initial training set and obtain the normal vector of the separating hyperplane

$$w^* = (w_1^*, \cdots, w_n^*)^{\mathrm{T}}. \tag{6.2.7}$$

If the $j$-th component $w_j^* = 0$, then we remove $j$-th feature $[x]_j$, because the decision function

$$f(x) = \mathrm{sgn}\left( \sum_{i=1}^{l} w_i^* [x]_i + b^* \right) = \mathrm{sgn}\left( \sum_{i \neq j} w_i^* [x]_i + b^* \right) \tag{6.2.8}$$

does not contain the $j$-th feature. Generally, some components of $w^*$ with the small absolute value can also be removed, and feature selection is implemented. In order to remove features more efficiently, the recursive feature elimination

(RFE) method was proposed in [65]. Its basic idea is to apply Algorithm 2.3.10 and find the normal vector $w^*$ several times. Each time, remove only one feature that corresponds to the component with the smallest absolute value of $w^*$. The specific process is as follows:

**Algorithm 6.2.2** *(Recursive feature elimination method)*

*(1) Input the training set $T$ defined by (6.2.1) and the number of selected features: $d$; set $k = 0$, and construct the training set $T_0 = T$;*

*(2) Apply Algorithm 2.3.10 on the training set $T_k$, and compute the normal vector $w^*$ of the separating hyperplane. Update the training set $T_{k+1}$ by eliminating the feature with the smallest absolute value of the components of $w^*$ in $T_k$.*

*(3) If $k + 1 = n - d$, then stop; the surviving features are the ones in $T_{k+1}$; otherwise, set $k = k + 1$, and go to step (2).*

### 6.2.2.3 Methods based on $p$-norm support vector classification ($0 \leq p \leq 1$)

It has been pointed out that in linear $C$-SVC, the $j$-th feature should be removed if the corresponding $j$-th component $w_j^*$ of the normal vector $w^*$ of the separating hyperplane is zero. In order to make $w^*$ have more zero components, the primal problem (2.3.4)~(2.3.6) is modified to the following problem:

$$\min_{w,b,\xi} \quad \|w\|_p^p + C \sum_{i=1}^{l} \xi_i , \tag{6.2.9}$$

$$\text{s.t.} \quad y_i((w \cdot x_i) + b) \geq 1 - \xi_i , \ i = 1, \cdots, l , \tag{6.2.10}$$

$$\xi_i \geq 0 , \ i = 1, \cdots, l, \tag{6.2.11}$$

where $p$ is a nonnegative parameter. For the case of $p = 0$, $\|w\|_0$ represents the number of nonzero components of $w$. For $p > 0$, $\|w\|_p^p$ is the $p$-th power of $\|w\|_p$, and

$$\|w\|_p = (|w_1|^p + \cdots + |w_n|^p)^{1/p}. \tag{6.2.12}$$

For the case of $p \geq 1$, $\|w\|_p$ is the p-norm of $w$. For example, when $p = 2$, the above primal problem is reduced to the one in the standard linear SVC. Strictly speaking, $\|w\|_p$ is not a norm when $p \in (0, 1)$, but we still follow this term.

Now we show intuitively the relationship between the sparsity of the solution $w^*$ w.r.t. $w$ to the problem (6.2.9)~(6.2.11) and the value $p$. Consider the problem (6.2.9)~(6.2.11) with $n = 2$ first, and denote its solution by $(w^*, b^*, \xi^*)$, the normal vector $w^*$ can be regarded as the solution to the problem

$$\min_{w \in R^2} \quad \|w\|_p , \tag{6.2.13}$$

$$\text{s.t.} \quad y_i((w \cdot x_i) + b^*) \geq 1 - \xi_i^* , \ i = 1, \cdots, l . \tag{6.2.14}$$

Generally, the feasible region of this problem is a polyhedron without the origin in $R^n$, and $w^*$ is the minimizer of $\|w\|_p$ in this polyhedron. In order to display the changes in the contour lines

$$\|w\|_p = k \qquad (6.2.15)$$

with different $p$ values, the corresponding counters with 2,1,0.5 and 0.01 are plotted in Figure 6.2. When $p = 2$, the contour line is a smooth circle; When $p$ decreases from 2 to 1, the contour lines gradually change from a circle to a prism and cusps appear. When $p$ decreases further, the cusps become more and more pointed. Note that the solution to the problem (6.2.13)$\sim$(6.2.14) with a fixed $p$ can be obtained in the following way: start from one contour line with a small $k$ but not intersect with the feasible region; then increase the values of $k$ gradually until the corresponding contour line intersects with the feasible region; thus, the crossing point is the solution $w^*$. Intuitively speaking, when $p = 2$, the crossing point lies in anywhere of the contour line (circle) with the same probability. When $p < 1$ , the smaller $p$, the more probability that the contour lines intersect with the feasible region at the cusp, i.e. the more probability that the solution $w^*$ has a zero component since a cusp solution is the one with one zero component. We can imagine that a similar situation is also true for the problems in $R^n$ with $n \geq 3$. Therefore, we can also get the conclusion: the smaller $p$, the more spare $w^*$. Hence, selecting an appropriate $p$ can conduct feature selection. This observation leads to the following general algorithm model.

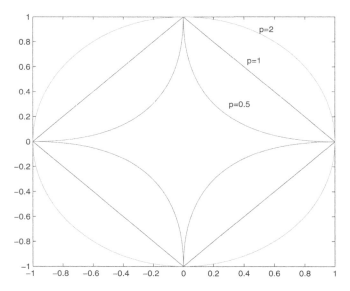

**FIGURE 6.2**: Contour lines of $\|w\|_p$ with different $p$.

**Algorithm 6.2.3** *(Feature selection based on p-norm SVC)*

*(1) Input the training set*

$$T = \{(x_1, y_1), \cdots, (x_l, y_l)\}, \tag{6.2.16}$$

*where $x_i \in R^n, y_i \in \mathcal{Y} = \{-1, 1\}, i = 1, \cdots, l$;*
*(2) Choose the parameters $p \geqslant 0$ and $C > 0$; find the solution $(w^{*T}, b^*, \xi^*) = ((w_1^*, \cdots, w_n^*)^T, \cdot, \cdot)$ to the problem (6.2.9)~(6.2.11);*
*(3) Select the feature set $\{i | w_i^* \neq 0, i = 1, \cdots, n\}$.*

Next we give some specific implementations of the above general algorithm model since there exist particular techniques for different $p$ selected.

### (1) Feature selection based on 1-norm SVC[197]

Selecting $p = 1$ in the above algorithm model (Algorithm 6.2.3) leads to the primal problem:

$$\min_{w, b, \xi} \quad \|w\|_1 + C \sum_{i=1}^{l} \xi_i, \tag{6.2.17}$$

$$\text{s.t.} \quad y_i((w \cdot x_i) + b) \geqslant 1 - \xi_i, \ i = 1, \cdots, l, \tag{6.2.18}$$

$$\xi_i \geqslant 0, \ i = 1, \cdots, l. \tag{6.2.19}$$

The objective function is not differentiable because of the absolute value in the first term: $\|w\|_1 = |w_1| + \cdots + |w_n|$. In order to eliminate the absolute value, we consider the following problem with the variable $\eta$:

$$\min \quad \eta, \tag{6.2.20}$$

$$\text{s.t.} \quad -\eta \leqslant \zeta \leqslant \eta, \tag{6.2.21}$$

where $\zeta$ is a parameter. This problem can be rewritten as:

$$\min \quad \eta, \tag{6.2.22}$$

$$\text{s.t.} \quad \eta \geqslant \zeta, \eta \geqslant -\zeta. \tag{6.2.23}$$

When $\zeta \geqslant 0$, the optimal value of the above problem is $\eta^* = \zeta$; when $\zeta \leqslant 0$, its optimal value is $\eta^* = -\zeta$. Therefore, its optimal value is $\eta^* = |\zeta|$. Furthermore, the optimal value of problem (6.2.20)~(6.2.21) is also $\eta^* = |\zeta|$. This implies that problem (6.2.17)~(6.2.19) can be transformed into the following linear programming:

$$\min_{w, b, \xi, v} \quad \sum_{i=1}^{n} v_i + C \sum_{i=1}^{l} \xi_i, \tag{6.2.24}$$

$$\text{s.t.} \quad y_i((w \cdot x_i) + b) \geqslant 1 - \xi_i, \ i = 1, \cdots, l, \tag{6.2.25}$$

$$\xi_i \geqslant 0, \ i = 1, \cdots, l, \tag{6.2.26}$$

$$-v \leqslant w \leqslant v, \tag{6.2.27}$$

where $v = (v_1, \cdots, v_n)^T$. The corresponding algorithm is summarized below.

**Algorithm 6.2.4** *(Feature selection based on 1-norm SVC)*
   *This algorithm is the same as Algorithm 6.2.3, except that step (2) is replaced by the following steps:*
   *(i) Choose the parameter $C > 0$;*
   *(ii) Find the solution $(w^{*\mathrm{T}}, b^*, \xi^*, v^*) = ((w_1^*, \cdots, w_n^*)^{\mathrm{T}}, \cdot, \cdot, \cdot)$ to the problem* (6.2.24)~(6.2.27).

**(2) Feature selection based on $p$-norm SVC $(0 < p < 1)$** [19, 26, 143, 149]
   Consider the algorithm model (Algorithm 6.2.3) with $p \in (0,1)$. Using the similar observation to problem (6.2.17)~(6.2.19), the problem (6.2.9)~(6.2.11) can be written as

$$\min_{w,b,\xi,v} \quad \sum_{i=1}^{n} v_i^p + C \sum_{i=1}^{l} \xi_i \,, \tag{6.2.28}$$

$$\text{s.t.} \quad y_i((w \cdot x_i) + b) \geqslant 1 - \xi_i \,, \ i = 1, \cdots, l \,, \tag{6.2.29}$$

$$\xi_i \geqslant 0 \,, \ i = 1, \cdots, l, \tag{6.2.30}$$

$$-v \leqslant w \leqslant v. \tag{6.2.31}$$

Introducing the first-order Taylor's expansion as the approximation of the nonlinear function:

$$v_i^p \approx \bar{v}_i^p + p\bar{v}_i^{p-1} v_i, \tag{6.2.32}$$

the problem can be solved by a successive linear approximation algorithm [19]. This leads to the algorithm below.

**Algorithm 6.2.5** *(Feature selection based on p-norm SVC $(0 < p < 1)$ )*
   *This algorithm is the same as Algorithm 6.2.3, except that step (2) is replaced by the following steps:*
   *(i) Choose the parameter $p \in (0,1)$, $C > 0$ and $\varepsilon > 0$;*
   *(ii) Start with a random choice $(w^0, b^0, \xi^0, v^0)$, and set $k = 1$;*
   *(iii) Find the solution $(w^k, b^k, \xi^k, v^k)$ to the linear programming:*

$$\min_{w,b,\xi,v} \quad p(\sum_{i=1}^{n} (v_i^{k-1})^{p-1} v_i) + C \sum_{i=1}^{l} \xi_i \,, \tag{6.2.33}$$

$$\text{s.t.} \quad y_i((w \cdot x_i) + b) \geqslant 1 - \xi_i \,, \ i = 1, \cdots, l \,, \tag{6.2.34}$$

$$\xi_i \geqslant 0 \,, \ i = 1, \cdots, l, \tag{6.2.35}$$

$$-v \leqslant w \leqslant v. \tag{6.2.36}$$

*(iv) If $|p \sum_{i=1}^{n} (v_i^k)^{p-1}(v_i^k - v_i^{k-1}) + C \sum_{i=1}^{l} (\xi_i^k - \xi_i^{k-1})| > \varepsilon$, then set $k = k+1$, and go to step (ii); otherwise stop, and set $w^* = w^k$.*

### (3) Feature selection based on 0-norm SVC[18]

Considering the algorithm model (Algorithm 6.2.3) with $p = 0$, we need to solve the problem (6.2.9)~(6.2.11). In order to compute $\|w\|_0$, introduce two transformations from $R^n$ to $R^n$

$$|\cdot|: \quad w = (w_1, \cdots, w_n)^{\mathrm{T}} \to |w| = (|w_1|, \cdots, |w_n|)^{\mathrm{T}} \qquad (6.2.37)$$

and

$$(\cdot)_*: \quad w = (w_1, \cdots, w_n)^{\mathrm{T}} \to w_* = (w_{*1}, \cdots, w_{*n})^{\mathrm{T}}, \qquad (6.2.38)$$

where

$$w_{*i} = \begin{cases} 1, & \text{when } w_i > 0; \\ 0, & \text{otherwise.} \end{cases} \qquad (6.2.39)$$

Then, we have $\|w\|_0 = e^{\mathrm{T}}|w|_*$. Therefore, problem (6.2.9)~(6.2.11) with $p = 0$ can be rewritten as

$$\min_{w,b,\xi} \quad e^{\mathrm{T}}|w|_* + C \sum_{i=1}^{l} \xi_i , \qquad (6.2.40)$$

$$\text{s.t.} \quad y_i((w \cdot x_i) + b) \geqslant 1 - \xi_i , \ i = 1, \cdots, l , \qquad (6.2.41)$$

$$\xi_i \geqslant 0 , \ i = 1, \cdots, l. \qquad (6.2.42)$$

Eliminating the absolute value in the above problem using the similar observation to the problem (6.2.17)~(6.2.19), we get the equivalent problem

$$\min_{w,b,\xi,v} \quad e^{\mathrm{T}}v_* + C \sum_{i=1}^{l} \xi_i , \qquad (6.2.43)$$

$$\text{s.t.} \quad y_i((w \cdot x_i) + b) \geqslant 1 - \xi_i , \ i = 1, \cdots, l , \qquad (6.2.44)$$

$$\xi_i \geqslant 0 , \ i = 1, \cdots, l. \qquad (6.2.45)$$

$$-v \leqslant w \leqslant v, \qquad (6.2.46)$$

where $v_* = (v_{*1}, \cdots, v_{*n})^{\mathrm{T}}$ is the image of $v = (v_1, \cdots, v_n)^{\mathrm{T}}$ under the transformation (6.2.38)~(6.2.39), i.e., for $i = 1, \cdots, n$,

$$v_{*i} = \begin{cases} 1, & \text{when } v_i > 0; \\ 0, & \text{otherwise.} \end{cases} \qquad (6.2.47)$$

Note that $v_{*i}$ is still the non-smooth function of $v_i$. So we introduce a smooth function as the approximation of $v_{*i}$. Since the constraint (6.2.46) implies $v_i \geqslant 0$, we only need to consider the case $v_i \in [0, \infty)$. It is easy to see that when $\alpha$ is large enough, we have

$$v_{*i} \approx t(v_i, \alpha) = 1 - \exp(-\alpha v_i), \quad i = 1, \cdots, n, \qquad (6.2.48)$$

see Figure 6.3, where the function $t(v_i, \alpha)$ with different values of $\alpha$ are plotted.

Replacing the corresponding component of $v_*$ in the objective function of the problem $(6.2.43)\sim(6.2.46)$ by the right hand of $(6.2.48)$, a smooth problem is given as follows:

$$\min_{w,b,\xi,v} \quad e^{\mathrm{T}}\left(e - \exp(-\alpha v)\right) + C\sum_{i=1}^{l}\xi_i, \tag{6.2.49}$$

$$\text{s.t.} \quad y_i((w \cdot x_i) + b) \geqslant 1 - \xi_i , \ i = 1, \cdots, l, \tag{6.2.50}$$

$$\xi_i \geqslant 0 , \ i = 1, \cdots, l, \tag{6.2.51}$$

$$-v \leqslant w \leqslant v, \tag{6.2.52}$$

where

$$\exp(-\alpha v) = (\exp(-\alpha v_1), \cdots, \exp(-\alpha v_n))^{\mathrm{T}}. \tag{6.2.53}$$

It can be expected to find an approximate solution to the problem

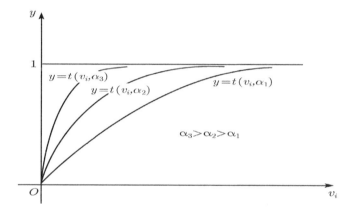

**FIGURE 6.3**: Function $t(v_i, \alpha)$ with different $\alpha$.

$(6.2.40)\sim(6.2.42)$ by solving the problem $(6.2.49)\sim(6.2.53)$ when $\alpha$ is large enough. This leads to the following algorithm.

**Algorithm 6.2.6** *(Feature selection based on 0-norm SVC)*
*This algorithm is the same as Algorithm 6.2.3, except that step (2) is replaced by the following steps:*
*(i) Choose the parameter $C > 0$ and the large number $\alpha$;*
*(ii) Find the solution $(w^{*\mathrm{T}}, b^*, \xi^*, v^*) = ((w_1^*, \cdots, w_n^*)^{\mathrm{T}}, \cdot, \cdot, \cdot)$ to the problem $(6.2.49)\sim(6.2.53)$.*

In the above Algorithm 6.2.4~Algorithm 6.2.6, only a single $p$-norm appears. However a combination of different norms, such as the mixture of 0-norm and 2-norm, is also a reasonable choice, see [167].

### 6.2.3   Feature extraction

Feature selection is to reduce the dimension of input space by removing some features. Feature extraction is also to reduce the dimension. However, unlike feature selection, it is conducted by transforming the input space $R^n$ to a low dimensional space $R^d$. So, feature extraction can be regarded as an extension of feature selection.

In the following, we introduce two types of feature extraction: linear dimensionality reduction and nonlinear dimensionality reduction.

#### 6.2.3.1   Linear dimensionality reduction

Linear dimensionality reduction is to transform $x$ in the input space $R^n$ into $\tilde{x}$ in the low dimensional space $R^d$ by the linear transformation:

$$\tilde{x} = Vx + u, \qquad (6.2.54)$$

where $V$ is a $d \times n$ matrix. There are numerous algorithms for linear dimensionality reduction including principle component analysis (PCA)[70], multidimensional scaling (MDS)[23,49,74], linear discriminate analysis (LDA)[113], independent component analysis (ICA)[23,47], nonnegative matrix factorization (NMF)[75] and so forth.

In this subsection, we provide an intuitive introduction to the classical method — PCA. Suppose we have an initial training set

$$T = \{(x_1, y_1), \cdots, (x_l, y_l)\}, \qquad (6.2.55)$$

where $x_i \in R^n$, $y_i \in \mathcal{Y} = \{1, -1\}, i = 1, \cdots, l$ and a new input $x$ to be classified. Construct the set

$$I = \{x_0, x_1, \cdots, x_l\}, \qquad (6.2.56)$$

where $x_0 = x$. A geometric interpretation of PCA is given in Figure 6.4, where the inputs in the set $I$ are the two-dimensional vectors and shown by the points in the plane $[x]_1 O[x]_2$ in Figure 6.4(a). Clearly, most of these points are close to a straight line $l$ through the origin. This implies that if these points in $[x]_1 O[x]_2$ are projected onto the straight line $l$, then the projections can be an approximate expression of the initial points. So, the two-dimensional inputs in Figure 6.4(a) can be replaced by the one-dimensional inputs on the straight line $l$ in Figure 6.4(b), i.e. the dimension of the input space is reduced from 2 to 1.

Based on the above geometric interpretation, we can imagine that in order to realize the dimension extraction, the inputs in $R^n$ should be projected onto a low-dimensional space $R^d$ such that the variance among the inputs in the subspace $R^d$ is large and the variance among the inputs beyond this subspace is small. This procedure is implemented as follows:

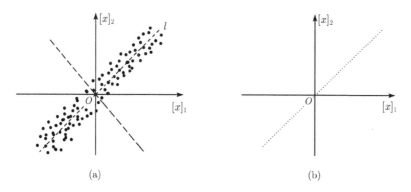

**FIGURE 6.4**: Principal component analysis.

**Algorithm 6.2.7** *(Principle component analysis)*

*(1) Input the initial training set $T$ defined by (6.2.55), a new input $x$, and the required dimension after dimensionality reduction: $d$, where $d < n$;*

*(2) Construct the set $I$ given by (6.2.56), and calculate its covariance matrix*

$$\Sigma = \frac{1}{l+1} \sum_{i=0}^{l} (x_i - \overline{x})(x_i - \overline{x})^{\mathrm{T}}, \qquad (6.2.57)$$

*where $\overline{x} = \dfrac{1}{l+1} \sum\limits_{i=0}^{l} x_i$;*

*(3) For the matrix $\sum$, compute its $d$ orthonormal eigenvectors $v_1, v_2, \cdots, v_d$ corresponding to $d$ largest eigenvalues;*

*(4) Construct the projective matrix $V = [v_1, v_2, \cdots, v_d]$;*

*(5) Computes*

$$\tilde{x}_i = V^{\mathrm{T}}(x_i - \overline{x}), \quad i = 0, 1, \cdots, l. \qquad (6.2.58)$$

*The $d$-dimensional vectors $\tilde{x}_0$ and $\tilde{x}_1, \cdots, \tilde{x}_l$ are the vectors after dimensionality reduction, corresponding to $x$ and $x_1, \cdots, x_l$ respectively.*

### 6.2.3.2  Nonlinear dimensionality reduction

The linear dimensionality reduction is limited to the linear or approximately linear structure of data. To deal with the nonlinear structure of data, many popular methods for nonlinear dimensionality reduction have been proposed, such as neural network, genetic algorithm, and manifold learning. Manifold learning has attracted a great deal of attention of the researchers in recent years [77, 7, 8, 67, 68, 123, 125, 145].

In the following, we provide a brief introduction to one of the manifold learning methods — locally linear embedding (LLE) [123]. Same to PCA, the set $I$ is constructed by the initial training set (6.2.55) and the input $x$ to be predicted, i.e.

$$I = \{x_0, x_1, \cdots, x_l\}, \tag{6.2.59}$$

where $x_0 = x$ and the inputs in the above set $I$ are vectors with high dimension. Suppose that these inputs lie on or close to a smooth nonlinear manifold with low dimension and any input can approximately be represented by the linear combination of inputs in its neighborhood. A toy example is given in Figure 6.5, where most inputs expressed by dots in two-dimensional space close to a one-dimensional curve, and any input, say $\bar{x}$, can be represented by the linear combination of three points in its neighborhood. LLE constructs a mapping that can preserve the neighborhood relations. More precisely, this mapping can not only map the original high-dimensional data into a global coordinate system of low dimension, but also maintain the linear combination as possible as it can. This adjacent properties is implemented through the overlapping of the neighborhoods. The algorithm is summarized as follows.

**Algorithm 6.2.8** *(Locally linear embedding)*

*(1) Input the training set $T$ defined by (6.2.55), a new input $x$, and dimension after dimensionality reduction: $d$, where $d < n$; Construct the set $I$ defined by (6.2.56);*

*(2) Assign the neighbor set $S_i$ to each input $x_i$, $i = 0, 1, \cdots, l$;*

*(3) For $i = 0, 1, \cdots, l$, construct the problems*

$$\min_{w_i \in R^{l+1}} \left\| x_i - \sum_{j=0}^{l} w_{ij} x_j \right\|^2, \tag{6.2.60}$$

$$\text{s.t.} \quad \sum_{j=0}^{l} w_{ij} = 1, \; w_{ii} = 0, \tag{6.2.61}$$

$$w_{ij} = 0, \text{for } x_j \notin S_i, j = 0, 1, \cdots, l, \tag{6.2.62}$$

*where $w_i = (w_{i0}, \cdots, w_{il})^{\mathrm{T}}$; Find its solution $w_i^*$, and construct the $(l+1) \times (l+1)$ matrix $W^* = (w_0^*, \cdots, w_l^*)$;*

*(4) Construct the problem:*

$$\min_{\tilde{X}} \left\| (I - W^{*T}) \tilde{X}^T \right\|^2, \tag{6.2.63}$$

$$\text{s.t.} \quad \sum_{i=0}^{l} \tilde{x}_i = 0, \tag{6.2.64}$$

$$\frac{1}{l} \sum_{i=0}^{l} \tilde{x}_i \tilde{x}_i^{\mathrm{T}} = \tilde{I}, \tag{6.2.65}$$

where $\tilde{X} = (\tilde{x}_0, \tilde{x}_1 \cdots, \tilde{x}_l) \in R^{d \times (l+1)}$, $I$ and $\tilde{I}$ are $(l+1) \times (l+1)$ and $d \times d$ identity matrix respectively, and $\| \cdot \|$ is the Frobenius norm; find its solution $(\tilde{x}_0^*, \tilde{x}_1^*, \cdots, \tilde{x}_l^*)$. Then the $d$-dimensional vectors $\tilde{x}_0^*$, $\tilde{x}_1^*, \cdots, \tilde{x}_l^*$ are the vectors after dimensionality reduction, corresponding to $x$, $x_1, \cdots, x_l$ respectively.

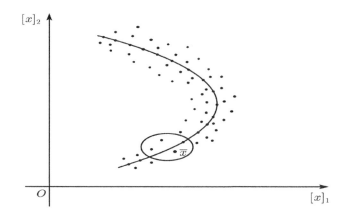

**FIGURE 6.5**: Locally linear embedding.

Now we show some explanations for the above algorithm: the neighbor set $S_i$ can be obtained, for example, by using $K$ nearest neighbors to find the $K$ closest inputs to $x_i$. Two optimization problems appeared in the above algorithm. The variables $w_{ij}(j = 0, 1, \cdots, l)$ in the problem $(6.2.60) \sim (6.2.62)$ summarize the contribution of the $j$-th input to the $i$-th reconstruction. The constraint $(6.2.62)$ requires that each input $x_i$ is reconstructed only from its neighbors. Now we rewrite the objective function $(6.2.60)$. Representing the column vector $x_i - displaystyle \sum_{j=0}^{l} w_{ij} x_j$ as the row vector and putting these vectors as together from top to bottom, we have

$$\begin{pmatrix} x_0^{\mathrm{T}} \\ \vdots \\ x_l^{\mathrm{T}} \end{pmatrix} - \begin{pmatrix} w_0^{\mathrm{T}} \\ \vdots \\ w_l^{\mathrm{T}} \end{pmatrix} \begin{pmatrix} x_0^{\mathrm{T}} \\ \vdots \\ x_l^{\mathrm{T}} \end{pmatrix} = (I - W^{\mathrm{T}}) X^{\mathrm{T}}, \qquad (6.2.66)$$

where $I$ is the $(l+1) \times (l+1)$ identity matrix, and $W = (w_0, \cdots, w_l)$, $X = (x_0, \cdots, x_l)$. Thus the objective functions $(6.2.60)$ with $i = 0, 1, \cdots, l$ can be summarized as:

$$\min \|(I - W^{\mathrm{T}}) X^{\mathrm{T}}\|^2, \qquad (6.2.67)$$

where $\| \cdot \|$ is the Frobenius norm of matrix. It is easy to see that the objective functions in $(6.2.63)$ and $(6.2.67)$ are very similar in form. Solving the problem $(6.2.60) \sim (6.2.62)$ is to compute the weight matrix $W^*$ from $X = (x_0, \cdots, x_l)$, while solving the problem (6.2.63)~(6.2.65) is to compute the low-dimensional embedding inputs $\tilde{X} = (\tilde{x}_0, \tilde{x}_1 \cdots, \tilde{x}_l)$ from the weight matrix $W^*$. This is the basic idea of LLE. The constraints (6.2.64) and (6.2.65) imply some restrictions on the inputs after dimensionality reduction. The former requires the inputs to be centered to the origin, and the letter requires the inputs to be stretched as far as possible in order to avoid the degenerate solutions.

Note that there are some differences between the feature extraction methods introduced here and the feature selection methods introduced in Section 6.2.2: (i) In feature selection, the inputs and outputs of training points are used, whereas in feature extraction, only the inputs of training points are used; (ii) in feature selection, only the training points are used, whereas; in feature extraction, both of the inputs of training points $x_1, \cdots, x_l$ and the input $x$ to be predicted are used.

### 6.2.4   Data compression

When we are given too many amounts of points in an initial training set, some techniques of data compression are required. One popular method is clustering. We first introduce one of the formulations of clustering problem.

**Clustering problem**: Given the set $X = \{x_1, \cdots, x_l\} \subset R^n$ and an integer $K > 0$, clustering is the task of assigning the points in $X$ into $K$ groups (called clusters): $S_1, S_2, \cdots, S_K$, so that every point in $X$ belongs in one and only one class, and points in the same cluster are close to each other but are far apart from points in other clusters.

There exists a large number of clustering algorithms in the literature ([13, 80]). We introduce only one popular method here — $K$-means clustering. Its basic idea is as follows: Select $K$ points as $K$ cluster centers and assign each point in $X$ to one of the clusters $S_1, S_2, \cdots, S_K$ based on the distance between the point and the cluster center. Then update the cluster centers by recalculating the mean value of each cluster. Relative to these new centers, points are redistributed to the clusters. This process is iterated until the following squared-error function is minimized:

$$E = \sum_{j=1}^{K} \sum_{x_i \in S_j} ||x_i - z_j||^2, \qquad (6.2.68)$$

where $z_j$ is the center of cluster $S_j$.

The $K$-means clustering is summarized as follows.

**Algorithm 6.2.9** *(K-means Clustering)*

*(1) Input the set $X = \{x_1, \cdots, x_l\}$ in $R^n$ and the number of clusters: $K$. Select $\varepsilon > 0$ and set $m = 0$. Arbitrarily choose $K$ points from $X$ as the initial cluster centers: $z_1^m, \cdots, z_K^m$; for example, select the points $x_1, \cdots, x_K$ as the initial cluster centers;*

*(2) Denote by $S_j^m$ the set of the j-th cluster. For $k = 1, \cdots, l$, we assign the point $x_k$ to the cluster $S_j^m$ based on the distance between $x_k$ and $z_j^m$, i.e. if $||x_k - z_j^m|| \leq ||x_k - z_i^m||$, $i = 1, \cdots, K$, then assign $x_k$ to the cluster $S_j^m$;*

*(3) Compute the new cluster centers:*

$$z_j^m = \frac{1}{n_j} \sum_{x_i \in S_j^m} x_i, \quad j = 1, 2, \cdots, K, \tag{6.2.69}$$

*where $n_j$ is the number of points in the cluster $S_j^m$;*

*(4) Compute the squared-error function:*

$$E_m = \sum_{j=1}^{K} \sum_{x_i \in S_j^m} ||x_i - z_j^m||^2; \tag{6.2.70}$$

*(5) If $m > 0$ and $|E_{m-1} - E_m| < \varepsilon$, then set $S_j = S_j^m$, $z_j = z_j^m$, $j = 1, \cdots, K$, and stop; otherwise, set $m = m + 1$, and go to step (2).*

Given a set $X$ in $R^n$ and the number of clusters: $K$, the $K$-means clustering algorithm assigns the points in $X$ into $K$ clusters: $S_1, \cdots, S_K$, and finds the centers of these clusters: $z_1, \cdots, z_K$.

**Example 6.2.10** *Consider a clustering problem in $R^2$. Given the set composed of the square points depicted in Figure 6.6(a). Group these points into two clusters by K-means clustering.*

*Firstly, we arbitrarily choose two points as two initial cluster centers shown in Figure 6.6(a). Secondly, each point is distributed to a cluster based on the cluster center to which it is the nearest. Such a distribution forms silhouettes encircled by curves. The cluster centers are updated, and marked by "$*$", as shown in Figure 6.6(b). This process iterates for two times, leading to Figure 6.6(c) and (d).*

Now let us return to the data compression of the initial training set by $K$-means clustering algorithm [98, 176]. Suppose that there are $l_+$ positive inputs and $l_-$ negative inputs in the initial training set, respectively, and it is required to reduce the numbers $l_+$ and $l_-$ to $K_+$ and $K_-$ respectively. Then $K$-means clustering algorithm with the cluster numbers $K_+$ and $K_-$ are used in the $l_+$ positive inputs and the $l_-$ negative inputs respectively, yielding $K_+$ positive cluster centers and $K_-$ negative cluster centers. These cluster centers with suitable labels would be the training points in the training set to be used in the SVM framework. So the initial training set is compressed by clustering.

## 6.2.5 Data rebalancing

SVMs are limited in their performance when the difference between the numbers of positive and negative training points is too large. So in order to

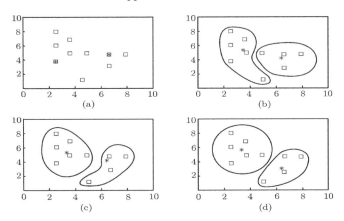

**FIGURE 6.6**: Clustering of a set based on $K$-means method.

reduce the difference, many methods have been proposed [69]. We introduce two of them below.

The first method is rebalancing the imbalanced training sets directly as follows.

**Algorithm 6.2.11** *(Rebalancing method based on support vectors)*

*(1) Input the initial training set*

$$T = T^+ \cup T^-, \tag{6.2.71}$$

*where $T^+$ and $T^-$ are positive set and negative set respectively, defined as*

$$\begin{align}
T^+ &= \{(x_1, y_1), \cdots, (x_p, y_p)\}, \tag{6.2.72}\\
T^- &= \{(x_{p+1}, y_{p+1}), \cdots, (x_{p+q}, y_{p+q})\}, \tag{6.2.73}
\end{align}$$

*where $x_i \in R^n, i = 1, \cdots, p+q, y_1 = \cdots = y_p = 1, y_{p+1} = \cdots = y_{p+q} = -1$, and $q \gg p$, which implies that the negative class is the majority class, and the positive class is the minority class. Set $k = 1, T_k = T$, $g_0 = 0$, $T_0^-$ to be the empty set;*

*(2) For the training set $T_k$, solve the dual problem (4.3.1)$\sim$(4.3.3) in Algorithm 4.3.1 (C-Support Vector Classification) and obtain its solution $\alpha^{k*}$. Construct the new negative set: $T_{sv}^- = \{(x_i, y_i) | x_i \text{ is the support vector, } y_i = -1\}$. Set $T_k^- = T_{k-1}^- \cup T_{sv}^-$;*

*(3) Set $\tilde{T}_k = T_k^- \cup T^+$. For the training set $\tilde{T}_k$, use the Algorithm 4.3.1 (C-Support Vector Classification), and obtain the decision function $f_k$; calculate the evaluation value $g_k$ of $f_k$ for the initial training set $T$;*

*(4) If $g_k \leq g_{k-1}$, then stop, and $\tilde{T}_{k-1}$ is the balanced training set; otherwise, let $T_{k+1} = T_k \backslash T_k^-, k = k + 1$, go to step (2).*

In step (3), an evaluation value of the decision functions is needed. A possible choice is the one of the accuracy measures given in next Section 6.3, e.g. $G$-mean value defined by (6.3.10).

The above algorithm can not only find a balanced training set, but also a decision function. In fact, if the algorithm is stopped at $k$-th iteration, the decision dinction $f_{k-1}$ is recommented for future classification.

The second method is based on ensemble [87, 163]. For the imbalanced classification problem, we first construct several balanced training sets by bootstrap, and then the corresponding decision functions are trained. At last, these decision functions are aggregated to make the final decision function. The corresponding algorithm is as follows:

**Algorithm 6.2.12** *(Ensemble method with bootstrap )*

*(1) Input the training set (6.2.71)$\sim$(6.2.73);*

*(2) Choose an integer $K$: the number of training sets with balanced classes;*

*(3) Bootstrapping builds $K$ replicate negative training sets: $T_1^-, \cdots, T_k^-$ by randomly re-sampling, but with replacement, from the initial training set (6.2.71)$\sim$(6.2.73) repeatedly;*

*(4) Construct $K$ training sets $T_k = T^+ \cup T_k^-, k = 1, \cdots, K$.*

*(5) Apply $C$-SVC on the training sets $T_k$ respectively, $k = 1, \cdots, K$, obtaining $K$ decision functions, named basic decision functions.*

*(6) The final decision function is given by the combination of $K$ basic decision functions. More precisely, if the outputs of basic decision function are 1 or $-1$, the output of the final decision function can be obtained by the majority voting; if the outputs of basic decision functions are the probabilities, the output is the mean of all probabilities[175].*

---

## 6.3 Model Selection

The performance of $C$-SVC models strongly depends on a proper setting of kernels and parameters. The main purpose of this section is to show a way to select kernels and parameters. Evaluating the effectiveness of a kernel and parameters is concerned with evaluating the accuracy of an algorithm.

### 6.3.1 Algorithm evaluation

In order to estimate the accuracy of an algorithm, we introduce some evaluation measures for a decision function firstly.

#### 6.3.1.1  Some evaluation measures for a decision function

Suppose that we have a testing set:

$$\tilde{T} = \{(\tilde{x}_1, \tilde{y}_1), \cdots, (\tilde{x}_{\tilde{l}}, \tilde{y}_{\tilde{l}})\}, \tag{6.3.1}$$

where $(\tilde{x}_i, \tilde{y}_i)$ are testing points, $\tilde{x}_i \in R^n, \tilde{y}_i \in \mathcal{Y} = \{-1, 1\}, i = 1, \cdots, \tilde{l}$. Suppose also that the 0-1 loss function is used and the decision function is in the form

$$f(x) = \text{sgn}(g(x)), \tag{6.3.2}$$

obtained by Algorithm 4.3.1 of Chapter 4, or in the form

$$f(x, cutoff) = \begin{cases} 1, & \text{when } g(x) \geqslant \text{cutoff}; \\ -1, & \text{otherwise}, \end{cases} \tag{6.3.3}$$

considered in Remark 4.3.2 of Chapter 4, where $g(x)$ is a given function. Thus some evaluation measures can be proposed as follows.

**(1) Accuracy rate $A_c$**

For a decision function in the form (6.3.2), the accuracy rate $A_c$ is the percentage of testing points in testing set $\tilde{T}$ that are correctly classified by $f(x)$. We can also introduce the error rate, which is simply $1 - A_c$.

The accuracy rate and the error rate take values in $[0, 1]$. Usually, a high accuracy rate or a low error rate may correspond to a good decision. However, they are not enough to judge a decision function, especially for the imbalanced testing sets. For example, suppose that the numbers of positive points and negative points in testing set $\tilde{T}$ are 100 and 900 respectively, and the following decision function

$$f(x) = -1 \tag{6.3.4}$$

is examined. The accuracy rate is $\dfrac{900}{100 + 900} = 90\%$. However, this decision function is not acceptable. So, we also need other evaluation measures.

**(2) MCC**

For a decision function in the form (6.3.2), the Matthew Correlation Coefficient (MCC) is defined as:

$$\text{MCC} = \frac{t_p \times t_n - f_n \times f_p}{\{(t_p + f_n) \times (t_n + f_p) \times (t_p + f_p) \times (t_n + f_n)\}^{1/2}}, \tag{6.3.5}$$

where $t_p, f_n, f_p,$ and $t_n$ are the number of true positives (the positive inputs that are correctly classified by $f(x)$), false negatives (the positive inputs that are incorrectly classified by $f(x)$), false positives (the negative inputs that are incorrectly classified by $f(x)$), and true negatives (the negative inputs that are correctly classified by $f(x)$) respectively.

Obviously, when all of testing points in testing set $\tilde{T}$ are incorrectly classified by the decision function, MCC is $-1$; MCC is 1 when all are correctly classified. So, the MCC takes values in $[-1, 1]$, and the bigger the better. Different from the accuracy rate $A_c$, MCC is an appropriate measure for imbalanced sets. For example, for any testing sets and the decision function shown by (6.3.4), the MCC always is zero because $t_p = f_p = 0$ even for the heavily imbalanced testing sets.

**(3) True positive rate $r_{tp}$, false negative rate $r_{fn}$, false positive rate $r_{fp}$, true negative rate $r_{tn}$, and $G$-mean value**

For the decision function in the form (6.3.2), using the four numbers $t_p, f_n, f_p$, and $t_n$ appeared in (6.3.5), we propose the following measures further:

True positive rate $r_{tp}$ is the proportion of positive inputs that are correctly classified, defined by

$$r_{tp} = t_p/(t_p + f_n), \tag{6.3.6}$$

that is also referred to as the sensitivity.

False negative rate $r_{fn}$ is the proportion of positive inputs that are incorrectly classified, defined by

$$r_{fn} = f_n/(t_p + f_n); \tag{6.3.7}$$

False positive rate $r_{fp}$ is the proportion of negative inputs that are incorrectly classified, defined by

$$r_{fp} = f_p/(f_p + t_n); \tag{6.3.8}$$

True negative rate $r_{tn}$ is the proportion of negative inputs that are correctly classified, defined by

$$r_{tn} = t_n/(f_p + t_n), \tag{6.3.9}$$

that is also referred to as the specificity.

Ideally, both the true positive rate $r_{tp}$ and true negative rate $r_{tn}$ should be 1, and the bigger the better; both the false negative rate $r_{fn}$ and false positive rate $r_{fp}$ should be 0, and the smaller the better.

Note that it is not suitable to evaluate a decision function if only one measure, say $r_{fp}$, of the above four measures is used. However, a pair of them, say $(r_{fp}, r_{tp})$ may be useful. In fact, for two decision functions $f_1$ and $f_2$, if their $r_{fp}$ and $r_{tp}$ values satisfy that $r_{fp}^1 < r_{fp}^2$ and $r_{tp}^1 > r_{tp}^2$, then $f_1$ is superior to $f_2$. But it is true that if $r_{fp}^1 < r_{fp}^2$ and $r_{tp}^1 < r_{tp}^2$, then we can say nothing. So a reasonable way is to propose a new measure by combining $r_{fp}$ and $r_{tp}$, e.g. the $G$-mean value, which is the geometric mean of true positive rate $r_{tp}$ and true negative rate $r_{tn}$, i.e.

$$G - mean = \sqrt{r_{tp} \cdot r_{tn}}. \tag{6.3.10}$$

This measure was proposed in [144] for imbalanced testing sets.

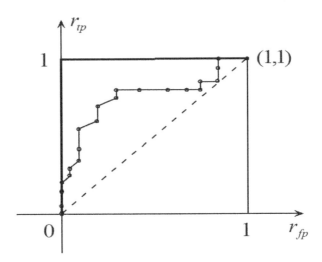

**FIGURE 6.7**: ROC curve.

### (4) ROC curve and AUC

Now we are concerned with the decision function $f(x, cutoff)$ with a parameter *cutoff* in the form (6.3.3). Consider the pair $(r_{fp}, r_{tp})$ defined by (6.3.8) and (6.3.6) and describe it by a plot of $r_{tp}$ versus $r_{fp}$. Clearly, the point $(r_{fp}, r_{tp})$ depends on the cutoff level. When the cutoff level increases from $-\infty$ to $+\infty$, the point $(r_{fp}, r_{tp})$ moves from $(1,1)$ to $(0,0)$. The receiver operating characteristic (ROC) curve is constructed by connecting all points obtained at all the possible cutoff levels (see Figure 6.7).

The ROC curve corresponds to a monotone nondecreasing function through the points $(0,0)$ and $(1,1)$ and can be used to evaluate the performance of a decision function $f(x; cutoff)$. Suppose there are two decision functions $f_1(x, cutoff)$ and $f_2(x, cutoff)$. We say that $f_1(x, cutoff)$ is better than $f_2(x, cutoff)$ if the ROC curve of $f_1(x, cutoff)$ is above the ROC curve of $f_2(x, cutoff)$ because this implies that the $r_{tp}$ value of $f_1(x, cutoff)$ is greater than that of $f_2(x, cutoff)$ when their $r_{fp}$ values are the same. The ideal ROC curve of $f(x; cutoff)$ is the broken line from the point $(0,0)$ to $(0,1)$ then $(1,1)$(the bold line shown in Figure 6.7).

The area under the ROC curve (AUC) is an important measure of the accuracy of a decision function in the form (6.3.3). A decision function with perfect accuracy will have an AUC of 1. The bigger the AUC, the more accurate the decision function.

### 6.3.1.2 Some evaluation measures for a concrete algorithm

Now we are concerned with a concrete classification algorithm — a completely determined algorithm, e.g. Algorithm 4.3.1 where the kernel and all parameters have been selected. Our aim is to evaluate a concrete classification algorithm and establish some evaluation measures. It is true that all measures corresponding to the evaluation measures for a decision function proposed above can be considered. However, to save the space, only the one corresponding to the accuracy rate $A_c$ is discussed here. Suppose that, for a given concrete classification algorithm, we have a training set

$$T = \{(x_1, y_1), \cdots, (x_l, y_l)\}, \tag{6.3.11}$$

where $x_i \in R^n$, $y_i \in \mathcal{Y} = \{1, -1\}(i = 1, \cdots, l)$. In order to establish an evaluation measure, the most natural way may be the following approach: first, using the set (6.3.11) as the training set, construct a decision function by the concrete algorithm; then, using the set (6.3.11) again as the testing set, calculate the accuracy rate $A_c$ of the decision function obtained; last, take the accuracy rate $A_c$ obtained as the evaluation measure of the concrete algorithm.

However, this approach suffers from a fatal flaw: the decision function depends on the testing set. The following example shows that it is not reasonable that the testing set is used when the decision function is constructed. Suppose that the training set (6.3.11) is also taken as the testing set. If the set (6.3.11) does not have the conflicting points, i.e., for $i, j = 1, \cdots, l$, if $x_i = x_j$, then $y_i = y_j$, then we are able to define directly a decision function:

$$\bar{f}(x) = \begin{cases} y_i, & x = x_i ; \\ 1, & x \neq x_i. \end{cases} \tag{6.3.12}$$

Obviously, it can classify all the testing inputs correctly and the accuracy rate $A_c$ arrives at the optimal value 1. However, it is absolutely not a good decision function since it is completely useless.

Note that, for a decision function $f(x)$, what we are concerned with is whether any other inputs $\bar{x}$ instead of the inputs in the training set can be correctly classified by $f(\bar{x})$. So, a testing set should be independent from the training set. In other words, in the process of constructing the decision function, we cannot use any information about the testing set. This consideration leads to the following strategy when the training set (6.3.11) is given: instead of using this set as the training set and testing set directly, we partition it into two subsets: one as the training set and the other as the testing set.

$k$-fold cross-validation is an implementation of the above strategy. In $k$-fold cross-validation, the training set is randomly partitioned into $k$ mutually exclusive subsets or "folds", $S_1, S_2, \cdots, S_k$, each of approximately equal size. Training and testing are performed $k$ iterations. In the $i$-th iteration, the $i$-th fold $S_i$ is reserved as the testing set, and the remaining folds

$S_1, \cdots, S_{i-1}, S_{i+1}, \cdots, S_k$ collectively serve as the training set used to find a decision function, which is tested on $S_i$.

Now we turn to derive an evaluation measure of a concrete classification algorithm. The combination of $k$-fold cross-validation and accuracy rate $A_c$ yields the following evaluation measure, called $k$-fold validation accuracy rate, defined as follows:

Partition the training set (6.3.11) into $k$ folds: $S_1, S_2, \cdots, S_k$, denote by $l_i$ the number of inputs in the $i$-th fold $S_i$ correctly classified. After $k$ iterations, we have $l_1, \cdots, l_k$. The overall number $\sum_{i=1}^{k} l_i$ divided by the total number $l$ of the training points is

$$\sum_{i=1}^{k} \frac{l_i}{l}. \tag{6.3.13}$$

We call it the $k$-fold cross-validation accuracy. This can be considered as an estimator of the accuracy of a concrete classification algorithm. The corresponding error rate $1 - \sum_{i=1}^{k} \frac{l_i}{l}$ can also be used. That is the overall number of inputs incorrectly classified, divided by the total number of the training points. We call it the $k$-fold cross-validation error.

The above $k$-fold cross-validation errors with $k = l$ or $k = 10$ are two commonly used evaluation measures: $l$-fold cross-validation error and ten-fold cross-validation error. In $l$-fold cross-validation, the training sets consists of $l - 1$ points by leaving one point out at a time for the testing set. This is commonly referred to as the leave-one-out (LOO). The cross-validation accuracy defined by (6.3.13) and the corresponding error are referred to as LOO accuracy and LOO error respectively. The formal definition of LOO error is as follows:

**Definition 6.3.1** *(LOO error) Consider the training set*

$$T = \{(x_1, y_1), \cdots, (x_l, y_l)\}, \tag{6.3.14}$$

*where $x_i \in R^n, y_i \in \mathcal{Y} = \{-1, 1\}$. Denote by $f_{T^i}$ the decision function obtained by a concrete classification algorithm, given the training set $T^i = T \setminus \{(x_i, y_i)\}$ i.e., remove the $i$-th point from $T$. Then the LOO error of the concrete classification algorithm on the training set $T$, or LOO error for short, is defined as*

$$R_{\text{LOO}}(T) = \frac{1}{l} \sum_{i=1}^{l} c(x_i, y_i, f_{T_i}(x_i)) \tag{6.3.15}$$

*where $c(x, y, f(x)$ is $0 - 1$ loss function.*

The following theorem shows that the LOO error is very close to the expected risk.

**Theorem 6.3.2** *Denote by $P(x, y)$ a distribution over $R^n \times \mathcal{Y}$, and by $T_l$ and $T_{l-1}$ training sets of size $l$ and $l-1$ respectively, drawn i.i.d. from $P(x, y)$. Moreover, denote by $R[f_{T_{l-1}}]$ the expected risk of a decision function derived from the training set $T_{l-1}$ by a concrete classification algorithm. Then, for this concrete classification algorithm, the LOO error $R_{LOO}(T_l)$ and the expected risk $R[f_{T_{l-1}}]$ satisfy:*

$$E_{T_{l-1}}[R[f_{T_{l-1}}]] = E_{T_l}[R_{LOO}(T_l)], \tag{6.3.16}$$

*where $E_T$ is the mathematical expectation.*

Theorem 6.3.2 shows that LOO error is an almost unbiased estimator of the expected risk (The term "almost" refers to the fact that the LOO error provides an estimate for training on sets $T_l$ and $T_{l-1}$ rather than $T$). Hence, we should consider it as a reliable estimator of the expected risk. This theorem provides us with the theoretical foundation of taking LOO error as one of the evaluation measures.

When $l$ is very large, the cost of computing LOO error is very expensive due to running a concrete classification algorithm $l$ times on the training sets sized $l-1$. This brings us to another question: how to find an appropriate estimation for the LOO error with cheap computation cost. The following theorems will provide us with two simple bounds that are computed by running a concrete classification algorithm only once on the original training set $T$ of size $l$. Both of them can be used as an evaluation measure for a concrete classification algorithm.

**Theorem 6.3.3** *(Jaakkola-Haussler bound[79]) Running Algorithm 4.3.1 (C-Support Vector Classification) with a fixed kernel and parameters on the training set (6.3.11) and using the $0-1$ loss function, the LOO error satisfies*

$$R_{LOO}(T) \leqslant \frac{1}{l}\sum_{t=1}^{l} \text{step}(-y_t g(x_t) + 2\alpha_t^* K(x_t, x_t)), \tag{6.3.17}$$

*where $K$ is a kernel, $\alpha^* = (\alpha_1^*, \cdots, \alpha_l^*)^T$ and $g(x)$ are the solution to the dual problem (4.3.1)~(4.3.3) and the function given by (4.3.6) respectively, step($\cdot$) is an one-variable function*

$$\text{step}(\eta) = \begin{cases} 1, & \eta \geqslant 0; \\ 0, & \eta < 0. \end{cases} \tag{6.3.18}$$

**Theorem 6.3.4** *(Joachims bound [82]) Running Algorithm 4.3.1 (C-Support Vector Classification) with a fixed kernel and parameters on the training set (6.3.11) and using the $0-1$ loss function, the LOO error satisfies*

$$R_{LOO}(T) \leqslant \frac{d}{l}, \tag{6.3.19}$$

*where $d$ is the size of the set $\{i : 2\alpha_i^* R^2 + \xi_i^* \geqslant 1\}$, $\alpha^* = (\alpha_1^*, \cdots, \alpha_l^*)^T$ is the solution to the dual problem (4.3.1)~(4.3.3), $R^2 = \max\{K(x_i, x_j) \mid i, j = 1, \cdots, l\}$, and $\xi^* = (\xi_1^*, \cdots, \xi_l^*)^T$ is the solution to the primal problem (4.1.6)~(4.1.8) with respect to $\xi$ that is obtained the following way:*

$$\xi_i^* = \max\left\{ 1 - y_i \left( \sum_{j=1}^{l} y_j \alpha_j^* K(x_j, x_i) + b^* \right), 0 \right\}. \qquad (6.3.20)$$

In the above, we mainly discussed one evaluation measure — the $k$-fold cross-validation accuracy rate, where the $k$-fold cross-validation is combined with accuracy rate $A_c$. It should be pointed out that the other evaluation measures from combinations of $k$-fold cross-validation and other evaluation measures proposed above are also interesting. In addition, the corresponding evaluation measures for regression algorithm are also useful; see e.g. [146, 177, 22, 180].

## 6.3.2    Selection of kernels and parameters

From the theoretical point of view, kernel selection contains feature selection since feature selection can be implemented by kernel selection. For simplicity, we explain it by the linear kernel $K(x, x') = (x \cdot x')$. Suppose that there are two features in the inputs of objects to be classified, i.e., $x = ([x]_1, [x]_2)^T$. The corresponding linear kernel function is:

$$K(x, x') = (x \cdot x') = [x]_1 [x']_1 + [x]_2 [x']_2. \qquad (6.3.21)$$

The result of applying Algorithm 4.3.1 with this kernel is the one without feature selection. If we select the feature $[x]_1$ and remove the feature $[x]_2$, i.e., the input $x$ becomes $\tilde{x} = [x]_1$, then the linear kernel function is changed into:

$$\tilde{K}(x, x') = (x \cdot x') = [x]_1 [x']_1, \qquad (6.3.22)$$

The result of applying Algorithm 4.3.1 with this kernel is the one after feature selection. Examining the process of Algorithm 4.3.1, it is easy to see that the above feature selection is equivalent to modify the kernel function (6.3.21) to (6.3.22) by removing the second feature $[x]_2$ and $[x']_2$ in the kernel function (6.3.21). The modification of kernel function (6.3.21) can also be implemented in the following way: first introduce the transformation

$$x = ([x]_1, [x]_2)^T \to \tilde{x} = ([x]_1, 0)^T, \qquad (6.3.23)$$

and then replace the kernel function $K(x, x')$ by $\tilde{K}(x, x') = K(\tilde{x}, \tilde{x}')$. So, feature selection of removing $[x]_2$ is achieved by modifying $K(x, x')$ to $\tilde{K}(x, x')$.

Similar conclusion is also true for a general feature selection and kernel function $K(x, x')$ with $x$ belonging to $R^n$. We introduce the transformation

$$x = ([x]_1, [x]_2, \cdots, [x]_n)^T \to \tilde{x} = \sigma * x, \qquad (6.3.24)$$

where $\sigma * x = (\sigma_1[x]_1, \sigma_2[x]_2, \cdots, \sigma_n[x]_n)^{\mathrm{T}}, \sigma = (\sigma_1, \sigma_2, \cdots, \sigma_n)^{\mathrm{T}}, \sigma_i = 0$ or $1, i = 1, \cdots, n$. The modification of $K(x, x')$ to $\widetilde{K}(x, x') = K(\tilde{x}, \tilde{x}')$ is equivalent to feature selection. More precisely, feature selection is conducted by choosing $n$ parameters $\sigma_1, \cdots, \sigma_n$. For example, $\sigma_i = 1$ and $\sigma_j = 0$ means that the $i$-th feature $[x]_i$ is maintained and the $j$-th feature $[x]_j$ is deleted, respectively. Hence, feature selection is contained in kernel selection.

Similarly, feature extraction is also contained in kernel selection. So kernel selection is very comprehensive.

Now let us turn to the main topic, kernel selection and parameter selection. Supposing that there are several candidates in our mind; what we need to do is to investigate the following three problems concerned with Algorithm 4.3.1:

(i) find the optimal kernel among several given kernels;

(ii) find the optimal parameters in a kernel among several given values;

(iii) find the optimal penalty parameter $C$ among several given values.

The above problems can be solved from a comparative perspective. We need only to find the best selection among different selections. Considering Algorithm 4.3.1 with a fixed selection as a concrete classification algorithm, this can be realized by comparing the evaluation measures of the concrete classification algorithms introduced above, such as:

(i) ten-fold cross-validation error;

(ii) LOO error;

(iii) the upper bound of LOO error.

For a small classification problem, ten-fold cross validation error and LOO error can be computed without any difficulty, and therefore can be used directly. Only for a large classification problem, the upper bound of LOO error is recommended due to its large computation cost.

A popular implementation of the above approach is as follows:

(i) Choose the Gaussian kernel: $K(x, x') = \exp(-\|x - x'\|^2/\sigma^2)$, where $\sigma$ is the parameter. The optimal combination of the parameter $\sigma$ in the kernel and the panelty parameter $C$ is selected by a grid search method among the corresponding concrete classification algorithms. A grid search is an iterative process that starts with the pre-specified ranges for each parameter, e.g. the ranges of parameters $\sigma$ and $C$ are assigned to be $\{2^{-5}, 2^{-4}, \cdots, 2^{15}\}$ and $\{2^{-15}, 2^{-14}, \cdots, 2^3\}$ respectively. In each iteration, a fixed pair of $(\sigma, C)$ in their ranges is tried and some evaluation measure such as LOO error are calculated. At last, the optimal parameters are picked with the best evaluation measure.

(ii) Choose other kernel functions. Find the optimal kernel and parameters in a way similar to the above process (i).

(iii) Comparing the above results obtained in (i) and (ii), the kernel and parameters finally selected are the ones with the best evaluation measure.

## 6.4 Rule Extraction

Support Vector Machines (SVMs) are popular methods for classification problems in a variety of applications. These classifiers, however, are hard to interpret by humans [47, 109, 113]. For instance, when an input is classified by the linear classifier as positive or negative, the only explanation that can be provided is that some linear weighted sum of the features of the input are lower (higher) than some threshold; such an explanation is completely non-intuitive to human experts. Humans are usually more comfortable dealing with rules that can be expressed as a hypercube with axis-parallel edges in the input space.

### 6.4.1 A toy example

Remember Example 2.1.1 in Chapter 2, where the data for heart disease are given in a training set

$$T = \{(x_1, y_1), \cdots, (x_{10}, y_{10})\}, \tag{6.4.1}$$

where $x_i \in R^2, y_i \in \{-1, 1\}, i = 1, \cdots, 10$, see Figure 2.1. Suppose that using the linear SVC we have found the decision function

$$f(x) = \text{sgn}((w \cdot x) + b), \tag{6.4.2}$$

with

$$w_1, \; w_2 > 0, \tag{6.4.3}$$

see Figure 6.8. Now the problem is to find some upright rectangles with axis-parallel edges where the inputs are predicted as negative (without heart disease), such that an input is predicted as negative (without heart disease) by the decision function when it falls into these upright rectangles. These upright rectangles are called rule rectangles.

First, let us restrict the region of interest on a big upright rectangle $\mathcal{C}$

$$\mathcal{C} = \{x \in R^2 | L_1 \leqslant [x]_1 \leqslant U_1, L_2 \leqslant [x]_2 \leqslant U_2\}, \tag{6.4.4}$$

where

$$L_j = \min_{i=1,\cdots,10} [x_i]_j, U_j = \max_{i=1,\cdots,10} [x_i]_j, j = 1, 2. \tag{6.4.5}$$

Note that an upright rectangle can be described by its lower vertex with the smallest components and its upper vertex with the largest components in Figure 6.8. For example, the rectangle $\mathcal{C}$ can be described by its lower vertex $(L_1, L_2)^T$ and its upper vertex $(U_1, U_2)^T$

$$\mathcal{C} = [(L_1, L_2)^T, (U_1, U_2)^T]; \tag{6.4.6}$$

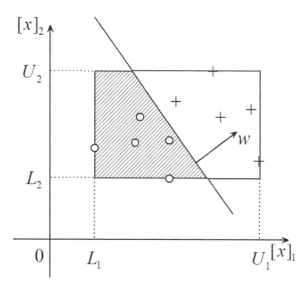

**FIGURE 6.8**: Rule extraction in Example 2.1.1.

see Figure 6.8. Now the problem becomes to find some rectangles in the shadow region. An interesting approach is based on the volume maximization criteria proposed in [60]. Its basic idea is to find an upright rectangle with the largest possible volume first, and then find as many upright rectangles as we require to describe adequately the region of interest by an iterative procedure. The union of these upright rectangles is our ultimate output.

In order to find the upright rectangle with the largest possible volume in the shadow region in Figure 6.8, it is sufficient to find its upper vertex $x^*$ on the line $(w \cdot x) + b = 0$ because its lower vertex is obviously $L = (L_1, L_2)^\mathrm{T}$. According to the volume maximization criteria the upper vertex $x^*$ should be the solution to the following optimization problem

$$\max \quad ([x]_1 - L_1)([x]_2 - L_2), \qquad (6.4.7)$$
$$\text{s.t.} \quad (w \cdot x) + b = 0, \qquad (6.4.8)$$
$$x \in \mathcal{C}, \qquad (6.4.9)$$

where $\mathcal{C}$ is given by (6.4.4) or (6.4.6). Introducing the transformation $T$ from $x$ to $\tilde{x}$:

$$\tilde{x} = T(x) = A(x - L), \qquad (6.4.10)$$

where

$$L = (L_1, L_2)^\mathrm{T}, \quad A = \mathrm{diag}(A_{jj}), \quad A_{jj} = \frac{1}{U_j - L_j}, \quad j = 1, 2, \qquad (6.4.11)$$

the problem (6.4.7)~(6.4.9) in $x$-space becomes the problem

$$\max \quad [\tilde{x}]_1 [\tilde{x}]_2, \tag{6.4.12}$$

$$\text{s.t.} \quad (\tilde{w} \cdot \tilde{x}) - 1 = 0, \tag{6.4.13}$$

$$\tilde{x} \in \tilde{\mathcal{C}} = [(0,0)^\mathrm{T}, (1,1)^\mathrm{T}], \tag{6.4.14}$$

or

$$\max \quad \log[\tilde{x}]_1 + \log[\tilde{x}]_2, \tag{6.4.15}$$

$$\text{s.t.} \quad (\tilde{w} \cdot \tilde{x}) - 1 = 0, \tag{6.4.16}$$

$$\tilde{x} \in \tilde{\mathcal{C}} = [(0,0)^\mathrm{T}, (1,1)^\mathrm{T}], \tag{6.4.17}$$

in $\tilde{x}$-space, where

$$\tilde{w} = \frac{1}{-((w \cdot L) + b)} \begin{pmatrix} (U_1 - L_1)w_1 \\ (U_2 - L_2)w_2 \end{pmatrix}. \tag{6.4.18}$$

After obtaining the solution $\tilde{x}^*$ to the problem (6.4.15)~(6.4.17), we are able to find the upright rectangle $[(0,0)^\mathrm{T}, \tilde{x}^*]$ in $\tilde{x}$-space, see Figure 6.9(a), and furthermore the required rule rectangle $[T^{-1}(0), T^{-1}(\tilde{x}^*)] = [T^{-1}(0), x^*]$ in $x$-space, where $T^{-1}$ is the inverse of the transformation (6.4.10), see Figure 6.9(b).

If more rule rectangles in $x$-space are needed, first we go back to the $\tilde{x}$-space and consider the remaining two rectangles

$$\tilde{I}_1 : \quad [([\tilde{x}^*]_1, 0)^\mathrm{T}, (1,1)^\mathrm{T}], \tag{6.4.19}$$

$$\tilde{I}_2 : \quad [(0, [\tilde{x}^*]_2)^\mathrm{T}, ([\tilde{x}^*]_1, 1)^\mathrm{T}], \tag{6.4.20}$$

see Figure 6.9(a), and then construct their counterparts in $x$-space

$$I_1 : \quad [(L_1 + (U_1 - L_1)[\tilde{x}^*]_1, L_2)^\mathrm{T}, (U_1, U_2)^\mathrm{T}], \tag{6.4.21}$$

$$I_2 : \quad [(L_1, L_2 + (U_2 - L_2)[\tilde{x}^*]_2)^\mathrm{T}, (L_1 + (U_1 - L_1)[\tilde{x}^*]_1, U_2)^\mathrm{T}]; \tag{6.4.22}$$

see Figure 6.9(b). Next we should find rule rectangles in both rectangle $I_1$ and rectangle $I_2$ by repeating the above procedure with replacing the big rectangle $\mathcal{C}$ by $I_1$ and $I_2$ respectively, and so forth.

## 6.4.2   Rule extraction

The above Example 2.1.1 is a rule extraction problem in two-dimensional space. Generally, there exists the rule extraction problem in the $n$-dimensional space. In order to formalize the problem mathematically, we first give a definition as follows.

**Definition 6.4.1** *(Upright hypercube and Rule hypercube) A hypercube is called an upright hypercube in the n-dimensional space if it is a hypercube with axis-parallel edges. An upright hypercube is called a rule hypercube if the class of an input can be predicted by the decision function when it falls into this upright hypercube.*

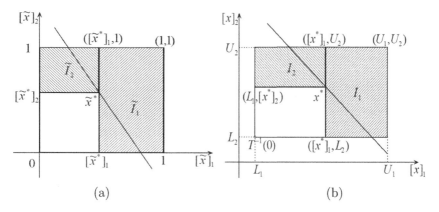

**FIGURE 6.9**: Rule rectangle.

Obviously an upright hypercube can always be described by its upper vertex with the largest components and its lower vertex with the smallest components. Thus the upright hypercube corresponding to the big rectangle $\mathcal{C}$ defined by (6.4.4) should be

$$\mathcal{C} = [(L_1, \cdots, L_n)^{\mathrm{T}}, (U_1, \cdots, U_n)^{\mathrm{T}}], \tag{6.4.23}$$

where

$$L_j = \min_i [x_i]_j, \ U_j = \max_i [x_i]_j, \ j = 1, \cdots, n. \tag{6.4.24}$$

Now let us turn to rule extraction problems described below, which is only concerned with the negative class since the positive class is similar.

**Rule extraction problem**: Given a training set

$$T - \{(x_1, y_1), \cdots, (x_l, y_l)\}, \tag{6.4.25}$$

where $x_i \in R^n, y \in \{-1, 1\}, i = 1, \cdots, l$, and a decision function

$$f(x) = \mathrm{sgn}((w \cdot x) + b), \tag{6.4.26}$$

find a set of rule hypercubes such that this set is an approximation of the region of interest, where the class of an input is predicted as negative by the decision function when it falls into any hypercube in the set.

First consider the problem $P(w, b, \mathcal{C})$ of finding a rule hypercube for the region:

$$I = \{x | (w \cdot x) + b < 0, x \in \mathcal{C}\} \tag{6.4.27}$$

where $(w \cdot x) + b$ and $\mathcal{C}$ are given by the decision function and (6.4.23). Without loss of generality, assume that the normal vector $w$ in the decision function satisfies

$$w_j \neq 0, i = 1, \cdots, n, \tag{6.4.28}$$

since the $j$th feature can be deleted if $w_j = 0$. Now the transformation corresponding to (6.4.10) with the condition (6.4.3) should be

$$\tilde{x} = T(x) = T(x, \mathcal{C}) = A(x - a), \tag{6.4.29}$$

where

$$A = \text{diag}(A_{jj}), \ A_{jj} = \frac{\text{sgn}(w_j)}{U_j - L_j}, \ j = 1, \cdots, n, \tag{6.4.30}$$

and

$$a = (a_1, \cdots, a_n)^{\mathrm{T}}, \ a_j = \begin{cases} L_j, & w_j > 0; \\ U_j, & \textit{otherwise}, \end{cases} \ j = 1, \cdots, n. \tag{6.4.31}$$

The above transformation transforms $\mathcal{C}$ into

$$\tilde{\mathcal{C}} = [(0, \cdots, 0)^{\mathrm{T}}, (1, \cdots, 1)^{\mathrm{T}}], \tag{6.4.32}$$

thus the problem $P(w, b, \mathcal{C})$ becomes the problem $P(\tilde{w}, 1, \tilde{\mathcal{C}})$, where

$$\tilde{w} = \tilde{w}(\mathcal{C}) = \frac{1}{-((w \cdot L) + b)} \begin{pmatrix} (U_1 - L_1)w_1 \\ \vdots \\ (U_n - L_n)w_n \end{pmatrix} \tag{6.4.33}$$

satisfying

$$\tilde{w}_j > 0, j = 1, \cdots, n. \tag{6.4.34}$$

And the optimization problem corresponding to (6.4.12)~(6.4.14) should be

$$\max \quad [\tilde{x}]_1 [\tilde{x}]_2 \cdots [\tilde{x}]_n, \tag{6.4.35}$$

$$\text{s.t.} \quad (\tilde{w} \cdot \tilde{x}) - 1 = 0, \tag{6.4.36}$$

$$\tilde{x} \in \tilde{\mathcal{C}} = [(0, \cdots, 0)^{\mathrm{T}}, (1, \cdots, 1)^{\mathrm{T}}], \tag{6.4.37}$$

or

$$\max \quad \sum_{j=1}^{n} \log[\tilde{x}]_j, \tag{6.4.38}$$

$$\text{s.t.} \quad (\tilde{w} \cdot \tilde{x}) - 1 = 0, \tag{6.4.39}$$

$$\tilde{x} \in \tilde{\mathcal{C}} = [(0, \cdots, 0)^{\mathrm{T}}, (1, \cdots, 1)^{\mathrm{T}}]. \tag{6.4.40}$$

After obtaining the solution $\tilde{x}^* = \tilde{x}^*(\mathcal{C})$ to the problem (6.4.38)~(6.4.40), we are able to find the rule hypercube

$$R = R(\mathcal{C}) = [x_{min}, x_{max}], \tag{6.4.41}$$

where

$$x_{min} = T^{-1}(0, \mathcal{C}), \tag{6.4.42}$$

$$x_{max} = T^{-1}(\tilde{x}^*, \mathcal{C}), \tag{6.4.43}$$

and $T^{-1}$ is the inverse of the transformation (6.4.29).

The above procedure for solving the problem $P(w, b, \mathcal{C})$ can be summarized as the following algorithm:

**Algorithm 6.4.2**

*(1) Input the training set (6.4.25), the decision function (6.4.26) and construct the big upright hypercube (6.4.23);*

*(2) Solve the problem (6.4.38)~(6.4.40) where $\tilde{w}(\mathcal{C})$ is given by (6.4.33), obtaining a solution $\tilde{x}^* = \tilde{x}^*(\mathcal{C})$;*

*(3) Construct a rule hypercube $R = R(\mathcal{C})$ by (6.4.41).*

If more rule hypercubes are needed, we should consider the remaining volume in $x$-space after extracting the rule hypercube $R(\mathcal{C})$ in the problem $P(w, b, \mathcal{C})$, which can be obtained from the corresponding remaining volume in $\tilde{x}$-space for the transformed problem $P(\tilde{w}, 1, \tilde{\mathcal{C}})$. In fact, in $\tilde{x}$-space extracting the rule hypercube $[0, \tilde{x}^*(\mathcal{C})]$ results in $n$ upright hypercubes $\tilde{I}_1, \cdots, \tilde{I}_n$, where

$$\tilde{I}_j(\mathcal{C}) = [\tilde{x}^j_{min}(\mathcal{C}), \tilde{x}^j_{max}(\mathcal{C})], \ j = 1, \cdots, n, \tag{6.4.44}$$

and

$$\tilde{x}^j_{min}(\mathcal{C}) = \underbrace{(0, \cdots, 0}_{j-1}, [\tilde{x}^*(\mathcal{C})]_j, 1, \cdots, 1)^{\mathrm{T}}, j = 1, \cdots, n. \tag{6.4.45}$$

$$\tilde{x}^j_{max}(\mathcal{C}) = \underbrace{([\tilde{x}^*(\mathcal{C})]_1, \cdots, [\tilde{x}^*(\mathcal{C})]_{j-1}}_{j-1}, 1, \cdots, 1)^{\mathrm{T}}, j = 1, \cdots, n. \tag{6.4.46}$$

Correspondingly, the counterparts of the above $n$ upright hypercubes $\tilde{I}_1, \cdots, \tilde{I}_n$ in the $x$-space are $I_1, \cdots, I_n$, where

$$I_j(\mathcal{C}) = [x^j_{min}(\mathcal{C}), x^j_{max}(\mathcal{C})], \ j = 1, \cdots, n, \tag{6.4.47}$$

and

$$x^j_{min}(\mathcal{C}) = T^{-1}(\tilde{x}^i_{min}(\mathcal{C})), \ x^j_{max}(\mathcal{C}) = T^{-1}(\tilde{x}^j_{max}(\mathcal{C})), \ j = 1, \cdots, n. \tag{6.4.48}$$

Thus an iterative procedure that extracts as many rule hypercubes as we require to describe adequately the region of interest is implemented in the following algorithm, where $d_{max}$ is the maximum depth pre-specified, $C$ is the set of the upright hypercubes, and $R$ is the set containing all the extracted rule hypercubes.

**Algorithm 6.4.3** *(Rule extraction)*

*(1) Input the training set (6.4.25), the decision function (6.4.26) and the maximum depth $d_{max}$. Set $d = 1$, $R = \Phi$;*

*(2) If $d = 1$, set $C$ to be the big upright hypercube defined by (6.4.23);*

*(3) Denote p be the number of the upright hypercubes belonging to the set $\mathcal{C}$ and containing at least one input in the training set. Denote the set $\mathcal{C}$ by $\mathcal{C} = \{\mathcal{C}_1, \cdots, \mathcal{C}_p\}$. For $i = 1, \cdots, p$, solve the problem $P(w, b, \mathcal{C}_i)$ by Algorithm 6.4.2, obtaining the solution $\tilde{x}^*(\mathcal{C}_i)$ and the rule hypercube $R(\mathcal{C}_i)$, construct the set*

$$R_{new} = \bigcup_{i=1}^{p} R(\mathcal{C}_i). \tag{6.4.49}$$

*Update R by*

$$R = R \cup R_{new}; \tag{6.4.50}$$

*(4) If $d = d_{max}$, stop; otherwise, for $i = 1, \cdots, p$, construct the next n upright hypercubes $I_1(\mathcal{C}_i), \cdots, I_n(\mathcal{C}_i)$ by (6.4.47)~(6.4.48), construct the set*

$$\mathcal{C} = \bigcup_{i=1}^{p} \bigcup_{j=1}^{n} I_j(\mathcal{C}_i); \tag{6.4.51}$$

*(5) Set $d = d + 1$ and go to step (3).*

# Chapter 7

## Implementation

This chapter gives an overview of the implementation of Support Vector Machines. We take Algorithm 4.3.1 ($C$-support vector classification) as the representative. Suppose the training set is given by

$$T = \{(x_1, y_1), \cdots, (x_l, y_l)\}, \tag{7.0.1}$$

where $x_i \in R^n, y_i \in \mathcal{Y} = \{1, -1\}, i = 1, \cdots, l$, now the convex quadratic programming problem $(4.3.1) \sim (4.3.3)$ w.r.t. variable $\alpha = (\alpha_1, \cdots, \alpha_l)^{\mathrm{T}}$

$$\min_{\alpha} \quad \frac{1}{2} \sum_{i=1}^{l} \sum_{j=1}^{l} y_i y_j \alpha_i \alpha_j K(x_i, x_j) - \sum_{i=1}^{l} \alpha_i, \tag{7.0.2}$$

$$\text{s.t.} \quad \sum_{i=1}^{l} y_i \alpha_i = 0, \tag{7.0.3}$$

$$0 \leqslant \alpha_i \leqslant C, \ i = 1, \cdots, l, \tag{7.0.4}$$

needs to be solved. This problem can be expressed compactly as

$$\min_{\alpha} \quad d(\alpha) = \frac{1}{2} \alpha^{\mathrm{T}} H \alpha - e^{\mathrm{T}} \alpha, \tag{7.0.5}$$

$$\text{s.t.} \quad y^{\mathrm{T}} \alpha = 0, \tag{7.0.6}$$

$$0 \leqslant \alpha \leqslant Ce, \tag{7.0.7}$$

where $H = (h_{ij})_{l \times l} = (y_i y_j K(x_i, x_j))_{l \times l}, e = (1, \cdots, 1)^{\mathrm{T}}, y = (y_1, \cdots, y_l)^{\mathrm{T}}$. This chapter mainly introduces the methods for solving problem $(7.0.5) \sim$ $(7.0.7)$. Although in principle, general optimization algorithms can be applied directly, they usually fail for real large scale problems due to the demands of the cache and computation. In fact, these algorithms all need to cache the kernel matrix corresponding to the training set, whereas the memory caching the kernel matrix increases with the square of the training points number $l$. When $l$ becomes thousands, the memory needed tends to be considerable. For example, if $l$ is larger than 4000, 128M memory is needed to cache the kernel matrix. In addition, these algorithms always involve amounts of matrix computation, which consume long computation time.

We note that the optimization problems in support vector machines are special; they have some very good features such as the convexity and the sparsity of the solution, which make it possible to construct less cache and fast algorithms. The basic approach of these special algorithms is: decompose the large scale original problem into a series of small scale sub-problems, then solve these sub-problems constantly following some iteration strategy, gradually increasing the accuracy of the approximate solution to the original problem. Different selection of sub-problem and iteration strategy leads to different methods. This chapter introduces the chunking method [155] and the decomposing method [114, 184], and a particular case of the decomposing method: sequential minimal optimization-SMO [118]. However, before introducing these methods, we first discuss the stopping criteria.

## 7.1 Stopping Criterion

Appropriate stopping criteria should be constructed when solving problem (7.0.5)∼(7.0.7) by some iteration method. Next we introduce three stopping criteria from different perspectives.

### 7.1.1 The first stopping criterion

The first stopping criterion is based on the following theorem:

**Theorem 7.1.1** *The feasible point* $\alpha^* = (\alpha_1^*, \cdots, \alpha_l^*)^{\mathrm{T}}$ *is the solution of the dual problem* (7.0.5)∼(7.0.7) *if and only if there exists* $b^*$, *such that*

$$0 \leqslant \alpha_j^* \leqslant C, \quad i = 1, \cdots, l, \quad \sum_{i=1}^{l} y_i \alpha_i^* = 0, \qquad (7.1.1)$$

$$\sum_{i=1}^{l} \alpha_i^* h_{ij} + b^* y_j \begin{cases} \geqslant 1, & j \in \{j | \alpha_j = 0\}; \\ = 1, & j \in \{j | 0 < \alpha_j < C\}; \\ \leqslant 1, & j \in \{j | \alpha_j = C\}. \end{cases} \qquad (7.1.2)$$

**Proof** Quadratic programming problem (7.0.5)∼(7.0.7) is convex, and satisfies Slater condition, so its KKT conditions are the solution's necessary and sufficient conditions. The KKT conditions at $\alpha^* = (\alpha_1^*, \cdots, \alpha_l^*)^{\mathrm{T}}$ are: there exist Lagrange multipliers $b^*, s^*$ and $\xi^*$ satisfying

$$0 \leqslant \alpha^* \leqslant Ce, \quad \alpha^{*\mathrm{T}} y = 0; \qquad (7.1.3)$$

$$H\alpha^* - e + b^* y - s^* + \xi^* = 0, \quad s^* \geqslant 0, \xi^* \geqslant 0; \qquad (7.1.4)$$

$$\xi^{*\mathrm{T}}(\alpha^* - Ce) = 0, \quad s^{*\mathrm{T}}\alpha^* = 0. \qquad (7.1.5)$$

For the case $\alpha_j^* = 0$, from (7.1.4)~(7.1.5) we know the $j$-th component of $\xi^*$ is zero, and the $j$-th component of $H\alpha^* - e + b^*y$ is nonnegative, i.e.

$$\sum_{i=1}^{l} \alpha_i^* h_{ij} + b^* y_j \geqslant 1. \qquad (7.1.6)$$

Similarly, for the case $0 < \alpha_j^* < C$, from (7.1.4)~(7.1.5), we have

$$\sum_{i=1}^{l} \alpha_i^* h_{ij} + b^* y_j = 1, \qquad (7.1.7)$$

and for the case $\alpha_j^* = C$, from (7.1.4)~(7.1.5), we have

$$\sum_{i=1}^{l} \alpha_i^* h_{ij} + b^* y_j \leqslant 1. \qquad (7.1.8)$$

Therefore, combining (7.1.6)~(7.1.8) and (7.1.3), we know the solution $\alpha^*$ of problem (7.0.5)~(7.0.7) should satisfy (7.1.1)~(7.1.2). ∎

The following stopping criterion can be established based on the above theorem.

**Stopping criterion 7.1.2** *Suppose the approximate solution* $\alpha^* = (\alpha_1^*, \cdots, \alpha_l^*)^{\mathrm{T}}$ *of problem (7.0.5)~(7.0.7) is obtained. Algorithm accepts this solution and stops iteration, if*

*(i) Approximate solution* $\alpha^*$ *is feasible within a certain range of accuracy, i.e. it satisfies (7.1.1) within a certain range of accuracy;*

*(ii) There exists* $b^*$ *such that* $\alpha^*$ *satisfies (7.1.2) within a certain range of accuracy.*

### 7.1.2   The second stopping criterion

The second stopping criterion is based on the following theorem:

**Theorem 7.1.3** *The feasible point* $\alpha^* = (\alpha_1^*, \cdots, \alpha_l^*)^{\mathrm{T}}$ *is the solution of optimization problem (7.0.5)~(7.0.7) if and only if*

$$m(\alpha^*) - M(\alpha^*) \leq 0, \qquad (7.1.9)$$

*where*

$$m(\alpha^*) = \max\{-y_i[\nabla d(\alpha^*)]_i \mid i \in I_{\mathrm{up}}(\alpha^*)\}, \qquad (7.1.10)$$
$$M(\alpha^*) = \min\{-y_i[\nabla d(\alpha^*)]_i \mid i \in I_{\mathrm{low}}(\alpha^*)\}, \qquad (7.1.11)$$

*where* $[\cdot]_i$ *denotes the* $i$-*th component of the vector in* $[]$, $\nabla d(\alpha^*) = H\alpha^* - e$

*is the gradient of the objective function $d(\alpha)$ at $\alpha^*$, $I_{up}(\alpha^*)$ and $I_{low}(\alpha^*)$ are the subsets of set $\{1, 2, \cdots, l\}$*

$$I_{up}(\alpha^*) = \{i | \alpha_i^* < C, y_i = 1 \text{ or } \alpha_i^* > 0, y_i = -1\}, \qquad (7.1.12)$$
$$I_{low}(\alpha^*) = \{i | \alpha_i^* < C, y_i = -1 \text{ or } \alpha_i^* > 0, y_i = 1\}. \qquad (7.1.13)$$

**Proof** *For the feasible point $\alpha^*$, KKT conditions $(7.1.3) \sim (7.1.5)$ are equivalent to*

$$\text{if } \alpha_i^* < C, \qquad [\nabla d(\alpha^*)]_i + by_i \geqslant 0; \qquad (7.1.14)$$
$$\text{if } \alpha_i^* > 0, \qquad [\nabla d(\alpha^*)]_i + by_i \leqslant 0. \qquad (7.1.15)$$

*Based on $(7.1.12)$ and $(7.1.13)$, the above $(7.1.14)$ and $(7.1.15)$ can be written as:*

$$-y_i[\nabla d(\alpha^*)]_i \leqslant b, \quad \forall i \in I_{up}(\alpha^*),$$
$$-y_i[\nabla d(\alpha^*)]_i \geqslant b, \quad \forall i \in I_{low}(\alpha^*).$$

*Therefore, the feasible point $\alpha^*$ is the solution of optimization problem $(7.0.5) \sim (7.0.7)$ if and only if: $m(\alpha^*)$ and $M(\alpha^*)$ defined respectively by $(7.1.10)$ and $(7.1.11)$ satisfy*

$$m(\alpha^*) \leqslant M(\alpha^*). \qquad (7.1.16)$$

■

The following stopping criterion can be established based on the above theorem.

**Stopping criterion 7.1.4** *Suppose the approximate solution $\alpha^* = (\alpha_1^*, \cdots, \alpha_l^*)^T$ of problem $(7.0.5) \sim (7.0.7)$ is obtained. Algorithm accepts this solution and stops iteration, if*
 *(i) Approximate solution $\alpha^*$ is feasible within a certain range of accuracy, i.e. it satisfies $(7.1.1)$ within a certain range of accuracy;*
 *(ii) Approximate solution $\alpha^*$ satisfies $(7.1.9)$ within a certain range of accuracy. For example, select an appropriate $\varepsilon > 0$, such that*

$$m(\alpha^*) - M(\alpha^*) \leqslant \varepsilon, \qquad (7.1.17)$$

*where $m(\alpha^*)$ and $M(\alpha^*)$ are given by $(7.1.10)$ and $(7.1.11)$ respectively.*

### 7.1.3  The third stopping criterion

The third stopping criterion is based on the following theorem.

**Theorem 7.1.5** *The feasible point* $\alpha^* = (\alpha_1^*, \cdots, \alpha_l^*)^{\mathrm{T}}$ *is the solution of optimization problem* $(7.0.5)\sim(7.0.7)$ *if and only if there exist* $\xi_1^*, \cdots, \xi_l^*$, *such that*

$$\frac{2d(\alpha^*) + \sum\limits_{i=1}^{l}\alpha_i^* + C\sum\limits_{i=1}^{l}\xi_i^*}{d(\alpha^*) + \sum\limits_{i=1}^{l}\alpha_i^* + C\sum\limits_{i=1}^{l}\xi_i^* + 1} = 0. \tag{7.1.18}$$

**Proof** *We know that optimization problem* $(7.0.5)\sim(7.0.7)$ *is equivalent to*

$$\max_{\alpha} \quad -d(\alpha) = e^{\mathrm{T}}\alpha - \frac{1}{2}\alpha^{\mathrm{T}}H\alpha, \tag{7.1.19}$$

$$\text{s.t.} \quad y^{\mathrm{T}}\alpha = 0, \tag{7.1.20}$$

$$0 \leqslant \alpha \leqslant Ce. \tag{7.1.21}$$

*while this problem is the dual problem of the primal problem*

$$\min_{w,b,\xi} \quad \frac{1}{2}\|w\|^2 + C\sum_{i=1}^{l}\xi_i, \tag{7.1.22}$$

$$\text{s.t.} \quad y_i((w \cdot \Phi(x_i)) + b) \geqslant 1 - \xi_i, \ i = 1, \cdots, l, \tag{7.1.23}$$

$$\xi_i \geqslant 0, \ i = 1, \cdots, l. \tag{7.1.24}$$

*The feasible point* $(w^*, b^*, \xi^*)$ *of problem* $(7.1.22)\sim(7.1.24)$ *can be constructed by the feasible point* $\alpha^*$ *of the dual problem:*

$$w^* = \sum_{i=1}^{l} \alpha_i^* y_i \Phi(x_i), \tag{7.1.25}$$

$$\xi_i^* = \max\left(0, 1 - \left(\sum_{j=1}^{l}\alpha_j^* h_{ji} + b^* y_i\right)\right), \quad i = 1, \cdots, l. \tag{7.1.26}$$

*Corollary 1.2.19 in Chapter 1 indicates that the feasible points* $\alpha^*$ *and* $(w^*, b^*, \xi^*)$ *are the solutions of the dual problem and primal problem respectively if and only if the corresponding objective function values are equal, i.e.*

*objective function value of the primal problem*

$$= \frac{1}{2}\|w\|^2 + C\sum_{i=1}^{l}\xi_i = -d(\alpha^*)$$

$$= \quad \textit{objective function value of the dual problem.} \tag{7.1.27}$$

*However, from* (7.1.25) *it is easy to get*

$$\frac{1}{2}\|w\|^2 = \frac{1}{2}\sum_{i,j=1}^{l} y_i\alpha_i^* y_j\alpha_j^* K(x_i, x_j) = d(\alpha^*) + \sum_{i=1}^{l}\alpha_i^*, \tag{7.1.28}$$

*hence, (7.1.27) is equivalent to*

$$\frac{\begin{array}{c} objective\ function\ value\\ (primal\ problem) \end{array} - \begin{array}{c} objective\ function\ value\\ (dual\ problem) \end{array}}{objective\ function\ value\ (primal\ problem)\ +1}$$

$$= \frac{2d(\alpha^*) + \sum\limits_{i=1}^{l} \alpha_i^* + C \sum\limits_{i=1}^{l} \xi_i}{d(\alpha^*) + \sum\limits_{i=1}^{l} \alpha_i^* + C \sum\limits_{i=1}^{l} \xi_i + 1} = 0. \qquad (7.1.29)$$

*Therefore (7.1.18) is the necessary and sufficient condition of $\alpha^*$ being the solution of problem (7.1.19)~(7.1.21).* ∎

The following stopping criterion can be established based on the above theorem:

**Stopping criterion 7.1.6** *Suppose the approximate solution $\alpha^* = (\alpha_1^*, \cdots, \alpha_l^*)^T$ of problem (7.0.5)~(7.0.7) is obtained. Algorithm accepts this solution and stops iteration, if*

*(i) Approximate solution $\alpha^*$ is feasible within a certain range of accuracy, i.e. it satisfies (7.1.1) within a certain range of accuracy;*

*(ii) Approximate solution $\alpha^*$ satisfies (7.1.18) within a certain range of accuracy. For example, select appropriate $\varepsilon > 0$, such that the left term of (7.1.18) is less than $\varepsilon$.*

It should be pointed out that the demand of stopping criterion testing accuracy significantly influences the algorithm execution time. High demands will be very time-consuming, but would not necessarily improve the decision function. So in real applications, we should carefully select the stopping criterion.

In addition, the above discussion of the stopping criteria will give us some inspiration to improve algorithms and the efficiency of the algorithms. For example, in the iterative process we can pay more attention to those training points that violate the stopping criteria mostly. We give a detailed description in the last sections.

---

## 7.2 Chunking

We have seen that in Algorithm 4.3.1 (*C*-support vector classification), the solution to the optimization problem (7.0.5)~(7.0.7) only depends on the training points corresponding to the support vectors (please refer to the discussion of sparsity in Section 4.3.1). Therefore if we know which inputs are the support vectors, we can keep the corresponding training points and delete other training points, and hence construct the corresponding optimization problem based on the reduced training set and get the decision function. Obviously it is very important for large scale real problems, since the problems usually have fewer support vectors and only smaller scale optimization problems need to be solved. However we do not know beforehand which exactly are the support vectors; generally the use of heuristic algorithms is required to be adjusted repeatedly to get the support vectors.

The simplest heuristic method is chunking. "Chunk" here means the working set, which is a subset in the training set $T$. "Chunking" means excluding the training points corresponding to the nonsupport vectors in the chunk by some iterative approach step by step, and selecting the training points corresponding to all support vectors into the chunk step by step. Specifically: start with an arbitrary chunk of the training set, then apply the standard optimization algorithm to solve the problem $(7.0.5)\sim(7.0.7)$, obtaining its solution $\alpha$, and adjust the current chunk for the new chunk in the following ways:

(i) Keep the training points corresponding to the nonzero components of $\alpha$ in the current chunk, while discarding other training points in the chunk;

(ii) Add several training points being not in the current chunk which violate the stopping criteria most seriously to the current chunk.

After getting the new chunk, solve the problem $(7.0.5)\sim(7.0.7)$ on it. Repeat the above process until satisfying one stopping criteria. More precisely, the main steps of solving the problem $(7.0.5)\sim(7.0.7)$ corresponding to the training set $(7.0.1)$ can be described as follows:

**Algorithm 7.2.1** *(Chunking)*

*(1) Choose positive integer parameter $M$, accuracy demand $\varepsilon$, and initial point $\alpha^0 = (\alpha_1^0, \cdots, \alpha_l^0)^{\mathrm{T}} = 0$, choose initial chunk (working set)$W_0 \subset T$, denote the subscripts set corresponding to the training set $J_0$, let $k = 0$;*

*(2) Choose the components from the point $\alpha^k$ whose subscript belongs to the set $J_k$, construct the point $\alpha^{J_k}$. Solve the convex quadratic programming subproblem*

$$\min_{\alpha} \quad W(\alpha) = \frac{1}{2}\sum_{i \in J_k}\sum_{j \in J_k}\alpha_i\alpha_j h_{ij} - \sum_{i \in J_k}\alpha_i , \tag{7.2.30}$$

$$\text{s.t.} \quad \sum_{i \in J_k} y_i\alpha_i = 0 , \tag{7.2.31}$$

$$0 \le \alpha_i \le C , \ i \in J_k , \tag{7.2.32}$$

*obtaining the solution $\hat{\alpha}^{J_k}$;*

*(3) Construct $\alpha^{k+1} = (\alpha_1^{k+1}, \cdots, \alpha_l^{k+1})^{\mathrm{T}}$ based on $\hat{\alpha}^{J_k}$ by the following approach: if $j \in J_k$, $\alpha_j^{k+1}$ takes the corresponding component of $\hat{\alpha}^{J_k}$; if $j \notin J_k$,*

$\alpha_j^{k+1} = \alpha_j^k$, *test whether $\alpha^{k+1}$ satisfies some stopping criteria within the accuracy $\varepsilon$; if so, get the approximate solution $\alpha^* = \alpha^{k+1}$ and stop; else go to step (4);*

*(4) Construct the set $S_k$ being composed of the training points corresponding to the support vectors based on $\hat{\alpha}^{J_k}$, and find out $M$ training points violating the stopping criteria most seriously from the set $T \backslash S_k$, such as finding out $M$ training points violating the conditions*

$$\sum_{i=1}^{l} \alpha_i^{k+1} h_{ij} + b y_j \begin{cases} \geqslant 1, & j \in \{j | \alpha_j^{k+1} = 0\}; \\ = 1, & j \in \{j | 0 < \alpha_j^{k+1} < C\}; \\ \leqslant 1, & j \in \{j | \alpha_j^{k+1} = C\}, \end{cases} \quad (7.2.33)$$

*then construct the new chunk $W_{k+1}$ by the $M$ points and the points in $S_k$, denoting corresponding subscript set $J_{k+1}$;*

*(5) Set $k = k + 1$, goto step (2).*

The advantage of chunking is that when the number of support vectors is far less than the number of training points, the computing speed can be greatly enhanced. However, if the number of support vectors increases, with the increase in the number of algorithm iterations, the selected chunk will be growing and the algorithm becomes very slow.

---

## 7.3  Decomposing

When solving the problem (7.0.5)~(7.0.7), chunking needs to find out the chunk being composed of the training points corresponding to all support vectors, hence the kernel function matrix corresponding to all support vectors needs to be cached as a final step. Thus, when there are many support vectors, chunking will encounter the difficulty of the required excessive storage. To overcome this difficulty, we use another technique ——"decomposing". Decomposing is characterized by updating several (a certain number of) components of $\alpha$ each time and keeping other components unchanged. The set of the training points corresponding to the updating components of $\alpha$ is the current working set. Thus adding several new training points in the current working set each time, the same number of training points should be discarded from the current working set. In other words, only a part of "worst case" points outside of the current working set exchange with the same number of the training points in the current working set in the iteration procedure; the working set size is fixed. This method solves the problem (7.0.5)~(7.0.7) repeatedly in accordance with the changing working set and aims to adjust the components of $\alpha$.

We now give the specific formulation of the convex quadratic programming problem $(7.0.5)\sim(7.0.7)$ corresponding to the working set. Denote $B$ the set being composed of the subscripts of the training points in the working set, appropriately exchange the order of the components of $\alpha$, $\alpha$ can be rewritten as

$$\alpha = \begin{pmatrix} \alpha_B \\ \alpha_N \end{pmatrix}, \tag{7.3.34}$$

where $N = \{1, \cdots, l\} \setminus B$. Correspondingly, $y$ and $H$ can be formulated as

$$y = \begin{pmatrix} y_B \\ y_N \end{pmatrix}, \quad H = \begin{pmatrix} H_{BB} & H_{BN} \\ H_{NB} & H_{NN} \end{pmatrix}. \tag{7.3.35}$$

Here we need to adjust $\alpha_B$ and fix $\alpha_N$. Since $H$ is symmetric, i.e. $H_{BN} = H_{NB}^{\mathrm{T}}$, the problem $(7.0.5)\sim(7.0.7)$ should be rewritten as

$$\min_{\alpha_B} \quad W(\alpha) = \frac{1}{2}\alpha_B^{\mathrm{T}} H_{BB}\alpha_B + \frac{1}{2}\alpha_N^{\mathrm{T}} H_{NN}\alpha_N$$
$$-\alpha_N^{\mathrm{T}} e - \alpha_B^{\mathrm{T}}(e - H_{BN}\alpha_N), \tag{7.3.36}$$
$$\text{s.t.} \quad \alpha_B^{\mathrm{T}} y_B + \alpha_N^{\mathrm{T}} y_N = 0, \tag{7.3.37}$$
$$0 \leqslant \alpha \leqslant Ce. \tag{7.3.38}$$

In the problem $(7.3.36)\sim(7.3.38)$, since $\alpha_N$ is fixed, the term $\frac{1}{2}\alpha_N^{\mathrm{T}} H_{NN}\alpha_N - \alpha_N^{\mathrm{T}} e$ is constant, then the problem is equivalent to the following problem

$$\min_{\alpha_B} \quad W(\alpha) = \frac{1}{2}\alpha_B^{\mathrm{T}} H_{BB}\alpha_B - \alpha_B^{\mathrm{T}}(e - H_{BN}\alpha_N), \tag{7.3.39}$$
$$\text{s.t.} \quad \alpha_B^{\mathrm{T}} y_B + \alpha_N^{\mathrm{T}} y_N = 0, \tag{7.3.40}$$
$$0 \leqslant \alpha_B \leqslant Ce. \tag{7.3.41}$$

The problem $(7.3.39)\sim(7.3.41)$ only needs to cache $|B|$ rows of the $l \times l$ matrix $H$ ($|B|$ is the size of the set $B$); usually $|B|$ is chosen to be far less than $l$.

Next we focus on how to select the subscript set $B$. Here an even number should be chosen to be $|B|$ in advance, and then choose the set $B$. Note that we aim to adjust the components of the current $\alpha$ corresponding to $B$ to make it to approximate the solution of the convex quadratic programming $(7.0.5)\sim(7.0.7)$; therefore this adjustment should make the objective function $d(\alpha)$ given by $(7.0.5)$ decrease as much as possible. Therefore, for simplicity, we only need to find out an appropriate feasible direction $d = (d_1, d_2, \cdots, d_l)^{\mathrm{T}}$ from current $\alpha$, then compose $B$ by the subscripts of these nonzero components of $d$. The direction $d$ should better satisfy the following conditions (i) along this direction, the objective function $(7.0.5)$ decreases fast; (ii) along this direction, a nonzero step can be achieved while not exceeding the feasible domain of the problem $(7.0.5)\sim(7.0.7)$; (iii) it has exactly $|B|$ nonzero components. Therefore finding the direction $d$ leads to solve the following linear programming problem:

$$\min \quad v(d) = (-e + H\alpha^k)^{\mathrm{T}}d \,, \tag{7.3.42}$$

$$\text{s.t.} \quad y^{\mathrm{T}}d = 0 \,, \tag{7.3.43}$$

$$d_i \geq 0, \quad i \in \{i|\ \alpha_i^k = 0\} \,, \tag{7.3.44}$$

$$d_i \leq 0, \quad i \in \{i|\ \alpha_i^k = C\} \,, \tag{7.3.45}$$

$$-1 \leqslant d_i \leqslant 1 \,, \tag{7.3.46}$$

$$|\{d_i|\ d_i \neq 0\}| = |B|, \tag{7.3.47}$$

where the objective function is dot product of $d$ with the gradient of the objective function (7.0.5)

$$v(d) = (-e + H\alpha^k)^{\mathrm{T}}d = \sum_{i=1}^{l} g_i d_i \,, \tag{7.3.48}$$

where $g_i = \left(-1 + \sum_{j=1}^{l} y_i y_j \alpha_j^k K(x_i, x_j)\right), v(d)$ states the rate of the descent of the objective function (7.0.5) along the direction $d$, the previous three constraints ensure that a nonzero step can be obtained along the direction $d$.

Note that solving the problem (7.3.42)$\sim$(7.3.47) aims to find out a subscript set of the nonzero components of $d$, and let the set be the working set $B$. Hence we do not need to solve it exactly or even get the approximate solution $\bar{d}$ of the problem (7.3.42)$\sim$(7.3.47), while only providing a rule of determining the subscripts (i.e. working set $B$) of the nonzero components of $d$, and explain that the determined subscript has a corresponding approximate solution $\bar{d}$ satisfying all constraints and has a negative objective value. Next we give the rule and then explain.

**Algorithm 7.3.1** *(Selecting working set $B$)*

(1) *Given the current* $\alpha^k = (\alpha_1^k, \cdots, \alpha_l^k)^{\mathrm{T}}$;

(2) *Choose the number* $|B|$ *of the working set* $B$, *where* $|B|$ *is an even number;*

(3) *Compute* $\vartheta_i = y_i g_i = y_i\left(-1 + \sum_{j=1}^{l} y_i y_j \alpha_j^k K(x_i, x_j)\right), i = 1, \cdots, l$. *For* $\vartheta_1, \cdots, \vartheta_l$, *rearrange them in decrease order to be* $\vartheta_{i_1}, \vartheta_{i_2}, \cdots, \vartheta_{i_l}$ *such that*

$$\vartheta_{i_1} \geqslant \vartheta_{i_2} \geq \cdots \geq \vartheta_{i_l}, \tag{7.3.49}$$

*correspondingly*

$$\alpha_{i_1}, \alpha_{i_2}, \cdots, \alpha_{i_l}; \tag{7.3.50}$$

(4) *Successively pick the* $\dfrac{|B|}{2}$ *elements from the top of the list* (7.3.50), *and the elements satisfy:* $0 < \alpha_{i_j} < C$, *or if* $\alpha_{i_j} = 0$, $y_{i_j} = -1$, *or* $\alpha_{i_j} = C$,

$y_{i_j} = 1$; then successively pick the $\dfrac{|B|}{2}$ elements from the bottom of the list (7.3.50), and the elements satisfy: $0 < \alpha_{i_j} < C$, or if $\alpha_{i_j} = 0$, $y_{i_j} = 1$, or if $\alpha_{i_j} = C$, $y_{i_j} = -1$. These subscripts corresponding to the $|B|$ elements variables compose the working set $B$.

In order to show the rationality of the selected $B$ by Algorithm 7.3.1, we only need to show that after restricting the components of $d$ to be nonzero only on the selected working set $B$, there still exists a feasible point $\bar{d}$ of the problem (7.3.42) ~(7.3.47) which has a negative objective value. In fact, we can construct $\bar{d}$ by the following rule: corresponding to the former $\dfrac{|B|}{2}$ subscripts $i$, let $\bar{d}_i = -y_i$; corresponding to the latter $\dfrac{|B|}{2}$ subscripts $i$, let $\bar{d}_i = y_i$, and other components are zero. It is easy to verity that $\bar{d}$ satisfies all constraints (7.3.43)~(7.3.47), and its objective value is negative.

Now we conclude the decomposing method solving the problem (7.0.5)~(7.0.7) corresponding to the training set (7.0.1) as follows:

**Algorithm 7.3.2** *(Decomposing)*

*(1) Select the number $|B|$ (even number) of the working set $B$ and the accuracy demand $\varepsilon$, choose the initial point $\alpha^0 = \begin{pmatrix} \alpha_B^0 \\ \alpha_N^0 \end{pmatrix}$, set $k = 0$;*

*(2) Select the working set $B$ by Algorithm 7.3.1 based on the current approximate solution $\alpha^k$;*

*(3) Solve the convex quadratic programming subproblem (7.3.39)~(7.3.41), obtaining the solution $\alpha_B^{k+1}$, update $\alpha^k$ to be $\alpha^{k+1} = \begin{pmatrix} \alpha_B^{k+1} \\ \alpha_N^k \end{pmatrix}$;*

*(4) If $\alpha^{k+1}$ satisfies one stopping criteria within the accuracy $\varepsilon$, obtaining the approximate solution $\alpha^* = \alpha^{k+1}$, and stop; else set $k = k + 1$, go to step (2).*

---

## 7.4 Sequential Minimal Optimization

A special type of decomposition method is the sequential minimal optimization (SMO), which restricts the working set $B$ to have only two elements, i.e. in each iteration only $\alpha_i$ and $\alpha_j$ corresponding to training points $(x_i, y_i)$ and $(x_j, y_j)$ need to be adjusted. Now the optimization subproblem (7.3.39)~(7.3.41) has only two variables. In fact, the size of the working set is the smallest, since the subproblem has the equality constraint $\displaystyle\sum_{i=1}^{l} \alpha_i y_i = 0$. If one multiplier $\alpha_i$ changes, then at least another multiplier should be adjusted at the same time to keep the constraints valid.

The scale of the subproblem and the required number of iterations of the whole algorithm is a contradiction. SMO reduces the size of the working set to the smallest, while it increases the number of the iterations directly. However, the advantage of this method is: this simple two-variable problem can be solved analytically without needing the iteration procedure of solving the convex quadratic programming problem. Each iteration chooses two variables, $\alpha_i$ and $\alpha_j$, to be adjusted while other variables fixed. After getting the solution $\alpha_i^*$ and $\alpha_j^*$ of the two variables optimization problem, the corresponding components of $\alpha$ are improved based on them. Compared with usual decomposing methods, though SMO needs more number of iterations, it often shows rapid convergence because of the small amount of computation in each iteration. Furthermore, this method has other important advantages, such as it does not require storage of kernel matrix, has no matrix operations, is easy to implement, and so on.

### 7.4.1  Main steps

The main steps of SMO solving the convex quadratic programming problem $(7.0.5) \sim (7.0.7)$ corresponding to the training set $(7.0.1)$ are sketched in the following algorithm:

**Algorithm 7.4.1** *(sequential minimal optimization, SMO)*

*(1) Choose accuracy demand $\varepsilon$, choose $\alpha^0 = (\alpha_1^0, \cdots, \alpha_l^0)^{\mathrm{T}} = 0$, set $k = 0$;*

*(2) Find a two-element working set $B = \{i, j\} \subset \{1, 2, \cdots, l\}$ based on the current feasible approximate solution $\alpha^k$;*

*(3) Solve the optimization problem $(7.3.39) \sim (7.3.41)$ corresponding to the working set $B$, getting the solution $\alpha_B^* = (\alpha_i^{k+1}, \alpha_j^{k+1})^{\mathrm{T}}$, then update the $i$-th and the $j$-th components of $\alpha^k$ to get the new feasible approximate solution $\alpha^{k+1}$;*

*(4) If $\alpha^{k+1}$ satisfies one stopping criteria within the accuracy $\varepsilon$, then set the approximate solution $\alpha^* = \alpha^{k+1}$, stop; otherwise, set $k = k + 1$, go to step (2).*

Two specific details implementing this algorithm are described below.

### 7.4.2  Selecting the working set

Suppose the current approximate solution $\alpha^k = (\alpha_1^k, \cdots, \alpha_l^k)^{\mathrm{T}}$. The question now is which two components should be adjusted. Referring to Theorem 7.1.3 introducing the second stopping criteria, we naturally hope that the adjustment can reduce the gap between $m(\alpha)$ and $M(\alpha)$, which induces the following heuristic algorithm selecting working set $B$:

**Algorithm 7.4.2** *(Selecting working set B)*

*(1) Suppose the current approximate solution of the problem* $(7.0.5) \sim (7.0.7)$ *is* $\alpha^k$; *compute the gradient of the objective function* $d(\alpha) = \dfrac{1}{2}\alpha^T H \alpha - e^T \alpha$ *at* $\alpha^k$

$$\nabla d(\alpha^k) = H\alpha^k - e; \qquad (7.4.51)$$

*(2) Compute*

$$i = \operatorname*{argmax}_{t}\{-y_t[\nabla d(\alpha^k)]_t \mid t \in I_{\text{up}}(\alpha^k)\}, \qquad (7.4.52)$$

$$j = \operatorname*{argmin}_{t}\{-y_t[\nabla d(\alpha^k)]_t \mid t \in I_{\text{low}}(\alpha^k)\}, \qquad (7.4.53)$$

*where*

$$I_{\text{up}}(\alpha) \equiv \{t \mid \alpha_t < C, y_t = 1 \ \text{or} \ \alpha_t > 0, y_t = -1\},$$
$$I_{\text{low}}(\alpha) \equiv \{t \mid \alpha_t < C, y_t = -1 \ \text{or} \ \alpha_t > 0, y_t = 1\};$$

*(3) Set* $B = \{i, j\}$.

An interesting fact is that it can be proved that the above algorithm is equivalent to the decomposing algorithm in which the working set is determined by solving the problem $(7.3.42) \sim (7.3.47)$ in the case of $|B| = 2$. Furthermore, the linear objective function of the problem $(7.3.42) \sim (7.3.47)$ is the first order approximation of the objective function $d(\alpha)$ given by $(7.0.5)$, therefore Algorithm 7.4.2 uses the first order approximation. So an approach further improving this algorithm is to use more accurate approximation; for example, change the objective function of the problem $(7.3.42) \sim (7.3.47)$ to be the quadratic objective function $d(\alpha)$ itself, or another approximating quadratic function; details can be found in [52].

### 7.4.3 Analytical solution of the two-variables problem

Now what needs to be addressed is how to search for the solution of the subproblem $(7.3.39) \sim (7.3.41)$ after selecting the working set $B = \{i, j\}$ in the $k + 1$-th iteration. Without loss of generality, suppose $B = \{1, 2\}$. Now the subproblem $(7.3.39) \sim (7.3.41)$ can be written as an optimization problem of two variables $\alpha_1$ and $\alpha_2$

$$\min \quad W(\alpha_1, \alpha_2) = \frac{1}{2}\beta_{11}\alpha_1^2 + \frac{1}{2}\beta_{22}\alpha_2^2 + y_1 y_2 \beta_{12}\alpha_1\alpha_2$$
$$-(\alpha_1 + \alpha_2) + y_1\beta_1\alpha_1 + y_2\beta_2\alpha_2, \qquad (7.4.54)$$

$$\text{s.t.} \quad \alpha_1 y_1 + \alpha_2 y_2 = -\sum_{i=3}^{l} y_i \alpha_i, \qquad (7.4.55)$$

$$0 \leqslant \alpha_i \leqslant C, i = 1, 2, \cdots, l, \qquad (7.4.56)$$

where

$$\beta_{11} = K(x_1, x_1), \quad \beta_{22} = K(x_2, x_2), \quad \beta_{12} = K(x_1, x_2),$$

$$\beta_1 = \sum_{i=3}^{l} y_i \alpha_i K(x_i, x_1), \quad \beta_2 = \sum_{i=3}^{l} y_i \alpha_i K(x_i, x_2). \qquad (7.4.57)$$

Considering that we update the feasible approximate solution continuously in the whole iteration procedure of this algorithm, there is already a feasible point $(\alpha_1^{\text{old}}, \alpha_2^{\text{old}})^{\text{T}}$ when the problem (7.4.4)~(7.4.7) is to be solved. For example, in the beginning of the $k+1$-th iteration, there is already a feasible approximate solution $\alpha^k = (\alpha_1^k, \alpha_2^k, \cdots, \alpha_l^k)^{\text{T}}$, so $\alpha_1^{\text{old}}$ and $\alpha_2^{\text{old}}$ can be chosen to be $\alpha_1^k$ and $\alpha_2^k$ respectively, we can start from the feasible point $(\alpha_1^{\text{old}}, \alpha_2^{\text{old}})^{\text{T}}$ to search for the solution $(\alpha_1^{\text{new}}, \alpha_2^{\text{new}})^{\text{T}}$ of this problem. Furthermore, in order to satisfy the linear constraint $\sum_{i=1}^{l} \alpha_i y_i = 0$, solution $(\alpha_1^{\text{new}}, \alpha_2^{\text{new}})^{\text{T}}$ should satisfy

$$\alpha_1 y_1 + \alpha_2 y_2 = \text{constant} = \alpha_1^{\text{old}} y_1 + \alpha_2^{\text{old}} y_2 \qquad (7.4.58)$$

and

$$0 \leqslant \alpha_1, \alpha_2 \leqslant C. \qquad (7.4.59)$$

Hence the variables of the objective function are restricted on a segment of $(\alpha_1, \alpha_2)$ space. The two-variables optimization problem turns to be a single-variable optimization problem on a finite interval, so it is easy to solve analytically. However, the derivation process is cumbersome and the details are omitted here. We describe the steps in the following algorithm:

**Algorithm 7.4.3** *(Solving the two-variables optimization problem)*

*(1) Suppose the optimization problem (7.4.54)~(7.4.57) is given, and the feasible point $(\alpha_1^{\text{old}}, \alpha_2^{\text{old}})^{\text{T}}$ is known;*

*(2) Compute*

$$\alpha_2^{\text{new,unc}} = \alpha_2^{\text{old}} + \frac{y_2 E}{\kappa}, \qquad (7.4.60)$$

*where*

$$E = \beta_1 - \beta_2 + \alpha_1^{\text{old}} y_1 (\beta_{11} - \beta_{12}) + \alpha_2^{\text{old}} y_2 (\beta_{21} - \beta_{22}) - y_1 + y_2, (7.4.61)$$

$$\kappa = \beta_{11} + \beta_{22} - 2\beta_{12}; \qquad (7.4.62)$$

*(3) Compute $\alpha_2^{\text{new}}$ based on $\alpha_2^{\text{new,unc}}$:*

$$\alpha_2^{\text{new}} = \begin{cases} V, & \text{if } \alpha_2^{\text{new,unc}} > V; \\ \alpha_2^{\text{new,unc}}, & \text{if } U \leqslant \alpha_2^{\text{new,unc}} \leqslant V; \\ U, & \text{if } \alpha_2^{\text{new,unc}} < U, \end{cases} \qquad (7.4.63)$$

*where $U$ and $V$ are determined by the following way: when $y_1 \neq y_2$,*

$$U = \max\{0, \alpha_2^{\text{old}} - \alpha_1^{\text{old}}\}, \qquad (7.4.64)$$

$$V = \min\{C, C - \alpha_1^{\text{old}} + \alpha_2^{\text{old}}\}; \qquad (7.4.65)$$

*when $y_1 = y_2$,*

$$U = \max\{0, \alpha_1^{\text{old}} + \alpha_2^{\text{old}} - C\} \,, \tag{7.4.66}$$
$$V = \min\{C, \alpha_1^{\text{old}} + \alpha_2^{\text{old}}\} \,; \tag{7.4.67}$$

*(4) Compute $\alpha_1^{\text{new}}$ based on $\alpha_2^{\text{new}}$:*

$$\alpha_1^{\text{new}} = \alpha_1^{\text{old}} + y_1 y_2 (\alpha_2^{\text{old}} - \alpha_2^{\text{new}}) \,; \tag{7.4.68}$$

*(5) Construct the solution $(\alpha_1^{\text{new}}, \alpha_2^{\text{new}})$ of the problem (7.4.54)~(7.4.57).*

---

## 7.5 Software

There are a lot of software programs about support vector machines, such as LIBSVM, LIBLINEAR[53], mySVM, SVM$^{\text{light}}$, etc. The free download websites and brief introductions of most software can be obtained from the website http://www.kernel-machines.org/software. Here we introduce the software LIBSVM briefly.

LIBSVM, developed by professor Lin Chih-Jen et al. of National Taiwan University, is a simple, easy-to-use, and efficient software for SVM classification and regression. The current release (Version 3.1, April 2011) of LIBSVM can be obtained free by downloading the zip file or tar.gz file from http://www.csie.ntu.edu.tw/~cjlin/libsvm/. The package includes the source code of the library in C++ and Java, and a simple program for scaling training data. LIBSVM also provides a simple interface that users can easily link with their own programs, such as Python, Java, R, MATLAB, Perl, Ruby, LabVIEW, and C♯.net; these are not only convenient to use in the Windows or UNIX platforms, but also to reform them according to their own need. LIBSVM also provides the executable files under the Windows operating system, including the training file *svmtrain.exe* for training support vector machine, the predicting file *svmpredict.exe* for predicting some dataset based on the trained support vector machine model, and the scaling file *svmscale.exe* for scaling both training set and testing set. All can be used directly in the DOS environment.

LIBSVM is an integrated software for support vector classification, such as Algorithm 4.3.1 (*C*-support vector classification), Algorithm 8.1.18 (*ν*-support vector classification), and support vector regression, such as Algorithm 4.3.5 (*ε*-support vector regression), Algorithm 8.2.6 (*ν*-support vector regression). Please refer to the website http://www.csie.ntu.edu.tw/~cjlin/libsvm/ for more details.

# Chapter 8

## Variants and Extensions of Support Vector Machines

The variants of classification and regression are proposed in this chapter. Some related problems are also discussed here. To save space, only main conclusions are given while almost all proofs of theorems are omitted.

## 8.1 Variants of Binary Support Vector Classification

Some variants of the standard $C$-SVC are introduced in this section. Remember the binary classification problem with the training set

$$T = \{(x_1, y_1), \cdots, (x_l, y_l)\}, \tag{8.1.1}$$

where $x_i \in R^n$, $y_i \in \mathcal{Y} = \{1, -1\}, i = 1, \cdots, l$. Our task is to find the decision function

$$f(x) = \operatorname{sgn}(g(x)), \tag{8.1.2}$$

where $g(x)$ is a real function in $R^n$.

### 8.1.1 Support vector classification with homogeneous decision function

Construct the linear classifier using a homogeneous hyperplane $(w \cdot x) = 0$ instead of a general hyperplane $(w \cdot x) + b = 0$. In other words, the decision function is in the form

$$f(x) = \operatorname{sgn}((w \cdot x)). \tag{8.1.3}$$

Following the derivation of the standard $C$-SVC, we start from the linearly separable problem in $R^2$, where the positive and negative inputs can be separated correctly by a straight line $(w \cdot x) = 0$ passing through the origin, see Figure 8.1. The maximal margin principle leads to the following primal problem

$$\min_{w} \quad \frac{1}{2} \|w\|^2, \tag{8.1.4}$$

$$\text{s.t.} \quad y_i(w \cdot x_i) \geqslant 1, \ i = 1, \cdots, l. \tag{8.1.5}$$

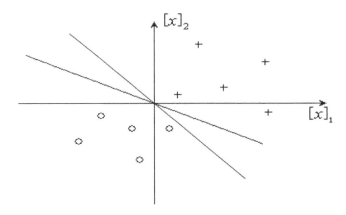

**FIGURE 8.1**: Linearly separable problem with homogeneous decision function.

The above problem can be illustrated geometrically as follows: First, let us suppose that the straight line $(w \cdot x) = 0$ separates the inputs correctly and consider the above problem when the direction of $w$ is fixed. Now the problem is only searching for $\|w\|$. Obviously, when $\|w\|$ is very large, the field between the two straight lines

$$l_1 : (w \cdot x) = 1 \text{ and } l_{-1} : (w \cdot x) = -1 \tag{8.1.6}$$

does not cover any inputs and separates all positive and negative inputs correctly. However, when $\|w\|$ becomes smaller, $l_1$ and $l_{-1}$ will move to opposite sides parallelly. Denote the straight lines $l_1$ and $l_{-1}$ as $l_+$ and $l_-$ respectively when $l_1$ and/or $l_{-1}$ touch inputs the first time. Obviously, the vector $w$ corresponding to $l_+$ and $l_-$ is the solution to the problem (8.1.4)~(8.1.5) with a fixed direction of $w$.

Denoting the distance between the straight lines $l_+$ and $l_-$ as $d(w)$, the aim of the problem (8.1.4)~(8.1.5) is to find a vector $w$ such that the distance $d(w)$ is maximized. So this problem also embodies the principle of maximal margin, but with a different measure.

Now extend the above problem to $R^n$ and introduce the slack variables $\xi$. We will get the general primal problem

$$\min_{w,\xi} \quad \frac{1}{2}\|w\|^2 + C\sum_{i=1}^{l} \xi_i, \tag{8.1.7}$$

$$\text{s.t.} \quad y_i(w \cdot x_i) \geq 1 - \xi_i, \ i = 1, \cdots, l, \tag{8.1.8}$$

$$\xi_i \geq 0, \ i = 1, \cdots, l. \tag{8.1.9}$$

If mapping $\mathrm{x} = \Phi(x) : R^n \to \mathcal{H}$ is introduced, then the primal problem turns out to be a convex quadratic programming in $\mathcal{H}$

$$\min_{w,\xi} \quad \frac{1}{2}\|w\|^2 + C\sum_{i=1}^{l}\xi_i, \tag{8.1.10}$$

$$\text{s.t.} \quad y_i(w \cdot \Phi(x_i)) \geqslant 1 - \xi_i, \ i = 1,\cdots,l, \tag{8.1.11}$$

$$\xi_i \geqslant 0, \ i = 1,\cdots,l. \tag{8.1.12}$$

**Theorem 8.1.1** *Optimization problem*

$$\max_{\alpha} \quad -\frac{1}{2}\sum_{i=1}^{l}\sum_{j=1}^{l}y_iy_jK(x_i,x_j)\alpha_i\alpha_j + \sum_{i=1}^{l}\alpha_i, \tag{8.1.13}$$

$$\text{s.t.} \quad 0 \leqslant \alpha_i \leqslant C, i = 1,\cdots,l \tag{8.1.14}$$

*is the dual problem of the primal problem (8.1.10)~(8.1.12), where $K(x,x') = (\Phi(x) \cdot \Phi(x'))$ is the kernel function.*

**Theorem 8.1.2** *Support that $\alpha^* = (\alpha_1^*,\cdots,\alpha_l^*)^{\mathrm{T}}$ is any solution to the dual problem (8.1.13)~(8.1.14); then the solution to the primal problem (8.1.10)~(8.1.12) w.r.t. w can be obtained by*

$$w^* = \sum_{i=1}^{l}\alpha_i^* y_i \Phi(x_i). \tag{8.1.15}$$

Thus we can establish the following algorithm:

**Algorithm 8.1.3** *(Support vector machine with homogeneous decision function)*

*(1) Input the training set $T = \{(x_1,y_1),\cdots,(x_l,y_l)\}$, where $x_i \in R^n, y_i \in \mathcal{Y} = \{-1,1\}, i = 1,\cdots,l$;*

*(2) Choose an appropriate kernel function $K(x,x')$ and a penalty parameter $C > 0$;*

*(3) Construct and solve the convex quadratic programming*

$$\min_{\alpha} \quad \frac{1}{2}\sum_{i=1}^{l}\sum_{j=1}^{l}y_iy_jK(x_i,x_j)\alpha_i\alpha_j - \sum_{i=1}^{l}\alpha_i, \tag{8.1.16}$$

$$\text{s.t.} \quad 0 \leqslant \alpha_i \leqslant C, i = 1,\cdots,l, \tag{8.1.17}$$

*obtaining a solution $\alpha^* = (\alpha_1^*,\cdots,\alpha_l^*)^{\mathrm{T}}$;*

*(4) Construct the decision function $f(x) = \mathrm{sgn}\left(\sum_{i=1}^{l}\alpha_i^* y_i K(x,x_i)\right)$.*

## 8.1.2    Bounded support vector classification

In the linear classifier of the above algorithm (Algorithm 8.1.3), the separating hyperplane is restricted to pass through the origin. Usually this is not reasonable, for instance for the two-dimensional problem with the training set

$$T = \{(x_1, y_1), \cdots, (x_{10}, y_{10})\} \tag{8.1.18}$$

shown by Figure 8.2(a). Now we propose a modification and explain it by

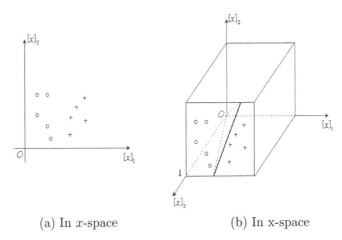

(a) In $x$-space                    (b) In x-space

**FIGURE 8.2**: Example form $x$-space to x-space with $\mathrm{x} = (x^{\mathrm{T}}, 1)^{\mathrm{T}}$.

taking the above problem as an example. Instead of dealing with the problem in $x$-space $R^2$ directly, introduce a transformation from $x = ([x]_1, [x]_2)^{\mathrm{T}}$-space $R^2$ into $\mathrm{x} = ([\mathrm{x}]_1, [\mathrm{x}]_2, [\mathrm{x}]_3)^{\mathrm{T}}$-space $R^3$

$$\mathrm{x} = (x^{\mathrm{T}}, 1)^{\mathrm{T}}. \tag{8.1.19}$$

Thus the training set $T$ in (8.1.18) is transformed into a new training set

$$T_1 = \{(\mathrm{x}_1, y_1), \cdots, (\mathrm{x}_{10}, y_{10})\} \tag{8.1.20}$$

where

$$\mathrm{x}_i = (x_i^{\mathrm{T}}, 1)^{\mathrm{T}}, i = 1, \cdots, 10, \tag{8.1.21}$$

see Figure 8.2(b). Now the classification problem with training set $T_1$ is a problem in x-space $R^3$. Corresponding to the primal problem (8.1.10)~(8.1.12), the primal problem in $\mathrm{x} = (x^{\mathrm{T}}, 1)^{\mathrm{T}}$-space is

$$\min_{\mathrm{w}, \xi} \quad \frac{1}{2} \|\mathrm{w}\|^2 + C \sum_{i=1}^{10} \xi_i, \tag{8.1.22}$$

$$\text{s.t.} \quad y_i(\mathrm{w} \cdot \mathrm{x}_i) \geqslant 1 - \xi_i, \ i = 1, \cdots, 10, \tag{8.1.23}$$

$$\xi_i \geqslant 0, \ i = 1, \cdots, 10. \tag{8.1.24}$$

This leads to the separating plane in $R^3$

$$(w^* \cdot x) = w_1^*[x]_1 + w_2^*[x]_2 + w_3^*[x]_3 = 0, \tag{8.1.25}$$

where $w^* = (w_1^*, w_2^*, w_3^*)^T$ is the solution to the problem (8.1.22)~(8.1.24) w.r.t. w. So the separating straight line on the plane $\Pi$: $[x]_3 = 1$ is

$$w_1^*[x]_1 + w_2^*[x]_2 + w_3^* = 0, \tag{8.1.26}$$

See Figure 8.2(b). Returning to the $x$-space $R^2$, the corresponding separating straight line should be

$$w_1^*[x]_1 + w_2^*[x]_2 + w_3^* = 0. \tag{8.1.27}$$

Replacing $w = (w_1, w_2, w_3)^T$ by $(w_1, w_2, b)^T = (w^T, b)^T$ and noticing (8.1.19), the problem (8.1.22)~(8.1.24) and the separating straight line (8.1.25) becomes

$$\min_{w,b,\xi} \quad \frac{1}{2}\|w\|^2 + \frac{1}{2}b^2 + C\sum_{i=1}^{10}\xi_i, \tag{8.1.28}$$

$$\text{s.t.} \quad y_i((w \cdot x_i) + b) \geqslant 1 - \xi_i, \ i = 1, \cdots, 10, \tag{8.1.29}$$

$$\xi_i \geqslant 0, \ i = 1, \cdots, 10. \tag{8.1.30}$$

and

$$(w^* \cdot x) + b^* = 0, \tag{8.1.31}$$

respectively, where $(w^*, b^*)$ is the solution to the problem (8.1.28)~(8.1.30) w.r.t. $(w, b)$. This implies that a new variant of support vector classification can be derived by considering the problem (8.1.28)~(8.1.30) as the primal problem. In fact, this is just what the Bounded SVC does, see [104].

Comparing with the standard $C$-support vector classification, linear bounded support vector classification has also the decision function in the form

$$f(x) = \text{sgn}((w \cdot x) + b), \tag{8.1.32}$$

and the only difference between their primal problems is that the term $\frac{1}{2}\|w\|^2$ is replaced by $\frac{1}{2}(\|w\|^2 + b^2)$. This difference comes from the maximal principle in different spaces considered; in the objective function, the term $\frac{1}{2}\|w\|^2$ corresponds to x-space while the term $\frac{1}{2}(\|w\|^2 + b^2)$ to the $x = (x^T, 1)^T$-space. Introducing the transformation $x = \Phi(x)$ and the corresponding kernel function $K(x, x') = (\Phi(x) \cdot \Phi(x'))$, the primal problem becomes the convex quadratic programming

$$\min_{w,b,\xi} \quad \frac{1}{2}(\|w\|^2 + b^2) + C\sum_{i=1}^{l}\xi_i, \tag{8.1.33}$$

$$\text{s.t.} \quad y_i((w \cdot \Phi(x_i)) + b) \geqslant 1 - \xi_i, \ i = 1, \cdots, l, \tag{8.1.34}$$

$$\xi_i \geqslant 0, \ i = 1, \cdots, l. \tag{8.1.35}$$

**Theorem 8.1.4** *There exists a unique solution* $(\mathrm{w}^*, b^*)$ *to the primal problem* (8.1.33)~(8.1.35).

**Theorem 8.1.5** *Optimization problem*

$$\max_{\alpha} \quad -\frac{1}{2}\sum_{i=1}^{l}\sum_{j=1}^{l}\alpha_i\alpha_j y_i y_j (K(x_i, x_j) + 1) + \sum_{i=1}^{l}\alpha_i, \qquad (8.1.36)$$

$$\text{s.t.} \quad 0 \leqslant \alpha_i \leqslant C, \; i = 1, \cdots, l \qquad (8.1.37)$$

*is the dual problem of the primal problem* (8.1.33)~(8.1.35).

**Theorem 8.1.6** *Suppose* $\alpha^* = (\alpha_1^*, \cdots, \alpha_l^*)^{\mathrm{T}}$ *is the solution to the dual problem* (8.1.36)~(8.1.37), *then the solution to the primal problem* (8.1.33)~(8.1.35) *w.r.t.* $(\mathrm{w}, b)$ *can be obtained by*

$$\mathrm{w}^* = \sum_{i=1}^{l}\alpha_i^* y_i \Phi(x_i), \qquad (8.1.38)$$

$$b^* = \sum_{i=1}^{l}\alpha_i^* y_i. \qquad (8.1.39)$$

Thus we can establish the following algorithm.

**Algorithm 8.1.7** *(Bounded C-support vector classification)*

*(1) Input the training set* $T = \{(x_1, y_1), \cdots, (x_l, y_l)\}$, *where* $x_i \in R^n, y_i \in \mathcal{Y} = \{-1, 1\}, i = 1, \cdots, l$;

*(2) Choose an appropriate kernel function* $K(x, x')$ *and a penalty parameter* $C > 0$;

*(3) Construct and solve the convex quadratic programming*

$$\min_{\alpha} \quad \frac{1}{2}\sum_{i=1}^{l}\sum_{j=1}^{l}\alpha_i\alpha_j y_i y_j (K(x_i, x_j) + 1) - \sum_{i=1}^{l}\alpha_i, \qquad (8.1.40)$$

$$\text{s.t.} \quad 0 \leqslant \alpha_i \leqslant C, \; i = 1, \cdots, l, \qquad (8.1.41)$$

*obtaining the solution* $\alpha^* = (\alpha_1^*, \cdots, \alpha_l^*)^{\mathrm{T}}$;

*(4) Construct the decision function* $f(x) = \mathrm{sgn}\left(\sum_{i=1}^{l}\alpha_i^* y_i (K(x, x_i) + 1)\right)$.

**Remark 8.1.8** *(The relationship between Algorithm 8.1.7 and Algorithm 8.1.3) It can be found by comparing the problems* (8.1.36)~(8.1.37) *and* (8.1.13)~(8.1.14) *that Algorithm 8.1.7 with the kernel* $K(x, x')$ *and Algorithm 8.1.3 with the kernel* $K(x, x') + 1$ *are identical.*

## 8.1.3 Least squares support vector classification

Just like the standard $C$-support vector classification, the starting point of least squares support vector classification (LSSVC)[141, 140] is also to find a separating hyperplane $(w \cdot x) + b = 0$, but with a different primal problem. In fact, introducing the transformation $x = \Phi(x)$ and the corresponding kernel $K(x, x') = (\Phi(x) \cdot \Phi(x'))$, the primal problem becomes the convex quadratic programming

$$\min_{w,\eta,b} \quad \frac{1}{2}\|w\|^2 + \frac{C}{2}\sum_{i=1}^{l} \eta_i^2, \tag{8.1.42}$$

$$\text{s.t.} \quad y_i((w \cdot \Phi(x_i)) + b) = 1 - \eta_i, i = 1, \cdots, l. \tag{8.1.43}$$

The geometric interpretation of the above problem with $x \in R^2$ is shown in Figure 8.3, where minimizing $\frac{1}{2}\|w\|^2$ realizes the maximal margin between the straight lines

$$(w \cdot x) + b = 1 \text{ and } (w \cdot x) + b = -1, \tag{8.1.44}$$

while minimizing $\sum_{i=1}^{l} \eta_i^2$ implies making the two straight lines (8.1.44) proximal to all inputs of positive points and negative points respectively.

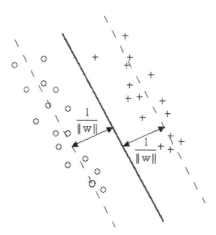

**FIGURE 8.3**: An interpretation of two-dimensional classification problem.

**Theorem 8.1.9** *Denoting*

$$\delta_{ij} = \begin{cases} 1, & i = j; \\ 0, & i \neq j, \end{cases} \tag{8.1.45}$$

*optimization problem*

$$\max_{\alpha} \quad -\frac{1}{2}\sum_{i=1}^{l}\sum_{j=1}^{l}\alpha_i\alpha_j y_i y_j \left(K(x_i, x_j) + \frac{\delta_{ij}}{C}\right) + \sum_{i=1}^{l}\alpha_i, \quad (8.1.46)$$

$$\text{s.t.} \quad \sum_{i=1}^{l}\alpha_i y_i = 0 \quad (8.1.47)$$

*is the dual problem of the primal problem (8.1.42)~(8.1.43).*

**Theorem 8.1.10** *Suppose* $\alpha^* = (\alpha_1^*, \cdots, \alpha_l^*)^{\mathrm{T}}$ *is any solution to the dual problem (8.1.46)~(8.1.47). Then a solution* $(\mathrm{w}^*, b^*)$ *to the primal problem (8.1.42)~(8.1.43) w.r.t.* $(\mathrm{w}, b)$ *can be obtained by*

$$\mathrm{w}^* = \sum_{i=1}^{l}\alpha_i^* y_i \Phi(x_i), \quad (8.1.48)$$

$$b^* = y_i\left(1 - \frac{\alpha_i^*}{C}\right) - \sum_{j=1}^{l}\alpha_j^* y_j K(x_j, x_i), \quad i \in \{1, \cdots, l\}. \quad (8.1.49)$$

Now we can establish the following algorithm according to above theorems:

**Algorithm 8.1.11** *(Least squares support vector classification, LSSVC)*

*(1) Input the training set* $T = \{(x_1, y_1), \cdots, (x_l, y_l)\}$, *where* $x_i \in R^n, y_i \in \mathcal{Y} = \{1, -1\}, i = 1, \cdots, l$;

*(2) Choose an appropriate kernel function* $K(x, x')$ *and a penalty parameter* $C > 0$;

*(3) Construct and solve the convex quadratic programming*

$$\min_{\alpha} \quad \frac{1}{2}\sum_{i=1}^{l}\sum_{j=1}^{l}\alpha_i\alpha_j y_i y_j \left(K(x_i, x_j) + \frac{\delta_{ij}}{C}\right) - \sum_{i=1}^{l}\alpha_i, \quad (8.1.50)$$

$$\text{s.t.} \quad \sum_{i=1}^{l}\alpha_i y_i = 0, \quad (8.1.51)$$

*obtaining a solution* $\alpha^* = (\alpha_1^*, \cdots, \alpha_l^*)^{\mathrm{T}}$;

*(4) Compute* $b^*$: *Choose a subscript* $i(1 \leqslant i \leqslant l)$, *then compute*

$$b^* = y_i\left(1 - \frac{\alpha_i^*}{C}\right) - \sum_{j=1}^{l}\alpha_j^* y_j K(x_j, x_i); \quad (8.1.52)$$

*(5) Construct the decision function*

$$f(x) = \text{sgn}(g(x)), \tag{8.1.53}$$

*where*

$$g(x) = \sum_{i=1}^{l} y_i \alpha_i^* K(x_i, x) + b^*. \tag{8.1.54}$$

**Remark 8.1.12** *There are two important differences between the above algorithm and Algorithm 4.3.1 (C-SVC):*

*(i) In C-SVC, the error is measured by the soft margin loss function (4.3.18). This leads to the fact that the decision function is decided only by the training points corresponding to support vectors and is unrelated to the training points corresponding to non-support vectors. However, in LSSVC, almost all training points contribute to the decision function, which makes the solution of LSSVC lose the sparseness.*

*(ii) The C-SVC needs to solve a quadratic programming with inequality constraints. However, LSSVC needs to solve a quadratic programming with only equality constraints, or equivalently a linear system of equations. Therefore, it is simpler and faster.*

For more discussion about least squares support vector machines, see [32, 33, 75, 81, 84, 99, 139, 138, 148, 185].

### 8.1.4 Proximal support vector classification

Proximal support vector classification (PSVC)[55] is very similar to least squares support vector classification. The only difference between their primal problems is that the term $\frac{1}{2}\|w\|^2$ in the latter is replaced by $\frac{1}{2}(\|w\|^2 + b^2)$ in the former, which is used and interpreted in Section 8.1.2 This makes the primal problem strictly convex quadratic programming

$$\min_{w,b,\eta} \quad \frac{1}{2}(\|w\|^2 + b^2) + \frac{C}{2} \sum_{i=1}^{l} \eta_i^2, \tag{8.1.55}$$

$$\text{s.t.} \quad y_i((w \cdot \Phi(x_i)) + b) = 1 - \eta_i, i = 1, \cdots, l. \tag{8.1.56}$$

**Theorem 8.1.13** *Unconstrained optimization problem*

$$\max_{\alpha} \quad -\frac{1}{2} \sum_{i=1}^{l} \sum_{j=1}^{l} \alpha_i \alpha_j y_i y_j (K(x_i, x_j) + 1) - \frac{1}{2C} \sum_{i=1}^{l} \alpha_i^2 + \sum_{i=1}^{l} \alpha_i \tag{8.1.57}$$

*is the dual problem of the primal problem (8.1.55)~(8.1.56).*

**Theorem 8.1.14** *Suppose that* $\alpha^* = (\alpha_1^*, \cdots, \alpha_l^*)^{\mathrm{T}}$ *is the solution to the dual problem (8.1.57). Then the unique solution* $(\mathrm{w}^*, b^*, \eta^*)$ *to the primal problem (8.1.55)~(8.1.56) can be expressed as*

$$\mathrm{w}^* = \sum_{i=1}^{l} \alpha_i^* y_i \Phi(x_i), \tag{8.1.58}$$

$$b^* = \sum_{i=1}^{l} y_i \alpha_i^*, \tag{8.1.59}$$

$$\eta^* = \alpha^*/C. \tag{8.1.60}$$

Thus, the following algorithm is established.

**Algorithm 8.1.15** *(Proximal support vector classification, PSVC)*

*(1) Input the training set* $T = \{(x_1, y_1), \cdots, (x_l, y_l)\}$, *where* $x_i \in R^n, y_i \in \mathcal{Y} = \{1, -1\}, i = 1, \cdots, l$;

*(2) Choose an appropriate kernel function* $K(x, x')$ *and a penalty parameter* $C > 0$;

*(3) Construct and solve the convex unconstrained optimization problem*

$$\min_{\alpha} \quad \frac{1}{2} \sum_{i=1}^{l} \sum_{j=1}^{l} \alpha_i \alpha_j y_i y_j (K(x_i, x_j) + 1) + \frac{1}{2C} \sum_{i=1}^{l} \alpha_i^2 - \sum_{i=1}^{l} \alpha_i, \tag{8.1.61}$$

*obtaining the solution* $\alpha^* = (\alpha_1^*, \cdots, \alpha_l^*)^{\mathrm{T}}$;

*(4) Compute* $b^*$:

$$b^* = \sum_{i=1}^{l} y_i \alpha_i^*; \tag{8.1.62}$$

*(5) Construct the decision function*

$$f(x) = \mathrm{sgn}(g(x)), \tag{8.1.63}$$

*where*

$$g(x) = \sum_{i=1}^{l} y_i \alpha_i^* K(x_i, x) + b^*. \tag{8.1.64}$$

Proximal support vector classification has the properties similar to Algorithm 8.1.11. In addition, another proximal support vector classification has been proposed in [55]. More references can refer to [56, 106, 153].

## 8.1.5   $\nu$-Support vector classification

In the above support vector classifications, the penalty parameter $C$ determines the tradeoff between two conflicting goals: maximizing the margin and minimizing the training error. The value of $C$ is qualitatively clear; the larger $C$ implies that more attention has been paid to minimizing the training error. However, it is gravely lacking in quantitative meaning. In order to overcome this drawback, the standard $C$-SVC is modified as $\nu$-support vector classification ($\nu$-SVC), where the penalty parameter $C$ is replaced by a parameter $\nu$.

### 8.1.5.1   $\nu$-Support vector classification

Introducing the transformation $\mathrm{x} = \Phi(x)$ and the corresponding kernel function $K(x, x') = (\Phi(x) \cdot \Phi(x'))$, the primal problem of $\nu$-SVC is the convex quadratic programming

$$\min_{\mathrm{w}, b, \xi, \rho} \quad \frac{1}{2}\|\mathrm{w}\|^2 - \nu\rho + \frac{1}{l}\sum_{i=1}^{l}\xi_i , \tag{8.1.65}$$

$$\text{s.t.} \quad y_i((\mathrm{w} \cdot \Phi(x_i)) + b) \geqslant \rho - \xi_i , i = 1, \cdots, l, \tag{8.1.66}$$

$$\xi_i \geqslant 0 , i = 1, \cdots, l ; \rho \geqslant 0 , \tag{8.1.67}$$

where $\nu \in (0, 1]$ is a preselected parameter.

**Theorem 8.1.16** *Optimization problem*

$$\max_{\alpha} \quad -\frac{1}{2}\sum_{i=1}^{l}\sum_{j=1}^{l}y_iy_j\alpha_i\alpha_jK(x_i, x_j) , \tag{8.1.68}$$

$$\text{s.t.} \quad \sum_{i=1}^{l}y_i\alpha_i = 0 , \tag{8.1.69}$$

$$0 \leqslant \alpha_i \leqslant \frac{1}{l}, \quad i = 1, \cdots, l , \tag{8.1.70}$$

$$\sum_{i=1}^{l}\alpha_i \geqslant \nu \tag{8.1.71}$$

*is the dual problem of the primal problem (8.1.65)~(8.1.67).*

**Theorem 8.1.17** *Suppose that $\alpha^* = (\alpha_1^*, \cdots, \alpha_l^*)^{\mathrm{T}}$ is any solution to the dual problem (8.1.68)~(8.1.71). If there exist two components of $\alpha^*$, $\alpha_j^*$ and $\alpha_k^*$, such that $\alpha_j^* \in \{\alpha_j^* | \alpha_i^* \in (0, 1/l), y_i = 1\}$ and $\alpha_k^* \in \{\alpha_i^* | \alpha_i^* \in (0, 1/l), y_i = -1\}$, then a solution $(\mathrm{w}^*, b^*, \rho^*)$ to the primal problem (8.1.65)~(8.1.67) w.r.t.*

$(w, b, \rho)$ *can be obtained by*

$$w^* = \sum_{i=1}^{l} \alpha_i^* y_i \Phi(x_i), \tag{8.1.72}$$

$$b^* = -\frac{1}{2} \sum_{i=1}^{l} \alpha_i^* y_i (K(x_i, x_j) + K(x_i, x_k)). \tag{8.1.73}$$

$$\rho^* = \sum_{i=1}^{l} \alpha_i^* y_i K(x_i, x_j) + b^* = -\sum_{i=1}^{l} \alpha_i^* y_i K(x_i, x_k) - b^*. \tag{8.1.74}$$

Thus we can establish the following algorithm:

**Algorithm 8.1.18** *($\nu$-support vector classification, $\nu$-SVC)*

*(1) Input the training set* $T = \{(x_1, y_1), \cdots, (x_l, y_l)\}$, *where* $x_i \in R^n, y_i \in \mathcal{Y} = \{1, -1\}, i = 1, \cdots, l;$

*(2) Choose an appropriate kernel function* $K(x, x')$ *and a parameter* $\nu \in (0, 1];$

*(3) Construct and solve the convex quadratic programming*

$$\min_{\alpha} \quad \frac{1}{2} \sum_{i=1}^{l} \sum_{j=1}^{l} y_i y_j \alpha_i \alpha_j K(x_i, x_j), \tag{8.1.75}$$

$$\text{s.t.} \quad \sum_{i=1}^{l} y_i \alpha_i = 0, \tag{8.1.76}$$

$$0 \leqslant \alpha_i \leqslant \frac{1}{l}, \quad i = 1, \cdots, l, \tag{8.1.77}$$

$$\sum_{i=1}^{l} \alpha_i \geqslant \nu, \tag{8.1.78}$$

*obtaining the solution* $\alpha^* = (\alpha_1^*, \cdots, \alpha_l^*)^{\mathrm{T}};$

*(4) Compute* $b^*$: *Choose two components of* $\alpha^*$, $\alpha_j^* \in \{\alpha_i^* | \alpha_i^* \in (0, 1/l), y_i = 1\}$ *and* $\alpha_k^* \in \{\alpha_i^* | \alpha_i^* \in (0, 1/l), y_i = -1\}$, *and compute*

$$b^* = -\frac{1}{2} \sum_{i=1}^{l} \alpha_i^* y_i (K(x_i, x_j) + K(x_i, x_k)); \tag{8.1.79}$$

*(5) Construct the decision function*

$$f(x) = \mathrm{sgn}\,(g(x)), \tag{8.1.80}$$

*where*

$$g(x) = \sum_{i=1}^{l} \alpha_i^* y_i K(x, x_i) + b^*. \tag{8.1.81}$$

**8.1.5.2 Relationship between $\nu$-SVC and $C$-SVC**

The following theorem shows that $\nu$-SVC is equivalent to $C$-SVC.

**Theorem 8.1.19** *There exists a non-increasing function $\nu = \varphi(C)$ : $(0, \infty) \to (0, 1]$ such that, for any $\overline{C} > 0$ and the corresponding $\overline{\nu} = \varphi(\overline{C})$, the decision functions obtained by $\nu$-SVC with $\nu = \overline{\nu}$ and $C$-SVC with $C = \overline{C}$ are identical if*
*(i) The same kernel function is chosen by both of them,*
*(ii) The decision functions can be computed by both of them, i.e. for $\nu$-SVC with $\nu = \overline{\nu}$ , two components $\alpha_j^*$ and $\alpha_k^*$ of $\alpha^*$ can be chosen such that $\alpha_j^* \in \{\alpha_i^* | \alpha_i^* \in (0, 1/l), y_i = 1\}$ and $\alpha_k^* \in \{\alpha_i^* | \alpha_i^* \in (0, 1/l), y_i = -1\}$, and for $C$-SVC with $C = \overline{C}$, one component $\alpha_j^*$ of $\alpha^*$ can be chosen such that $\alpha_j^* \in (0, C)$.*

**8.1.5.3 Significance of the parameter $\nu$**

The significance of the parameter $\nu$ is concerned with the terms of "support vector" and "training point with margin error". Suppose that $\alpha^* = (\alpha_1^*, \cdots, \alpha_l^*)^{\mathrm{T}}$ is the solution to the dual problem (8.1.68)~(8.1.71) obtained using Algorithm 8.1.18 ($\nu$-SVC). The input $x_i$ associated with the training point $(x_i, y_i)$ is still called a support vector if the corresponding component $\alpha_i^*$ of $\alpha^*$ is nonzero. The definition of training point with margin error is given below.

**Definition 8.1.20** *(Training point with margin error) Suppose that $\alpha^*$ is the solution to the dual problem (8.1.68)~(8.1.71), and the corresponding solution to the primal problem (8.1.65)~(8.1.67) is $(w^*, b^*, \rho^*, \xi^*) = (\cdot, \cdot, \rho^*, \cdot)$. The training point $(x_i, y_i)$ is called training point with margin error if the function $g(x)$ given by (8.1.81) satisfies*

$$y_i g(x_i) = y_i \left( \sum_{j=1}^{l} \alpha_j^* y_j K(x_j, x_i) + b^* \right) < \rho^*. \tag{8.1.82}$$

*Roughly speaking, a training point is the one whose input is not separated "sufficient" correctly.*

The significance of $\nu$ is shown by the following theorem.

**Theorem 8.1.21** *Suppose that Algorithm 8.1.18 ($\nu$-SVC) is performed on the training set (8.1.1) and the value $\rho^*$ is also computed by (8.1.74). If $\rho^* > 0$, then*
*(i) Denoting the number of the training points with margin error as $p$, we have $\nu \geqslant p/l$, i.e. $\nu$ is an upper bound on the fraction of the training points with margin error.*
*(ii) Denoting the number of support vectors as $q$, we have $\nu \leqslant q/l$, i.e. $\nu$ is a lower bound on the fraction of support vectors.*

In addition, it can also be shown under certain conditions that, with probability 1, both the fraction of training points with margin error and the fraction of support vectors approach to $\nu$ when the number $l$ of the training points tends to infinity.

For detailed discussions of $\nu$-support vector classification, we refer the reader to [21] and [126].

## 8.1.6 Linear programming support vector classifications (LPSVC)

In the above support vector classifications, quadratic programming problems need to be solved. However, it is also possible to formulate classification problems in linear programming, replacing the quadratic objective function by a linear function.

### 8.1.6.1 LPSVC corresponding to $C$-SVC

Remember the standard $C$-SVC. Introducing the transformation $\mathrm{x} = \Phi(x)$ and the corresponding kernel function $K(x, x') = (\Phi(x) \cdot \Phi(x'))$, the primal problem is

$$\min_{\mathrm{w},b,\xi} \quad \frac{1}{2}\|\mathrm{w}\|^2 + C\sum_{i=1}^{l} \xi_i, \tag{8.1.83}$$

$$\text{s.t.} \quad y_i((\mathrm{w} \cdot \Phi(x_i)) + b) \geqslant 1 - \xi_i \,, i = 1, \cdots, l \,, \tag{8.1.84}$$

$$\xi_i \geqslant 0, i = 1, \cdots, l, \tag{8.1.85}$$

and the corresponding dual problem is

$$\max_{\alpha} \quad \sum_{i=1}^{l} \alpha_i - \frac{1}{2}\sum_{i=1}^{l}\sum_{j=1}^{l} y_i y_j \alpha_i \alpha_j K(x_i, x_j) \,, \tag{8.1.86}$$

$$\text{s.t.} \quad \sum_{i=1}^{l} y_i \alpha_i = 0 \,, \tag{8.1.87}$$

$$0 \leqslant \alpha_i \leqslant C, \quad i = 1, \cdots, l. \tag{8.1.88}$$

After having solved the above dual problem, we can find the solution to the primal problem w.r.t. w

$$\mathrm{w}^* = \sum_{i=1}^{l} \alpha_i^* y_i \Phi(x_i), \tag{8.1.89}$$

and furthermore, construct the decision function.

It is well known that the optimal values of the primal problem and the dual problem are equal, i.e. if $(w^*, b^*, \xi^*)$ and $\alpha^* = (\alpha_1^*, \cdots, \alpha_l^*)^{\mathrm{T}}$ are the solutions to the primal problem (8.1.83)~(8.1.85) and dual problem (8.1.86)~(8.1.88) respectively, then

$$\frac{1}{2}\|w^*\|^2 + C\sum_{i=1}^{l}\xi_i^* = \sum_{i=1}^{l}\alpha_i^* - \frac{1}{2}\sum_{i=1}^{l}\sum_{j=1}^{l}y_iy_j\alpha_i^*\alpha_j^*K(x_i, x_j). \qquad (8.1.90)$$

On the other hand, equation (8.1.89) implies that

$$\|w^*\|^2 = \left(\sum_{i=1}^{l}\alpha_i^*y_i x_i \cdot \sum_{i=1}^{l}\alpha_i^*y_i x_i\right) = \sum_{i=1}^{l}\sum_{j=1}^{l}y_iy_j\alpha_i^*\alpha_j^*K(x_i, x_j). \qquad (8.1.91)$$

From (8.1.90) and (8.1.91), we get that

$$\sum_{i=1}^{l}\alpha_i^* = \|w^*\|^2 + C\sum_{i=1}^{l}\xi_i^*. \qquad (8.1.92)$$

or

$$\sum_{i=1}^{l}\alpha_i^* + C\sum_{i=1}^{l}\xi_i^* = 2\left(\frac{1}{2}\|w^*\|^2 + C\sum_{i=1}^{l}\xi_i^*\right). \qquad (8.1.93)$$

Now let us convert the problem (8.1.83)~(8.1.85) into a linear programming by a heuristic approach: first, looking at (8.1.93), replace the objective function (8.1.83) by $\sum_{i=1}^{l}\alpha_i + C\sum_{i=1}^{l}\xi_i$; then substitute w in (8.1.89) into the constraint (8.1.84); at last, add the constraint $\alpha \geqslant 0$. This leads to the problem

$$\min_{\alpha,b,\xi} \quad \sum_{i=1}^{l}\alpha_i + C\sum_{i=1}^{l}\xi_i, \qquad (8.1.94)$$

$$\text{s.t.} \quad y_i\left(\sum_{j=1}^{l}\alpha_jy_jK(x_j, x_i) + b\right) \geqslant 1 - \xi_i, i = 1, \cdots, l, \qquad (8.1.95)$$

$$\alpha_i, \xi_i \geqslant 0, i = 1, \cdots, l. \qquad (8.1.96)$$

After having solved the above problem and gotten its solution $\alpha^*$ w.r.t. $\alpha$, the decision function can be constructed in the same way as *C*-SVC does. Therefore, the corresponding algorithm can be established from Algorithm 4.3.1 (*C*-SVC) by replacing the convex quadratic programming (4.3.1)~(4.3.3) with the linear programming (8.1.94)~(8.1.96).

Corresponding to the primal problem (8.1.83)~(8.1.85), there is another linear programming

$$\min_{\alpha,\alpha^*,b,\xi} \quad \sum_{i=1}^{l}(\alpha_i + \alpha_i^*) + C\sum_{i=1}^{l}\xi_i , \tag{8.1.97}$$

$$\text{s.t.} \quad y_i\left(\sum_{j=1}^{l}(\alpha_j - \alpha_j^*)K(x_j,x_i) + b\right) \geq 1 - \xi_i , i = 1,\cdots,l, \tag{8.1.98}$$

$$\alpha_i,\alpha_i^*,\xi_i \geq 0, i = 1,\cdots,l . \tag{8.1.99}$$

See [124, 168] for details.

### 8.1.6.2 LPSVC corresponding to $\nu$-SVC

In the linear programming support vector classification (LPSVC) corresponding to $\nu$-SVC, the linear programming is

$$\min_{\alpha,\alpha^*,\xi,b,\rho} \quad \frac{1}{l}\sum_{i=1}^{l}\xi_i - \nu\rho , \tag{8.1.100}$$

$$\text{s.t.} \quad \frac{1}{l}\sum_{i=1}^{l}(\alpha_i + \alpha_i^*) = 1 , \tag{8.1.101}$$

$$y_i\left(\sum_{j=1}^{l}(\alpha_j - \alpha_j^*)K(x_j,x_i) + b\right) \geq \rho - \xi_i , i = 1,\cdots,l, \tag{8.1.102}$$

$$\alpha_i,\alpha_i^*,\xi_i, i = 1,\cdots,l, \; \rho \geq 0 . \tag{8.1.103}$$

The corresponding algorithm can be established from Algorithm 8.1.18 ($\nu$-SVC) by replacing the problem (8.1.68)~(8.1.71) with the problem (8.1.100)~(8.1.103); see [124] for details.

### 8.1.7 Twin support vector classification

For convenience, rewrite the training set by putting the negative training points after the positive training points as

$$T = \{(x_1,y_1),...,(x_p,y_p),(x_{p+1},y_{p+1}),...,(x_{p+q},y_{p+q})\}, \tag{8.1.104}$$

where $y_1 = ... = y_p = 1$, $y_{p+1} = ... = y_{p+q} = -1$.

Let us introduce the linear twin classifier first. Remember least squares SVC and Proximal SVC, their basic steps can be understood as follows: (i) Find two parallel hyperplanes, a positive hyperplane and a negative hyperplane such that they are proximal to all positive inputs and all negative inputs respectively as far as possible; (ii) construct the decision function from these two hyperplanes; an input $x$ is assigned to the positive class if the positive hyperplane is closer to the input $x$; the negative class otherwise.

The basic steps in linear twin SVC are similar to the above ones. The only difference is that it allows the two hyperplanes are not parallel. This idea was first proposed in [108], but the following approach comes from [86] and [129].

Suppose the two non-parallel hyperplanes are the positive hyperplane

$$(w_+ \cdot x) + b_+ = 0, \tag{8.1.105}$$

and the negative hyperplane

$$(w_- \cdot x) + b_- = 0. \tag{8.1.106}$$

The primal problems for finding these two hyperplanes are

$$\min_{w_+, b_+, \xi_-} \quad \frac{1}{2}c_1(\|w_+\|^2 + b_+^2) + \frac{1}{2}\sum_{i=1}^{p}((w_+ \cdot x_i) + b_+)^2 + c_2 \sum_{j=p+1}^{p+q} \xi_j,$$

$$\tag{8.1.107}$$

$$\text{s.t.} \quad (w_+ \cdot x_j) + b_+ \leq -1 + \xi_j, j = p+1, ..., p+q, \tag{8.1.108}$$

$$\xi_j \geq 0, j = p+1, ..., p+q \tag{8.1.109}$$

and

$$\min_{w_-, b_-, \xi_+} \quad \frac{1}{2}c_3(\|w_-\|^2 + b_-^2) + \frac{1}{2}\sum_{i=p+1}^{p+q} ((w_- \cdot x_i) + b_-)^2 + c_4 \sum_{j=1}^{p} \xi_j,$$

$$\tag{8.1.110}$$

$$\text{s.t.} \quad (w_- \cdot x_j) + b_- \geq 1 - \xi_j, j = 1, ..., p, \tag{8.1.111}$$

$$\xi_j \geq 0, j = 1, ..., p \tag{8.1.112}$$

respectively, where $c_1 > 0$, $c_2 > 0$, $c_3 > 0$, $c_4 > 0$ are parameters, $\xi_- = (\xi_{p+1}, ..., \xi_{p+q})^T$, $\xi_+ = (\xi_1, ..., \xi_p)^T$.

For both of the above primal problems, an interpretation can be offered in the same way, so only the former one is considered here. Among the three terms in the objective function (8.1.107), the second term makes the positive hyperplane proximal to all positive inputs, the third term with the constraints (8.1.108) and (8.1.109) require the positive hyperplane to be at a distance from the negative inputs by pushing the negative inputs to the other side of the bounding hyperplane $(w_+ \cdot x) + b_+ = -1$, where a set $\xi$ of variables is used to measure the error whenever the positive hyperplane is close to the negative inputs. The first term realizes the maximal margin between the positive hyperplane $(w_+ \cdot x) + b_+ = 0$ and the bounding hyperplane $(w_+ \cdot x) + b_+ = -1$. However, similar to the discussion in bounded support vector classification and proximal support vector classification, this margin is measured by the distance $d$ between these two hyperplanes in $R^{n+1}$ space

$$(\bar{w}_+ \cdot \mathrm{x}) = 0 \; and \; (\bar{w}_+ \cdot \mathrm{x}) = -1, \tag{8.1.113}$$

where $\bar{w}_+^{\mathrm{T}} = (w_+^{\mathrm{T}}, b_+)^{\mathrm{T}}$. Obviously, the distance $d$ can be expressed as

$$\frac{1}{\|\bar{w}\|} = \frac{1}{\sqrt{\|w_+\|^2 + b_+^2}}. \qquad (8.1.114)$$

Therefore, the first term in (8.1.107) embodies the maximal margin principle. Introducing the matrices

$$A = (x_1, ..., x_p)^{\mathrm{T}} \in R^{p \times n}, B = (x_{p+1}, ..., x_{p+q})^{\mathrm{T}} \in R^{q \times n}, \qquad (8.1.115)$$

the problems (8.1.107)~(8.1.109) and (8.1.110)~(8.1.112) can be written as

$$\min_{w_+, b_+, \xi_-} \quad \frac{1}{2}c_1(\|w_+\|^2 + b_+^2) + \frac{1}{2}\|Aw_+ + e_1b_+\|^2 + c_2 e_2^{\mathrm{T}} \xi_-, (8.1.116)$$

$$\text{s.t.} \quad -(Bw_+ + e_2b_+) + \xi_- \geq e_2, \ \xi_- \geq 0, \qquad (8.1.117)$$

and

$$\min_{w_-, b_-, \xi_+} \quad \frac{1}{2}c_3(\|w_-\|^2 + b_-^2) + \frac{1}{2}\|Bw_- + e_2b_-\|^2 + c_4 e_1^{\mathrm{T}} \xi_+, (8.1.118)$$

$$\text{s.t.} \quad Aw_- + e_1b_- + \xi_+ \geq e_1, \ \xi_+ \geq 0, \qquad (8.1.119)$$

respectively, where $e_1$ and $e_2$ are vectors of ones of appropriate dimension.

**Theorem 8.1.22** *Optimization problems*

$$\max_{\alpha} \quad e_2^{\mathrm{T}} \alpha - \frac{1}{2} \alpha^{\mathrm{T}} G(H^{\mathrm{T}}H + c_1 I)^{-1}G^{\mathrm{T}}\alpha, \qquad (8.1.120)$$

$$\text{s.t.} \quad 0 \leq \alpha \leq c_2 \qquad (8.1.121)$$

*and*

$$\max_{\gamma} \quad e_1^{\mathrm{T}} \gamma - \frac{1}{2} \gamma^{\mathrm{T}} H(G^{\mathrm{T}}G + c_3 I)^{-1}H^{\mathrm{T}}\gamma, \qquad (8.1.122)$$

$$\text{s.t.} \quad 0 \leq \gamma \leq c_4 \qquad (8.1.123)$$

*are the dual problems of the problems (8.1.107)~(8.1.109) and (8.1.110)~(8.1.112) respectively, where $H = [A \ \ e_1]$, $G = [B \ \ e_2]$.*

**Theorem 8.1.23** *Suppose that $\alpha^*$ and $\gamma^*$ are the solutions to the dual problems (8.1.120)~(8.1.121) and (8.1.122)~(8.1.123) respectively, then the solutions $(w_+^*, b_+^*)$ and $(w_-^*, b_-^*)$ to the primal problems w.r.t. $(w_+, b_+)$ and $(w_-, b_-)$ can be obtained by*

$$(w_+^{*\mathrm{T}}, \ b_+^*)^{\mathrm{T}} = -(H^{\mathrm{T}}H + c_1 I)^{-1}G^{\mathrm{T}}\alpha^*, \qquad (8.1.124)$$

*and*

$$(w_-^{*\mathrm{T}}, \ b_-^*)^{\mathrm{T}} = (G^{\mathrm{T}}G + c_3 I)^{-1}H^{\mathrm{T}}\gamma^*, \qquad (8.1.125)$$

*respectively.*

Once the positive hyperplane $(w_+^* \cdot x) + b_+^* = 0$ and the negative hyperplane $(w_-^* \cdot x) + b_-^* = 0$ are obtained, the decision function can be easily constructed: a new input is assigned to the positive class if the positive hyperplane is closer to the new input; the negative class otherwise. Thus the following algorithm is established.

**Algorithm 8.1.24** *(Linear twin support vector classification, LTSVC)*

*(1) Input the training set* $T = \{(x_1, y_1), ..., (x_p, y_p), (x_{p+1}, y_{p+1}), ..., (x_{p+q}, y_{p+q})\}$, *where* $x_i \in R^n, i = 1, ..., p + q$, $y_1 = ... = y_p = 1$, $y_{p+1} = ... = y_{p+q} = -1$.

*(2) Choose appropriate parameters* $c_1 > 0$, $c_2 > 0$, $c_3 > 0$, $c_4 > 0$;

*(3) Construct and solve the strictly convex quadratic programming problems*

$$\min_{\alpha} \quad \frac{1}{2}\alpha^T G(H^T H + c_1 I)^{-1} G^T \alpha - e_2^T \alpha, \quad (8.1.126)$$

$$s.t. \quad 0 \le \alpha \le c_2 \quad (8.1.127)$$

*and*

$$\min_{\gamma} \quad \frac{1}{2}\gamma^T H(G^T G + c_3 I)^{-1} H^T \gamma - e_1^T \gamma, \quad (8.1.128)$$

$$s.t. \quad 0 \le \gamma \le c_4 \quad (8.1.129)$$

*where* $H = [A \ \ e_1]$, $G = [B \ \ e_2]$, $A = [x_1, ..., x_p]^T$, $B = [x_{p+1}, ..., x_{p+q}]^T$, $e_1$ *and* $e_2$ *are vectors of ones of appropriate dimension, obtaining the solutions* $\alpha^* = (\alpha_1^*, \cdots, \alpha_q^*)$ *and* $\gamma^* = (\gamma_1^*, \cdots, \gamma_p^*)$ *respectively;*

*(4) Compute* $(w_+^*, b_+^*)$ *and* $(w_-^*, b_-^*)$:

$$\begin{pmatrix} w_+^* \\ b_+^* \end{pmatrix} = -(H^T H + c_1 I)^{-1} G^T \alpha^*, \quad \begin{pmatrix} w_-^* \\ b_-^* \end{pmatrix} - (G^T G + c_3 I)^{-1} H^T \gamma^*.$$

$$(8.1.130)$$

*(5) Construct the decision function*

$$f(x) = \begin{cases} 1, & if \ \frac{|(w_+^* \cdot x) + b_+^*|}{\|w_+^*\|} \le \frac{|(w_-^* \cdot x) + b_-^*|}{\|w_-^*\|}; \\ -1 & otherwise, \end{cases} \quad (8.1.131)$$

Corresponding to the above linear classifier, the nonlinear classifier can also be established. Introducing the transformation $x = \Phi(x) : R^n \to \mathcal{H}$ and the kernel function $K(x, x') = (\Phi(x) \cdot \Phi(x'))$, we need to find the positive and negative hyperplanes

$$(w_+ \cdot x) + b_+ = 0 \quad (8.1.132)$$

and

$$(w_- \cdot x) + b_- = 0. \tag{8.1.133}$$

For the positive hyperplane (8.1.132), we should solve the primal problem

$$\min_{w_+, b_+, \xi_-} \quad \frac{1}{2}c_1(\|w_+\|^2 + b_+^2) + \frac{1}{2}\sum_{i=1}^{p}((w_+ \cdot x_i) + b_+)^2 + c_2 \sum_{j=p+1}^{p+q} \xi_j, \tag{8.1.134}$$

$$\text{s.t.} \quad ((w_+ \cdot x_j) + b_+) \leq -1 + \xi_j, j = p+1, ..., p+q, \tag{8.1.135}$$

$$\xi_j \geq 0, j = p+1, ..., p+q \tag{8.1.136}$$

Thus, a natural approach is to derive the dual problem of the above primal problem and obtain $(w_+^*, b_+^*)$ from the solution of the dual problem, as we did for the problem (4.1.6)~(4.1.8). Unfortunately, this approach does not work here. In fact, it can be found that, in the dual problem (4.1.10)~(4.1.14) of the problem (4.1.6)~(4.1.8), $\Phi$ appears always in the form of inner products $(\Phi(x_i) \cdot \Phi(x_j))$, instead of any single $\Phi$. This is the reason that enables us to express the dual problem by the kernel function $K$. However, the situation is different for the problem (8.1.134)~(8.1.136) where the single $\Phi$ appears in its dual problem, and therefore this approach fails in this setting.

Due to the above difficulty in solving the problem (8.1.134)~(8.1.136), we introduce a general approach to find its approximate solution.

Suppose that $w_+$ can be expressed as

$$w_+ = \sum_{k=1}^{p+q} u_+^k \Phi(x_k), \tag{8.1.137}$$

where $x_k$, $k = 1, ..., p+q$ are the inputs of the training points, $u_+^1, ..., u_+^{p+q}$ are the undetermined coefficients. This implies that $w_+$ is restricted in the subspace spanned by $\{\Phi(x_1), \cdots, \Phi(x_{p+q})\}$ although we should find $w_+$ in the whole space $\mathcal{H}$. Thus the problem (8.1.134)~(8.1.136) becomes

$$\min_{u_+, b_+, \xi_-} \quad \frac{1}{2}c_1(\|\sum_{k=1}^{p+q} u_+^k \Phi(x_k)\|^2 + b_+^2)$$

$$+ \frac{1}{2}\sum_{i=1}^{p}(\sum_{k=1}^{p+q} u_+^k K(x_i, x_k) + b_+)^2 + c_2 \sum_{j=p+1}^{p+q} \xi_j, \tag{8.1.138}$$

$$\text{s.t.} \quad -(\sum_{k=1}^{p+q} u_+^k K(x_j, x_k) + b_+) + \xi_j \geq 1, j = p+1, ..., p+q, \tag{8.1.139}$$

$$\xi_j \geq 0, j = p+1, ..., p+q, \tag{8.1.140}$$

where $u_+ = (u_+^1, ..., u_+^{p+q})^{\mathrm{T}}$ and $\xi_- = (\xi_{p+1}, ..., \xi_{p+q})^{\mathrm{T}}$. Introducing

$$\widetilde{A} = \begin{pmatrix} K(x_1, x_1) & ... & K(x_1, x_{p+q}) \\ ... & ... & ... \\ K(x_p, x_1) & ... & K(x_p, x_{p+q}) \end{pmatrix},$$

$$\widetilde{B} = \begin{pmatrix} K(x_{p+1}, x_1) & ... & K(x_{p+1}, x_{p+q}) \\ ... & ... & ... \\ K(x_{p+q}, x_1) & ... & K(x_{p+q}, x_{p+q}) \end{pmatrix} \tag{8.1.141}$$

and taking the approximation

$$\|\sum_{k=1}^{p+q} u_+^k \Phi(x_k)\|^2 \approx \|u_+\|^2, \tag{8.1.142}$$

the problem (8.1.138)$\sim$(8.1.140) can be written as

$$\min_{w_+, b_+, \xi_-} \quad \frac{1}{2} c_1(\|u_+\|^2 + b_+^2) + \frac{1}{2}\|\widetilde{A}u_+ + e_1 b_+\|^2 + c_2 e_2^{\mathrm{T}} \xi_-, \tag{8.1.143}$$

$$\text{s.t.} \quad -(\widetilde{B}u_+ + e_2 b_+) + \xi_- \geq e_2, \tag{8.1.144}$$

$$\xi_- \geq 0. \tag{8.1.145}$$

The form of the above problem is exactly the same as that of the problem (8.1.116)$\sim$(8.1.117) and can be solved in the same way, obtaining its solution $(u_+^{*\mathrm{T}}, b_+^*) = ((u_+^{*1}, ..., u_+^{*p+q}), b_+^*)$ w.r.t. $(u_+, b_+)$ and the positive hyperplane in Hilbert space $\mathcal{H}$

$$(\sum_{k=1}^{p+q} u_+^{*k} \Phi(x_k) \cdot x) + b_+^* = 0. \tag{8.1.146}$$

Similarly, we can also obtain the negative hyperplane

$$(\sum_{k=1}^{p+q} u_-^{*k} \Phi(x_k) \cdot x) + b_-^* = 0. \tag{8.1.147}$$

Obviously, the above two hyperplanes formed the basis of the decision function: a new input is assigned to the positive class if the positive hyperplane is closer; to the negative class otherwise. Thus the following algorithm is established.

**Algorithm 8.1.25** *(Twin support vector classification, TSVC)*

*(1) Input the training set* $T = \{(x_1, y_1), ..., (x_p, y_p), (x_{p+1}, y_{p+1}), ..., (x_{p+q}, y_{p+q})\}$, *where* $x_i \in R^n, i = 1, ..., p + q$, $y_1 = ... = y_p = 1$, $y_{p+1} = ... = y_{p+q} = -1$;

*(2) Choose an appropriate kernel function* $K(x, x')$ *and parameters* $c_1 > 0$, $c_2 > 0$, $c_3 > 0$, $c_4 > 0$;

*(3) Construct and solve the strictly convex quadratic programming*

$$\max_{\alpha} \quad e_2^{\mathrm{T}} \alpha - \frac{1}{2} \alpha^{\mathrm{T}} \widetilde{G} (\widetilde{H} \widetilde{H}^{\mathrm{T}} + c_1 I)^{-1} \widetilde{G}^{\mathrm{T}} \alpha, \tag{8.1.148}$$

$$\text{s.t.} \quad 0 \leq \alpha \leq c_2, \tag{8.1.149}$$

*and*

$$\max_{\gamma} \quad e_1^{\mathrm{T}} \gamma - \frac{1}{2} \gamma^{\mathrm{T}} \widetilde{H} (\widetilde{G} \widetilde{G}^{\mathrm{T}} + c_3 I)^{-1} \widetilde{H}^{\mathrm{T}} \gamma, \tag{8.1.150}$$

$$\text{s.t.} \quad 0 \leq \gamma \leq c_4, \tag{8.1.151}$$

*where* $\widetilde{H} = [\widetilde{A}, e_1]$, $\widetilde{G} = [\widetilde{B}, e_2]$, $e_1$ *and* $e_2$ *are vectors of ones of appropriate dimension,* $\widetilde{A} = \begin{pmatrix} K(x_1, x_1) & \dots & K(x_1, x_{p+q}) \\ \dots & \dots & \dots \\ K(x_p, x_1) & \dots & K(x_p, x_{p+q}) \end{pmatrix}$, $\widetilde{B} = \begin{pmatrix} K(x_{p+1}, x_1) & \dots & K(x_{p+1}, x_{p+q}) \\ \dots & \dots & \dots \\ K(x_{p+q}, x_1) & \dots & K(x_{p+q}, x_{p+q}) \end{pmatrix}$, *obtaining the solutions* $\alpha^* = (\alpha_1^*, \cdots, \alpha_q^*)$, $\gamma^* = (\gamma_1^*, \cdots, \gamma_p^*)$ *respectively;*

*(4) Compute* $(u_+^{*\mathrm{T}}, b_+^*) = ((u_+^{*1}, ..., u_+^{*p+q}), b_+^*)$ *and* $(u_-^{*\mathrm{T}}, b_-^*) = ((u_-^{*1}, ..., u_-^{*p+q}), b_-^*)$:

$$\begin{pmatrix} u_+^* \\ b_+^* \end{pmatrix} = -(\widetilde{H}^{\mathrm{T}} \widetilde{H} + c_1 I)^{-1} \widetilde{G}^{\mathrm{T}} \alpha^*, \quad \begin{pmatrix} u_-^* \\ b_-^* \end{pmatrix} = (\widetilde{G}^{\mathrm{T}} \widetilde{G} + c_3 I)^{-1} \widetilde{H}^{\mathrm{T}} \gamma^*; \tag{8.1.152}$$

*(5) Construct the decision function*

$$f(x) = \begin{cases} 1, & if \ \frac{\sum_{k=1}^{p+q} u_+^{*k} K(x_k, x) + b_+^*|}{\sqrt{u_+^{*\mathrm{T}} C u_+^*}} \leq \frac{\sum_{k=1}^{p+q} u_-^{*k} K(x_k, x) + b_-^*|}{\sqrt{u_-^{*\mathrm{T}} C u_-^*}}; \\ -1, & otherwise, \end{cases} \tag{8.1.153}$$

*where* $C = [\widetilde{A}, \widetilde{B}]^{\mathrm{T}}$.

Twin support vector machines have been studied extensively recently; see references [85, 92, 93, 117, 119].

---

## 8.2 Variants of Support Vector Regression

Some variants of $\varepsilon$-SVR are introduced in this section. Remember the regression problem with the training set

$$T = \{(x_1, y_1), \cdots, (x_l, y_l)\}, \tag{8.2.1}$$

where $x_i \in R^n$, $y_i \in \mathcal{Y} = R$, $i = 1, \cdots, l$, our task is to find a real function $g(x)$ in $R^n$, to derive the value of $y$ for any input $x$ by the function $y = g(x)$.

## 8.2.1   Least squares support vector regression

Just like $\varepsilon$-support vector regression, the starting point of least squares support vector regression (LSSVR) [140]) is also to find a decision function $y = (w \cdot x) + b$, but with different primal problems. In fact, introducing the transformation $\mathrm{x} = \Phi(x)$ and the corresponding kernel $K(x, x') = (\Phi(x) \cdot \Phi(x'))$, the primal problem becomes the convex quadratic programming

$$\min_{\mathrm{w},b,\eta} \quad \frac{1}{2}\|\mathrm{w}\|^2 + \frac{C}{2}\sum_{i=1}^{l}\eta_i^2 \, , \tag{8.2.2}$$

$$\text{s.t.} \quad y_i - ((\mathrm{w} \cdot \Phi(x_i)) + b) = \eta_i \, , \ i = 1, \cdots, l \, . \tag{8.2.3}$$

**Theorem 8.2.1**   *Denoting*

$$\delta_{ij} = \left\{ \begin{array}{ll} 1, & i = j; \\ 0, & i \neq j, \end{array} \right. \tag{8.2.4}$$

*optimization problem*

$$\max_{\alpha} \quad -\frac{1}{2}\sum_{i=1}^{l}\sum_{j=1}^{l}\alpha_i\alpha_j\left(K(x_i, x_j) + \frac{\delta_{ij}}{C}\right) + \sum_{i=1}^{l}\alpha_i y_i \, , \tag{8.2.5}$$

$$\text{s.t.} \quad \sum_{i=1}^{l}\alpha_i = 0 \tag{8.2.6}$$

*is the dual problem of the primal problem (8.2.2)~(8.2.3).*

**Theorem 8.2.2** *Suppose $\alpha^* = (\alpha_1^*, \cdots, \alpha_l^*)^{\mathrm{T}}$ is any solution to the dual problem (8.2.5)~(8.2.6). Then a solution $(\bar{\mathrm{w}}, \bar{b})$ to the primal problem (8.2.2)~(8.2.3) w.r.t. $(\mathrm{w}, b)$ can be obtained by*

$$\bar{\mathrm{w}} = \sum_{i=1}^{l}\alpha_i^*\Phi(x_i), \tag{8.2.7}$$

$$\bar{b} = y_i - \frac{\alpha_i^*}{C} - \sum_{j=1}^{l}\alpha_j^* K(x_j, x_i). \tag{8.2.8}$$

Now we can establish the following algorithm according to above theorems.

**Algorithm 8.2.3** *(Least squares support vector regression, LSSVR)*

*(1) Input the training set $T = \{(x_1, y_1), \cdots, (x_l, y_l)\}$, where $x_i \in R^n, y_i \in R, i = 1, \cdots, l$;*

*(2) Choose an appropriate kernel function $K(x, x')$ and a penalty parameter $C > 0$;*

*(3) Construct and solve the convex quadratic programming*

$$\min_{\alpha} \quad \frac{1}{2} \sum_{i=1}^{l} \sum_{j=1}^{l} \alpha_i \alpha_j \left( K(x_i, x_j) + \frac{\delta_{ij}}{C} \right) - \sum_{i=1}^{l} \alpha_i y_i , \qquad (8.2.9)$$

$$s.t. \quad \sum_{i=1}^{l} \alpha_i = 0 \qquad (8.2.10)$$

*obtaining a solution $\alpha^* = (\alpha_1^*, \cdots, \alpha_l^*)^{\mathrm{T}}$;*

*(4) Compute $\bar{b}$: Choose a subscript $i(1 \leqslant i \leqslant l)$, then compute*

$$\bar{b} = y_i - \frac{\alpha_i^*}{C} - \sum_{j=1}^{l} \alpha_j^* K(x_j, x_i) ; \qquad (8.2.11)$$

*(5) Construct the decision function*

$$g(x) = \sum_{i=1}^{l} \alpha_i^* K(x_i, x) + \bar{b}. \qquad (8.2.12)$$

**Remark 8.2.4** *There are two important differences between the above algorithm and Algorithm 4.3.6 ($\varepsilon$-SVR):*

*(i) In $\varepsilon$-SVR, the decision function is decided only by the training points corresponding to support vectors and is unrelated to the training points corresponding to non-support vectors. However, in LSSVR, almost all of the training points contribute to the decision function. This leads to the fact that the solution of LSSVR loses the sparseness.*

*(ii) $\varepsilon$-SVR needs to solve a quadratic programming with inequality constraints. However, LSSVR needs to solve a quadratic programming with only equality constraints, or equivalently a linear system of equations. Therefore, it is simpler and faster.*

### 8.2.2 $\nu$-Support vector regression

Compared with $C$-SVC, $\nu$-SVC discussed in Section 8.1.5 proposes a parameter $\nu$ of the significance to replace the penalty parameter $C$. We can deal with $\varepsilon$-SVR in the similar way. $\varepsilon$-SVR is modified as the equivalent $\nu$-support vector regression ($\nu$-SVR) [88], where the parameter $\varepsilon$ is replaced by a meaningful parameter $\nu$.

### 8.2.2.1 $\nu$-Support vector regression

Introducing the transformation $\mathrm{x} = \Phi(x)$ and the corresponding kernel $K(x, x') = (\Phi(x) \cdot \Phi(x'))$, the primal problem of $\nu$-SVR is

$$\min_{\mathrm{w}, b, \xi^{(*)}, \varepsilon} \quad \frac{1}{2}\|\mathrm{w}\|^2 + C \cdot \left( \nu\varepsilon + \frac{1}{l}\sum_{i=1}^{l}(\xi_i + \xi_i^*) \right), \tag{8.2.13}$$

$$\text{s.t.} \quad ((\mathrm{w} \cdot \Phi(x_i)) + b) - y_i \leqslant \varepsilon + \xi_i \,, i = 1, \cdots, l \,, \tag{8.2.14}$$

$$y_i - ((\mathrm{w} \cdot \Phi(x_i)) + b) \leqslant \varepsilon + \xi_i^* \,, i = 1, \cdots, l \,, \tag{8.2.15}$$

$$\xi_i^{(*)} \geqslant 0 \,, i = 1, \cdots, l \,, \ \varepsilon \geqslant 0 \,, \tag{8.2.16}$$

where $\xi^{(*)}=(\xi_1, \xi_1^*, \cdots, \xi_l, \xi_l^*)^{\mathrm{T}}$. Note that $\varepsilon$ is a variable and its value is decided by the solution to the above problem. This is different than the primal problem $(4.1.45)\sim(4.1.48)$ of $\varepsilon$-SVR, where $\varepsilon$ is a prespecified parameter.

**Theorem 8.2.5** *Optimization problem*

$$\max_{\alpha^{(*)}} \quad -\frac{1}{2}\sum_{i,j=1}^{l}(\alpha_i^* - \alpha_i)(\alpha_j^* - \alpha_j)K(x_i, x_j) + \sum_{i=1}^{l}(\alpha_i^* - \alpha_i)y_i \,, \tag{8.2.17}$$

$$\text{s.t.} \quad \sum_{i=1}^{l}(\alpha_i - \alpha_i^*) = 0 \,, \tag{8.2.18}$$

$$0 \leqslant \alpha_i^{(*)} \leqslant C/l \,, i = 1, \cdots, l \,, \tag{8.2.19}$$

$$\sum_{i=1}^{l}(\alpha_i + \alpha_i^*) \leqslant C\nu \tag{8.2.20}$$

*is the dual problem of the primal problem $(8.2.13)\sim(8.2.16)$.*

**Theorem 8.2.6** *Suppose that $\bar{\alpha}^{(*)} = (\bar{\alpha}_1, \bar{\alpha}_1^*, \cdots, \bar{\alpha}_l, \bar{\alpha}_l^*)^{\mathrm{T}}$ is any solution to the dual problem $(8.2.17)\sim(8.2.20)$. If there exist two components of $\bar{\alpha}^{(*)}$, $\bar{\alpha}_j$ and $\bar{\alpha}_k^*$, such that $\bar{\alpha}_j \in (0, C/l)$ and $\bar{\alpha}_k^* \in (0, C/l)$, then a solution $(\bar{\mathrm{w}}, \bar{b})$ to the primal problem $(8.2.13)\sim(8.2.16)$ w.r.t. $(\mathrm{w}, b)$ can be obtained by*

$$\bar{\mathrm{w}} = \sum_{i=1}^{l}(\bar{\alpha}_i^* - \bar{\alpha}_i)\Phi(x_i), \tag{8.2.21}$$

$$\bar{b} = \frac{1}{2}\left[ y_j + y_k - \left( \sum_{i=1}^{l}(\bar{\alpha}_i^* - \bar{\alpha}_i)K(x_i, x_j) + \sum_{i=1}^{l}(\bar{\alpha}_i^* - \bar{\alpha}_i)K(x_i, x_k) \right) \right]. \tag{8.2.22}$$

Thus we can establish the following algorithm:

**Algorithm 8.2.7** *(ν-support vector regression, ν-SVR)*

*(1) Input the training set $T = \{(x_1, y_1), \cdots, (x_l, y_l)\}$, where $x_i \in R^n, y_i \in R, i = 1, \cdots, l$;*

*(2) Choose an appropriate kernel function $K(x, x')$ and two parameters $C > 0$ and $\nu \in (0, 1]$;*

*(3) Construct and solve the convex quadratic programming*

$$\min_{\alpha^{(*)}} \quad \frac{1}{2} \sum_{i,j=1}^{l} (\alpha_i^* - \alpha_i)(\alpha_j^* - \alpha_j)K(x_i, x_j) - \sum_{i=1}^{l}(\alpha_i^* - \alpha_i)y_i \,, \quad (8.2.23)$$

$$\text{s.t.} \quad \sum_{i=1}^{l}(\alpha_i - \alpha_i^*) = 0 \,, \quad (8.2.24)$$

$$0 \leqslant \alpha_i^{(*)} \leqslant C/l \,, \ i = 1, \cdots, l \,, \quad (8.2.25)$$

$$\sum_{i=1}^{l}(\alpha_i + \alpha_i^*) \leqslant C\nu \quad (8.2.26)$$

*obtaining the solution $\bar{\alpha}^{(*)} = (\bar{\alpha}_1, \bar{\alpha}_1^*, \cdots, \bar{\alpha}_l, \bar{\alpha}_l^*)^{\mathrm{T}}$;*

*(4) Compute $\bar{b}$: Choose two components of $\bar{\alpha}^{(*)}$, $\bar{\alpha}_j \in (0, C/l)$ and $\bar{\alpha}_k^* \in (0, C/l)$, and compute*

$$\bar{b} = \frac{1}{2} \left[ y_j + y_k - \left( \sum_{i=1}^{l}(\bar{\alpha}_i^* - \bar{\alpha}_i)K(x_i, x_j) + \sum_{i=1}^{l}(\bar{\alpha}_i^* - \bar{\alpha}_i)K(x_i, x_k) \right) \right];$$
$$(8.2.27)$$

*(5) Construct the decision function*

$$g(x) = \sum_{i=1}^{l}(\bar{\alpha}_i^* - \bar{\alpha}_i)K(x_i, x) + \bar{b} \,. \quad (8.2.28)$$

**Remark 8.2.8** *A solution $\bar{\varepsilon}$ to the primal problem (8.2.13)~(8.2.16) w.r.t. $\varepsilon$ can be obtained by*

$$\bar{\varepsilon} = \sum_{i=1}^{l}(\bar{\alpha}_i^* - \bar{\alpha}_i)K(x_i, x_j) + \bar{b} - y_j \,, \quad (8.2.29)$$

*or*

$$\bar{\varepsilon} = y_k - \sum_{i=1}^{l}(\bar{\alpha}_i^* - \bar{\alpha}_i)K(x_i, x_k) - \bar{b} \,, \quad (8.2.30)$$

*where the indexes $j$ and $k$ are the same as the ones in (8.2.27).*

### 8.2.2.2 Relationship between $\nu$-SVR and $\varepsilon$-SVR

There are two parameters $\varepsilon$ and $C$ in $\varepsilon$-SVR, while there are two parameters $\nu$ and $C$ in $\nu$-SVR. Roughly speaking, the relationship between $\nu$-SVR and $\varepsilon$-SVR is as follows: The decision functions obtained by two methods are identical if the values of parameter $C$ are same, and the parameter $\varepsilon$ has a relationship with the parameter $\nu$. For a detailed discussion, we refer the reader to [42].

### 8.2.2.3 The significance of the parameter $\nu$

The significance of the parameter $\nu$ is concerned with "support vector" and "training point classified incorrectly". Suppose that $\bar{\alpha}^{(*)} = (\bar{\alpha}_1, \bar{\alpha}_1^*, \cdots, \bar{\alpha}_l, \bar{\alpha}_l^*)^{\mathrm{T}}$ is the solution to the dual problem (8.2.17)~(8.2.20) obtained using Algorithm 8.2.7. The input $x_i$ associated with the training point $(x_i, y_i)$ is still called a support vector if the corresponding component $\bar{\alpha}_i$ or $\bar{\alpha}_i^*$, of $\alpha^{(*)}$ is nonzero. The definition of training point classified incorrectly is given below.

**Definition 8.2.9** *(Training point classified incorrectly) Suppose that $\bar{\alpha}^{(*)}$ is the solution to the dual problem (8.2.17)~(8.2.20), and the corresponding solution to the primal problem (8.2.13)~(8.2.16) is $(\bar{w}, \bar{b}, \bar{\varepsilon}, \bar{\xi}^{(*)}) = (\cdot, \cdot, \bar{\varepsilon}, \cdot)$. The training point $(x_i, y_i)$ is called a training point classified incorrectly if the decision function $g(x)$ obtained by Algorithm 8.2.7 satisfies*

$$|g(x_i) - y_i| > \bar{\varepsilon}. \tag{8.2.31}$$

The significance of $\nu$ is shown by the following theorem.

**Theorem 8.2.10** *Suppose that Algorithm 8.2.7($\nu$-SVR) is performed on the training set (8.2.1), and the value of $\bar{\varepsilon}$ is also computed by (8.2.29) or (8.2.30). If $\nu$ is nonzero, then*

*(i) Denoting the number of the training points classified incorrectly as $q$, we have $\nu \geqslant q/l$, i.e. $\nu$ is an upper bound on the fraction of the training points classified incorrectly;*

*(ii) Denoting the number of the support vectors as $p$, we have $\nu \leqslant p/l$, i.e. $\nu$ is a lower bound on the fraction of the support vectors.*

In addition, it can be shown under certain conditions that, with probability 1, both the fraction of the training points classified incorrectly and the fraction of the support vectors approach to $\nu$ when the number $l$ of the training points tends to infinity.

### 8.2.2.4 Linear programming support vector regression (LPSVR)

In the above support vector regressions, quadratic programming problem need to be solved. However, it is also possible to formulate regression problems in linear programming, replacing the quadratic objective function by a linear function.

Remember the regression machine based on nonlinear classification discussed in Section 4.1.3. The relationship between the primal problem (4.1.45)~(4.1.48) and the dual problem (4.1.59)~(4.1.61) is as follows: Suppose that $\bar{\alpha}^{(*)} = (\bar{\alpha}_1, \bar{\alpha}_1^*, \cdots, \bar{\alpha}_l, \bar{\alpha}_l^*)^{\mathrm{T}}$ is the solution to the latter, then the solution to the former w.r.t. $w$ can be obtained:

$$\bar{w} = \sum_{i=1}^{l} (\bar{\alpha}_i^* - \bar{\alpha}_i) \Phi(x_i). \tag{8.2.32}$$

Based on the above results, we modify the objective function in the primal problem, replacing the term $\frac{1}{2}\|w\|_2^2$ with $l_2$-norm by the term $\|\alpha^{(*)}\| = \sum_{i=1}^{l}(|\alpha_i| + |\alpha_i^*|)$ with $l_1$-norm. Note that the constraints of (4.1.59)~(4.1.61)

$$\alpha_i, \ \alpha_i^* \geqslant 0, \quad i = 1, \cdots, l, \tag{8.2.33}$$

so the above term with $l_1$-norm is equivalent to

$$\|\alpha^{(*)}\|_1 = \sum_{i=1}^{l} (\alpha_i + \alpha_i^*). \tag{8.2.34}$$

Introducing the kernel $K(x, x') = (\Phi(x), \Phi(x'))$, the linear programming is

$$\min_{\alpha^{(*)}, \xi^{(*)}, b} \quad \sum_{i=1}^{l}(\alpha_i + \alpha_i^*) + C \sum_{i=1}^{l}(\xi_i + \xi_i^*), \tag{8.2.35}$$

$$\text{s.t.} \quad \sum_{j=1}^{l}(\alpha_j^* - \alpha_j)K(x_j, x_i) + b - y_i \leqslant \varepsilon + \xi_i, \ i = 1, \cdots, l, \tag{8.2.36}$$

$$y_i - \sum_{j=1}^{l}(\alpha_j^* - \alpha_j)K(x_j, x_i) - b \leqslant \varepsilon + \xi_i^*, \ i = 1, \cdots, l, \tag{8.2.37}$$

$$\alpha_i^{(*)}, \xi_i^{(*)} \geqslant 0, \ i = 1, \cdots, l. \tag{8.2.38}$$

After solving the above problem and getting its solution $(\bar{\alpha}^{(*)}, \bar{b})$ w.r.t. $(\alpha^{(*)}, b)$, the decision function can be constructed as follows:

$$g(x) = \sum_{i=1}^{l} (\bar{\alpha}_i^* - \bar{\alpha}_i)K(x_i, x) + \bar{b}. \tag{8.2.39}$$

Thus we can establish the following algorithm.

**Algorithm 8.2.11** *(Linear programming $\varepsilon$-support vector regression, $\varepsilon$-LPSVR)*

*(1) Input the training set $T = \{(x_1, y_1), \cdots, (x_l, y_l)\}$, where $x_i \in R^n, y_i \in R, i = 1, \cdots, l$;*

*(2) Choose an appropriate kernel function $K(x, x')$ and two parameters $C > 0$ and $\varepsilon > 0$;*

*(3) Construct and solve the linear programming (8.2.35)~(8.2.38), obtaining the solution $(\bar{\alpha}^{(*)}, \bar{b})$ w.r.t. $(\alpha^{(*)}, b)$, where $\bar{\alpha}^{(*)} = (\bar{\alpha}_1, \bar{\alpha}_1^*, \cdots, \bar{\alpha}_l, \bar{\alpha}_l^*)^{\mathrm{T}}$;*

*(4) Construct the decision function*

$$g(x) = \sum_{i=1}^{l} (\bar{\alpha}_i^* - \bar{\alpha}_i) K(x_i, x) + \bar{b} . \tag{8.2.40}$$

$\varepsilon$-SVR can be modified to $\nu$-SVR. The linear programming $\varepsilon$-SVR can also be modified to linear programming $\nu$-SVR in the similar way. The algorithm is summarized as follows.

**Algorithm 8.2.12** *(Linear programming $\nu$-support vector regression, $\nu$-LPSVR)*

*(1) Input the training set $T = \{(x_1, y_1), \cdots, (x_l, y_l)\}$, where $x_i \in R^n, y_i \in R, i = 1, \cdots, l$;*

*(2) Choose an appropriate kernel function $K(x, x')$ and two parameters $C > 0$ and $\nu \in (0, 1]$;*

*(3) Construct and solve the linear programming*

$$\min_{\alpha^{(*)}, \xi^{(*)}, \varepsilon, b} \quad \frac{1}{l} \sum_{i=1}^{l} (\alpha_i + \alpha_i^*) + \frac{C}{l} \sum_{i=1}^{l} (\xi_i + \xi_i^*) + C\nu\varepsilon , \tag{8.2.41}$$

$$\text{s.t.} \quad \sum_{j=1}^{l} (\alpha_j^* - \alpha_j) K(x_j, x_i) + b - y_i \leqslant \varepsilon + \xi_i , i = 1, \cdots, l , \tag{8.2.42}$$

$$y_i - \sum_{j=1}^{l} (\alpha_j^* - \alpha_i) K(x_j, x_i) - b \leqslant \varepsilon + \xi_i^* , i = 1, \cdots, l , \tag{8.2.43}$$

$$\alpha_i^{(*)}, \xi_i^{(*)} , i = 1, \cdots, l , \varepsilon \geqslant 0 , \tag{8.2.44}$$

*obtaining the solution $(\bar{\alpha}^{(*)}, \bar{b})$ w.r.t. $(\alpha^{(*)}, b)$, where $\bar{\alpha}^{(*)} = (\bar{\alpha}_1, \bar{\alpha}_1^*, \cdots, \bar{\alpha}_l, \bar{\alpha}_l^*)^{\mathrm{T}}$;*

*(4) Construct the decision function*

$$g(x) = \sum_{i=1}^{l} (\bar{\alpha}_i^* - \bar{\alpha}_i) K(x_i, x) + \bar{b} . \tag{8.2.45}$$

## 8.3 Multiclass Classification

A natural extension of the binary classification problem is the multiclass classification problem, which is formulated mathematically as follows.

**Multiclass classification problem**: Given a training set

$$T = \{(x_1, y_1), \cdots, (x_l, y_l)\}, \qquad (8.3.1)$$

where $x_i \in R^n, y_i \in \mathcal{Y} = \{1, 2, \cdots, M\}, i = 1, \cdots, l$. Find a decision function $f(x)$ in $R^n$, such that the class number $y$ for any $x$ can be predicted by $y = f(x)$.

Thus it can be seen that solving the above multiclass classification problem is to find a criterion to separate the $R^n$ space into $M$ regions according to the training set.

### 8.3.1 Approaches based on binary classifiers

Multiclass classification problems are typically solved using voting scheme methods based on combining many binary classification decision functions. Different collection of binary classification problems leads to different approach, see [76].

#### 8.3.1.1 One versus one

Consider the multiclass classification problem with the training set (8.3.1). For each pair $(i, j) \in \{(i, j)|i < j ,\ i, j = 1, \cdots, M\}$, construct a binary classification problem to separate the $i$-th class from the $j$-th class, resulting a function $g^{i-j}(x)$ and the corresponding decision function

$$f^{i-j}(x) = \begin{cases} i, & g^{i-j}(x) > 0 ; \\ j, & \text{otherwise.} \end{cases} \qquad (8.3.2)$$

There are $M(M-1)/2$ decision functions for different $i, j$. These decision functions are used to predict the class label $y$ for any input $x$ according to which of the classes gets the highest number of votes; a vote for a given class is defined as a decision function putting the input $x$ into the class. Note that when there are two or more than two classes with the same number of votes, the input $x$ is unclassified in this approach.

#### 8.3.1.2 One versus the rest

For a multiclass classification problem with training set (8.3.1), "one versus the rest" is another way to construct the set of binary classification problems. The set consists of $M$ binary problems. The $j$-th one separates the $j$-th class from the rest, yielding the decision function $f^j(x) = \text{sgn}(g^j(x)), j = 1, \cdots, M$.

The next step is doing multiclass classification according to $g^1(x), \cdots, g^M(x)$. Obviously, if these decision functions are exactly correct, for any input $x$ there exists a unique value $g^J(x) > 0$ among the $M$ values $g^1(x), \cdots, g^M(x)$ and the input $x$ can be predicted in class $J$. However, due to the errors in these decision functions, it may happen that none are positive or there is more than one that is positive. In order to deal with these cases, the input $x$ should be predicted in class $J$, where $J$ is the superscript of the largest among $g^1(x), \cdots, g^M(x)$. This leads to the following algorithm.

**Algorithm 8.3.1** *(One versus the rest classification)*

*(1) Input the training set*

$$T = \{(x_1, y_1), \cdots, (x_l, y_l)\}, \tag{8.3.3}$$

*where* $x_i \in R^n, y_i \in \mathcal{Y} = \{1, \cdots, M\}, i = 1, \cdots, l;$

*(2) For* $j = 1, \cdots, M$, *construct the training set of the* $j$-*th binary problem with the training set*

$$T^j = \{(x_1, y_1^j), \cdots, (x_l, y_l^j)\}, \tag{8.3.4}$$

*where*

$$y_i^j = \begin{cases} 1, & if \ y_i = j; \\ 0, & otherwise. \end{cases} \tag{8.3.5}$$

*Find the corresponding decision function*

$$f^j(x) = \text{sgn}(g^j(x)); \tag{8.3.6}$$

*(3) Construct the decision function*

$$f(x) = \text{argmax}_{j=1,\cdots,M} g^j(x). \tag{8.3.7}$$

A puzzle appears when the two largest $g^j(x)$ are equal. In fact, the difference between the two largest $g^j(x)$ can be considered as a measure of confidence in the classification of $x$; it would not be reliable to give any prediction when the difference is very small. So a reasonable remedy is to assign an input $x$ a class when this difference is larger than a threshold otherwise refuse to give any prediction.

Note that a difficulty in the above algorithm may come from the fact that the datasets in the binary classification problems are imbalanced. For example, for the ten-class digit recognition problem, we need to solve binary classification problems which separate one digit (positive class) from the rest (negative class), thus positive class would be the minority class and the negative class would be majority class. The characteristic of class imbalance often leads to unsatisfactory results from the standard SVC. A simple remedy to tackle the imbalance problem is to select different penalty parameters for different classes; larger penalty for minority class and smaller penalty for majority class. Thus the primal problem becomes

$$\min_{w,b,\xi} \quad \frac{1}{2}\|w\|^2 + \sum_{i=1}^{l} C_i \xi_i , \qquad (8.3.8)$$

$$\text{s.t.} \quad y_i((w \cdot \Phi(x_i)) + b) \geqslant 1 - \xi_i , \ i = 1, \cdots, l , \qquad (8.3.9)$$

$$\xi_i \geqslant 0 , \ i = 1, \cdots, l, \qquad (8.3.10)$$

where $C_i$ is selected according to the above principle. The corresponding dual problem is

$$\max_{\alpha} \quad -\frac{1}{2} \sum_{i=1}^{l} \sum_{j=1}^{l} y_i y_j \alpha_i \alpha_j K(x_i, x_j) + \sum_{j=1}^{l} \alpha_j , \qquad (8.3.11)$$

$$\text{s.t.} \quad \sum_{i=1}^{l} y_i \alpha_i = 0 , \qquad (8.3.12)$$

$$0 \leqslant \alpha_i \leqslant C_i , \ i = 1, \cdots, l . \qquad (8.3.13)$$

For more efficient approaches for the imbalance problem, see Section 6.2.5.

### 8.3.1.3 Error-correcting output coding

For an $M$-class classification problem, the above "one versus one" and "one versus the rest" construct and use $M(M-1)/2$ and $M$ binary classification problems respectively. Obviously, many more binary classification problems can be considered. For example, include the class 1 and 2 in the positive class, and include the rest $M-2$ classes in the negative class, or include the classes with odd label in the positive class and include the classes with even label in the negative class. In most applications, the binary classification problems have been chosen to be meaningful. For example, consider the ten-class digit recognition problem. The first positive and negative class can be obtained by examining whether the digit contains vertical line (vl); the digit containing a vertical line is included in positive class. Thus the second column in Table 8.3.1 is obtained. The other five columns are obtained by examining if the digit contains horizontal line (hl), diagonal line (dl), close curve (cc), curve open to left (ol), and curve open to right (or). The $10 \times 6$ binary numbers in the right lower part form a $10 \times 6$ matrix, called code matrix[48]. This matrix can be used to construct 6 binary classification problems and predict the class label for any input $x$ by the corresponding 6 decision functions.

The above example can be extended to the general $M$-class classification problem. Suppose the number of the binary classification problem is $L$; then we will have a $M \times L$ code matrix $S = (s_{ij})_{M \times L}$, where $s_{ij}$, the element in the $i$-th row and the $j$-th column, is defined as follows: $s_{ij} = 1$ if the class $i$ is included in positive class of the $j$-th binary classification problem; $s_{ij} = -1$ otherwise.

**TABLE 8.1:**   Binary classification problems in ten-class digit recognition.

| class | vl | hl | dl | cc | ol | or |
|-------|-----|-----|-----|-----|-----|-----|
| 0 | $-1$ | $-1$ | $-1$ | $1$ | $-1$ | $-1$ |
| 1 | $1$ | $-1$ | $-1$ | $-1$ | $-1$ | $-1$ |
| 2 | $-1$ | $1$ | $1$ | $-1$ | $1$ | $-1$ |
| 3 | $-1$ | $-1$ | $-1$ | $-1$ | $1$ | $-1$ |
| 4 | $1$ | $1$ | $-1$ | $-1$ | $-1$ | $1$ |
| 5 | $1$ | $1$ | $-1$ | $-1$ | $1$ | $-1$ |
| 6 | $-1$ | $-1$ | $1$ | $1$ | $-1$ | $1$ |
| 7 | $-1$ | $1$ | $1$ | $-1$ | $1$ | $-1$ |
| 8 | $-1$ | $-1$ | $1$ | $1$ | $-1$ | $-1$ |
| 9 | $-1$ | $-1$ | $1$ | $1$ | $1$ | $-1$ |

Once the code matrix $S$ is constructed, we need to solve the $L$ binary classification problems and find the corresponding decision functions $f^j (j = 1, \cdots, L)$. In order to predict the label for an input $x$, compute the $L$-dimensional row vector $\hat{f}(x) = (f^1(x), \cdots, f^L(x))$ and compare it to each of the rows in the code matrix $S$. It is not difficult to imagine that there should exist one and only one row in $S$ which is identical to the vector $\hat{f}(x)$ if the code matrix is suitable and the decision functions $f^j (j = 1, \cdots, L)$ are correct exactly, and the input $x$ should be assigned to the class corresponding to that row in $S$. Generally, due to the possible computational error, the input $x$ should be assigned to the class corresponding to the row in $S$ which is closest to the vector $\hat{f}(x)$. In order to measure the proximity between two row vectors $u = (u_1, \cdots, u_L)$ and $v = (v_1, \cdots, v_L)$ with components 1 and $-1$, we can use Hamming distance $d(u, v)$ defined by

$$d(u, v) = |\{i | u_i \neq v_i\}|, \tag{8.3.14}$$

where $|\cdot|$ stands for the number of elements in the set.

For a practical problem, constructing a suitable code matrix is a technical job. However, when $M$ is small, e.g when $3 \leqslant M \leqslant 7$, we can use the exhaustive coding scheme by introducing all of the possible binary classification problems with $L = 2^{M-1} - 1$. The $M \times (2^{M-1} - 1)$ code matrix is constructed as follows. Row 1 is all ones. Row 2 consists of $2^{M-2}$ minus ones followed by $2^{M-2} - 1$ ones. In row $i$, there are alternating runs of $2^{M-i}$ minus ones and ones. The code matrix for a four-class problem is given by

$$S = \begin{pmatrix} 1 & 1 & 1 & 1 & 1 & 1 & 1 \\ -1 & -1 & -1 & -1 & 1 & 1 & 1 \\ -1 & -1 & 1 & 1 & -1 & -1 & 1 \\ -1 & 1 & -1 & 1 & -1 & 1 & -1 \end{pmatrix}. \tag{8.3.15}$$

The algorithm using code matrix is given as follows.

**Algorithm 8.3.2** *(Error-correcting output coding classification)*

*(1) Input the training set*

$$T = \{(x_1, y_1), \cdots, (x_l, y_l)\}, \tag{8.3.16}$$

*where $x_i \in R^n, y_i \in \{1, \cdots, M\}, i = 1, \cdots, l$;*

*(2) Construct a $M \times L$ code matrix $S$ with elements ones or minus ones;*

*(3) For $i = 1, \cdots, L$, construct the $i$-th binary classification problem according to the $i$-th column of $S$ as follows: Its positive inputs consist of the inputs of the classes whose corresponding element in the $i$-th row is one and its negative inputs consist of the inputs of the classes whose corresponding element in the $i$-th row is minus one;*

*(4) For the above $L$ binary classification problems, find the corresponding decision functions $f^1(x), \cdots, f^L(x)$. Define a $L$-dimensional row vector $\hat{f}(x) = (f^1(x), \cdots, f^L(x))$;*

*(5) Construct the decision function*

$$f(x) = \arg_k \min d(\hat{f}(x), s_k), \tag{8.3.17}$$

*where $s_k$ is the row vector in the $i$-th row in the code matrix $S$ and $d(\cdot, \cdot)$ is the Hamming distance given by (8.3.14).*

The name "error-correcting output coding" of the above algorithm comes from the fact that it may be able to recover from errors. Consider the case where the exhaustive code matrix $S$ given by (8.3.15) is used. It is easy to see that Hamming distance between any pair of the rows in $S$ is 4. This implies that the final prediction is still correct even if a single component error in the row vector $\hat{f}(x) = (f^1(x), \cdots, f^7(x))$. Generally speaking, if the minimum Hamming distance between any pair of the rows is $d$ in $S$, then the algorithm can correct at least $[\frac{d-1}{2}]$ single component errors, where $[\cdot]$ is the integer part. Note that "the one versus the rest" strategy does not have the ability to recover from any error. In fact, for a four-class problem, the code matrix is

$$S = \begin{pmatrix} 1 & -1 & -1 & -1 \\ -1 & 1 & -1 & -1 \\ -1 & -1 & 1 & -1 \\ -1 & -1 & -1 & 1 \end{pmatrix} \tag{8.3.18}$$

and the Hamming distance between any pair of the rows in $S$ is $d = 2$, resulting $[\frac{d-1}{2}] = 0$.

## 8.3.2   Approach based on ordinal regression machines

Ordinal regression machine is a method for solving a specialization of the multiclass classification problem. Here it is emphasized for use in the context of solving general multiclass classification problems although it has many applications itself[72].

### 8.3.2.1   Ordinal regression machine

**(1) Ordinal regression problem**
Ordinal regression problem is a special multiclass classification problem when there exists an ordering among the inputs in $R^n$. More precisely, for the problem with $M$ classes, the inputs in class $j$ adjoin only to the inputs in class $j-1$ and class $j+1$, not to any others, $j = 2, \cdots, M-1$. In fact, what we are considering is the following more particular case: Suppose that the inputs in $M$ classes can be or almost can be separated by $M-1$ parallel hyperplanes in $R^n$; a geometric interpretation in $R^2$ is given in Figure 8.4, where "o", "□", "●", "■" and "+" stand for the inputs in different classes.

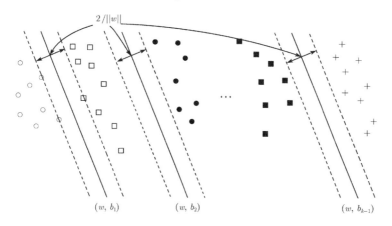

**FIGURE 8.4**: An ordinal regression problem in $R^2$.

Essentially, the training set of the ordinal regression problem can be represented in the form (8.3.1) of the general multiclass classification problem; however, for convenience, it is formulated as

$$T = \{x_i^j\}_{i=1,\cdots,l^j}^{j=1,\cdots,M},\qquad(8.3.19)$$

where $x_i^j$ is an input of a training point, the superscript $j = 1, \cdots, M$ denotes the corresponding class number, $i = 1, \cdots, l^j$ is the index within each class, and $l^j$ is the number of the training points in class $j$.

Now let us formulate an ordinal regression problem mathematically as follows.

**Ordinal regression problem**: Given a training set shown by (8.3.19), find $M-1$ parallel hyperplanes in $R^n$

$$(w \cdot x) - b_r = 0, \quad r = 1, \cdots, M-1,\qquad(8.3.20)$$

where $w \in R^n$, $b_1 \leqslant b_2 \leqslant \cdots \leqslant b_{M-1}$, $b_0 = -\infty$, $b_M = +\infty$, such that the class number for any $x$ can be predicted by

$$f(x) = \arg \min_{r=1,\cdots,M} \{(w \cdot x) - b_r\}.\qquad(8.3.21)$$

It can be seen that the above $M - 1$ hyperplanes (8.3.20) separate the $R^n$ space into $M$ ranked regions. The decision function (8.3.21) assigns the class number $r$ to the input $x$ in the $r$-th region.

### (2) Ordinal regression machine

Similar to the binary classification, we first consider the problem with a training set where the inputs in different classes can be separated by the parallel hyperplanes correctly, e.g. the problem shown in Figure 8.4. As an extension of the principle of maximal margin in binary classification problem, the margin to be maximized is associated with the two closest neighbor classes. This leads to the primal problem

$$\min_{w,b} \quad \frac{1}{2}\|w\|^2, \tag{8.3.22}$$

$$\text{s.t.} \quad (w \cdot x_i^j) - b_j \leqslant -1, \ j = 1, \cdots, M, i = 1, \cdots, l^j, \tag{8.3.23}$$

$$\quad (w \cdot x_i^j) - b_{j-1} \geqslant 1, \ j = 1, \cdots, M, i = 1, \cdots, l^j, \tag{8.3.24}$$

where $b = (b_1, \cdots, b_{M-1})^{\mathrm{T}}$, $b_0 = -\infty$, $b_M = +\infty$.

For general training set, we should introduce slack variables $\xi^{(*)} = (\xi_1^1, \cdots, \xi_{l^1}^1, \cdots, \xi_1^M, \cdots, \xi_{lM}^M, \xi_1^{*1}, \cdots, \xi_{l^1}^{*1}, \cdots, \xi_1^{*M}, \cdots, \xi_{lM}^{*M})^{\mathrm{T}}$ and a penalty parameter $C > 0$, thus the primal problem becomes

$$\min_{w,b,\xi^{(*)}} \quad \frac{1}{2}\|w\|^2 + C \sum_{j=1}^{M} \sum_{i=1}^{l^j} (\xi_i^j + \xi_i^{*j}), \tag{8.3.25}$$

$$\text{s.t.} \quad (w \cdot x_i^j) - b_j \leqslant -1 + \xi_i^j, \ j = 1, \cdots, M, i = 1, \cdots, l^j, \tag{8.3.26}$$

$$\quad (w \cdot x_i^j) - b_{j-1} \geqslant 1 - \xi_i^{*j}, \ j = 1, \cdots, M, i = 1, \cdots, l^j, \tag{8.3.27}$$

$$\quad \xi_i^j \geqslant 0, \ \xi_i^{*j} \geqslant 0, \ j = 1, \cdots, M, i = 1, \cdots, l^j, \tag{8.3.28}$$

where $b = (b_1, \cdots, b_{M-1})^{\mathrm{T}}$, $b_0 = -\infty$, $b_M = +\infty$.

The dual problem of the above problem can be obtained by introducing Lagrange function

$$L(w, b, \xi^{(*)}, \alpha^{(*)}, \eta^{(*)}) = \frac{1}{2}\|w\|^2 + C \sum_{j=1}^{M} \sum_{i=1}^{l^j} (\xi_i^j + \xi_i^{*j})$$

$$+ \sum_{j,i} \alpha_i^j ((w \cdot x_i^j) - b_j + 1 - \xi_i^j)$$

$$- \sum_{j,i} \alpha_i^{*j} ((w \cdot x_i^j) - b_{j-1} - 1 + \xi_i^{*j})$$

$$- \sum_{j,i} \eta_i^j \xi_i^j - \sum_{j,i} \eta_i^{*j} \xi_i^{*j}, \tag{8.3.29}$$

where $\quad \alpha^{(*)} \quad = \quad (\alpha_1^1, \cdots, \alpha_{l^1}^1, \cdots, \alpha_1^M, \cdots, \alpha_{lM}^M, \alpha_1^{*1}, \cdots, \alpha_{l^1}^{*1}, \cdots, \alpha_1^{*M}, \cdots,$

$$\alpha_{lM}^{*M})^{\mathrm{T}}, \quad \eta^{(*)} \quad = \quad (\eta_1^1, \cdots, \eta_{l1}^1, \cdots, \eta_1^M, \cdots, \eta_{lM}^M, \eta_1^{*1}, \cdots, \eta_{l1}^{*1}, \cdots, \eta_1^{*M}, \cdots,$$
$$\eta_{lM}^{*M})^{\mathrm{T}}.$$

**Theorem 8.3.3** *Convex quadratic programming*

$$\min_{\alpha^{(*)}} \quad \frac{1}{2}\sum_{j,i}\sum_{j',i'}(\alpha_i^{*j} - \alpha_i^j)(\alpha_{i'}^{*j'} - \alpha_{i'}^{j'})(x_i^j \cdot x_{i'}^{j'}) - \sum_{j,i}(\alpha_i^j + \alpha_i^{*j}),$$

$$(8.3.30)$$

$$\text{s.t.} \quad \sum_{i=1}^{l^j}\alpha_i^j = \sum_{i=1}^{l^{j+1}}\alpha_i^{*j+1}, \quad j = 1, \cdots, M-1, \tag{8.3.31}$$

$$0 \leqslant \alpha_i^j, \alpha_i^{*j} \leqslant C, \quad j = 1, \cdots, M, \quad i = 1, \cdots, l^j, \tag{8.3.32}$$

$$\alpha_i^{*1} = 0, \quad i = 1, \cdots, l^1, \tag{8.3.33}$$

$$\alpha_i^M = 0, \quad i = 1, \cdots, l^M \tag{8.3.34}$$

*is the dual problem of the primal problem* (8.3.25)~(8.3.28).

As expected, the solution to the primal problem (8.3.25)~(8.3.28) can be obtained by solving the dual problem (8.3.30)~(8.3.34), and the following algorithm is therefore established.

**Algorithm 8.3.4** *(Ordinal regression machine)*

*(1) Input the training set*

$$T = \{x_i^j\}_{i=1,\cdots,l^j}^{j=1,\cdots,M}, \tag{8.3.35}$$

*where $x_i^j$ is an input of a training point, the superscript $j = 1, \cdots, M$ denotes the corresponding class number, $i = 1, \cdots, l^j$ is the index within each class, and $l^j$ is the number of the training points in class $j$;*

*(2) Choose an appropriate penalty parameter $C > 0$, construct and solve the convex quadratic programming* (8.3.30)~(8.3.34), *obtaining a solution $\bar{\alpha}^{(*)} = (\bar{\alpha}_1^1, \cdots, \bar{\alpha}_{l1}^1, \cdots, \bar{\alpha}_1^M, \cdots, \bar{\alpha}_{lM}^M, \bar{\alpha}_1^{*1}, \cdots, \bar{\alpha}_{l1}^{*1}, \cdots, \bar{\alpha}_1^{*M}, \cdots, \bar{\alpha}_{lM}^{*M})^{\mathrm{T}}$;*

*(3) Compute*

$$g_0(x) = \sum_{j=1}^{M}\sum_{i=1}^{l^j}(\bar{\alpha}_i^{*j} - \bar{\alpha}_i^j)(x_i^j \cdot x); \tag{8.3.36}$$

*(4) For $j = 1, \cdots, M-1$:*

  *(4.1) If there exists a component of $\bar{\alpha}^{(*)}$, $\bar{\alpha}_i^j \in (0, C)$, compute*

$$\bar{b}_j = 1 + \sum_{j'=1}^{M}\sum_{i'=1}^{l^{j'}}(\bar{\alpha}_{i'}^{*j'} - \bar{\alpha}_{i'}^{j'})(x_{i'}^{j'} \cdot x_i^j). \tag{8.3.37}$$

*(4.2) If there exists a component of $\bar{\alpha}^{(*)}$, $\bar{\alpha}_i^{*j+1} \in (0, C)$, compute*

$$\bar{b}_j = \sum_{j'=1}^{M} \sum_{i'=1}^{l^{j'}} (\bar{\alpha}_{i'}^{*j'} - \bar{\alpha}_{i'}^{j'})(x_{i'}^{j'} \cdot x_i^{j+1}) - 1. \tag{8.3.38}$$

*(4.3) Compute*

$$\bar{b}_j = \frac{1}{2}(b_j^{dn} + b_j^{up}), \tag{8.3.39}$$

*where*

$$b_j^{dn} = \max\{\max_{i \in I_1^j}(g(x_i^j) + 1), \max_{i \in I_4^j}(g(x_i^{j+1}) - 1)\}, \tag{8.3.40}$$

$$b_j^{up} = \min\{\min_{i \in I_3^j}(g(x_i^j) + 1), \min_{i \in I_2^j}(g(x_i^{j+1}) - 1)\}, \tag{8.3.41}$$

*with*

$$I_1^j = \{i \in \{1, \cdots, l^j\} | \bar{\alpha}_i^j = 0\}, \quad I_2^j = \{i \in \{1, \cdots, l^{j+1}\} | \bar{\alpha}_i^{*j+1} = 0\},$$
$$I_3^j = \{i \in \{1, \cdots, l^j\} | \bar{\alpha}_i^j = C\}, \quad I_4^j = \{i \in \{1, \cdots, l^{j+1}\} | \bar{\alpha}_i^{*j+1} = C\};$$

*(5) If there exists $\bar{b}_j \leqslant \bar{b}_{j-1}$, stop (Algorithm fails), or go to step (2) to try again;*

*(6) Construct the decision function*

$$f(x) = \min_{r \in \{1, \cdots, M\}} \{r : g_0(x) - \bar{b}_r < 0\}, \tag{8.3.42}$$

*where $\bar{b}_M = +\infty$.*

Obviously, ordinal regression machine reduces to the standard $C$-SVC when the class number $M = 2$. For further information on ordinal regression machines, consult the literature [2, 30, 31, 72, 71, 74, 133].

### 8.3.2.2   Approach based on ordinal regression machines

Now we are in a position to show how to use ordinal regression machine to solve multiclass classification problem.

#### (1) Ordinal regression machine with kernel

Note that the ordinal regression problem is a special multiclass classification problem where there exists an ordering among the inputs. Therefore, it may not be suitable to use ordinal regression machine directly for solving a general multiclass classification problem due to the lack of ordering. However, if the inputs in the training set are transformed into a space with high dimension, the probability of having an ordering would be increased. Let us explain this fact by an intuitive example. Consider a one-dimensional three-class classification problem with a training set given in Figure 8.5(a), where "o", "□", and "*" represent the inputs of training points in class 1, class 2, and class 3 respectively. It is easy to see that the ordering condition in ordinal regression problem is not satisfied since the input "□" (in class 2) does not adjoin the input "○" (in class 1). However, if the three inputs in $R$ are transformed into $R^2$ by a suitable transformation, e.g. $x = ([x]_1, [x]_2) = (x, x^2)^T$, the three inputs in $R^2$ would satisfy the ordering condition, see Figure 8.5(b). Therefore, it can be expected that ordinal regression machine can be modified to solve general multiclass classification problem if a suitable transformation $\Phi(x)$ and the corresponding kernel $K(x, x') = (\Phi(x) \cdot \Phi(x'))$ is introduced as the following algorithm does.

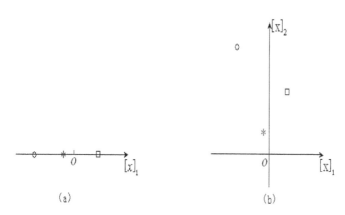

(a)                              (b)

**FIGURE 8.5**: An ordinal regression problem.

**Algorithm 8.3.5** *(Kernel ordinal regression machine) The same with Algorithm 8.3.4 (Ordinal regression machine) except the inner project $(x \cdot x')$ in the $x$-space is replaced by the kernel function $K(x, x')$, where $K(x, x')$ is chosen by the user.*

**(2) The approach based on ordinal regression machines**

For solving a general multiclass classification problem, the performance of the above kernel regression machine can be improved if it is used several times instead of only once. Remind the approach based on binary classifiers in Section 8.3.1, where the binary classifiers are used many times as a basic classifier. Similarly, the kernel ordinal regression machine can also be used as a basic classifier. Obviously there are many choices since any $p$-class kernel ordinal regression machine with different order can be a candidate, where $p = 2, 3, \cdots, M$. When $p = 2$, this approach reduces to the approach based on binary classifiers.

Next, for simplicity, we only describe the strategy with $p = 3$ (based on 3-class kernel ordinal regression machines) restricting to the counterpart corresponding to "one versus the rest" — "one versus one versus the rest"[5, 179]. For a general $M$-class classification problem with the training set (8.3.1), there are $M(M-1)/2$ training sets:

$$\tilde{T}(s_1, t_1), \cdots, \tilde{T}(s_{M(M-1)/2}, t_{M(M-1)/2}),\qquad(8.3.43)$$

where $s_m, t_m \in \{1, \cdots, M\}$, $(s_m, t_m)$ means taking class $s_m$ and class $t_m$ as the first class and the third class respectively, and taking the rest as the second class, and

$$\tilde{T}_m = \tilde{T}(s_m, t_m),\qquad(8.3.44)$$

is the corresponding training set. For each training set (8.3.44), the 3-class kernel ordinal regression machine yields a decision function $f_{s_m, t_m}(x)$. So there are $M(M-1)/2$ decision functions. The final decision function to the $M$-class classification problem can be obtained from these decision functions as shown in the following algorithm.

**Algorithm 8.3.6** *(Multiclass classification based on 3-class kernel ordinal regression machines)*

*(1) Input the training set*

$$T = \{(x_1, y_1), \cdots, (x_l, y_l)\},\qquad(8.3.45)$$

*where $x_i \in R^n$, $y_i \in \mathcal{Y} = \{1, 2, \cdots, M\}$, $i = 1, \cdots, l$;*

*(2) Construct a set $P$ containing $M(M-1)/2$ pairs of the class labels*

$$P = \{(s_1, t_1), \cdots, (s_{M(M-1)/2}, t_{M(M-1)/2})\} = \{(s, t) | s < t; s, t \in \{1, \cdots, M\}\},\qquad(8.3.46)$$

*set $m = 1$;*

*(3) Construct the training set (8.3.44) from the training set (8.3.45) and rewrite the training set in the form (8.3.19)*

$$\tilde{T} = \{\tilde{x}_i^j\}_{i=1,\cdots,l^j}^{j=1,2,3},\qquad(8.3.47)$$

*where*

$$\{\tilde{x}_i^1, i = 1, \cdots, l^1\} = \{x_i | y_i = s\},$$
$$\{\tilde{x}_i^2, i = 1, \cdots, l^2\} = \{x_i | y_i \in \mathcal{Y} \setminus \{s, t\}\},$$
$$\{\tilde{x}_i^3, i = 1, \cdots, l^3\} = \{x_i | y_i = t\};$$

*(4) For the training set (8.3.47), execute Algorithm 8.3.5 with $M = 3$ and obtain a decision function $f_{s_m, t_m}(x)$;*

*(5) If $m \neq M(M-1)/2$, set $m = m+1$, go to step (2);*

*(6) The decision functions $f_{s_m, t_m}(x)$, $m = 1, \cdots, M(M-1)/2$, are used to predict the class label $\bar{y}$ for any input $\bar{x}$ according to which of the classes gets the highest number of votes; a vote for class $s_m$ is defined as $f_{s_m, t_m}(x)(\bar{x}) = 1$, a vote for class $t_m$ is defined as $f_{s_m, t_m}(\bar{x}) = 3$, and a negative vote for class $s_m$ and a negative vote for class $t_m$ are defined as $f_{s_m, t_m}(\bar{x}) = 2$, $m = 1, \cdots, M(M-1)/2$.*

### 8.3.3 Crammer-Singer multiclass support vector classification

#### 8.3.3.1 Basic idea

Unlike previous approaches which decompose a multiclass problem into multiple independent classification tasks, Crammer-Singer method is an all-at-once support vector classification, see [37, 38]. For a $M$-class classification problem with the training set (8.3.1), its basic idea is to find $M$ vectors $w_1, \cdots, w_M$, and establish the decision function in the form

$$f(x) = \underset{r=1,\cdots,M}{\operatorname{argmax}} (w_r \cdot x). \tag{8.3.48}$$

Here the value of the inner product of $w_r$ with the input $x$ is interchangeably considered as the similarity score for the class $r$. Therefore the predicted label is the subscript of $w_r$ attaining the highest similarity score with $x$. Geometrically speaking, the decision function separates the $R^n$ space into $M$ regions by $C_M^2 = M(M-1)/2$ hyperplanes passing through the origin

$$(w_i \cdot x) = (w_j \cdot x), i, j = 1, \cdots, M, \tag{8.3.49}$$

where the $r$-th region is an unbounded polyhedron defined by

$$(w_r \cdot x) > (w_j \cdot x), j \in \{1, \cdots, M\} \setminus \{r\}. \tag{8.3.50}$$

The label for an input $x$ will be assigned to class $r$ if it falls into the $r$-th region. So the key point is to find $M$ vectors $w_1, \cdots, w_M$.

#### 8.3.3.2 Primal problem

For simplicity, let us start from a 3-class classification problem in the $R^2$ space with the training set

$$T = \{(x_1, y_1), \cdots, (x_l, y_l)\}, \tag{8.3.51}$$

where $x_i \in R^2, y_i \in \{1, 2, 3\}, i = 1, \cdots, l_i$. Now we should find three vectors $w_1, w_2$, and $w_3$ and the corresponding three regions according to the principle of maximal margin, see Figure 8.6(a), where the first region corresponding to $w_1$ is the shaded part. Similar to the discussion for the linearly separable binary problems in Section 2.2.2, we know that for the linearly separable case there exist the vectors $w_1, w_2$, and $w_3$ such that

$$(w_{y_i} \cdot x_i) - (w_r \cdot x_i) \geqslant 1, \quad \forall r \in \{1, 2, 3\} \setminus \{y_i\}, \tag{8.3.52}$$

or

$$(w_{y_i} \cdot x_i) - (w_r \cdot x_i) \geqslant 1 - \delta_{y_i r}, \quad i = 1, \cdots, l; \ r = 1, 2, 3, \tag{8.3.53}$$

where

$$\delta_{jk} = \begin{cases} 1, & j = k; \\ 0, & \text{otherwise,} \end{cases} \tag{8.3.54}$$

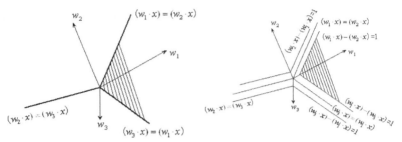

(a) The geometric interpretation     (b) The three margins
     of the decision function

**FIGURE 8.6**: Crammer-Singer method for a linearly separable three-class problem in $R^2$.

These inequalities imply that the inputs of the training points fall into the corresponding region respectively; for example the input $x_i$ with $y_i = 1$ falls into the shaded region in Figure 8.6(b). Note that there exist three margins, margin $d_{12}, d_{23}, d_{31}$ between class 1 and class 2, class 2 and class 3, as well as class 3 and class 1. Margin $d_{12}$ is the distance between the straight line

$$(w_1 \cdot x) - (w_2 \cdot x) = 1 \text{ or } ((w_1 - w_2) \cdot x) = 1 \qquad (8.3.55)$$

and the straight line

$$(w_2 \cdot x) - (w_1 \cdot x) = 1 \text{ or } ((w_1 - w_2) \cdot x) = -1. \qquad (8.3.56)$$

It is not difficult to see that $d_{12} = 2/\|w_1 - w_2\|$. Similarly, we have $d_{23} = 2/\|w_2 - w_3\|$ and $d_{31} = 2/\|w_3 - w_1\|$. Accordingly, the total margin can be measured by

$$D = \|w_1 - w_2\|^2 + \|w_2 - w_3\|^2 + \|w_3 - w_1\|^2 = \sum_{r<s\leqslant 3} \|w_r - w_s\|^2. \quad (8.3.57)$$

Thus using (8.3.57) and (8.3.53), the principle of maximal margin leads to the primal problem

$$\min_{w_1,w_2,w_3} \quad \sum_{r<s\leqslant 3} \|w_r - w_s\|^2, \qquad (8.3.58)$$

$$\text{s.t.} \quad (w_{y_i} \cdot x_i) - (w_r \cdot x_i) \geqslant 1 - \delta_{y_i r}, \ i = 1, \cdots, l; \ r = 1, 2, 3. \ (8.3.59)$$

It is easy to imagine that the above results for linearly separable three-class classification problem can be extended to general $M$-class classification problem by introducing slack variables and the total margin

$$D = \sum_{r<s\leqslant M} \|w_r - w_s\|^2, \qquad (8.3.60)$$

and constructing the optimization problem

$$\min_{w_1,\cdots,w_M,\xi} \quad \sum_{r<s\leqslant M} \|w_r - w_s\|^2 + \bar{C}\sum_{i=1}^{l}\xi_i, \tag{8.3.61}$$

$$\text{s.t.} \quad (w_{y_i}\cdot x_i) - (w_r\cdot x_i) \geqslant 1 - \delta_{y_i r} - \xi_i,$$
$$i = 1,\cdots,l;\ r = 1,\cdots,M, \tag{8.3.62}$$

where $\bar{C}$ is a penalty parameter. It can be seen that the constraints $\xi_i \geqslant 0, i = 1,\cdots,l$ are included in (8.3.62) when $r = y_i$. Noting that

$$\sum_{r<s\leqslant M} \|w_r - w_s\|^2 < M\sum_{r=1}^{M}\|w_r\|^2, \tag{8.3.63}$$

optimization problem (8.3.61)~(8.3.62) can be simplified approximately by substituting its first term in the objective function by the upper bound as the primal problem

$$\min_{w_1,\cdots,w_M,\xi} \quad \frac{1}{2}\sum_{r=1}^{M}\|w_r\|^2 + C\sum_{i=1}^{l}\xi_i, \tag{8.3.64}$$

$$\text{s.t.} \quad (w_{y_i}\cdot x_i) - (w_r\cdot x_i) \geqslant 1 - \delta_{y_i r} - \xi_i,$$
$$i = 1,\cdots,l;\ r = 1,\cdots,M, \tag{8.3.65}$$

where $C$ is a penalty parameter.

### 8.3.3.3 Crammer-Singer support vector classification

The solution to the primal problem (8.3.64)~(8.3.65) can also be obtained by solving its dual problem. Introducing Lagrange function

$$L(w_1,\cdots,w_M,\xi,\eta) = \frac{1}{2}\sum_{r=1}^{M}\|w_r\|^2 + C\sum_{i=1}^{l}\xi_i$$
$$-\sum_{i=1}^{l}\sum_{r=1}^{M}\eta_{ir}[(w_{y_i}\cdot x_i) - (w_r\cdot x_i) - 1 + \delta_{y_i r} + \xi_i], \tag{8.3.66}$$

where $\eta$ is the Lagrange multiplier matrix

$$\eta = \begin{pmatrix} \eta_{11} & \cdots & \eta_{l1} \\ \vdots & & \vdots \\ \eta_{1M} & \cdots & \eta_{lM} \end{pmatrix}. \tag{8.3.67}$$

We can obtain the dual problem with variable $\eta$. Replacing the variable $\eta$ by

$$\alpha = \begin{pmatrix} \alpha_1^1 & \cdots & \alpha_l^1 \\ \vdots & & \vdots \\ \alpha_1^M & \cdots & \alpha_l^M \end{pmatrix}, \tag{8.3.68}$$

where
$$\alpha_i^r = C\delta_{y_i r} - \eta_{ir}, \quad i = 1, \cdots, l; \ r = 1, \cdots, M, \tag{8.3.69}$$

the dual problem is written equivalently as the convex quadratic programming

$$\min_{\alpha} \quad \frac{1}{2}\sum_{i=1}^{l}\sum_{j=1}^{l}(x_i \cdot x_j)\bar{\alpha}_i^{\mathrm{T}}\bar{\alpha}_j + \sum_{i=1}^{l}\bar{\alpha}_i^{\mathrm{T}}\bar{e}_i, \tag{8.3.70}$$

$$\text{s.t.} \quad \sum_{r=1}^{M}\alpha_i^r = 0, i = 1, \cdots, l, \tag{8.3.71}$$

$$\alpha_i^r \leqslant 0 \ \text{if} \ y_i \neq r; \ \alpha_i^r \leqslant C, \ \text{if} \ y_i = r,$$
$$i = 1, \cdots, l, \ r = 1, \cdots, M, \tag{8.3.72}$$

where

$$\bar{\alpha}_i = [\alpha_i^1, \cdots, \alpha_i^M]^{\mathrm{T}}, \tag{8.3.73}$$

$$\bar{e}_i = [e_i^1, \cdots, e_i^M]^{\mathrm{T}}, \quad e_i^r = 1 - \delta_{y_i r}, \tag{8.3.74}$$

$$\alpha = (\bar{\alpha}_1, \cdots, \bar{\alpha}_l) = \begin{pmatrix} \alpha_1^1 & \cdots & \alpha_l^1 \\ \vdots & & \vdots \\ \alpha_1^M & \cdots & \alpha_l^M \end{pmatrix}. \tag{8.3.75}$$

**Theorem 8.3.7** *Suppose that* $\alpha^* = (\alpha_i^{r*})_{M \times l}$ *is any solution to problem* (8.3.70)~(8.3.75). *Then a solution to the primal problem* (8.3.64)~(8.3.65) *w.r.t.* $w_1, \cdots, w_M$ *can be obtained by*

$$w_r = \sum_{i=1}^{l}\alpha_i^{r*}x_i, \quad r = 1, \cdots, M. \tag{8.3.76}$$

This theorem is easily extended to the case with kernel $K(x, x') = (\Phi(x) \cdot \Phi(x'))$, yielding the following algorithm:

**Algorithm 8.3.8** *(Crammer-Singer multiclass support vector classification)*
*(1) Input the training set*

$$T = \{(x_1, y_1), \cdots, (x_l, y_l)\}, \tag{8.3.77}$$

*where* $x_i \in R^n, y_i \in \mathcal{Y} = \{1, \cdots, M\}, i = 1, \cdots, l;$
*(2) Choose an appropriate kernel function* $K(x, x')$ *and penalty parameter* $C > 0$;
*(3) Construct and solve convex quadratic programming problem* (8.3.70)~(8.3.75), *obtaining a solution*

$$\alpha^* = \begin{pmatrix} \alpha_1^{1*} \cdots \alpha_l^{1*} \\ \vdots \quad \vdots \\ \alpha_1^{M*} \cdots \alpha_l^{M*} \end{pmatrix}; \tag{8.3.78}$$

*(4) Construct the decision function*

$$f(x) = \underset{r=1,\cdots,M}{\operatorname{argmax}} \sum_{i=1}^{l} \alpha_i^{r*} K(x_i, x). \tag{8.3.79}$$

---

## 8.4 Semisupervised Classification

### 8.4.1 PU classification problem

In the standard binary classification problem, the training set consists of a collection of positive inputs and a collection of negative inputs. Now let us consider a different case where the training set consists of a collection of positive inputs and a collection of unlabeled inputs known to belong to one of the two classes: PU binary classification problem (P and U stand for "positive" and "unlabeled" respectively). It is formulated mathematically as follows:

**PU classification problem**: Given a training set

$$T = \{(x_1, y_1), \cdots, (x_l, y_l)\} \cup \{x_{l+1}, \cdots, x_{l+q}\}, \tag{8.4.1}$$

where $x_i \in R^n$, $y_i = 1$, i.e. $x_i$ is a positive input, $i = 1, \cdots, l$; $x_i \in R^n$, i.e. $x_i$ is an unlabeled input known to belong to one of the two classes, $i = l+1, \cdots, l+q$, find a real function $g(x)$ in $R^n$ such that the output $y$ for any input $x$ can be predicted by

$$f(x) = \operatorname{sgn}(g(x)). \tag{8.4.2}$$

Obviously, different from the standard binary classification problem, there are no labeled negative inputs for training, see [44, 45, 61, 96, 102]. So traditional support vector classifications are thus not directly applicable because they all require both labeled positive and labeled negative inputs to build a classifier.

### 8.4.2 Biased support vector classification[101]

#### 8.4.2.1 Optimization problem

Let us consider a PU problem in $R^2$ shown in Figure 8.7, where positive inputs are represented with "+"s, and unlabeled inputs with "∘"s. First, assume that the positive inputs in the training set have no error, i.e. all positive inputs are positive indeed. In order to find the best separating line $(w \cdot x) + b = 0$, consider three candidates $l_1, l_2$, and $l_3$ in Figure 8.7. Every input on the top right of each line will be labeled (classified) by the line as positive, and every input on the down left will be labeled as negative. Line $l_1$ is clearly not suitable because it does not separate the positive inputs complete correctly. Line $l_3$ is poor too because there seems no reason to allow too many unlabeled

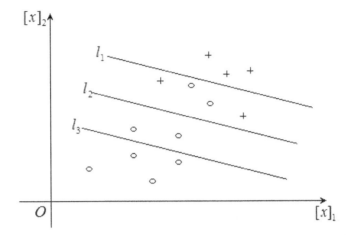

**FIGURE 8.7**: A PU problem.

inputs labeled as positive. Therefore line $l_2$ should be the optimal, where no positive input is labeled negative, and the number of unlabeled inputs labeled as positive is minimized. This intuitive observation leads to the following conclusion: minimizing the number of unlabeled inputs classified as positive while constraining the positive inputs to be correctly classified. This conclusion has also been shown in [101] from a theoretical point of view when the training set is large enough. Following the conclusion with maximal margin principle, we have the following primal optimization problem

$$\min_{w,b,\xi} \quad \frac{1}{2}\|w\|^2 + C_- \sum_{i=l+1}^{l+q} \xi_i, \tag{8.4.3}$$

$$\text{s.t.} \quad (w \cdot x_i) + b \geqslant 1, i = 1, \cdots, l, \tag{8.4.4}$$

$$-((w \cdot x_i) + b) \geqslant 1 - \xi_i, i = l+1, \cdots, l+q, \tag{8.4.5}$$

$$\xi_i \geqslant 0, i = l+1, \cdots, l+q, \tag{8.4.6}$$

where $\xi = (\xi_{l+1}, \cdots, \xi_{l+q})$. Note that this formulation is for the noiseless case: There is no error in the positive inputs. Here we do not allow any mistake in the positive inputs, which is the first constraint, but some unlabeled inputs are allowed to be labeled as positive inputs, which is the second constraint. Clearly, the formulation follows the above conclusion, minimizing the number of unlabeled inputs classified as positive, exactly due to the second term in the objective function. The subscript in the second term starts from $l + 1$, which is the index of the first unlabeled input.

However, in practice, the positive inputs may also contain some errors. Thus, if we allow noise (or error) in positive inputs, we have the following soft margin version which uses an extra parameter $C_+$

$$\min_{w,b,\xi} \quad \frac{1}{2}\|w\|^2 + C_+ \sum_{i=1}^{l} \xi_i + C_- \sum_{i=l+l}^{l+q} \xi_i, \tag{8.4.7}$$

$$\text{s.t.} \quad y_i((w \cdot x_i) + b) \geqslant 1 - \xi_i, i = 1, \cdots, l + q, \tag{8.4.8}$$

$$\xi_i \geqslant 0, i = 1, \cdots, l + q, \tag{8.4.9}$$

where $y_i = 1, i = 1, \cdots, l, y_i = -1, i = l + 1, \cdots, l + q, \xi = (\xi_1, \cdots, \xi_{l+q})^{\mathrm{T}}$. We can vary $C_+$ and $C_-$ to achieve our objective. Intuitively, we give a bigger value for $C_+$ and a smaller value for $C_-$ because the unlabeled set, which is assumed to be negative, contains positive inputs.

### 8.4.2.2  The selection of the parameters $C_+$ and $C_-$

When biased support vector classification is implemented in practice, there exists a difficulty for selecting the parameters $C_+$ and $C_-$. Note that the common approach is to try a range of values for both $C_+$ and $C_-$. The $C_+$ and $C_-$ values that give the optimal classification results are selected as the final parameter values of them. The optimality usually depends on an evaluation measure on a testing set. Unfortunately it is not clear how to estimate the evaluation measure here. For example, try to calculate the evaluation measure $G$-mean

$$G\text{-mean} = \sqrt{r_{tp} \cdot r_{tn}} \tag{8.4.10}$$

introduced by (6.3.10) in Chapter 6. Corresponding the training set (8.4.1), on the testing set is in the form

$$\tilde{T} = \{(\tilde{x}_1, \tilde{y}_1), \cdots, (\tilde{x}_{\tilde{l}}, \tilde{y}_{\tilde{l}})\} \cup \{(\tilde{x}_{\tilde{l}+1}, \cdots, \tilde{x}_{\tilde{l}+\tilde{q}})\}, \tag{8.4.11}$$

where $\tilde{x}_i \in R^n, i = 1, \cdots, \tilde{l} + \tilde{q}, \tilde{y}_i = 1, i = 1, \cdots, \tilde{l}$. For a decision function $f(x)$, the values of the true positive rate $r_{tp}$ and the true negative rate $r_{tn}$ are needed. Note that the former factor $r_{tp}$ can be calculated directly by considering the positive inputs in the testing set (8.4.11); but the latter one $r_{tn}$ cannot be obtained directly since there are no labeled negative inputs. So instead of using $G$-mean directly, we define a new combined evaluation measure

$$r_{tp} \cdot p, \tag{8.4.12}$$

where the factor $r_{tn}$ in $G$-mean is replaced by another evaluation measure $p$ defined by

$$p = \frac{t_p}{t_p + f_p}, \tag{8.4.13}$$

where $t_p$ and $f_p$ are respectively the number of true positives and false positives defined in (6.3.5) in Chapter 6. Obviously, the larger the product $r_{tp} \cdot p$, the better. Next we show that starting from this product we are able to obtain a quantity which can be used to compare different decision functions when the testing set is large enough. In fact, when the testing set is large, we can write $r_{tp}$ and $p$ in terms of probability

$$r_{tp} \approx P(f(x) = 1 | y = 1), \quad p \approx P(y = 1 | f(x) = 1). \qquad (8.4.14)$$

It is easy to see that

$$P(y = 1 | f(x) = 1) \cdot P(f(x) = 1) = P(f(x) = 1 | y = 1) \cdot P(y = 1) \qquad (8.4.15)$$

since both sides of the equality are the probability of the case where $f(x) = 1$ and $y = 1$. Using (8.4.14), the above equality can approximately be written as

$$p \approx P(y = 1) \frac{r_{tp}}{P(f(x) = 1)}, \qquad (8.4.16)$$

or

$$r_{tp} \cdot p \approx P(y = 1) \cdot L, \qquad (8.4.17)$$

where

$$L = \frac{r_{tp}^2}{P(f(x) = 1)}. \qquad (8.4.18)$$

Noting that $P(y = 1)$ does not depend on the decision function, the quantity $L$ can be used to compare the performance of different decisions; the bigger, the better. On the other hand, the quantity $L$ can be estimated based on the testing set (8.4.11) which contains both positive and unlabeled inputs since $r_{tp}$ can be calculated using the positive inputs and $P(f(x) = 1)$ can be estimated approximately from the whole testing set. Therefore, an estimation of the $L$ is an evaluation measure in the sense that it can be used to compare the performance of biased support vector classifications with different parameters $C_+$ and $C_-$ ; the larger the quantity $L$, the better. So, in this way the optimal values of the parameters $C_+$ and $C_-$ can be selected.

Additionally, it can be seen that the quantity $L$ is large when $r_{tp}$ is large and $Pr(f(x) = 1)$ is small, which means that the number of unlabeled inputs labeled as positive should be small. This is also a support to the conclusion which is used to derive the primal problem of biased support vector classification.

The above primal optimization problem is very similar to the one in the standard support vector classification, and therefore it is easy to derive the corresponding classification algorithm. The detail is omitted.

### 8.4.3  Classification problem with labeled and unlabeled inputs

Another semisupervised classification problem is formulated mathematically as follows.

**Classification problem with labeled and unlabeled inputs**: Given a training set

$$T = \{(x_1, y_1), \cdots, (x_l, y_l)\} \bigcup \{x_{l+1}, \cdots, x_{l+q}\}, \qquad (8.4.19)$$

where $x_i \in R^n$, $y_i \in \{-1,1\}$, $i = 1,\cdots,l$, $x_i \in R^n$, $i = l+1,\cdots,l+q$, and the set $\{x_{l+1},\cdots,x_{l+q}\}$ is a collection of unlabeled inputs known to belong to one of the two classes, predict the outputs $y_{l+1},y_{l+2},\cdots,y_{l+q}$ for $\{x_{l+1},\cdots,x_{l+q}\}$ and find a real function $g(x)$ in $R^n$ such that the output $y$ for any input $x$ can be predicted by

$$f(x) = \mathrm{sgn}(g(x)). \tag{8.4.20}$$

Here we have a labeled training set $\{(x_1,y_1),\cdots,(x_l,y_l)\}$ as well as an unlabeled training set $\{x_{l+1},\cdots,x_{l+q}\}$. The goal is to combine the information in these two data sets to produce a more accurate classifier; see [25, 196, 198, 199].

## 8.4.4 Support vector classification by semidefinite programming

### 8.4.4.1 Optimization problem

It is obvious that there will be no essential difficulty to get the decision function if the output vector

$$y = (y_{l+1},y_{l+2},\cdots,y_{l+q})^{\mathrm{T}} \tag{8.4.21}$$

is obtained. So next we investigate how to find this vector. To avoid the complicated computation, only a clue is provided below.

Suppose that output vector (8.4.21) is given and consider a transformation $\mathrm{x} = \Phi(x)$ with the kernel $K(x,x')$. Corresponding to the primal problem (8.1.33)$\sim$(8.1.35) and the dual problem (8.1.36)$\sim$(8.1.37), we have the optimization problem

$$\min_{\mathrm{w},b,\xi} \quad h_1(\mathrm{w},b,\xi) = \frac{1}{2}\|\mathrm{w}\|^2 + \frac{1}{2}b^2 + C\sum_{i=1}^{l+q}\xi_i, \tag{8.4.22}$$

$$\text{s.t.} \quad y_i((\mathrm{w}\cdot\Phi(x_i))+b) \geqslant 1-\xi_i, i = 1,\cdots,l+q, \tag{8.4.23}$$

$$\xi_i \geqslant 0, i = 1,\cdots,l+q, \tag{8.4.24}$$

and its dual problem

$$\max_{\alpha} \quad d_1(\alpha,y) = \sum_{i=1}^{l+q}\alpha_j - \frac{1}{2}\sum_{i=1}^{l+q}\sum_{j=1}^{l+q}y_iy_j\alpha_i\alpha_j(K(x_i,x_j)+1), \tag{8.4.25}$$

$$\text{s.t.} \quad 0 \leqslant \alpha_i \leqslant C, i = 1,\cdots,l+q. \tag{8.4.26}$$

Obviously, both their solutions $(\bar{\mathrm{w}},\bar{b},\bar{\xi})$ and $\bar{\alpha}$ depend on $y$

$$\bar{\mathrm{w}} = \bar{\mathrm{w}}(y), \quad \bar{b} = \bar{b}(y), \quad \bar{\xi} = \bar{\xi}(y), \quad \bar{\alpha} = \bar{\alpha}(y). \tag{8.4.27}$$

By the strong duality theorem mentioned in Section 1.3.3, we have

$$h_1(\bar{\mathrm{w}}(y),\bar{b}(y),\bar{\xi}(y)) = d_1(\bar{\alpha}(y),y). \tag{8.4.28}$$

Now we are in a position to establish the optimization problem to find the output vector $y$. Noting that solving problem (8.4.22)~(8.4.24) implies to select $w, b, \xi$ such that the objective function $h_1(w, b, \xi)$ is minimized. Here the optimal value $h_1(\bar{w}, \bar{b}, \bar{\xi})$ is a function of $y$

$$h_2(y) = h_1(\bar{w}(y), \bar{b}(y), \bar{\xi}(y)). \tag{8.4.29}$$

Therefore, a natural idea is to select $y$, such that $h_2(y)$ is minimized. This leads to the optimization problem

$$\min_{y} \quad h_2(y) = h_1(\bar{w}(y), \bar{b}(y), \bar{\xi}(y)), \tag{8.4.30}$$

$$\text{s.t.} \quad -\varepsilon \leqslant \sum_{i=1}^{l+q} y_i \leqslant \varepsilon, \tag{8.4.31}$$

where $(\bar{w}(y), \bar{b}(y), \bar{\xi}(y))$ is a solution to problem (8.4.22)~(8.4.24) and $\varepsilon$ is a parameter. Looking at (8.4.28), the above problem can be written as

$$\min_{y} \quad d_2(y) = d_1(\bar{\alpha}(y), y), \tag{8.4.32}$$

$$\text{s.t.} \quad -\varepsilon \leqslant \sum_{i=1}^{l+q} y_i \leqslant \varepsilon, \tag{8.4.33}$$

where $d_1(\cdot, \cdot)$ is given by (8.4.25) and $\bar{\alpha}(y)$ is the solution to the problem (8.4.25)~(8.4.26). The desired output vector can be obtained by solving the above optimization problem.

### 8.4.4.2  Approximate solution via semidefinite programming

In order to solve problem (8.4.32)~(8.4.33), introduce the matrix

$$W = \tilde{y}\tilde{y}^{\mathrm{T}}, \tag{8.4.34}$$

where

$$\tilde{y} = (y_1, \cdots, y_l, y^{\mathrm{T}})^{\mathrm{T}}, \quad y = (y_{l+1}, y_{l+2}, \cdots, y_{l+q})^{\mathrm{T}}, \tag{8.4.35}$$

and define

$$A \circ B = (a_{ij})_{n \times n} \circ (b_{ij})_{n \times n} = (a_{ij} b_{ij})_{n \times n}, \tag{8.4.36}$$

$$\langle A, B \rangle = \langle (a_{ij})_{n \times n}, (b_{ij})_{n \times n} \rangle = \sum_{ij} a_{ij} b_{ij}. \tag{8.4.37}$$

Thus the problem can be written as

$$\min_{\tilde{y}, W} \max_{\alpha} \quad \alpha^{\mathrm{T}} e - \frac{1}{2} \langle (K + e e^{\mathrm{T}}) \circ W, \alpha \alpha^{\mathrm{T}} \rangle, \tag{8.4.38}$$

$$\text{s.t.} \quad 0 \leqslant \alpha \leqslant Ce, \tag{8.4.39}$$

$$\quad -\varepsilon e \leqslant We \leqslant \varepsilon e, \tag{8.4.40}$$

$$\quad W - \tilde{y}\tilde{y}^{\mathrm{T}} = 0. \tag{8.4.41}$$

Relaxing the constraint $W - \widetilde{y}\widetilde{y}^{\mathrm{T}} = 0$ as

$$W_{ij} = y_i y_j, \quad i, j = 1, \cdots, l, \quad \mathrm{diag}(W) = e, \quad W \succeq 0, \tag{8.4.42}$$

the above problem is expressed approximately as

$$\min_{W} \quad h_4(W) = h_3(W, \bar{\alpha}), \tag{8.4.43}$$

$$\text{s.t.} \quad -\varepsilon e \leqslant We \leqslant \varepsilon e, \tag{8.4.44}$$

$$W \succeq 0, W_{ij} = y_i y_j, i, j = 1, 2, \cdots, l, \tag{8.4.45}$$

$$\mathrm{diag}(W) = e, \tag{8.4.46}$$

where

$$h_3(W, \alpha) = \alpha^{\mathrm{T}} e - \frac{1}{2} \langle (K + ee^{\mathrm{T}}) \circ W, \alpha\alpha^{\mathrm{T}} \rangle, \tag{8.4.47}$$

and $\bar{\alpha}$ is the solution to

$$\max_{\alpha} \quad h_3(W, \alpha), \tag{8.4.48}$$

$$\text{s.t.} \quad 0 \leqslant \alpha \leqslant Ce. \tag{8.4.49}$$

The above problem is a min-max problem. In order to change it into a min-min problem, replace problem (8.4.48)~(8.4.49) by its dual problem

$$\min_{u,v} \quad \frac{1}{2}(e - u + v)^{\mathrm{T}}((K + ee^{\mathrm{T}}) \circ W)^{\dagger}(e - u + v) + u^{\mathrm{T}}Ce, \tag{8.4.50}$$

$$\text{s.t.} \quad u \geqslant 0, v \geqslant 0, \tag{8.4.51}$$

where $(\cdot)^{\dagger}$ stands for the Moore-Penrose inverse, and rewrite problem (8.4.43)~(8.4.49) as the following min-min problem

$$\min_{W} \min_{u,v} \quad \frac{1}{2}(e - u + v)^{\mathrm{T}}((K + ee^{\mathrm{T}}) \circ W)^{\dagger}(e - u + v) + u^{\mathrm{T}}Ce,$$

$$\tag{8.4.52}$$

$$\text{s.t.} \quad -\varepsilon e \leqslant We \leqslant \varepsilon e, \tag{8.4.53}$$

$$W \succeq 0, \mathrm{diag}(W) = e, W_{ij} = y_i y_j, \ i, j = 1, \cdots, l, \tag{8.4.54}$$

$$u \geqslant 0, v \geqslant 0. \tag{8.4.55}$$

This problem can be further transformed equivalently into a semidefinite programming problem

$$\min_{W,\delta,u,v} \quad \frac{1}{2}\delta, \tag{8.4.56}$$

$$\text{s.t.} \quad \begin{pmatrix} (K + ee^{\mathrm{T}}) \circ W & (e - u + v) \\ (e - u + v)^{\mathrm{T}} & \delta - 2u^{\mathrm{T}}Ce \end{pmatrix} \succeq 0, \tag{8.4.57}$$

$$-\varepsilon e \leqslant We \leqslant \varepsilon e, \tag{8.4.58}$$

$$W \succeq 0, \mathrm{diag}(W) = e, W_{ij} = y_i y_j, i, j = 1, 2, \cdots, l, \tag{8.4.59}$$

$$u \geqslant 0, v \geqslant 0. \tag{8.4.60}$$

To get the output vector $y$ from a solution $W^*$ to the problem (8.4.56)∼(8.4.60) w.r.t. $W$, the following conclusion is helpful.

**Theorem 8.4.1** *Suppose that the matrix $W^*$ is a solution to the problem (8.4.56) ∼(8.4.60), and the rank of $W^*$ is one, i.e there exists a vector $\tilde{y}^* = (\tilde{y}_1^*, \cdots, \tilde{y}_l^*, \tilde{y}_{l+1}^*, \cdots, \tilde{y}_{l+q}^*)^{\mathrm{T}}$, such that $W^* = \tilde{y}^* \tilde{y}^{*\mathrm{T}}$, then $\tilde{y}^*$ is the solution to the problem (8.4.30)∼(8.4.31).*

Note that the matrix $W^*$ has only one nonzero (positive) eigenvalue if rank($W^*$)=1. So the above theorem can be understood to get the output vector $y$ from the eigenvector corresponding to the largest eigenvalue of $W^*$. Extending this rule to the general case even the rank of $W^*$ is not 1, the output vector $y = (y_{l+1}^*, \cdots, y_{l+q}^*)$ is reasonably defined by

$$y_i^* = \mathrm{sgn}(\nu_{1i}), i = l+1, \cdots, l+q, \tag{8.4.61}$$

where $\nu_1 = (\nu_{11}, \cdots, \nu_{1l}, \nu_{1,l+1}, \cdots, \nu_{1,l+q})^{\mathrm{T}}$ is the eigenvector corresponding to the largest eigenvalue.

### 8.4.4.3    Support vector classification by semidefinite programming

Once the output vector $y$ is defined, the decision function $f(x) = \mathrm{sgn}(\sum_{i=1}^{l+q} \alpha_i^* y_i (K(x, x_i) + 1))$ can be obtained by considering the problem as a standard binary classification problem with full outputs $y_1, \cdots, y_l, y_{l+1}, \cdots, y_{l+q}$, and finding $\alpha^* = (\alpha_1^*, \cdots, \alpha_{l+q}^*)$ from the dual problem corresponding to the problem (8.1.36)∼(8.1.37) in bounded support vector classification. However, in order to reduce the computational error, a better technique is to find $\alpha^*$ by solving the problem (8.4.48)∼(8.4.49) where $W$ is replaced by the solution $W^*$ to the problem (8.4.56) ∼(8.4.60) w.r.t $W$:

$$\alpha^* = ((K + ee^{\mathrm{T}}) \circ W)^{\dagger} (e - u^* + v^*). \tag{8.4.62}$$

Thus we establish the following algorithm.

**Algorithm 8.4.2** *(Support vector classification by semidefinite programming)*

*(1) Input the training set $T = \{(x_1, y_1), \cdots, (x_l, y_l)\} \bigcup \{x_{l+1}, \cdots, x_{l+q}\}$, where $x_i \in R^n$, $i = 1, \cdots, l+q$, $y_i \in \{1, -1\}, i = 1, \cdots, l$;*

*(2) Choose an appropriate kernel function $K(x, x')$ and parameters $C > 0$ and $\varepsilon > 0$;*

*(3) Construct and solve the semidefinite programming problem*

$$\min_{W,\delta,u,v} \quad \frac{1}{2}\delta, \tag{8.4.63}$$

$$\text{s.t.} \quad \begin{pmatrix} (K + ee^{\mathrm{T}}) \circ W & (e - u + v) \\ (e - u + v)^{\mathrm{T}} & \delta - 2u^{\mathrm{T}}Ce \end{pmatrix} \succeq 0, \tag{8.4.64}$$

$$-\varepsilon e \leqslant We \leqslant \varepsilon e, \tag{8.4.65}$$

$$W \succeq 0, \mathrm{diag}(W) = e, W_{ij} = y_i y_j, i, j = 1, 2, \cdots, l, \tag{8.4.66}$$

$$u \geqslant 0, v \geqslant 0, \tag{8.4.67}$$

*obtaining the solution $W^*$, $u^*$, $v^*$ w.r.t $(W, u, v)$;*

*(4) Let $y_i = \mathrm{sgn}(v_{1i})$, $i = l + 1, \cdots, l + q$, where $v_1 = (v_{11}, \cdots, v_{1(l+q)})^{\mathrm{T}}$ is the eigenvector corresponding to the largest eigenvalue of $W^*$ ;*

*(5) Construct the decision function $f(x) = \mathrm{sgn}\left( \sum_{i=1}^{l+q} \alpha_i^* y_i (K(x, x_i) + 1) \right)$,*

*where $\alpha^* = ((K + ee^{\mathrm{T}}) \circ W^*)^{\dagger}(e - u^* + v^*)$.*

The above algorithm based on bounded support vector classification comes from [174]. The counterparts based on $v$-support vector classification and Lagrange support vector classification are also interesting[190, 191]. In addition, for multiclass classification problems and robust classification problem, the corresponding topics have also been investigated, see [24, 173, 174, 189, 192].

---

## 8.5 Universum Classification

### 8.5.1 Universum classification problem

**Universum classification problem**: Given a training set

$$T = \{(x_1, y_1), \cdots, (x_l, y_l)\} \bigcup \{x_1^*, \cdots, x_u^*\}, \tag{8.5.1}$$

where $x_i \in R^n, y_i \in \{-1, 1\}, i = 1, \cdots, l, x_j^* \in R^n, j = 1, \cdots, u$, and the set

$$U = \{x_1^*, \cdots, x_u^*\} \tag{8.5.2}$$

is a collection of unlabeled inputs known not to belong to either class, find a real function $g(x)$ in $R^n$ such that the value of $y$ for any $x$ can be predicted by the decision function

$$f(x) = \mathrm{sgn}(g(x)). \tag{8.5.3}$$

Set (8.5.2) is called the Universum and is expected to represent meaningful information related to the classification task at hand.

Training set (8.5.1) is similar to training set (8.4.19) of the semisupervised classification problem. However there is an important difference: the input $x_i$ in (8.4.19) belongs to one of the two classes concerned, $i = l + 1, \cdots, l + q$, while $x_j^*$ in (8.5.1) does not, $j = 1, \cdots, u$.

## 8.5.2 Primal problem and dual problem

Introducing the transformation, from $R^n$ to Hilbert space $\mathcal{H}$

$$\Phi : \begin{array}{l} R^n \to \mathcal{H} , \\ x \mapsto \mathrm{x} = \Phi(x) , \end{array} \tag{8.5.4}$$

training set (8.5.1) is transformed into

$$\begin{aligned} \tilde{T} &= \{(\mathrm{x}_1, y_1), \cdots, (\mathrm{x}_l, y_l)\} \bigcup \{\mathrm{x}_1^*, \cdots, \mathrm{x}_u^*\} \\ &= \{(\Phi(x_1), y_1), \cdots, (\Phi(x_l), y_l)\} \bigcup \{\Phi(x_1^*), \cdots, \Phi(x_u^*)\} , \end{aligned} \tag{8.5.5}$$

According to [156], the goal is to find a separating hyperplane $(\mathrm{w} \cdot \mathrm{x}) + b = 0$ such that, on one hand, it separates the inputs $\{x_1, \cdots, x_l\}$ with maximal margin, and on the other hand, it approximates to the inputs $\{x_1^*, \cdots, x_u^*\}$. This leads to the primal problem

$$\min_{\mathrm{w}, b, \xi, \psi^{(*)}} \quad \frac{1}{2} \|\mathrm{w}\|_2^2 + C_t \sum_{i=1}^{l} \xi_i + C_u \sum_{s=1}^{u} (\psi_s + \psi_s^*), \tag{8.5.6}$$

$$\text{s.t.} \quad y_i((\mathrm{w} \cdot \mathrm{x}_i) + b) \geq 1 - \xi_i, \xi_i \geq 0, i = 1, \cdots, l, \tag{8.5.7}$$

$$-\varepsilon - \psi_s^* \leq (\mathrm{w} \cdot \mathrm{x}_s^*) + b \leq \varepsilon + \psi_s, s = 1, \cdots, u, \tag{8.5.8}$$

$$\psi_s, \psi_s^* \geq 0, s = 1, \cdots, u, \tag{8.5.9}$$

where $\psi^{(*)} = (\psi_1, \psi_1^*, \cdots, \psi_u, \psi_u^*)^{\mathrm{T}}$ and $C_t, C_u \in [0, +\infty)$ and $\varepsilon \in [0, +\infty)$ are parameters.

Introduce the Lagrange function

$$\begin{aligned} L(\mathrm{w}, b, \xi, \xi^*, \alpha, \mu, \nu, \gamma, \gamma^*) &= \frac{1}{2} \|\mathrm{w}\|_2^2 + C_t \sum_{i=1}^{l} \xi_i + C_u \sum_{s=1}^{u} (\psi_s + \psi_s^*) \\ &\quad - \sum_{i=1}^{l} \alpha_i [y_i((\mathrm{w} \cdot \mathrm{x}_i) + b) - 1 + \xi_i] - \sum_{i=1}^{l} \eta_i \xi_i \\ &\quad - \sum_{s=1}^{u} \nu_s [\varepsilon + \psi_s - (\mathrm{w} \cdot \mathrm{x}_s^*) - b] - \sum_{s=1}^{u} \gamma_s \psi_s \\ &\quad - \sum_{s=1}^{u} \mu_s [(\mathrm{w} \cdot \mathrm{x}_s^*) + b + \varepsilon + \psi_s^*] - \sum_{s=1}^{u} \gamma_s^* \psi_s^* \end{aligned} \tag{8.5.10}$$

where $\alpha = (\alpha_1, \cdots, \alpha_l)^{\mathrm{T}}$, $\mu = (\mu_1, \cdots, \mu_u)^{\mathrm{T}}$, $\nu = (\nu_1, \cdots, \nu_u)^{\mathrm{T}}$, $\eta = (\eta_1, \cdots, \eta_l)^{\mathrm{T}}$, $\gamma = (\gamma_1, \cdots, \gamma_u)^{\mathrm{T}}$ and $\gamma^* = (\gamma_1^*, \cdots, \gamma_u^*)^{\mathrm{T}}$ are multiplier vectors, the following two theorems can be obtained.

**Theorem 8.5.1** *Optimization problem*

$$
\max_{\alpha,\mu,\nu,\eta,\gamma,\gamma^*} \quad -\frac{1}{2}\sum_{i,j=1}^{l}\alpha_i\alpha_j y_i y_j K(x_i,x_j) - \frac{1}{2}\sum_{s,t=1}^{u}(\mu_s-\nu_s)(\mu_t-\nu_t)K(x_s^*,x_t^*)
$$

$$
-\sum_{i=1}^{l}\sum_{s=1}^{u}\alpha_i y_i(\mu_s-\nu_s)K(x_i,x_s^*) + \sum_{i=1}^{l}\alpha_i - \varepsilon\sum_{s=1}^{u}(\mu_s+\nu_s),
$$

$$(8.5.11)$$

$$
s.t. \quad \sum_{i=1}^{l}y_i\alpha_i + \sum_{s=1}^{u}(\mu_s-\nu_s) = 0, \tag{8.5.12}
$$

$$
C_t - \alpha_i - \eta_i = 0, \quad i=1,\cdots,l\,, \tag{8.5.13}
$$

$$
C_u - \nu_s - \gamma_s = 0, \quad s=1,\cdots,u\,, \tag{8.5.14}
$$

$$
C_u - \mu_s - \gamma_s^* = 0, \quad s=1,\cdots,u\,, \tag{8.5.15}
$$

$$
\alpha_i \ge 0,\ \eta_i \ge 0, \quad i=1,\cdots,l\,, \tag{8.5.16}
$$

$$
\nu_s \ge 0,\ \gamma_s \ge 0, \quad s=1,\cdots,u\,, \tag{8.5.17}
$$

$$
\mu_s \ge 0,\ \gamma_s^* \ge 0, \quad s=1,\cdots,u \tag{8.5.18}
$$

*is the dual problem of the primal problem* (8.5.6)∼(8.5.9).

**Theorem 8.5.2** *Suppose* $\hat{\alpha} = (\hat{\alpha}_1,\cdots,\hat{\alpha}_l)^{\mathrm{T}}$, $\hat{\mu} = (\hat{\mu}_1,\cdots,\hat{\mu}_u)^{\mathrm{T}}$, $\hat{\nu} = (\hat{\nu}_1,\cdots,\hat{\nu}_u)^{\mathrm{T}}$ *is a solution to the dual problem* (8.5.11)∼(8.5.18) *w.r.t.* $(\alpha,\mu,\nu)$. *If there exists a component* $\hat{\alpha}_j \in (0,C_t)$ *of* $\hat{\alpha}$, *or a component* $\hat{\mu}_m \in (0,C_u)$ *of* $\hat{\mu}$, *or a component of* $\hat{\nu}_t \in (0,C_u)$ *of* $\hat{\nu}$, *then a solution* $(\hat{w},\hat{b})$ *to the problem* (8.5.6)∼(8.5.9) *w.r.t.* (w, b) *can be obtained in the following way*

$$
\hat{w} = \sum_{i=1}^{l}\hat{\alpha}_i y_i \Phi(x_i) - \sum_{s=1}^{u}(\hat{\nu}_s-\hat{\mu}_s)\Phi(x_s^*) \tag{8.5.19}
$$

*and*

$$
\hat{b} = y_j - \sum_{i=1}^{l}\hat{\alpha}_i y_i K(x_i,x_j) + \sum_{s=1}^{u}(\hat{\nu}_s-\hat{\mu}_s)K(x_s^*,x_j), \tag{8.5.20}
$$

*or*

$$
\hat{b} = \varepsilon - \sum_{i=1}^{l}\hat{\alpha}_i y_i K(x_i,x_m^*) + \sum_{s=1}^{u}(\hat{\nu}_s-\hat{\mu}_s)K(x_s^*,x_m^*), \tag{8.5.21}
$$

*or*

$$
\hat{b} = -\varepsilon - \sum_{i=1}^{l}\hat{\alpha}_i y_i K(x_i,x_t^*) + \sum_{s=1}^{u}(\hat{\nu}_s-\hat{\mu}_s)K(x_s^*,x_t^*). \tag{8.5.22}
$$

### 8.5.2.1 Algorithm and its relationship with three-class classification

According to the above theorem, we can establish the following algorithm.

**Algorithm 8.5.3** *(Universum support vector classification, USVC)*

*(1) Input the training set* $T \bigcup U = \{(x_1, y_1), \cdots, (x_l, y_l)\} \cup \{x_1^*, \cdots, x_u^*\}$, *where* $x_i \in R^n, y_i \in \mathcal{Y} = \{1, -1\}, i = 1, \cdots, l, x_i^* \in R^n, i = 1, \cdots, u;$

*(2) Choose an appropriate kernel function* $K(x, x')$ *and parameters* $C_t, C_u, \varepsilon > 0;$

*(3) Construct and solve the optimization problem* (8.5.11)$\sim$(8.5.18), *obtaining a solution w.r.t.* $(\alpha, \mu, \nu)$: $\hat{\alpha} = (\hat{\alpha}_1, \cdots, \hat{\alpha}_l)^{\mathrm{T}}, \hat{\mu} = (\hat{\mu}_1, \cdots, \hat{\mu}_u)^{\mathrm{T}}, \hat{\nu} = (\hat{\nu}_1, \cdots, \hat{\nu}_u)^{\mathrm{T}};$

*(4) Compute* $\hat{b}$: *Choose a component of* $\hat{\alpha}, \hat{\alpha}_j \in (0, C_t)$ , *or a component of* $\hat{\mu}$, $\hat{\mu}_m \in (0, C_u)$, *or a component of of* $\hat{\nu}, \hat{\nu}_t \in (0, C_u)$, *compute* $\hat{b}$ *by* (8.5.20) *or* (8.5.21) *or* (8.5.22);

*(5) Construct the decision function*

$$f(x) = \mathrm{sgn}(g(x)), \tag{8.5.23}$$

*where*

$$g(x) = \sum_{i=1}^{l} \hat{\alpha}_i y_i K(x_i, x) - \sum_{s=1}^{u} (\hat{\nu}_s - \hat{\mu}_s) K(x_s^*, x) + \hat{b}. \tag{8.5.24}$$

Note that the inputs in Universum belong to neither positive class nor negative class. So there are three classes. It is natural to consider the relationship between Universum support vector classification and some three-class classifications. In fact, it can be shown that under some assumptions, Universum support vector classification is also equivalent to $K$-SVCR[4, 194], and is equivalent to the ordinal regression machine with $M = 3$ described in Section 8.3.3 with slight modification. Please see [63] for details.

Universum support vector classification proposes an interesting way for solving a binary classification problem by solving a three-class classification problem.

### 8.5.2.2 Construction of Universum

In order to show that it may not be difficult to collect Universum in applications, we give a simple example in [168] as follows: Consider the binary classification problem to separate digit "5" from digit "8". The Universum can be selected to be examples of the other digit ("0","1","2","3","4","6","7", or "9"). The preliminary experiments show an improvement of Universum support vector classification over the standard support vector classification, and indicate that the digits "3" and "6" are the most useful. This seems to match our intuition as these digits seem somehow "in between" the digits "5" and "8". Another possible way to construct Universum is to create an artificial image by first selecting a random "5" and a random "8" from the training set, and then constructing the mean of these two digits. This trick can be extended to many practical problems. From a practical point, a good Universum dataset needs to be carefully chosen, please refer to [136].

---

## 8.6 Privileged Classification

In many real-world problems, we are not only given the traditional training set, but also provided with some prior information such as some additional descriptions of the training points. In this section, we will focus on the algorithms proposed in [159] for such scenario where prior knowledge is only available for the training data but not available for the testing data. More precisely, the problem is formulated mathematically as follows:

**Privileged classification problem**: Given a training set

$$T = \{(x_1, x_1^*, y_1), \cdots, (x_l, x_l^*, y_l)\} \tag{8.6.1}$$

where $x_i \in R^n$, $x_i^* \in R^m$, $y_i \in \{-1, 1\}$, $i = 1, \cdots, l$, find a real valued function $g(x)$ in $R^n$, such that the value of $y$ for any $x$ can be predicted by the decision function

$$f(x) = \mathrm{sgn}(g(x)). \tag{8.6.2}$$

Since the additional information $x_i^* \in R^m$ is included in the training input $(x_i, x_i^*)$, but not in any testing input $x$, we call it privileged information.

### 8.6.1 Linear privileged support vector classification

Let us start from the standard $C$-SVC with the training set

$$T = \{(x_1, y_1), \cdots, (x_l, y_l)\}. \tag{8.6.3}$$

In order to show the basic idea of privileged support vector classification, we first introduce the definition of Oracle function [159].

**Definition 8.6.1** *(Oracle function) Given a traditional classification problem, suppose there exists the best but unknown linear hyperplane:*

$$(w_0 \cdot x) + b_0 = 0. \tag{8.6.4}$$

*The oracle function $\xi(x)$ of the input $x$ is defined as follows:*

$$\xi^0 = \xi(x) = [1 - y((w_0 \cdot x) + b_0)]_+, \tag{8.6.5}$$

*where*

$$[\eta]_+ = \begin{cases} \eta, & \text{if } \eta \geqslant 0; \\ 0, & \text{otherwise}. \end{cases} \tag{8.6.6}$$

If we could know the value of the oracle function on each training input $x_i$ such as we know the triplets $(x_i, \xi_i^0, y_i)$ with $\xi_i^0 = \xi(x_i), i = 1, \cdots, l$, we can get improved classifier. However, in reality, such a thing is impossible. Instead we use a so-called correcting function to approximate the Oracle function. We construct a simple linear function:

$$\phi(x) = (w^* \cdot x) + b^* \tag{8.6.7}$$

as the correcting function. Replacing $\xi_i(i = 1, \cdots, l)$ by $\phi(x_i^*)$ in the primal problem of $C$-SVC, we get the following primal problem:

$$\min_{w,w^*,b,b^*} \quad \frac{1}{2}\|w\|^2 + C\sum_{i=1}^{l}[(w^* \cdot x_i^*) + b^*], \tag{8.6.8}$$

$$\text{s.t.} \quad y_i[(w \cdot x_i) + b] \geq 1 - [(w^* \cdot x_i^*) + b^*], \tag{8.6.9}$$

$$(w^* \cdot x_i^*) + b^* \geq 0, i = 1, \cdots, l. \tag{8.6.10}$$

**Theorem 8.6.2** *Optimization problem*

$$\max_{\alpha,\beta} \quad \sum_{j=1}^{l}\alpha_j - \frac{1}{2}\sum_{i=1}^{l}\sum_{j=1}^{l}y_iy_j\alpha_i\alpha_j(x_i \cdot x_j), \tag{8.6.11}$$

$$\text{s.t.} \quad \sum_{i=1}^{l}\alpha_iy_i = 0, \tag{8.6.12}$$

$$\sum_{i=1}^{l}(\alpha_i + \beta_i - C) = 0, \tag{8.6.13}$$

$$\sum_{i=1}^{l}(\alpha_i + \beta_i - C)x_i^* = 0, \tag{8.6.14}$$

$$\alpha_i \geq 0, \beta_i \geq 0, i = 1, \cdots, l \tag{8.6.15}$$

*is the dual problem of the problem (8.6.8) $\sim$ (8.6.10).*

**Theorem 8.6.3** *Suppose that $(\alpha^*, \beta^*)$ is a solution to the dual problem (8.6.11) $\sim$ (8.6.15). If there exist two positive components of $\alpha^*$ and $\beta^*$, $\alpha_j^*$ and $\beta_j^*$, then the solution $(\tilde{w}, \tilde{b})$ to the primal problem (8.6.8) $\sim$ (8.6.10) w.r.t. $(w, b)$ can be obtained by*

$$\tilde{w} = \sum_{i=1}^{l}\alpha_i^*y_ix_i, \tag{8.6.16}$$

$$\tilde{b} = y_j - \sum_{i=1}^{l} \alpha_i^* y_i (x_i \cdot x_j). \tag{8.6.17}$$

Once the optimal solution $(\tilde{w}, \tilde{b})$ is obtained, the decision function can be easily constructed: a new input is assigned to the positive class if $g(x) = (\tilde{w} \cdot x) + \tilde{b}$ is greater than zero; the negative class otherwise. Thus the following linear SVM+ algorithm is constructed.

**Algorithm 8.6.4** *(Linear privileged support vector classification)*

*(1) Input the training set given by (8.6.1);*

*(2) Choose an appropriate penalty parameters $C > 0$;*

*(3) Construct and solve the convex quadratic programming problem (8.6.11)~ (8.6.15), obtaining a solution $(\alpha^*, \beta^*)$;*

*(4) Compute*

$$\tilde{w} = \sum_{i=1}^{l} \alpha_i^* y_i x_i; \tag{8.6.18}$$

*Choose two positive components of $\alpha^*$ and $\beta^*$, $\alpha_j^*$ and $\beta_j^*$, then compute*

$$\tilde{b} = y_j - \sum_{i=1}^{l} \alpha_i^* y_i (x_i \cdot x_j); \tag{8.6.19}$$

*(5) Construct the decision function:*

$$f(x) = \operatorname{sgn}(g(x)), \tag{8.6.20}$$

*where*

$$g(x) = (\tilde{w} \cdot x) + \tilde{b}. \tag{8.6.21}$$

## 8.6.2 Nonlinear privileged support vector classification

Similar to nonlinear $C$-SVC, we can introduce kernel function to get nonlinear classifier.

Introducing two transformations: $\mathrm{x} = \Phi(x) : R^n \to \mathcal{H}$ and $\mathrm{x}^* = \Phi^*(x^*) : R^m \to \mathcal{H}^*$, according to the problem (8.6.8)~(8.6.10), the primal problem is constructed as follows:

$$\min_{w, w^*, b, b^*} \quad \frac{1}{2} \|\mathrm{w}\|^2 + C \sum_{i=1}^{l} [(\mathrm{w}^* \cdot \Phi(x_i^*)) + b^*], \tag{8.6.22}$$

$$\text{s.t.} \quad y_i[(\mathrm{w} \cdot \Phi(x_i)) + b] \geq 1 - [(\mathrm{w}^* \cdot \Phi^*(x_i^*)) + b^*], \tag{8.6.23}$$

$$(\mathrm{w}^* \cdot \Phi^*(x_i^*)) + b^* \geq 0, i = 1, \cdots, l. \tag{8.6.24}$$

Similarly, we can give its dual programming.

**Theorem 8.6.5** *Optimization problem*

$$\min_{\alpha,\beta} \quad \frac{1}{2}\sum_{i=1}^{l}\sum_{j=1}^{l}y_iy_j\alpha_i\alpha_jK(x_i,x_j) - \sum_{j=1}^{l}\alpha_j, \qquad (8.6.25)$$

$$s.t. \quad \sum_{i=1}^{l}\alpha_iy_i = 0, \qquad (8.6.26)$$

$$\sum_{i=1}^{l}(\alpha_i + \beta_i - C) = 0, \qquad (8.6.27)$$

$$\sum_{i=1}^{l}(\alpha_i + \beta_i - C)\Phi^*(x_i^*) = 0, \qquad (8.6.28)$$

$$\alpha_i \geq 0, \beta_i \geq 0, i = 1, \cdots, l. \qquad (8.6.29)$$

*is the dual problem of the problem* (8.6.22)~(8.6.24), *where* $K(x_i, x_j) = (\Phi(x_i) \cdot \Phi(x_j))$.

In order to replace the single $\Phi^*$ by the corresponding kernel $K^*$, we need the following observation: Suppose $z_i \in \mathcal{H}, i = 1, \cdots, l$, and $z$ is a linear combination of $z_1, \cdots, z_l$

$$z = \sum_{i=1}^{l}r_iz_i. \qquad (8.6.30)$$

Then $z = 0$ if and only if

$$(z \cdot z_j) = 0, j = 1, \cdots, l. \qquad (8.6.31)$$

Using this observation, the constraint (8.6.28) can be written as

$$\sum_{i=1}^{l}(\alpha_i + \beta_i - C)K^*(x_i^*, x_j^*) = 0, j = 1, \cdots, l, \qquad (8.6.32)$$

where $K^*(x_i^*, x_j^*) = (\Phi^*(x_i^*) \cdot \Phi^*(x_j^*))$.

Thus, replacing (8.6.28) by the above equations, the problem (8.6.25)~ (8.6.29) becomes

$$\min_{\alpha,\beta} \quad \frac{1}{2}\sum_{i=1}^{l}\sum_{j=1}^{l}y_iy_j\alpha_i\alpha_jK(x_i,x_j) - \sum_{j=1}^{l}\alpha_j, \qquad (8.6.33)$$

$$s.t. \quad \sum_{i=1}^{l}\alpha_iy_i = 0, \qquad (8.6.34)$$

$$\sum_{i=1}^{l}(\alpha_i + \beta_i - C) = 0, \qquad (8.6.35)$$

$$\sum_{i=1}^{l}(\alpha_i + \beta_i - C)K^*(x_i^*, x_j^*) = 0, j = 1, \cdots, l \qquad (8.6.36)$$

$$\alpha_i \geq 0, \beta_i \geq 0, i = 1, \cdots, l. \tag{8.6.37}$$

**Theorem 8.6.6** *Suppose that $(\alpha^*, \beta^*)$ is a solution to the dual problem (8.6.25)~(8.6.29). If there exist two positive components of $\alpha^*$ and $\beta^*$, $(\alpha_j^*$ and $\beta_j^*)$, then the solution $(\tilde{w}, \tilde{b})$ to the primal problem (8.6.22)~(8.6.24) w.r.t $(w, b)$ can be obtained by*

$$\tilde{w} = \sum_{i=1}^{l} \alpha_i^* y_i \Phi(x_i), \tag{8.6.38}$$

$$\tilde{b} = y_j - \sum_{i=1}^{l} \alpha_i^* y_i K(x_i, x_j). \tag{8.6.39}$$

According to the above theorems, the general privileged support vector classification called SVM+ is constructed.

**Algorithm 8.6.7** *(Privileged support vector classification)*
*(1) Input the training set $T$ given by (8.6.1);*
*(2) Choose two appropriate kernels $K(x, x')$ and $K^*(x^*, x^{*'})$, and a parameter $C > 0$;*
*(3) Construct and solve the convex quadratic programming problem (8.6.33)~ (8.6.37), obtaining the solution $(\alpha^*, \beta^*)$;*
*(4) Choose two positive components of $\alpha^*$ and $\beta^*$, $\alpha_j^*$ and $\beta_j^*$, compute*

$$\tilde{b} = y_j - \sum_{i=1}^{l} \alpha_i^* y_i K(x_i, x_j), \tag{8.6.40}$$

*(5) Construct the decision function:*

$$f(x) = \text{sgn}(g(x)), \tag{8.6.41}$$

*where*

$$g(x) = \sum_{i=1}^{l} y_i \alpha_i^* K(x_i, x) + \tilde{b}. \tag{8.6.42}$$

### 8.6.3   A variation

A variation, called SVM$_\gamma$+, was proposed in [156] by introducing an extra item $\frac{\gamma}{2}\|w^*\|^2$ in the primal problem (8.6.22)~(8.6.24), so it becomes:

$$\min_{w, w^*, b, b^*} \quad \frac{1}{2}(\|w\|^2 + \gamma\|w^*\|^2) + C\sum_{i=1}^{l}[(w^* \cdot \Phi^*(x_i^*)) + b^*], \tag{8.6.43}$$

$$\text{s.t.} \quad y_i[(w \cdot \Phi(x_i)) + b] \geq 1 - [(w^* \cdot \Phi^*(x_i^*)) + b^*], \tag{8.6.44}$$

$$(w^* \cdot \Phi^*(x_i^*)) + b^* \geq 0, i = 1, \cdots, l. \tag{8.6.45}$$

where $C > 0$ and $\gamma > 0$ are parameters. Its solution can be obtained by solving its dual problem:

$$\min_{\alpha,\beta} \quad \frac{1}{2}\sum_{i=1}^{l}\sum_{j=1}^{l}y_iy_j\alpha_i\alpha_j K(x_i, x_j)$$

$$+\frac{1}{2\gamma}\sum_{i=1}^{l}\sum_{j=1}^{l}(\alpha_i + \beta_i - C)(\alpha_j + \beta_j - C)K^*(x_i^*, x_j^*) - \sum_{j=1}^{l}\alpha_j,$$

$$(8.6.46)$$

$$\text{s.t.} \quad \sum_{i=1}^{l}\alpha_i y_i = 0, \tag{8.6.47}$$

$$\sum_{i=1}^{l}(\alpha_i + \beta_i - C) = 0, \tag{8.6.48}$$

$$\alpha_i \geq 0, \beta_i \geq 0, i = 1, \cdots, l. \tag{8.6.49}$$

This approach can be summarized as the following algorithm:

**Algorithm 8.6.8** *(Privileged support vector classification with $\gamma$-term)*

*(1) Input the training set $T$ given by (8.6.1);*

*(2) Choose two appropriate kernels $K(x, x')$ and $K^*(x^*, x^{*\prime})$ and parameters $C > 0, \gamma > 0$;*

*(3) Construct and solve the optimization problem (8.6.46)~(8.6.49), obtaining the solution $\alpha^*, \beta^*$;*

*(4) Choose two positive components $\alpha^*$ and $\beta^*$, $\alpha_j^*$ and $\beta_j^*$, then compute*

$$\tilde{b} = \frac{1}{\gamma}\sum_{i=1}^{l}(\alpha_i^* + \beta_i^* - C)K(x_i^*, x_j^*) \tag{8.6.50}$$

*(5) Construct the decision function:*

$$f(x) = \text{sgn}(g(x)), \tag{8.6.51}$$

*where*

$$g(x) = \sum_{i=1}^{l}y_i\alpha_i^* K(x_i, x) + \tilde{b}. \tag{8.6.52}$$

See [115, 116, 160] for more details about privileged support vector machines.

## 8.7 Knowledge-based Classification

Similar to the previous section, we continuously consider the classification problem by using prior information. The prior information considered here is quite different from the previous one. There we used additional informative features to describe the training data set while here we introduce some advised classification rules as prior information. Now the problem can be considered as an extension of the standard classification problem in the following way: the single input points in the training points are extended to input sets, called knowledge sets since they come from some special prior knowledge. Note that the input sets are restricted to be polyhedrons. More precisely the problem is formulated mathematically as follows:

**Knowledge-based classification problem**: Given a training set

$$T = \{(\mathcal{X}_1, y_1), \cdots, (\mathcal{X}_p, y_p), (\mathcal{X}_{p+1}, y_{p+1}), \cdots, (\mathcal{X}_{p+q}, y_{p+q})\}, \qquad (8.7.1)$$

where $\mathcal{X}_i$ is a polyhedron in $R^n$ defined by

$$\mathcal{X}_i = \{x | Q_i x \le d_i\},$$

where $Q_i \in R^{l_i \times n}$, $d_i \in R^{l_i}$, $y_1 = \cdots = y_p = 1, y_{p+1} = \cdots = y_{p+q} = -1$, and the label $y_i = 1$ or $y_i = -1$ corresponding to each $\mathcal{X}_i$ means all the points in the set $\mathcal{X}_i$ belong to positive or negative class respectively, $i = 1, ...p+q$. Find a real valued function $g(x)$ in $R^n$, such that the value of $y$ for any $x$ can be predicted by the decision function

$$f(x) = \text{sgn}(g(x)). \qquad (8.7.2)$$

### 8.7.1 Knowledge-based linear support vector classification

We first consider the linearly separable problem where the input sets can be separated by a hyperplane correctly, and try to find the separating hyperplane $(w \cdot x) + b = 0$. Corresponding to the problem $(2.2.8) \sim (2.2.9)$ in Chapter 2, we can get the primal problem:

$$\min_{w,b} \quad \frac{1}{2} \|w\|^2, \qquad (8.7.3)$$

$$\text{s.t.} \quad (w \cdot x) + b \ge 1, \text{for } x \in \mathcal{X}_i, \ i = 1, \cdots, p, \qquad (8.7.4)$$

$$(w \cdot x) + b \le -1, \text{for } x \in \mathcal{X}_i, \ i = p+1, \cdots, p+q. \qquad (8.7.5)$$

Obviously there are infinite constraints, leading the above problem to a semi-infinite program which is hard to be solved. However, it will be shown that the constraints $(8.7.4) \sim (8.7.5)$ can be converted into a set of limited constraints and the problem becomes a quadratic programming ([57],[58],[107]).

**Theorem 8.7.1** *Consider the polyhedron* $\mathcal{X} = \{x|Qx \leq d\}$ *where* $Q \in R^{l \times n}$ *and* $d \in R^l$. *If* $\mathcal{X}$ *is nonempty, then the polyhedron* $\mathcal{X} = \{x|Qx \leq d\}$ *lies in the half-space* $(w \cdot x) + b \geq 1$ *if and only if the system*

$$Q^{\mathrm{T}}u + w = 0, \tag{8.7.6}$$
$$d^{\mathrm{T}}u - b + 1 \leq 0, \tag{8.7.7}$$
$$u \geq 0 \tag{8.7.8}$$

*has a solution* $u \in R^l$.

**Proof** The fact that the polyhedron $\mathcal{X}$ lies in the half-space $(w \cdot x) + b \geq 1$ means that for each $x$ in $\mathcal{X} = \{Qx \leq q\}$, we have $(w \cdot x) + b - 1 \geq 0$. This is equivalent to that the linear programming

$$\min_{x} \quad (w \cdot x) + b - 1, \tag{8.7.9}$$
$$\text{s.t.} \quad Qx \leq d \tag{8.7.10}$$

has a solution and its optimal value is great than or equal to 0.

By Definition 1.2.16 in Chapter 1, the dual problem of the problem (8.7.9) $\sim$ (8.7.10) is

$$\max_{u} \quad -(d \cdot u) + b - 1, \tag{8.7.11}$$
$$\text{s.t.} \quad Q^{\mathrm{T}}u + w = 0, \tag{8.7.12}$$
$$u \geq 0. \tag{8.7.13}$$

From the dual theorem, the primal problem (8.7.9)$\sim$(8.7.10) and dual problem (8.7.11)$\sim$(8.7.13) have the same optimal values. Thus "the optimal value of problem (8.7.9 )$\sim$ (8.7.10) is great than or equal to 0" is equivalent to the fact that "the optimal value of problem (8.7.11)$\sim$(8.7.13) is greater than or equal to 0". Obviously, the latter is valid if and only if system (8.7.6)$\sim$(8.7.8) has a solution. So we get the conclusion.  ∎

According to the above theorem, the constraint "$(w \cdot x) + b \geq 1$, for $x \in \mathcal{X} = \{x|Qx \leq d\}$" could be rewritten as follows:

$$Q^{\mathrm{T}}u + w = 0, \tag{8.7.14}$$
$$d^{\mathrm{T}}u - b + 1 \leq 0, \tag{8.7.15}$$
$$u \geq 0, \tag{8.7.16}$$

while the constraint "$(w \cdot x) + b \leq -1$, for $x$ in $\mathcal{X}$" could be rewritten as follows:

$$Q^{\mathrm{T}}u - w = 0, \tag{8.7.17}$$
$$d^{\mathrm{T}}u + b + 1 \leq 0, \tag{8.7.18}$$
$$u \geq 0. \tag{8.7.19}$$

Then finally we could reformulate the problem (8.7.4)~(8.7.5) as

$$\min_{w,b,u} \quad \frac{1}{2}\|w\|^2, \tag{8.7.20}$$

$$\text{s.t.} \quad Q_i^T u_i + w = 0, i = 1, \cdots, p, \tag{8.7.21}$$

$$d_i^T u_i - b + 1 \le 0, i = 1, \cdots, p, \tag{8.7.22}$$

$$Q_i^T u_i - w = 0, i = p+1, \cdots, p+q, \tag{8.7.23}$$

$$d_i^T u_i + b + 1 \le 0, i = p+1, \cdots, p+q, \tag{8.7.24}$$

$$u = (u_1^T, \cdots, u_{p+q}^T)^T \ge 0. \tag{8.7.25}$$

In order to deal with a more general case including the non-separable problem, we introduce slack variables $\xi$ and $\eta$, and modify the above formulation into the following primal program with the variables $w, b, \xi = (\xi_1^T, \cdots, \xi_{p+q}^T)^T, \xi_i = (\xi_{i_1}, \cdots, \xi_{i_n})^T, \eta = (\eta_1, \cdots, \eta_{p+q})^T$, and $u = (u_1^T, \cdots, u_{p+q}^T)^T$ with $u_i \in R^{l_i}, i = 1, \cdots, p+q$:

$$\min_{w,b,u,\xi,\eta} \quad \frac{1}{2}\|w\|^2 + C\sum_{i=1}^{p+q}((\sum_{j=1}^{n}\xi_{i_j}) + \eta_i), \tag{8.7.26}$$

$$\text{s.t.} \quad -\xi_i \le Q_i^T u_i + w \le \xi_i, i = 1, \cdots, p, \tag{8.7.27}$$

$$d_i^T u_i - b + 1 \le \eta_i, i = 1, \cdots, p, \tag{8.7.28}$$

$$-\xi_i \le Q_i^T u_i - w \le \xi_i, i = p+1, \cdots, p+q, \tag{8.7.29}$$

$$d_i^T u_i + b + 1 \le \eta_i, i = p+1, \cdots, p+q, \tag{8.7.30}$$

$$\xi, \eta, u \ge 0. \tag{8.7.31}$$

**Theorem 8.7.2** *Optimization problem*

$$\max_{\alpha,\beta,r} \quad \sum_{i=1}^{p+q} r_i - \frac{1}{2}\sum_{i=1}^{p+q}\sum_{j=1}^{p+q} y_i y_j (\alpha_i - \beta_i)^T(\alpha_j - \beta_j), \tag{8.7.32}$$

$$\text{s.t.} \quad \sum_{i=1}^{p+q} y_i r_i = 0, \tag{8.7.33}$$

$$Q_i(\alpha_i - \beta_i) + r_i d_i \ge 0, i = 1, \cdots, p+q, \tag{8.7.34}$$

$$0 \le \alpha_i + \beta_i \le Ce, i = 1, \cdots, p+q, \tag{8.7.35}$$

$$0 \le r_i \le C, i = 1, \cdots, p+q, \tag{8.7.36}$$

$$\alpha_i, \beta_i \ge 0, i = 1, \cdots, p+q, \tag{8.7.37}$$

*is the dual problem of the problem (8.7.26) ~ (8.7.31), where* $r = (r_1, \cdots, r_{p+q})^T$, $\alpha = (\alpha_1^T, \cdots, \alpha_{p+q}^T)^T$, $\beta = (\beta_1^T, \cdots, \beta_{p+q}^T)^T$, $\alpha_i, \beta_i \in R^n, i = 1, \cdots, p+q$ *and* $e$ *is a vector of ones in* $R^n$.

**Theorem 8.7.3** *Suppose that* $(\alpha^*, \beta^*, r^*)$ *is the solution to the dual problem* $(8.7.32)\sim(8.7.37)$. *If there exist three components* $\alpha_i^*, \beta_i^*$ *and* $r_i^*$, *such that* $0 < \alpha_i^* + \beta_i^* < C$, $0 < r_i^* < C$, *then the solution* $(w^*, b^*)$ *to the primal problem* $(8.7.26)\sim(8.7.31)$ *w.r.t.* $(w, b)$ *can be obtained by*

$$w^* = -\sum_{j=1}^{p+q} y_j(\alpha_j^* - \beta_j^*), \qquad (8.7.38)$$

$$b^* = y_i(1 + d_i^T u_i^*), \qquad (8.7.39)$$

*where* $u_i^*$ *can be obtained by solving* $Q_i^T u_i + y_i w^* = 0$.

Once the optimal solution $(w^*, b^*)$ is obtained, the separating hyperplane $g(x) = (w^* \cdot x) + b^* = 0$ can be easily constructed. Thus the following knowledge-based linear algorithm is constructed.

**Algorithm 8.7.4** *(Knowledge-based linear Support Vector Classification)*

*(1) Input the training data set* $T = \{(\mathcal{X}_1, y_1), \cdots, (\mathcal{X}_p, y_p), (\mathcal{X}_{p+1}, y_{p+1}), \cdots, (\mathcal{X}_{p+q}, y_{p+q})\}$, *where* $y_1 = \cdots = y_p = 1, y_{p+1} = \cdots = y_{p+q} = -1$, *and* $\mathcal{X}_i = \{x | Q_i x \le d_i\}, i = 1, 2, ..., p + q$;

*(2) Choose an appropriate penalty parameter* $C > 0$;

*(3) Construct and solve the convex quadratic programming problem* $(8.7.32)\sim$ $(8.7.37)$, *obtaining a solution* $\alpha^*, \beta^*, r^*$;

*(4) Choose three components* $\alpha_i^*, \beta_i^*$ *and* $r_i^*$, *such that* $0 < \alpha_i^* + \beta_i^* < C$, $0 < r_i^* < C$, *then compute* $w^* = -\sum_{j=1}^{p+q} y_j(\alpha_j^* - \beta_j^*)$ *and* $b^* = y_i(1 + d_i^T u_i^*)$, *where* $u_i^*$ *is obtained by solving* $Q_i^T u_i + y_i w^* = 0$.

*(5) Construct the decision function*

$$f(x) = \text{sgn}(g(x)), \qquad (8.7.40)$$

*where* $g(x) = (w^* \cdot x) + b^*$.

## 8.7.2 Knowledge-based nonlinear support vector classification

Corresponding to the knowledge-based linear classifier, the nonlinear classifier can also be established by employing the "kernel trick".

Introducing the transformation $x = \Phi(x)$: $R^n \to \mathcal{H}$ and the kernel function $K(x, x') = (\Phi(x) \cdot \Phi(x'))$, we need to find the separating hyperplane $(w \cdot x) + b = 0$.

Now the key point is to deal with the constraint in x-space $\mathcal{H}$

$$(w \cdot x) + b \ge 1, \text{for } x \in X = \{x = \Phi(x) | x \in \{x | Qx \le d, x \in R^n\}\}. \qquad (8.7.41)$$

First, a random sample set of input set $\{x_1, x_2, \cdots, x_m\}$ are taken from the knowledge sets $\mathcal{X}_1, \cdots, \mathcal{X}_l$, and make the following two approximation assumptions ([59]):

(i) Any x $= \Phi(x)$ in x-space $\mathcal{H}$ can be expressed as

$$\Phi(x) = \tilde{A}^{\mathrm{T}} z \qquad (8.7.42)$$

where $z = (z_1, \cdots, z_m)^{\mathrm{T}}$, and

$$\tilde{A} = \begin{pmatrix} \Phi(x_1)^{\mathrm{T}} \\ \cdots \\ \Phi(x_m)^{\mathrm{T}} \end{pmatrix}. \qquad (8.7.43)$$

(ii) Any polyhedron X $= \{\Phi(x)| x \in \{x | Qx \leq d, x \in R^n\}\}$ with

$$Q = \begin{pmatrix} q_1^{\mathrm{T}} \\ \cdots \\ q_l^{\mathrm{T}} \end{pmatrix}$$

in x-space $\mathcal{H}$ can be expressed as

$$X = \{\Phi(x)| \tilde{Q}\Phi(x) \leq d\}, \qquad (8.7.44)$$

where

$$\tilde{Q} = \begin{pmatrix} \Phi(q_1)^{\mathrm{T}} \\ \cdots \\ \Phi(q_l)^{\mathrm{T}} \end{pmatrix}.$$

The above assumption (i) is similar to the trick used in twin support vector classification; see Section 8.1. Now, we try to explain the assumption (ii). If the kernel function $K(x, x') = (x \cdot x')$, then

$$\tilde{Q}\Phi(x) = \begin{pmatrix} \Phi(q_1)^{\mathrm{T}} \\ \cdots \\ \Phi(q_l)^{\mathrm{T}} \end{pmatrix} \Phi(x) = \begin{pmatrix} K(q_1, x) \\ \cdots \\ K(q_l, x) \end{pmatrix} = Qx.$$

So, the set X given by (8.7.44) is equivalent to the set $X$ defined by (8.7.41), when $K(x, x') = (x \cdot x')$. This implies that the assumption (ii) is true for the case $K(x, x') = (x \cdot x')$. Furthermore, we consider the Gaussian kernel, i.e., $K(x, x') = \exp(\frac{-(\|x - x'\|)^2}{2\sigma^2})$. If $\sigma^2 \to \infty$ and $C = \tilde{C}\sigma^2$ where $\tilde{C}$ is fixed then the SVM classifier with the Gaussian kernel converges to the linear SVM classifier with the parameter $\tilde{C}$. From this point of view, the assumption (ii) is reasonable.

According to the above two assumptions, the set X can be written as

$$X = \{\Phi(x) = \tilde{A}^{\mathrm{T}} z | \tilde{K} z \leq d\}, \qquad (8.7.45)$$

where

$$\tilde{K} = \begin{pmatrix} \Phi(q_1)^{\mathrm{T}} \\ \cdots \\ \Phi(q_l)^{\mathrm{T}} \end{pmatrix} (\Phi(x_1), \cdots, \Phi(x_m)) = \begin{pmatrix} K(q_1, x_1) & \cdots & K(q_1, x_m) \\ \cdots & \cdots & \cdots \\ K(q_l, x_1) & \cdots & K(q_l, x_m) \end{pmatrix}.$$
(8.7.46)

Now let us return to the constraint (8.7.41). From (8.7.42), (8.7.43), and (8.7.45), it can be written as the constraint in x-space $\mathcal{H}$:

$$(\mathrm{w} \cdot \mathrm{x}) + b \geq 1, \text{ for } \mathrm{x} \in \{\Phi(x) = \tilde{A}^{\mathrm{T}} z | z \in \{z | \tilde{K}z \leq d\}\}, \tag{8.7.47}$$

or the constraint in $z$-space:

$$(\tilde{A}\mathrm{w} \cdot z) + b \geq 1, \text{ for } z \in \{z | \tilde{K}z \leq d\}, \tag{8.7.48}$$

since $(\mathrm{w} \cdot \tilde{A}^{\mathrm{T}} z) = (\tilde{A}\mathrm{w} \cdot z)$, where $\tilde{A}\mathrm{w}$ is considered as a vector in $z$-space, $\tilde{A}$ and $\tilde{K}$ are given by (8.7.43) and (8.7.46) respectively.

By Theorem 8.7.1 and the equivalence between (8.7.41) and (8.7.48), the primal problem can be obtained from the problem (8.7.26)∼(8.7.31) by replacing $w$ by w, $Q_i$ and $w$ by $\tilde{K}_i$ and $\tilde{A}\mathrm{w}$ respectively.

$$\min_{\mathrm{w}, b, u, \xi, \eta} \quad \frac{1}{2} \|\mathrm{w}\|^2 + C \sum_{i=1}^{p+q} ((\sum_{j=1}^{n} \xi_{i_j}) + \eta_i), \tag{8.7.49}$$

$$\text{s.t.} \quad -\xi_i \leq \tilde{K}_i^{\mathrm{T}} u_i + \tilde{A}\mathrm{w} \leq \xi_i, i = 1, \cdots, p, \tag{8.7.50}$$

$$d_i^{\mathrm{T}} u_i - b + 1 \leq \eta_i, i = 1, \cdots, p, \tag{8.7.51}$$

$$-\xi_i \leq \tilde{K}_i^{\mathrm{T}} u_i - \tilde{A}\mathrm{w} \leq \xi_i, i = p+1, \cdots, p+q, \tag{8.7.52}$$

$$d_i^{\mathrm{T}} u_i + b + 1 \leq \eta_i, i = p+1, \cdots, p+q, \tag{8.7.53}$$

$$\xi, \eta, u \geq 0, \tag{8.7.54}$$

where $\tilde{A}$ is given by (8.7.43) and $\tilde{K}_i$ is defined by

$$\tilde{K}_i = \begin{pmatrix} K(q_1^i, x_1) & \cdots & K(q_1^i, x_m) \\ \cdots & \cdots & \cdots \\ K(q_l^i, x_1) & \cdots & K(q_l^i, x_m) \end{pmatrix}.$$

**Theorem 8.7.5** *Optimization problem*

$$\max_{\alpha, \beta, r} \quad \sum_{i=1}^{p+q} r_i - \frac{1}{2} \sum_{i=1}^{p+q} \sum_{j=1}^{p+q} y_i y_j (\alpha_i - \beta_i)^{\mathrm{T}} \tilde{H} (\alpha_j - \beta_j), \tag{8.7.55}$$

$$\text{s.t.} \quad \sum_{i=1}^{p} r_i - \sum_{i=p+1}^{p+q} r_i = 0, \tag{8.7.56}$$

$$\tilde{K}_i(\alpha_i - \beta_i) + r_i d_i \geq 0, i = 1, \cdots, p+q, \tag{8.7.57}$$

$$0 \leq \alpha_i + \beta_i \leq Ce, i = 1, \cdots, p+q, \tag{8.7.58}$$

$$0 \leq r_i \leq C, i = 1, \cdots, p+q, \tag{8.7.59}$$

$$\alpha_i, \beta_i \geq 0, i = 1, \cdots, p+q, \tag{8.7.60}$$

is the dual problem of the problem (8.7.49)~(8.7.54), where $r = (r_1, \cdots, r_{p+q})^T$, $\alpha = (\alpha_1^T, \cdots, \alpha_{p+q}^T)^T$, $\beta = (\beta_1^T, \cdots, \beta_{p+q}^T)^T$, $\alpha_i, \beta_i \in R^m, i = 1, \cdots, p+q$, $e$ is a vector of ones in $R^m$, and

$$\tilde{H} = \begin{pmatrix} K(x_1, x_1) & \cdots & K(x_1, x_m) \\ \cdots & \cdots & \cdots \\ K(x_m, x_1) & \cdots & K(x_m, x_m) \end{pmatrix}.$$

**Theorem 8.7.6** *Suppose that $(\alpha^*, \beta^*, r^*)$ is the solution to the dual problem (8.7.55)~(8.7.60). Suppose there exist three components $\alpha_i^*$, $\beta_i^*$, and $r_i^*$, such that $0 < \alpha_i^* + \beta_i^* < C$, and $0 < r_i^* < C$, then the solution $(w^*, b^*)$ to the primal problem (8.7.49)~(8.7.54) w.r.t. $(w, b)$ can be obtained by*

$$w^* = -\sum_{j=1}^{p+q} y_j \tilde{A}^T (\alpha_j^* - \beta_j^*), \tag{8.7.61}$$

$$b^* = y_i (1 + d_i^T u_i^*), \tag{8.7.62}$$

*where $u_i^*$ can be obtained by solving $\tilde{K}_i^T u_i + y_i \tilde{A} w^* = 0$.*

Once the optimal solution $(w^*, b^*)$ is obtained, the separating hyperplane $g(x) = (w^* \cdot x) + b^* = 0$ can be easily constructed. Thus the following knowledge-based nonlinear algorithm is constructed.

**Algorithm 8.7.7** *(Knowledge-based nonlinear Support Vector Classification)*

*(1) Given a training data set $T = \{(\mathcal{X}_1, y_1), \cdots, (\mathcal{X}_p, y_p), (\mathcal{X}_{p+1}, y_{p+1}), \cdots, (\mathcal{X}_{p+q}, y_{p+q})\}$, where $y_1 = \cdots = y_p = 1, y_{p+1} = \cdots = y_{p+q} = -1$, and $\mathcal{X}_i = \{x | Q_i x \le d_i\}, i = 1, 2, ..., p+q$.*

*(2) Choose an appropriate kernel and a parameter $C > 0$;*

*(3) Construct and solve the convex quadratic programming problem (8.7.55)~(8.7.60), obtaining the solution $\alpha^*, \beta^*, r^*$.*

*(4) Choose three components $\alpha_i^*, \beta_i^*$ and $r_i^*$, such that $0 < \alpha_i^* + \beta_i^* < C$, $0 < r_i^* < C$, compute $b^* = y_i (1 + d_i^T u_i^*)$, where $u_i^*$ is obtained by solving*

$$\tilde{K}_i^T u_i - y_i \sum_{j=1}^{p+q} y_j \tilde{H} (\alpha_j^* - \beta_j^*) = 0 .$$

*(5) Construct the decision function*

$$f(x) = \text{sgn}(g(x)), \tag{8.7.63}$$

*where $g(x) = -\sum_{i=1}^{p+q} \sum_{j=1}^{m} y_i (\alpha_{ij}^* - \beta_{ij}^*) K(x_j, x) + b^*$.*

## 8.8    Robust Classification

### 8.8.1    Robust classification problem

Remember that the training set of the standard binary classification problem is given by

$$T = \{(x_1, y_1), \cdots, (x_l, y_l)\}, \tag{8.8.1}$$

where it is assumed that the inputs are precisely known, and therefore can be described by points $x_i \in R^n, i = 1, \cdots, l$. However some uncertainty is often present in many real-world problems. For example, when the inputs are subjected to measurement errors, it would be better to describe the inputs by uncertainty sets $\mathcal{X}_i \subset R^n, i = 1, \cdots, l$, since all we know is that the input belongs to the set $\mathcal{X}_i$. In this section we investigate two kinds of the uncertainty sets. In the first one the set $\mathcal{X}_i$ is a polyhedron obtained from perturbation of a point $x_i$

$$\mathcal{X}_i = \{x \mid [x]_j = [x_i]_j + [\Delta x_i]_j [z_i]_j, j = 1, \cdots, n,$$
$$z_i = ([z_i]_1, \cdots, [z_i]_n)^{\mathrm{T}}, \|z_i\|_1 \leqslant \Omega\}, \tag{8.8.2}$$

where $x_i$ is the nominal value, $\Delta x_i = ([\Delta x_i]_1, \cdots, [\Delta x_i]_n)^{\mathrm{T}}$ is a direction of perturbation, $\Omega$ is the magnitude of perturbation, $z_i$ is the variation, and $\| \cdot \|_1$ is the 1-norm, i.e. $\|z_i\|_1 = \sum_{j=1}^{n} |[z_i]_j|$. In the second one, the set $\mathcal{X}_i$ is a supersphere obtained from perturbation of a point $x_i$

$$\mathcal{X}_i = \{x \mid \|x - x_i\| \leqslant r_i\}, \tag{8.8.3}$$

where $x_i$ is the nominal value and $r_i$ is the magnitude of perturbation.

Extending the input point $x_i$ into an input set $\mathcal{X}_i$, the training set should become

$$T = \{(\mathcal{X}_1, \mathcal{Y}_1), \cdots, (\mathcal{X}_l, \mathcal{Y}_l)\}. \tag{8.8.4}$$

If the set $\mathcal{X}_i$ is defined by either (8.8.2) or (8.8.3) and the pair $(x_i, y_i)$ is known in advance, a reasonable consideration is to take $\mathcal{Y}_i = y_i$, meaning that the label of all input points in $\mathcal{X}_i$ is $\mathcal{Y}_i = y_i$. This leads to the following problem.

**Robust binary classification problem**: Given a training set

$$T = \{(\mathcal{X}_1, \mathcal{Y}_1), \cdots, (\mathcal{X}_l, \mathcal{Y}_l)\}, \tag{8.8.5}$$

where $\mathcal{X}_i$ is a set in $R^n$, $\mathcal{Y}_i \in \{-1, 1\}$. The pair $(\mathcal{X}_i, \mathcal{Y}_i)$ with $\mathcal{Y}_i = 1$ means that $\mathcal{X}_i$ is a positive input set where every $x$ in $\mathcal{X}_i$ belongs to the positive class, and $(\mathcal{X}_i, \mathcal{Y}_i)$ with $\mathcal{Y}_i = -1$ means that $\mathcal{X}_i$ is a negative input set where every $x$ in $\mathcal{X}_i$ belongs to the negative class, $i = 1, \cdots, l$. Find a real function $g(x)$ in $R^n$, such that the value of $y$ for any $x$ can be predicted by the decision function

$$f(x) = \mathrm{sgn}(g(x)). \tag{8.8.6}$$

## 8.8.2 The solution when the input sets are polyhedrons

Consider the robust binary classification problem with the training set given by (8.8.5) and (8.8.2). It is easy to see that the equality (8.8.2) can be expressed as

$$\mathcal{X}_i = \{x \mid \sum_{j=1}^{n} \left| \frac{[x]_j - [x_i]_j}{[\Delta x_i]_j} \right| \leqslant \Omega\}, \quad i = 1, \cdots, l. \tag{8.8.7}$$

For the problem in $R^n$ with $n = 2$, the set $\mathcal{X}_i$ is a diamond, whose horizontal length and vertical length are $2|[\Delta x_i]_1|\Omega$ and $2|[\Delta x_i]_2|\Omega$ respectively. A toy example in $R^2$ is shown in Figure 8.8, where the diamonds with "+"and "o" are positive and negative input sets respectively.

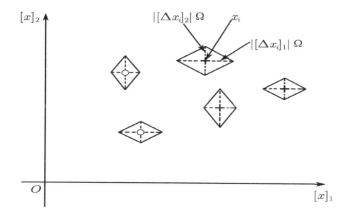

**FIGURE 8.8**: A robust classification problem with polyhedron input sets in $R^2$.

### 8.8.2.1 Linear robust support vector classification

It is easy to see that the problem given in Figure 8.8 is linearly separable since there exists a straight line such that it separates all input sets correctly: all positive and negative diamonds lie in the upper right and the lower left of the straight line respectively. Noticing the principle of maximal margin, its separating line $(w^* \cdot x) + b^* = 0$ should be obtained from the optimization problem

$$\min_{w,b} \quad \frac{1}{2}\|w\|^2, \tag{8.8.8}$$

$$\text{s.t.} \quad y_i \left( \sum_{j=1}^{2} w_j([x_i]_j + [\Delta x_i]_j[z_i]_j) + b \right) \geqslant 1, \forall \, \|z_i\|_1 \leqslant \Omega, i = 1, \cdots, 5. \tag{8.8.9}$$

As for the general problem in $R^n$ without the assumption of linear separability, we only need to introduce slack variables $\xi$ and penalty parameter $C$, and then get the optimization problem

$$\min_{w,b,\xi} \frac{1}{2}\|w\|^2 + C\sum_{i=1}^{l}\xi_i, \tag{8.8.10}$$

$$\text{s.t. } y_i\left(\sum_{j=1}^{n}w_j([x_i]_j + [\Delta x_i]_j[z_i]_j) + b\right) \geqslant 1 - \xi_i, \quad \forall\|z_i\|_1 \leqslant \Omega, i = 1,\cdots,l, \tag{8.8.11}$$

$$\xi_i \geqslant 0, \quad i = 1,\cdots,l. \tag{8.8.12}$$

where $w = (w_1,\cdots,w_n)^{\mathrm{T}}, \xi = (\xi_1,\cdots,\xi_l)^{\mathrm{T}}$. This problem does not belong to the problems discussed in Chapter 1. In fact, it is a semi-infinite programming problem since the $\forall\|z_i\|_1 \leqslant \Omega$ clause in the constraint (8.8.11) implies that there are infinitely many constraints. However, following [11], the constraint (8.8.11) can be rewritten as the one with only finitely many constraints as shown in the following theorem.

**Theorem 8.8.1** *Constraint* (8.8.11) *is equivalent to*

$$y_i((w \cdot x_i) + b) + \xi_i - 1 \geqslant \Omega t_i, \quad i = 1,\cdots,l, \tag{8.8.13}$$

$$t_i - y_i[\Delta x_i]_j w_j \geqslant 0, \quad j = 1,\cdots,n; \quad i = 1,\cdots,l, \tag{8.8.14}$$

$$t_i + y_i[\Delta x_i]_j w_j \geqslant 0, \quad j = 1,\cdots,n; \quad i = 1,\cdots,l, \tag{8.8.15}$$

$$t_i \geqslant 0, \quad i = 1,\cdots,l. \tag{8.8.16}$$

**Proof** We only list the main steps of the proof as follows:
(i) Prove that the constraint (8.8.11) is equivalent to

$$\min_{\nu,\omega\in\vartheta}\left\{y_i(w \cdot x_i) + y_ib - 1 + \xi_i + \sum_{j=1}^{n}(y_iw_j[\Delta x_i]_j\nu_j - y_iw_j[\Delta x_i]_j\omega_j)\right\} \geqslant 0, \tag{8.8.17}$$

where $\vartheta = \{(\nu,\omega) \in R_+^n \times R_+^n | \|\nu + \omega\|_1 \leqslant \Omega\}$.
(ii) Prove that the optimal values of the problems

$$\max \quad a^{\mathrm{T}}\nu + b^{\mathrm{T}}\omega, \tag{8.8.18}$$

$$\text{s.t.} \quad \|\nu + \omega\|_1 \leqslant \Omega, \quad \nu,\omega \geqslant 0 \tag{8.8.19}$$

and

$$\max \quad \sum_{j=1}^{n}\max\{a_j, b_j, 0\}r_j, \tag{8.8.20}$$

$$\text{s.t.} \quad \|r\|_1 \leqslant \Omega \tag{8.8.21}$$

are equal.

(iii) Prove that the constraint (8.8.17) is equivalent to

$$y_i((w \cdot x_i) + b) + \xi_i - 1 \geqslant \Omega \|s\|_1^*, \tag{8.8.22}$$

where $\|s\|_1^* = \max_{\|r\|_1 \leqslant 1} s^T r$, $s = (s_1, \cdots, s_n)^T$, $s_j = \max\{-y_i w_j [\Delta x_i]_j$, $y_i w_j [\Delta x_i]_j\}$, $j = 1, \cdots, n$.

(iv) Prove that the constraint (8.8.22) is equivalent to

$$y_i((w \cdot x_i) + b) + \xi_i - 1 \geqslant \Omega \eta, \tag{8.8.23}$$
$$-y_i w_j [\Delta x_i]_j + \eta \geqslant 0, \quad j = 1, \cdots, n, \tag{8.8.24}$$
$$y_i w_j [\Delta x_i]_j + \eta \geqslant 0, \quad j = 1, \cdots, n, \tag{8.8.25}$$
$$\eta \geqslant 0. \tag{8.8.26}$$

(v) Prove the conclusion by the above (iii) and (iv).
Please see [11] for the detail. ∎

Using the above theorem the problem (8.8.10)~(8.8.12) can be rewritten as a convex quadratic programming

$$\min_{w,b,t,\xi} \quad \frac{1}{2}\|w\|^2 + C\sum_{i=1}^{l} \xi_i, \tag{8.8.27}$$

$$\text{s.t.} \quad y_i((w \cdot x_i) + b) + \xi_i - 1 \geqslant \Omega t_i, \quad i = 1, \cdots, l, \tag{8.8.28}$$
$$t_i - y_i [\Delta x_i]_j w_j \geqslant 0, \quad j = 1, \cdots, n; \quad i = 1, \cdots, l, \tag{8.8.29}$$
$$t_i + y_i [\Delta x_i]_j w_j \geqslant 0, \quad j = 1, \cdots, n; \quad i = 1, \cdots, l. \tag{8.8.30}$$
$$\xi_i \geqslant 0, t_i \geqslant 0, \quad i = 1, \cdots, l, \tag{8.8.31}$$

or

$$\min_{w,b,t,\xi} \quad \frac{1}{2}\|w\|^2 + C\sum_{i=1}^{l} \xi_i, \tag{8.8.32}$$

$$\text{s.t.} \quad y_i((w \cdot x_i) + b) + \xi_i - 1 \geqslant \Omega t_i, \quad i = 1, \cdots, l, \tag{8.8.33}$$
$$t_i e - y_i \Delta_i w \geqslant 0, \quad i = 1, \cdots, l, \tag{8.8.34}$$
$$t_i e + y_i \Delta_i w \geqslant 0, \quad i = 1, \cdots, l, \tag{8.8.35}$$
$$\xi_i \geqslant 0, t_i \geqslant 0, \quad i = 1, \cdots, l, \tag{8.8.36}$$

where

$$\Delta_i = \text{diag}([\Delta x_i]_1, [\Delta x_i]_2, \cdots, [\Delta x_i]_n). \tag{8.8.37}$$

This is the primal problem.

**Theorem 8.8.2** *Optimization problem*

$$\max_{\alpha,\beta,\beta^*,\gamma,\eta} \quad -\frac{1}{2}\left\{\sum_{i=1}^{l}\sum_{j=1}^{l}\alpha_i\alpha_j y_i y_j(x_i \cdot x_j) + \sum_{i=1}^{l}\sum_{j=1}^{l} y_i y_j (\beta_i^* - \beta_i)^{\mathrm{T}} A^{ij}(\beta_j^* - \beta_j)\right.$$

$$\left. +2\sum_{i=1}^{l}\sum_{j=1}^{l} y_i y_j \alpha_i {B^{ij}}^{\mathrm{T}}(\beta_j^* - \beta_j)\right\} + \sum_{i=1}^{l}\alpha_i, \tag{8.8.38}$$

s.t. 
$$\sum_{i=1}^{l}\alpha_i y_i = 0, \tag{8.8.39}$$

$$\Omega\alpha_i - \beta_i^{\mathrm{T}}e - \beta_i^{*\mathrm{T}}e - \eta_i = 0, \ i = 1,\cdots,l, \tag{8.8.40}$$

$$C - \alpha_i - \gamma_i = 0, \ i = 1,\cdots,l, \tag{8.8.41}$$

$$\beta_i, \beta_i^* \geqslant 0, \ i = 1,\cdots,l, \tag{8.8.42}$$

$$\alpha_i, \gamma_i, \eta_i \geqslant 0, \ i = 1,\cdots,l \tag{8.8.43}$$

*is the dual problem of the problem* (8.8.32)~(8.8.36), *where*

$$(A^{ij})_{p,q} = ((\Delta_i)_{\cdot,p} \cdot (\Delta_j)_{\cdot,q}), \quad p = 1,\cdots,n; q = 1,\cdots,n, \tag{8.8.44}$$

$$(B^{ij})_q = (x_i \cdot (\Delta_j)_{\cdot,q}), \quad q = 1,\cdots,n, \tag{8.8.45}$$

*and* $(\Delta_i)_{\cdot,p}$ *is the vector obtained from the p-th column of the matrix* $\Delta_i$.

It is easy to see that the solution set to the problem (8.8.38)~(8.8.43) w.r.t. $\alpha, \beta, \beta^*$ is the same with the one of the problem

$$\min_{\alpha,\beta,\beta^*} \quad \frac{1}{2}\left\{\sum_{i=1}^{l}\sum_{j=1}^{l}\alpha_i\alpha_j y_i y_j(x_i \cdot x_j) + \sum_{i=1}^{l}\sum_{j=1}^{l} y_i y_j (\beta_i^* - \beta_i)^{\mathrm{T}} A^{ij}(\beta_j^* - \beta_j)\right.$$

$$\left. +2\sum_{i=1}^{l}\sum_{j=1}^{l} y_i y_j \alpha_i {B^{ij}}^{\mathrm{T}}(\beta_j^* - \beta_j)\right\} - \sum_{i=1}^{l}\alpha_i, \tag{8.8.46}$$

s.t 
$$\sum_{i=1}^{l}\alpha_i y_i = 0, \tag{8.8.47}$$

$$\beta_i^{\mathrm{T}}e + \beta_i^{*\mathrm{T}}e \leqslant \Omega\alpha_i, i = 1,\cdots,l, \tag{8.8.48}$$

$$0 \leqslant \alpha_i \leqslant C, i = 1,\cdots,l, \tag{8.8.49}$$

$$\beta_i, \beta_i^* \geqslant 0, i = 1,\cdots,l, \tag{8.8.50}$$

*where* $A^{ij}$ *and* $B^{ij}$ *are given by* (8.8.44)~(8.8.45).

**Theorem 8.8.3** *Suppose that* $\bar{\alpha} = (\bar{\alpha}_1,\cdots,\bar{\alpha}_l)^{\mathrm{T}}, \bar{\beta}^{(*)} = (\bar{\beta}_1^{\mathrm{T}},\cdots,\bar{\beta}_l^{\mathrm{T}},\bar{\beta}_1^{*\mathrm{T}},$ $\cdots,\bar{\beta}_l^{*\mathrm{T}})^{\mathrm{T}}$ *is a solution to the problem* (8.8.46)~(8.8.50); *if there exists a subscript* $j \in \{i | 0 < \bar{\alpha}_i < C, \bar{\beta}_i^{\mathrm{T}}e + \bar{\beta}_i^{*\mathrm{T}}e < \Omega\bar{\alpha}_i\}$, *then a solution to the* *problem (8.8.32)~(8.8.36) w.r.t. (w,b) can be obtained by*

$$\bar{w} = \sum_{i=1}^{l} \bar{\alpha}_i y_i x_i + \sum_{i=1}^{l} y_i \Delta_i (\bar{\beta}_i^* - \bar{\beta}_i), \tag{8.8.51}$$

$$\bar{b} = y_j - (\bar{w} \cdot x_j). \tag{8.8.52}$$

**Algorithm 8.8.4** *(Linear robust support vector classification for polyhedron perturbation)*

*(1) Input the training set given by (8.8.5) and (8.8.2);*

*(2) Choose an appropriate penalty parameter $C > 0$;*

*(3) Construct and solve the convex quadratic programming (8.8.46)~(8.8.50), obtaining a solution $\bar{\alpha} = (\bar{\alpha}_1, \cdots, \bar{\alpha}_l)^T, \bar{\beta}^{(*)} = (\bar{\beta}_1^T, \cdots, \bar{\beta}_l^T, \bar{\beta}_1^{*T}, \cdots, \bar{\beta}_l^{*T})^T;$*

*(4) Compute $\bar{b}$: Choose a subscript $j \in \{i|0 < \bar{\alpha}_i < C, \bar{\beta}_i^T e + \bar{\beta}_i^{*T} e < \Omega \bar{\alpha}_i\}$, compute $\bar{b}$ by (8.8.51)~(8.8.52);*

*(5) Construct the decision function*

$$f(x) = \operatorname{sgn}\left( \sum_{i=1}^{l} \alpha_i y_i (x_i \cdot x) + \sum_{i=1}^{l} y_i B^{i^T} (\bar{\beta}_i^* - \bar{\beta}_i) + \bar{b} \right), \tag{8.8.53}$$

*where*

$$(B^i)_q = (x \cdot (\Delta_i)_{.,q}), \quad q = 1, \cdots, n. \tag{8.8.54}$$

### 8.8.2.2    Robust support vector classification

It is easy to extend Algorithm 8.8.4 to the nonlinear case.

**Algorithm 8.8.5** *We only need to introduce the kernel function $K(x, x')$, and change the inner products $((\Delta_i)_{.,p} \cdot (\Delta_j)_{.,q}), (x_i \cdot (\Delta_j)_{.,q})$ and $(x \cdot (\Delta_i)_{.,q})$ to $K((\Delta_i)_{.,p}, (\Delta_j)_{.,q}), K(x_i, (\Delta_j)_{.,q})$ and $K(x, (\Delta_i)_{.,q})$ respectively.*

## 8.8.3    The solution when the input sets are superspheres

Consider the robust binary classification problem with the training set given by (8.8.5) and (8.8.3). A toy example in $R^2$ is shown in Figure 8.9, where the circles with "+" and "∘" are positive and negative input sets respectively.

### 8.8.3.1    Linear robust support vector classification

First consider the linearly separable problems with the training set (8.8.5) and (8.8.3), where all positive input sets and negative input sets can be separated by a hyperplane correctly, e.g. the problem shown in Figure 8.8. In

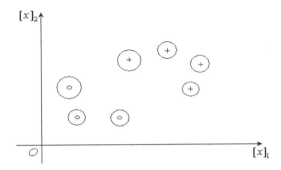

**FIGURE 8.9**: Robust classification problem with circle input sets in $R^2$.

order to find the optimal hyperplane $(w^* \cdot x) + b^* = 0$, the principle of maximal margin leads to the optimization problem

$$\min_{w,b} \quad \frac{1}{2}\|w\|^2, \tag{8.8.55}$$

$$\text{s.t.} \quad y_i((w \cdot (x_i + r_i u_i)) + b) \geqslant 1, \ \forall \ \|u_i\| \leqslant 1, i = 1, \cdots, 7. \tag{8.8.56}$$

Obviously for general robust classification without the linear separability, the above optimization problem can be modified by introducing slack variables as

$$\min_{w,b,\xi} \quad \frac{1}{2}\|w\|^2 + C\sum_{i=1}^{l}\xi_i, \tag{8.8.57}$$

$$\text{s.t.} \quad y_i((w \cdot (x_i + r_i u_i)) + b) \geqslant 1 - \xi_i, \ \forall \ \|u_i\| \leqslant 1, i = 1, \cdots, l, \tag{8.8.58}$$

$$\xi_i \geqslant 0, i = 1, \cdots, l. \tag{8.8.59}$$

Next two theorems convert the above problem into a second order cone programming.

**Theorem 8.8.6** *The triple $(w^*, b^*, \xi^*)$ is a solution to the problem (8.8.57)~(8.8.59) if and only if it is a solution to the second order cone programming w.r.t. $(w, b, \xi)$*

$$\min_{w,b,\xi,u,v,t} \quad \frac{1}{2}(u - v) + C\sum_{i=1}^{l}\xi_i, \tag{8.8.60}$$

$$\text{s.t.} \quad y_i((w \cdot x_i) + b) - r_i t \geqslant 1 - \xi_i, i = 1, \cdots, l, \tag{8.8.61}$$

$$\xi_i \geqslant 0, i = 1, \cdots, l, \tag{8.8.62}$$

$$u + v = 1, \tag{8.8.63}$$

$$\tag{8.8.64}$$

$$\begin{pmatrix} u \\ t \\ v \end{pmatrix} \in L^3, \tag{8.8.65}$$

$$\begin{pmatrix} t \\ w \end{pmatrix} \in L^{n+1}. \tag{8.8.66}$$

**Proof** Since

$$\min\{y_i r_i(w \cdot u_i), \|u_i\| \leqslant 1\} = -r_i\|w\|, \tag{8.8.67}$$

the problem $(8.8.57)\sim(8.8.59)$ is equivalent to

$$\min_{w,b,\xi} \quad \frac{1}{2}\|w\|^2 + C\sum_{i=1}^{l}\xi_i, \tag{8.8.68}$$

$$\text{s.t.} \quad y_i((w \cdot x_i) + b) - r_i\|w\| \geqslant 1 - \xi_i, i = 1, \cdots, l, \tag{8.8.69}$$

$$\xi_i \geqslant 0, i = 1, \cdots, l. \tag{8.8.70}$$

In order to convert the above problem into a second order cone programming, introduce a variable $t$ with $\|w\| \leqslant t$, and write it as

$$\min_{w,b,\xi,t} \quad \frac{1}{2}t^2 + C\sum_{i=1}^{l}\xi_i, \tag{8.8.71}$$

$$\text{s.t.} \quad y_i((w \cdot x_i) + b) - r_i t \geqslant 1 - \xi_i, i = 1, \cdots, l, \tag{8.8.72}$$

$$\xi_i \geqslant 0, i = 1, \cdots, l, \tag{8.8.73}$$

$$\|w\| \leqslant t. \tag{8.8.74}$$

Furthermore, introduce two variables $u$ and $v$ with the constraints $u + v = 1$ and $\sqrt{t^2 + v^2} \leqslant u$. Therefore, we have $t^2 = u^2 - v^2 = u - v$. Problem $(8.8.60)\sim(8.8.66)$ can be obtained from problem $(8.8.71)\sim(8.8.74)$ by replacing $t^2$ by $u - v$ and rewriting the constraints. ■

For the problem $(8.8.60)\sim(8.8.66)$, introducing the Lagrange function

$$L = \frac{1}{2}(u - v) + C\sum_{i=1}^{l}\xi_i - \sum_{i=1}^{l}\alpha_i(y_i((w \cdot x_i) + b) - r_i t - 1 + \xi_i) - \sum_{i=1}^{l}\eta_i\xi_i$$

$$- \beta(u + v - 1) - z_u u - z_v v - \gamma t - z_t t - z_w^{\mathrm{T}} w, \tag{8.8.75}$$

where $\alpha, \eta \in R^l, \beta, z_u, z_v, \gamma, z_t \in R, z_w \in R^n$ are the multiplier vectors, we can get its dual problem. In fact, the problem $(8.8.76)\sim(8.8.82)$ in the next theorem is an equivalent version of the dual problem. Furthermore, we have the following theorem.

**Theorem 8.8.7** *Suppose that $(\alpha^{*\mathrm{T}}, \gamma^*) = ((\alpha_1^*, \cdots, \alpha_l^*), \gamma^*)$ is a solution to* *the following second order cone programming w.r.t. $(\alpha, \gamma)$*

$$\max_{\alpha, \beta, \gamma, z_u, z_v} \quad \beta + \sum_{i=1}^{l} \alpha_i, \tag{8.8.76}$$

$$\text{s.t.} \quad \gamma \leqslant \sum_{i=1}^{l} r_i \alpha_i - \sqrt{\sum_{i=1}^{l} \sum_{j=1}^{l} \alpha_i \alpha_j y_i y_j (x_i \cdot x_j)}, \tag{8.8.77}$$

$$\beta + z_u = \frac{1}{2}, \tag{8.8.78}$$

$$\beta + z_v = -\frac{1}{2}, \tag{8.8.79}$$

$$\sum_{i=1}^{l} y_i \alpha_i = 0, \tag{8.8.80}$$

$$0 \leqslant \alpha_i \leqslant C, i = 1, \cdots, l, \tag{8.8.81}$$

$$\sqrt{\gamma^2 + z_v^2} \leqslant z_u. \tag{8.8.82}$$

*If there exists a component of $\alpha^*$, $\alpha_j^* \in (0, C)$, then a solution $(w^*, b^*)$ to the problem $(8.8.60) \sim (8.8.66)$ w.r.t. $(w, b)$ can be obtained by*

$$w^* = \frac{\gamma^*}{\left(\gamma^* - \sum_{i=1}^{l} r_i \alpha_i^*\right)} \sum_{i=1}^{l} \alpha_i^* y_i x_i, \tag{8.8.83}$$

$$b^* = y_j - \frac{\gamma^*}{\left(\gamma^* - \sum_{i=1}^{l} r_i \alpha_i^*\right)} \sum_{i=1}^{l} \alpha_i^* y_i (x_i \cdot x_j) - y_j r_j \gamma^*. \tag{8.8.84}$$

Thus we can establish the following algorithm.

**Algorithm 8.8.8** *(Linear robust support vector classification for supersphere perturbation)*

*(1) Input the training set $T$ given by $(8.8.5)$ and $(8.8.3)$;*

*(2) Choose an appropriate penalty parameter $C > 0$;*

*(3) Construct and solve second order cone programming $(8.8.76) \sim (8.8.82)$, obtaining a solution $(\alpha^*, \gamma^*)$ w.r.t. $(\alpha, \gamma)$;*

*(4) Compute $b^*$: Choose a component of $\alpha^*$, $\alpha_j^* \in (0, C)$, and compute*

$$b^* = y_j - \frac{\gamma^*}{\left(\gamma^* - \sum_{i=1}^{l} r_i \alpha_i^*\right)} \sum_{i=1}^{l} \alpha_i^* y_i (x_i \cdot x_j) - y_j r_j \gamma^*; \tag{8.8.85}$$

*(5) Construct the decision function*

$$f(x) = \text{sgn}\left(\frac{\gamma^*}{\left(\gamma^* - \sum_{i=1}^{l} r_i \alpha_i^*\right)} \sum_{i=1}^{l} \alpha_i^* y_i (x_i \cdot x) + b^*\right). \tag{8.8.86}$$

### 8.8.3.2   Robust support vector classification

The above linear classifier can be extended to a nonlinear classifier by introducing the Gaussian kernel function

$$K(x, x') = \exp(-\|x - x'\|^2/2\sigma^2). \qquad (8.8.87)$$

Denote the corresponding transformation as

$$\mathrm{x} = \Phi(x), \qquad (8.8.88)$$

it is easy to see that if $\tilde{\mathrm{x}} = \Phi(\tilde{x})$, $\hat{\mathrm{x}} = \Phi(\hat{x})$ and $\|\tilde{x} - \hat{x}\| = r$, then we have

$$\begin{aligned}
\|\tilde{\mathrm{x}} - \hat{\mathrm{x}}\|^2 = \|\Phi(\tilde{x}) - \Phi(\hat{x})\|^2 &= ((\Phi(\tilde{x}) - \Phi(\hat{x})) \cdot (\Phi(\tilde{x}) - \Phi(\hat{x})) \\
&= K(\tilde{x}, \tilde{x}) - 2K(\tilde{x}, \hat{x}) + K(\hat{x}, \hat{x}) \\
&= 2 - 2\exp(-\|\tilde{x} - \hat{x}\|^2/2\sigma^2) \\
&= \mathrm{r}^2, \qquad (8.8.89)
\end{aligned}$$

where

$$\mathrm{r} = (2 - 2\exp(-r^2/2\sigma^2))^{1/2}. \qquad (8.8.90)$$

Therefore, under transformation (8.8.88) the hypersphere $\mathcal{X}_i$ in $R^n$ becomes the hypersphere in $\mathcal{H}$,

$$\mathrm{X}_i = \{\tilde{\mathrm{x}}|\ \|\tilde{\mathrm{x}} - \Phi(x_i)\| \leqslant \mathrm{r}_i\}. \qquad (8.8.91)$$

where

$$\mathrm{r}_i = (2 - 2\exp(-r_i^2/2\sigma^2))^{1/2}. \qquad (8.8.92)$$

Using the above observation and considering the primal and dual problems, we arrive the counterparts of the problem (8.8.60)~(8.8.66) and problem (8.8.76)~(8.8.82), and furthermore construct the decision function; see [64, 177] for details.

**Algorithm 8.8.9** *(Nonlinear robust support vector classification)*
*The same with Algorithm 8.8.8 except:*
*(i) Introduce the Gaussian kernel function $K(x, x') = \exp(-\|x-x'\|^2/2\sigma^2)$ in step (2), and replace the inner products $(x_i \cdot x_j)$ and $(x_i \cdot x)$ by $K(x_i, x_j)$ and $K(x_i, x)$ respectively;*
*(ii) Replace $r_i$ in the problem (8.8.76)~(8.8.82) by $\mathrm{r}_i = (2 - 2\exp(-r_i^2/2\sigma^2))^{1/2}$.*

## 8.9    Multi-instance Classification

### 8.9.1    Multi-instance classification problem

Similar to both the robust and knowledge-based classification problems, the training set of the multi-instance classification problem is in the form

$$T = \{(\mathcal{X}_1, \mathcal{Y}_1), \cdots, (\mathcal{X}_l, \mathcal{Y}_l)\}, \qquad (8.9.1)$$

where $\mathcal{X}_i$ is a set containing a number of points in $R^n$, $\mathcal{X}_i = \{x_{i1}, \cdots, x_{il_i}\}$, $x_{ij} \in R^n$, $j = 1, \cdots, l_i$, $\mathcal{Y}_i \in \{-1, 1\}$, $i = 1, \cdots, l$. Here a point in $R^n$ is called an instance and a set containing a number of points in $R^n$ is called a bag, so the problem is to classify the bags. Note that the label of a bag is related with the labels of the instances in the bag and decided by the following way: a bag is positive if and only if there is at least one instance in the bag is positive; a bag is negative if and only if all instances in the bag are negative.

Now we are in a position to formulate the problem as follows:

**Multi-instance binary classification problem**: Suppose that there is a training set

$$T = \{(\mathcal{X}_1, \mathcal{Y}_1), \cdots, (\mathcal{X}_l, \mathcal{Y}_l)\}, \qquad (8.9.2)$$

where $\mathcal{X}_i = \{x_{i1}, \cdots, x_{il_i}\}$, $x_{ij} \in R^n$, $j = 1, \cdots, l_i$, $\mathcal{Y}_i \in \{-1, 1\}$. The pair $(\mathcal{X}_i, \mathcal{Y}_i)$ with $\mathcal{Y}_i = 1$ means that $\mathcal{X}_i$ is a positive bag where at least one instance $x_{ij}$ in $\mathcal{X}_i = \{x_{i1}, \cdots, x_{il_i}\}$ belongs to positive class and $(\mathcal{X}_i, \mathcal{Y}_i)$ with $\mathcal{Y}_i = -1$ means that $\mathcal{X}_i$ is a negative bag where all instances $x_{ij}$ in $\mathcal{X}_i = \{x_{i1}, \cdots, x_{il_i}\}$ belong to negative class, $i = 1, \cdots, l$. Find a real function $g(x)$ in $R^n$, such that the label $y$ for any instance $x$ can be predicted by the decision function

$$f(x) = \text{sgn}(g(x)). \qquad (8.9.3)$$

Obviously, the above decision function can be used to predict the label of any bag $\tilde{\mathcal{X}} = \{\tilde{x}_1, \cdots, \tilde{x}_m\}$. In fact, the bag is assigned to the negative class if the labels of all instances $\tilde{x}_1, \cdots, \tilde{x}_m$ predicted by (8.9.3) are $-1$; to the positive class otherwise. That is the label $\tilde{y}$ of $\tilde{\mathcal{X}}$ is computed by

$$\tilde{y} = \text{sgn}\Big( \max_{i=1,\cdots,m} f(\tilde{x}_i) \Big). \qquad (8.9.4)$$

The above multi-instance problem was proposed in the application domain of drug activity prediction[49] and a toy example in $R^2$ is shown in Figure 8.10, where every enclosure stands for a bag; a bag with "+" is positive and a bag with "o" is negative, and both "+" and "o" stand for instances. Multi-instance learning has been found useful in diverse domains and attracted a great deal of research such as [3, 28, 29, 105, 120, 127, 195].

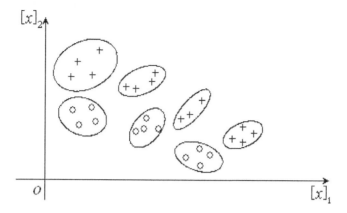

**FIGURE 8.10**: A multi-instance classification problem in $R^2$.

## 8.9.2 Multi-instance linear support vector classification

Let us introduce an algorithm proposed in [178] based on [3, 105]. Reorder training set (8.9.1) by putting the negative bags after the positive bags as

$$T = \{(\mathcal{X}_1, \mathcal{Y}_1), \cdots, (\mathcal{X}_p, \mathcal{Y}_p), (\mathcal{X}_{p+1}, \mathcal{Y}_{p+1}), \cdots, (\mathcal{X}_{p+q}, \mathcal{Y}_{p+q})\}, \qquad (8.9.5)$$

where $\mathcal{Y}_1 = \cdots = \mathcal{Y}_p = 1$, $\mathcal{Y}_{p+1} = \cdots = \mathcal{Y}_{p+q} = -1$. Denote all instances in all positive bags $\mathcal{X}_1, \cdots, \mathcal{X}_p$ and all negative bags $\mathcal{X}_{p+1}, \cdots, \mathcal{X}_{p+q}$ as the sets $S_+$ and $S_-$

$$S_+ = \{x_1, \cdots, x_r\}, \text{ and } S_- = \{x_{r+1}, \cdots, x_{r+s}\}, \qquad (8.9.6)$$

respectively, where $r$ and $s$ are respectively the number of the instances in all positive bags and all negative bags. Introduce the subscript set $I(i)$, such that

$$\mathcal{X}_i = \{x_j | x_j \in S_+, j \in I(i)\}, \quad i = 1, \cdots, p. \qquad (8.9.7)$$

Thus the training set can be equivalently written as

$$T = \{(\mathcal{X}_1, y_1), \cdots, (\mathcal{X}_p, y_p), (x_{r+1}, y_{r+1}), \cdots, (x_{r+s}, y_{r+s})\} \qquad (8.9.8)$$

with $\mathcal{X}_i = \{x_j | j \in I(i)\}$, where $y_1 = \mathcal{Y}_1 = \cdots = y_p = \mathcal{Y}_p = 1$, $y_{r+1} = \cdots = y_{r+s} = -1$, and the pair $(\mathcal{X}_i, y_i) = (\mathcal{X}_i, 1)$ means that there is at least one positive instance $x_k$ in the bag $\mathcal{X}_i, i = 1, \cdots, p$, and the pair $(x_i, y_i) = (x_i, -1)$ means that $x_i$ is a negative instance, $i = r + 1, \cdots, r + s$.

### 8.9.2.1 Optimization problem

First consider the linearly separable problem described in the following definition.

**Definition 8.9.1** (*Linearly separable multi-instance classification problem*)
*We say the training set (8.9.8) and the corresponding classification problem are linearly separable if there exist $w \in R^n$, $b \in R$ and a positive number $\varepsilon$, such that for any subscript $i$ with $y_i = 1$, the bag $\mathcal{X}_i$ includes at least one instance $x_k$ satisfying $(w \cdot x_k) + b \geq \varepsilon$; and for any subscript $i$ with $y_i = -1$, $x_i$ satisfies $(w \cdot x_i) + b \leq -\varepsilon$.*

Intuitively, a linearly separable problem is such a problem whose training set can be separated correctly by a hyperplane. A simple linearly separable problem in $R^2$ is shown in Figure 8.11 where any positive bag has at least one instance lying in the upper right of the separating line, and any negative instance lies in the lower left of the separating line.

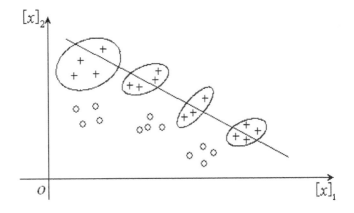

**FIGURE 8.11**: A linearly separable multi-instance classification problem in $R^2$.

For the linearly separable problem, find a separating hyperplane

$$(w \cdot x) + b = 0. \tag{8.9.9}$$

Similar to the formulation of the optimization problem (2.2.8)~(2.2.9), the principle of maximal margin leads to the optimization problem

$$\min_{w,b} \quad \frac{1}{2}\|w\|^2, \tag{8.9.10}$$

$$\text{s.t.} \quad \max_{j \in I(i)} \ (w \cdot x_j) + b \geq 1, \ i = 1, \cdots, p, \tag{8.9.11}$$

$$(w \cdot x_i) + b \leq -1, \ i = r+1, \cdots, r+s. \tag{8.9.12}$$

The next step will be based on the simple observation that a positive bag will be classified as being in the positive halfspace $\{x | (w \cdot x) + b - 1 \geqslant 0\}$ by separating hyperplane (8.9.9) if and only if some convex combination of the instances in the bag lies in the positive halfspace. This implies that, for

$i = 1, \cdots, p$, the inequality

$$\max_{j \in I(i)} (w \cdot x_j) + b \geq 1 \tag{8.9.13}$$

is equivalent to that there exists a set $\{v_j^i | j \in I(i)\}$, such that

$$v_j^i \geq 0, \quad \sum_{j \in I(i)} v_j^i = 1, \quad \left(w \cdot \sum_{j \in I(i)} v_j^i x_j\right) + b \geq 1. \tag{8.9.14}$$

Thus problem $(8.9.10) \sim (8.9.12)$ is transformed into the problem

$$\min_{w,b,v} \quad \frac{1}{2}\|w\|^2, \tag{8.9.15}$$

$$\text{s.t.} \quad \left(w \cdot \sum_{j \in I(i)} v_j^i x_j\right) + b \geq 1, \; i = 1, \cdots, p, \tag{8.9.16}$$

$$(w \cdot x_i) + b \leq -1, \; i = r+1, \cdots, r+s, \tag{8.9.17}$$

$$v_j^i \geq 0, j \in I(i), i = 1, \cdots, p, \tag{8.9.18}$$

$$\sum_{j \in I(i)} v_j^i = 1, i = 1, \cdots, p, \tag{8.9.19}$$

where

$$v = \{v_j^i | j \in I(i), \; i = 1, \cdots, p\}. \tag{8.9.20}$$

As for the problem without the assumption of linear separability, we need only to introduce slack variables $\xi = (\xi_1, \cdots, \xi_p, \xi_{r+1}, \cdots, \xi_{r+s})^{\mathrm{T}}$ and penalty parameters $C_1$, $C_2$, and then get the final optimization problem

$$\min_{w,b,v,\xi} \quad \frac{1}{2}\|w\|^2 + C_1 \sum_{i=1}^{p} \xi_i + C_2 \sum_{i=r+1}^{r+s} \xi_i, \tag{8.9.21}$$

$$\text{s.t.} \quad \left(w \cdot \sum_{j \in I(i)} v_j^i x_j\right) + b \geq 1 - \xi_i, \; i = 1, \cdots, p, \tag{8.9.22}$$

$$(w \cdot x_i) + b \leq -1 + \xi_i, \; i = r+1, \cdots, r+s, \tag{8.9.23}$$

$$\xi_i \geq 0, \; i = 1, \cdots, p, r+1, \cdots, r+s, \tag{8.9.24}$$

$$v_j^i \geq 0, j \in I(i), \; i = 1, \cdots, p, \tag{8.9.25}$$

$$\sum_{j \in I(i)} v_j^i = 1, \; i = 1, \cdots, p. \tag{8.9.26}$$

The decision function can be obtained from the solution $(w^*, b^*)$ to the above problem w.r.t. $(w, b)$

$$f(x) = \text{sgn}((w^* \cdot x) + b^*). \tag{8.9.27}$$

### 8.9.2.2    Linear support vector classification

Consider solving the problem $(8.9.21)\sim(8.9.26)$. It is easy to see that, among its constraints, only the first one is nonlinear, and in fact is bilinear. An obvious method of solution suggests itself as follows: Alternatively, hold one set of variables which constitute the bilinear terms constant while varying the other set. More precisely, it contains two steps:

(i) Update $(w, b)$ as given $v$. For a given $v$, define the series $\{\bar{x}_1, \cdots, \bar{x}_p, \bar{x}_{r+1}, \cdots, \bar{x}_{r+s}\}$:

$$\bar{x}_i = \sum_{j \in I(i)} v^i_j x_j, \quad i = 1, \cdots, p, \tag{8.9.28}$$

$$\bar{x}_i = x_i, \quad i = r + 1, \cdots, r + s, \tag{8.9.29}$$

then the problem $(8.9.21)\sim(8.9.26)$ can be written as

$$\min_{w,b,\xi} \quad \frac{1}{2}\|w\|^2 + C_1 \sum_{i=1}^{p} \xi_i + C_2 \sum_{i=r+1}^{r+s} \xi_i, \tag{8.9.30}$$

$$\text{s.t.} \quad y_i((w \cdot \bar{x}_i) + b) \geq 1 - \xi_i, \; i = 1, \cdots, p, r + 1, \cdots, r + s, \tag{8.9.31}$$

$$\xi_i \geq 0, \; i = 1, \cdots, p, r + 1, \cdots, r + s. \tag{8.9.32}$$

This problem corresponds to the problem $(2.3.4)\sim(2.3.6)$ in Chapter 2. Corresponding to the problem $(2.3.31)\sim(2.3.33)$, it is easy to get the optimization problem equivalent to the dual problem of problem $(8.9.30)\sim(8.9.32)$

$$\min_{\alpha} \quad \frac{1}{2}\sum_{i=1}^{p}\sum_{j=1}^{p} y_i y_j (\bar{x}_i \cdot \bar{x}_j)\alpha_i\alpha_j + \frac{1}{2}\sum_{i=1}^{p}\sum_{j=r+1}^{r+s} y_i y_j (\bar{x}_i \cdot \bar{x}_j)\alpha_i\alpha_j$$

$$[1mm] \quad + \frac{1}{2}\sum_{i=r+1}^{r+s}\sum_{j=1}^{p} y_i y_j (\bar{x}_i \cdot \bar{x}_j)\alpha_i\alpha_j + \frac{1}{2}\sum_{i=r+1}^{r+s}\sum_{j=r+1}^{r+s} y_i y_j (\bar{x}_i \cdot \bar{x}_j)\alpha_i\alpha_j$$

$$- \sum_{i=1}^{p}\alpha_i - \sum_{i=r+1}^{r+s}\alpha_j, \tag{8.9.33}$$

$$\text{s.t.} \quad \sum_{i=1}^{p} y_i\alpha_i + \sum_{i=r+1}^{r+s} y_i\alpha_i = 0, \tag{8.9.34}$$

$$0 \leq \alpha_i \leq C_1, i = 1, \cdots, p, \tag{8.9.35}$$

$$0 \leq \alpha_i \leq C_2, i = r + 1, \cdots, r + s. \tag{8.9.36}$$

According to the proof of Theorem 2.3.9, the solution $(\bar{w}, \bar{b})$ to the problem $(8.9.30)\sim(8.9.32)$ w.r.t. $(w, b)$ can be obtained from the solution $\bar{\alpha} =$

$(\bar{\alpha}_1, \cdots, \bar{\alpha}_p, \bar{\alpha}_{r+1}, \cdots, \bar{\alpha}_{r+s})^{\mathrm{T}}$ to the problem (8.9.33)~(8.9.36) by

$$\bar{w} = \sum_{i=1}^{p} \bar{\alpha}_i y_i \bar{x}_i + \sum_{i=r+1}^{r+s} \bar{\alpha}_i y_i \bar{x}_i, \tag{8.9.37}$$

$$\bar{b} = y_j - \sum_{i=1}^{p} \bar{\alpha}_i y_i (\bar{x}_i \cdot \bar{x}_j) - \sum_{i=r+1}^{r+s} \bar{\alpha}_i y_i (\bar{x}_i \cdot \bar{x}_j), \tag{8.9.38}$$

if there exists a component $\bar{\alpha}_j \in (0, C_1)$ with $1 \leqslant j \leqslant p$ or a component $\bar{\alpha}_j \in (0, C_2)$ with $r+1 \leqslant j \leqslant r+s$. The pair $(\bar{w}, \bar{b})$ is used to update the old value.

(ii) Update $(v, b)$ as given $w$. For a given $w$, problem (8.9.21)~(8.9.26) becomes a linear programming

$$\min_{v,b,\xi} \quad C_1 \sum_{i=1}^{p} \xi_i + C_2 \sum_{i=r+1}^{r+s} \xi_i, \tag{8.9.39}$$

$$\text{s.t.} \quad \left( w \cdot \sum_{j \in I(i)} v_j^i x_j \right) + b \geq 1 - \xi_i, \ i = 1, \cdots, p, \tag{8.9.40}$$

$$(w \cdot x_i) + b \leq -1 + \xi_i, i = r+1, \cdots, r+s, \tag{8.9.41}$$

$$\xi_i \geq 0, i = 1, \cdots, p, r+1, \cdots, r+s, \tag{8.9.42}$$

$$v_j^i \geq 0, \ j \in I(i), \ i = 1, \cdots, p, \tag{8.9.43}$$

$$\sum_{j \in I(i)} v_j^i = 1, \ i = 1, \cdots, p. \tag{8.9.44}$$

Its solution $(\bar{v}, \bar{b})$ w.r.t. $(v, b)$ enable us to update the old values.

Thus we can establish the following algorithm.

**Algorithm 8.9.2** *(Linear multi-instance support vector classification)*

*(1) Input the training set given by (8.9.8);*

*(2) Choose appropriate penalty parameters $C_1, C_2 > 0$.*

*(3) Choose an initial guess $v(1) = \{v_j^i(1) | j \in I(i), \ i = 1, \cdots, p\}$, e.g.*

$$v_j^i(1) = \frac{1}{|I(i)|}, \quad j \in I(i), \quad i = 1, \cdots, p, \tag{8.9.45}$$

*where $|I(i)|$ stands for the number of the elements in the set $I(i)$, i.e. the number of the instances in the positive bag $\mathcal{X}_i$. Set $k = 1$;*

*(4) For a fixed $v(k) = \{v_j^i(k)\}$, compute $w(k)$: First construct the series $\bar{x}_1, \cdots, \bar{x}_p, \bar{x}_{r+1}, \cdots, \bar{x}_{r+s}$ by (8.9.28)~(8.9.29), where $v_j^i$ is replaced by $v_j^i(k)$. Then solve the convex quadratic programming (8.9.33)~(8.9.36), obtaining the solution $\bar{\alpha} = (\bar{\alpha}_1, \cdots, \bar{\alpha}_p, \bar{\alpha}_{r+1}, \cdots, \bar{\alpha}_{r+s})^{\mathrm{T}}$. Last, compute $\bar{w}$ from (8.9.37), and set $w(k) = \bar{w}$;*

*(5) For fixed $w(k)$, compute $v(k + 1)$: Solve the linear programming $(8.9.39)\sim(8.9.44)$ with the variables $v = \{v_j^i\}$ and $b$, $\xi$, obtaining the solution $(\bar{v} = \{\bar{v}_j^i\}, \bar{b})$ w.r.t. $(v, b)$. Set $v(k + 1) = \{v_j^i(k + 1)\} = \bar{v}$ and $b(k) = \bar{b}$;*

*(6) If the difference between $v(k + 1)$ and $v(k)$ is less than some desired tolerance, construct the decision function*

$$f(x) = \text{sgn}((w^* \cdot x) + b^*), \tag{8.9.46}$$

*where $w^* = w(k)$, $b^* = b(k)$, stop; set $k = k + 1$, go to (4) otherwise.*

### 8.9.3   Multi-instance support vector classification

The above linear classifiers can be extended to general classifier by introducing a transformation

$$\Phi : \begin{array}{l} R^n \to \mathcal{H}, \\ x \to \mathrm{x} = \Phi(x). \end{array} \tag{8.9.47}$$

Suppose that the separating hyperplane in Hilbert space $\mathcal{H}$ is

$$(\mathrm{w} \cdot \mathrm{x}) + b = 0. \tag{8.9.48}$$

Replacing $x_i$ and $\sum_{j \in I(i)} v_j^i x_j$ by $\Phi(x_i)$ and $\sum_{j \in I(i)} v_j^i \Phi(x_j)$ respectively, $i = 1, \cdots, p$, problem $(8.9.21)\sim(8.9.26)$ becomes

$$\min_{\mathrm{w}, b, v, \xi} \quad \frac{1}{2}\|\mathrm{w}\|^2 + C_1 \sum_{i=1}^{p} \xi_i + C_2 \sum_{i=r+1}^{r+s} \xi_i, \tag{8.9.49}$$

$$\text{s.t.} \quad \left(\mathrm{w} \cdot \sum_{j \in I(i)} v_j^i \Phi(x_j)\right) + b \geq 1 - \xi_i, \ i = 1, \cdots, p, \tag{8.9.50}$$

$$(\mathrm{w} \cdot \Phi(x_i)) + b \leq -1 + \xi_i, \ i = r + 1, \cdots, r + s, \tag{8.9.51}$$

$$\xi_i \geq 0, \ i = 1, \cdots, p, r + 1, \cdots, r + s, \tag{8.9.52}$$

$$v_j^i \geq 0, j \in I(i), \ i = 1, \cdots, p, \tag{8.9.53}$$

$$\sum_{j \in I(i)} v_j^i = 1, \ i = 1, \cdots, p. \tag{8.9.54}$$

This problem can also be solved by using the following two steps alternatively:

(i) Update $(\mathrm{w}, b)$ as given $v$. For a given $v = \{v_j^i\} = \{v_j^i | j \in I(i)\}$, problem $(8.9.49)\sim(8.9.54)$ reduces to a problem similar to the problem $(8.9.30)\sim(8.9.32)$. Similar to the solution to the problem $(8.9.30)\sim(8.9.32)$ via the problem $(8.9.33)\sim(8.9.36)$, the current problem can be solved via the problem

$$\min_{\alpha} \quad \frac{1}{2}\sum_{i=1}^{p}\sum_{j=1}^{p} y_i y_j \alpha_i \alpha_j \left( \sum_{k\in I(i)} v_k^i \Phi(x_k) \cdot \sum_{l\in I(j)} v_l^j \Phi(x_l) \right)$$

$$+\frac{1}{2}\sum_{i=1}^{p}\sum_{j=r+1}^{r+s} y_i y_j \alpha_i \alpha_j \left( \sum_{k\in I(i)} v_k^i \Phi(x_k) \cdot \Phi(x_j) \right)$$

$$+\frac{1}{2}\sum_{i=r+1}^{r+s}\sum_{j=1}^{p} y_i y_j \alpha_i \alpha_j \left( \Phi(x_i) \cdot \sum_{k\in I(j)} v_k^j \Phi(x_k) \right)$$

$$+\frac{1}{2}\sum_{i=r+1}^{r+s}\sum_{j=r+1}^{r+s} y_i y_j \alpha_i \alpha_j (\Phi(x_i) \cdot \Phi(x_j))$$

$$-\sum_{i=1}^{p}\alpha_i - \sum_{i=r+1}^{r+s}\alpha_i, \tag{8.9.55}$$

$$\text{s.t.} \quad \sum_{i=1}^{p} y_i\alpha_i + \sum_{i=r+1}^{r+s} y_i\alpha_i = 0, \tag{8.9.56}$$

$$0 \le \alpha_i \le C_1, \ i = 1, \cdots, p, \tag{8.9.57}$$

$$0 \le \alpha_i \le C_2, \ i = r+1, \cdots, r+s. \tag{8.9.58}$$

or

$$\min_{\alpha} \quad \frac{1}{2}\sum_{i=1}^{p}\sum_{j=1}^{p} y_i y_j \alpha_i \alpha_j \left( \sum_{k\in I(i)} v_k^i \sum_{l\in I(j)} v_l^j K(x_k, x_l) \right)$$

$$+\frac{1}{2}\sum_{i=1}^{p}\sum_{j=r+1}^{r+s} y_i y_j \alpha_i \alpha_j \left( \sum_{k\in I(i)} v_k^i K(x_k, x_j) \right)$$

$$+\frac{1}{2}\sum_{i=r+1}^{r+s}\sum_{j=1}^{p} y_i y_j \alpha_i \alpha_j \left( \sum_{k\in I(j)} v_k^j K(x_i, x_k) \right)$$

$$+\frac{1}{2}\sum_{i=r+1}^{r+s}\sum_{j=r+1}^{r+s} y_i y_j \alpha_i \alpha_j K(x_i, x_j)$$

$$-\sum_{i=1}^{p}\alpha_i - \sum_{i=r+1}^{r+s}\alpha_i, \tag{8.9.59}$$

$$\text{s.t.} \quad \sum_{i=1}^{p} y_i\alpha_i + \sum_{i=r+1}^{r+s} y_i\alpha_i = 0, \tag{8.9.60}$$

$$0 \le \alpha_i \le C_1, \ i = 1, \cdots, p, \tag{8.9.61}$$

$$0 \le \alpha_i \le C_2, \ i = r+1, \cdots, r+s. \tag{8.9.62}$$

A solution $(\bar{w}, \bar{b})$ to the problem $(8.9.49) \sim (8.9.54)$ w.r.t. $(w, b)$ can be obtained from the solution $\bar{\alpha} = (\bar{\alpha}_1, \cdots, \bar{\alpha}_p, \bar{\alpha}_{r+1}, \cdots, \bar{\alpha}_{r+s})^{\mathrm{T}}$ to the problem $(8.9.59) \sim (8.9.62)$ by computing

$$\bar{w} = \sum_{i=1}^{p} \bar{\alpha}_i y_i \left( \sum_{j \in I(i)} v_j^i \Phi(x_j) \right) + \sum_{i=r+1}^{r+s} \bar{\alpha}_i y_i \Phi(x_i), \qquad (8.9.63)$$

and selecting a component of $\bar{\alpha}$, $\bar{\alpha}_j \in (0, C_1)$ with $1 \leqslant j \leqslant p$ and computing

$$\bar{b} = y_j - \sum_{i=1}^{p} y_i \bar{\alpha}_i \left( \sum_{k \in I(j)} v_k^j K(x_i, x_k) \right) - \sum_{i=r+1}^{r+s} y_i \bar{\alpha}_i \left( \sum_{l \in I(i)} v_l^i \sum_{k \in I(j)} v_k^j K(x_l, x_k) \right);$$
$$(8.9.64)$$

or selecting a component of $\bar{\alpha}$, $\bar{\alpha}_j \in (0, C_2)$ with $r+1 \leqslant j \leqslant r+s$ and computing

$$\bar{b} = y_j - \sum_{i=1}^{p} y_i \bar{\alpha}_i K(x_i, x_j) - \sum_{i=r+1}^{r+s} y_i \bar{\alpha}_i \left( \sum_{l \in I(i)} v_l^i K(x_l, x_j) \right). \qquad (8.9.65)$$

The pairs $(\bar{w}, \bar{b})$ obtained from $(8.9.63)$ and $(8.9.65)$ or $(8.9.63)$ and $(8.9.65)$ are used to update the old ones.

(ii) Update $(v, b)$ as given w in the form

$$\bar{w} = \sum_{i=1}^{p} \bar{\alpha}_i y_i \left( \sum_{j \in I(i)} v_j^i \Phi(x_j) \right) + \sum_{i=r+1}^{r+s} \bar{\alpha}_i y_i \Phi(x_i). \qquad (8.9.66)$$

Substituting $(8.9.66)$ into the problem $(8.9.49) \sim (8.9.54)$ yields the linear programming

$$\min_{v,b,\xi} \quad C_1 \sum_{i=1}^{p} \xi_i + C_2 \sum_{i=r+1}^{r+s} \xi_i, \qquad (8.9.67)$$

$$\text{s.t.} \quad \sum_{j=1}^{p} y_j \bar{\alpha}_j \left( \sum_{k \in I(i)} v_k^i K(x_j, x_k) \right)$$

$$+ \sum_{j=r+1}^{r+s} y_j \bar{\alpha}_j \left( \sum_{l \in I(j)} \tilde{v}_l^j \sum_{k \in I(i)} v_k^i K(x_l, x_k) \right) + b \geq 1 - \xi_i, \quad i = 1, \cdots, p,$$
$$(8.9.68)$$

$$\sum_{j=1}^{p} \bar{\alpha}_j y_j K(x_j, x_i) + \sum_{j=r+1}^{r+s} \bar{\alpha}_j y_j \left( \sum_{k \in I(j)} \tilde{v}_l^j K(x_l, x_i) \right) + b \leq -1 + \xi_i,$$

$$i = r+1, \cdots, r+s, \quad (8.9.69)$$

$$\xi_i \geq 0, \ i = 1, \cdots, p, r+1, \cdots, r+s, \qquad (8.9.70)$$

$$v_j^i \geq 0, j \in I(i), \ i = 1, \cdots, p, \qquad (8.9.71)$$

$$\sum_{j \in I(i)} v_j^i = 1, \ i = 1, \cdots, p. \qquad (8.9.72)$$

where $\bar{\alpha} = (\bar{\alpha}_1, \cdots, \bar{\alpha}_p, \alpha_{r+1}, \cdots, \bar{\alpha}_{r+s})^{\mathrm{T}}$ and $\tilde{v} = \{\tilde{v}_j^i | j \in I(i), \ i = 1, \cdots, p\}$ are known. Its solution $(\bar{v}, \bar{b})$ w.r.t. $(v, b)$ is used to update the old one.

At last corresponding to the separating hyperplane (8.9.48) in $\mathcal{H}$, the separating hypersurface in $R^n$ is given by

$$g(x) = 0, \tag{8.9.73}$$

where

$$g(x) = \sum_{i=1}^{p} \bar{\alpha}_i y_i \left( \sum_{j \in I(i)} v_j^i K(x_j, x) \right) + \sum_{i=r+1}^{r+s} \bar{\alpha}_i y_i K(x_i, x) + \bar{b}. \tag{8.9.74}$$

Thus the following algorithm is established.

**Algorithm 8.9.3** *(Multi-instance support vector classification)*

*(1) Input the training set given by (8.9.8);*

*(2) Choose an appropriate kernel function $K(x, x')$ and penalty parameters $C_1, C_2 > 0$;*

*(3) Choose an initial guess $v = \{v_j^i\} = \{v_j^i | j \in I(i), \ i = 1, \cdots, p\}$, e.g.*

$$v_j^i = \frac{1}{|I(i)|}, \quad j \in I(i), \quad i = 1, \cdots, p, \tag{8.9.75}$$

*where $|I(i)|$ stands for the number of the elements in the set $I(i)$, i.e. the number of the instances in the positive bag $\mathcal{X}_i$, $i = 1, \cdots, p$;*

*(4) For a fixed $v = \{v_j^i\}$ compute $\bar{\alpha}$: Solve the convex quadratic programming (8.9.59)∼(8.9.62), obtaining the solution $\bar{\alpha} = (\bar{\alpha}_1, \cdots, \bar{\alpha}_p, \bar{\alpha}_{r+1}, \cdots, \bar{\alpha}_{r+s})^{\mathrm{T}}$. Set $\tilde{v} \equiv \{\tilde{v}_j^i\} = \{v_j^i\} \equiv v$;*

*(5) For fixed $\alpha, \tilde{v}$, compute $\bar{v} = \{\bar{v}_j^i\}$: Solve the linear programming (8.9.67)∼(8.9.72) with the variables $v = \{v_j^i\}$, $b$ and $\xi$, obtaining the solution $\bar{v} = \{\bar{v}_j^i\}$ w.r.t. $v = \{v_j^i\}$;*

*(6) If the difference between $\bar{v} = \{\bar{v}_j^i\}$ and $\tilde{v} = \{\tilde{v}_j^i\}$, is less than some desired tolerance, construct the decision function*

$$f(x) = \mathrm{sgn}(g(x)), \tag{8.9.76}$$

*where $g(x)$ comes from (8.9.74) and (8.9.64) or (8.9.74) and (8.9.65), here the last $\bar{\alpha}$ and $v = \{v_j^i\}$ are used, stops; Set $v \equiv \{v_j^i\} = \{\bar{v}_j^i\} \equiv \bar{v}$, go to (4) otherwise.*

Algorithm 8.9.3 is an extension of Algorithm 8.9.2, they get the same decision function if the linear kernel is chosen in the former. However, when the linear classifier is required, Algorithm 8.9.2 is recommended since it needs a little less computation cost.

## 8.10    Multi-label Classification

Multi-label classification was mainly motivated by the tasks of medical diagnosis and text categorization. In medical diagnosis, a patient may be suffering, for example, from diabetes and prostate cancer at the same time. Similarly, text documents usually belong to more than one conceptual class. For example, a document describing the politics involved in the sport of cricket could be classified as Sports/Cricket, as well as Society/Politics. When a document can belong to more than one class, it is called multi-labeled. Nowadays, multi-label classification methods are increasingly required by modern applications, such as protein function classification, music categorization, and semantic scene classification [128, 151]. Multi-label classification is a more difficult problem than just choosing one out of many classes. This problem can be considered as an extension of the standard classification problem in the following way: the single labels in the training points are extended to a set of labels. More precisely, the problem is formulated mathematically as follows:

**Multi-label classification problem** Suppose that there is a training set

$$T = \{(x_1, Y_1), \ldots, (x_l, Y_l)\} \tag{8.10.1}$$

where the vector $x_i \in R^n$, the set $Y_i \subseteq \{1, 2, ..., M\}$, $i = 1, \cdots, l$. Find a decision function $f(x)$ in $R^n$, such that the label set $Y$ for any input $x$ can be predicted by the decision function.

The existing methods for multi-label classification problems can be grouped into two main categories [151]: 1) problem transformation methods, which transform the multi-label classification problem either into one or more single-label classification or regression problems, for both of which there exists a huge bibliography of learning algorithms; and 2) algorithm adaptation methods, which extend specific learning algorithms in order to handle multi-label data directly.

### 8.10.1    Problem transformation methods

Here we briefly introduce two algorithms of this category [128]. The first is the standard method which creates an ensemble of $M$ numbers of yes/no binary classifiers, one for each label. This method is called one-vs-others. For each label, a binary classification problem is constructed, in which the positive class includes all training points having this label as one of their labels and the negative side includes all other training points. During application, this method outputs a label set which is the union of the labels outputted by the $M$ classifiers for any $x$. Thus the following algorithm is established.

**Algorithm 8.10.1** *(Multi-label support vector classification based on problem transformation[51])*

*(1) Input the training set $T$ given by (8.10.1), set $k = 1$;*

*(2) Construct the $k$-th training set $T_k$ for the binary classification problem: for $x_i, i = 1, \cdots, l$, if $k \in Y_i$, set its corresponding output label $y(k)_i = 1$, otherwise $y(k)_i = -1$. Let $T_k = \{(x(k)_1, y(k)_1), \cdots, (x(k)_l, y(k)_l)\}$, where $x(k)_i = x_i \in R^n$, $y(k)_i \in \{-1, +1\}, i = 1, \cdots, l$;*

*(3) For the training set $T_k$, apply standard binary support vector classification, get the decision function $f_k(x) = \text{sgn}(g_k(x))$; if $k < M$, set $k = k + 1$, go to step (2), otherwise go to step (4);*

*(4) Construct the decision function*

$$f(x) = (f_1(x), \cdots, f_M(x)), \tag{8.10.2}$$

*for any $x$, $f_i(x) = 1$ means that $x$ belongs to the class $i$, while $f_j(x) = -1$ means that $x$ does not belong to the class $j$.*

Algorithm 8.10.1 does not take into account the correlation between labels. However, multi-labeled data, by its very nature, consists of highly correlated and overlapping classes. For instance, in the Reuters-21578 dataset, there are classes like wheat-grain, crude-fuel, where one class is almost a parent of the other class although this knowledge is not explicitly available to the classifier. Therefore, as a remedial measure, Algorithm 8.10.1 was improved by extending the original training set with $M$ extra features containing the predictions of each binary classifier since these predictions may imply some correlation information between labels.

**Algorithm 8.10.2** *(Improved multi-label support vector classification)*

*(1) Input the training set $T$ given by (8.10.1);*

*(2) Apply Algorithm 8.10.1 and get the decision function*

$$f(x) = (f_1(x), \cdots, f_M(x)); \tag{8.10.3}$$

*(3) Extend the training set $T$ to be*

$$\tilde{T} = \{(\tilde{x}_1, \tilde{Y}_1), \ldots, (\tilde{x}_l, \tilde{Y}_l)\}, \tag{8.10.4}$$

*where $\tilde{x}_i = (x_i^T, f(x_i))^T = (x_i^T, f_1(x_i), \cdots, f_M(x_i))^T \in R^{n+M}$, $\tilde{Y}_i = Y_i \subseteq Y = \{1, 2, \ldots, M\}, i = 1, \cdots, l$;*

*(4) For the extended training set $\tilde{T}$, apply Algorithm 8.10.1 again and get the final decision function*

$$\tilde{f}(x) = (\tilde{f}_1(\tilde{x}), \cdots, \tilde{f}_M(\tilde{x})). \tag{8.10.5}$$

*For any $x$, first extend it to $\tilde{x}$ by step (3) and $\tilde{f}_i(\tilde{x}) = 1$ means that $x$ belongs to the class $i$, while $\tilde{f}_j(\tilde{x}) = -1$ means that $x$ does not belong to the class $j$.*

## 8.10.2   Algorithm adaptation methods

One of the algorithm adaptation methods is ranking support vector classification proposed in [51], which can be considered as a modification and extension of Crammer-Singer support vector classification introduced in Section 8.3.3.

### 8.10.2.1   A ranking system

Remember that for an $M$-class classification problem, linear Crammer-Singer support vector classification find vectors $w_1, \cdots, w_M$. And for any input $x$, the corresponding output is obtained by comparing $(w_1 \cdot x), \cdots, (w_M \cdot x)$, i.e.

$$f(x) = \underset{r=1,\cdots,M}{\operatorname{argmax}}(w_r \cdot x). \tag{8.10.6}$$

Intuitively speaking, this strategy can be understood that the larger the value of $(w_r \cdot x)$, the more possible the corresponding $x$ will be in class $r$. Similarly, for a multi-label classification problem with the training set (8.10.1), linear ranking support vector classification find vectors $w_1, \cdots, w_M$ and $b_1, \cdots, b_M$. Corresponding to the values $(w_1 \cdot x), \cdots, (w_M \cdot x)$, the values $(w_1 \cdot x) + b_1, \cdots, (w_M \cdot x) + b_M$ are compared; the larger the value of $(w_r \cdot x) + b_r$, the more possible the corresponding $x$ will be in class $r$.

For a system that ranks the values of $(w_r \cdot x) + b$, the decision boundaries for $x$ are defined by the hyperplanes whose equations are $(w_r - w_p, x) + b_r - b_p = 0$, where $r$ belongs to the label set of $x$ and $p$ does not. So, the margin of $(x, Y)$ can be expressed as

$$\min_{r \in Y, p \in \bar{Y}} \frac{(w_r - w_p, x) + b_r - b_p}{\|w_r - w_p\|}, \tag{8.10.7}$$

where $\bar{Y}$ is the complementary set of $Y$ in $\{1, ..., M\}$. It represents the signed 2-norm distance of $x$ to the boundaries. Assuming that the training set $T$ is linearly separable, we can normalize the parameters $w_r$ such that

$$(w_r - w_p, x) + b_r - b_p \geqslant 1 \tag{8.10.8}$$

with equality for some input $x_i$ of $T$, and $(r, p) \in Y \times \bar{Y}$. So the maximal margin on the whole training set leads to the following problem

$$\max_{w_j, b_j, j=1,\cdots,M} \min_{(x_i, Y_i), i=1,\cdots,l} \min_{r \in Y_i, p \in \bar{Y}_i} \frac{1}{\|w_r - w_p\|^2}, \tag{8.10.9}$$

$$\text{s.t.} \quad (w_r - w_p, x_i) + b_r - b_p \geqslant 1, \ (r, p) \in Y_i \times \bar{Y}_i,$$

$$i = 1, \cdots, l. \tag{8.10.10}$$

In the case where the problem is not ill-conditioned (two labels are always co-occurring), the objective function can be replaced by $\max\limits_{w_j} \min\limits_{r,p} \dfrac{1}{\|w_r - w_p\|^2} =$

$\min_{w_j} \max_{r,p} \|w_r - w_p\|^2$. In order to get a simpler optimization problem we approximate this maximum by the sum and, after some calculations, obtain

$$\max_{w_j, b_j, j=1,\cdots,M} \quad \frac{1}{2} \sum_{k=1}^{M} \|w_k\|^2, \tag{8.10.11}$$

$$\text{s.t.} \quad (w_r - w_p, x_i) + b_r - b_p \geqslant 1, \ (r,p) \in Y_i \times \bar{Y}_i,$$
$$i = 1, \cdots, l. \tag{8.10.12}$$

To generalize this problem in the case where the training set may be linearly nonseparable, we introduce the slack variables $\xi_{irp} \geqslant 0$ and get the primal problem:

$$\max_{w_j, b_j, j=1,\cdots,M} \quad \frac{1}{2} \sum_{k=1}^{M} \|w_k\|^2 + C \sum_{i=1}^{l} \frac{1}{|Y_i||\bar{Y}_i|} \sum_{(r,p)\in Y_i\times\bar{Y}_i} \xi_{irp} \tag{8.10.13}$$

$$\text{s.t.} \quad (w_r - w_p, x_i) + b_r - b_p \geqslant 1 - \xi_{irp}, \ (r,p) \in Y_i \times \bar{Y}_i,$$
$$i = 1, \cdots, l, \tag{8.10.14}$$

$$\xi_{irp} \geqslant 0, \ (r,p) \in (Y_i \times \bar{Y}_i), \ i = 1, \cdots, l, \tag{8.10.15}$$

where $|Y_i|$ and $|\bar{Y}_i|$ are the numbers of the elements in $Y_i$ and $\bar{Y}_i$ respectively, the term $\dfrac{1}{|Y_i||\bar{Y}_i|}$ is used to normalize the sum of slack variables for each $i$.

The solution to the primal problem (8.10.13)~(8.10.15) can also be obtained by solving its dual problem. Introducing the Lagrange function

$$\begin{aligned} L \ = \ & \frac{1}{2} \sum_{k=1}^{M} \|w_k\|^2 + C \sum_{i=1}^{l} \frac{1}{|Y_i||\bar{Y}_i|} \sum_{(r,p)\in Y_i\times\bar{Y}_i} \xi_{irp} \\ & - \sum_{i=1}^{l} \sum_{(r,p)\in Y_i\times\bar{Y}_i} \alpha_{irp}\big((w_r - w_p, x_i) + b_r - b_p - 1 + \xi_{irp}\big) \\ & - \sum_{i=1}^{l} \sum_{(r,p)\in Y_i\times\bar{Y}_i} \eta_{irp}\xi_{irp}, \end{aligned} \tag{8.10.16}$$

where $\alpha$ and $\eta$ are the corresponding Lagrange multipliers, we get the dual problem, which can be written equivalently as

$$\max_{\alpha} \quad W(\alpha) = \frac{1}{2} \sum_{k=1}^{M} \sum_{i,j=1}^{l} \beta_{ki}(\alpha)\beta_{kj}(\alpha)(x_i \cdot x_j) - \sum_{i=1}^{l} \sum_{(r,p)\in Y_i\times\bar{Y}_i} \alpha_{irp},$$
$$\tag{8.10.17}$$

$$\text{s.t.} \quad \sum_{i=1}^{l} \sum_{(r,p)\in Y_i\times\bar{Y}_i} c_{irpk}\alpha_{irp} = 0, \ k = 1, \cdots, M, \tag{8.10.18}$$

$$0 \leqslant \alpha_{irp} \leqslant C/C_i, \ (r,p) \in Y_i \times \bar{Y}_i, \ i = 1, \cdots, l, \tag{8.10.19}$$

where $C_i = |Y_i||\bar{Y}_i|$ and

$$\beta_{kq}(\alpha) = \sum_{(r,p) \in Y_i \times \bar{Y}_i} c_{qrpk} \alpha_{qrp}, \quad k = 1, \cdots, M, \quad q = 1, \cdots, l,$$

$$(8.10.20)$$

$$c_{irpk} = \begin{cases} 0 & if\ r \neq k\ and\ p \neq k, \\ +1 & if\ r = k, \\ -1 & if\ p = k. \end{cases} \qquad (8.10.21)$$

**Theorem 8.10.3** *Suppose that $\alpha^*$ is any solution to the problem* (8.10.17)$\sim$
(8.10.21). *Then a solution* $(w_1^*, \cdots, w_M^*, b_1^*, \cdots, b_M^*)$ *to the primal problem*
(8.10.13)$\sim$(8.10.15) *w.r.t.* $(w, \cdots, w_M, b_1, \cdots, b_M)$ *such that*

$$(w_k^* \cdot x) = \sum_{i=1}^{l} \Big( \sum_{(r,p) \in (Y_i \times \bar{Y}_i)} c_{irpk} \alpha_{irp}^* \Big)(x_i \cdot x), \quad k = 1, \cdots, M, \quad (8.10.22)$$

*and if $\alpha_{irp}^* \in (0, C/C_i)$,*

$$b_k^* - b_q^* = 1 - ((w_k^* - w_q^*) \cdot x_i), \quad i = 1, \cdots, l;\ k, q = 1, \cdots, M. \quad (8.10.23)$$

This theorem can be used to establish the ranking system by comparing
any pair $g_k(x) = (w_k^* \cdot x) + b_k^*$ and $g_q(x) = (w_q^* \cdot x) + b_q^*$. In addition, this
system is easily extended to the case with kernel $K(x, x') = (\Phi(x) \cdot \Phi(x'))$ by
replacing (8.10.22) and (8.10.23) by

$$g_k(x) = \sum_{i=1}^{l} \Big( \sum_{(r,p) \in Y_i \times \bar{Y}_i} c_{irpk} \alpha_{irp}^* \Big) K(x_i, x) + b_k^*, \quad k = 1, \cdots, M, \quad (8.10.24)$$

and

$$b_k^* - b_q^* = 1 - \Big( \sum_{i=1}^{l} \Big( \sum_{(r,p) \in Y_i \times \bar{Y}_i} c_{irpk} \alpha_{irp}^* \Big) K(x_i, x) -$$

$$\sum_{i=1}^{l} \Big( \sum_{(r,p) \in Y_i \times \bar{Y}_i} c_{irpq} \alpha_{irp}^* \Big) K(x_i, x) \Big),$$

$$i = 1, \cdots, l;\ k, q = 1, \cdots, M. \qquad (8.10.25)$$

### 8.10.2.2  Label set size prediction

So far we have only developed a ranking system. To obtain a complete algorithm we need to design a label set size predictor $s(x)$, the number of elements
in the label set for any input $x$. A natural way of doing this is to look for inspiration from Algorithm 8.10.1, where the output is $f(x) = \{f_1(x), \cdots, f_M(x)\}$,
$f_k(x) = \text{sgn}(g_k(x)), k = 1, \cdots, M$. It can indeed be interpreted as a ranking

system whose ranks are derived from the real values $(g_1(x), \cdots, g_M(x))$. The predictor of the label set size is then quite simple: $s(x) = |\{g_k(x) > 0\}|$ is the number of $g_k$ greater than 0. The function $s(x)$ is computed from a threshold value that differentiates labels in the target set from others. For the current ranking system we generalize this idea by designing a function $s(x) = |g_k(x) > t(x)|$. The remaining problem now is to choose $t(x)$ which is done by solving a regression problem. The corresponding training set $T_r = \{(x_1, y_1), \cdots, (x_l, y_l)\}$ can be obtained from the training set (8.10.1) and the equations (8.10.24)~(8.10.25):

$$y_i = \mathrm{argmin}_t |\{k \in Y \mid g_k(x_i) \leqslant t\}| + |\{k \in \bar{Y} \mid g_k(x_i) \geqslant t\}|, \quad i = 1, \cdots, l.$$
$$(8.10.26)$$

When the minimum is not unique and the optimal values are a segment, we choose the middle of this segment.

## 8.10.3    Algorithm

Combining the above ranking system and label set size prediction yields the following algorithm.

**Algorithm 8.10.4** *(Ranking support vector classification)*

*(1) Input the training set $T$ given by (8.10.1);*

*(2) Choose an appropriate penalty parameter $C > 0$;*

*(3) Construct and solve the convex quadratic programming (8.10.17)~(8.10.21), obtaining a solution $\alpha^*$;*

*(4) Construct $M$ functions $\{g_1(x), \cdots, g_M(x)\}$ by (8.10.24) and (8.10.25);*

*(5) Construct the training set*

$$T_r = \{(x_1, y_1), \cdots, (x_l, y_l)\} \qquad (8.10.27)$$

*where $y_1, \cdots, y_l$ are given by (8.10.26);*

*(6) Construct a decision function $y = t(x)$ by a regression algorithm, e.g Algorithm 4.3.6 from the training set $T_r$;*

*(7) For any input $x$, all integer $k$ such that $g_k(x) > t(x)$ are considered to belong to its label set.*

An efficient implementation of the above algorithm is also proposed in [51].

In conclusion, multi-label classification problem is a rather difficult problem and has attracted significant attention from many researchers. Please see [62, 122, 151, 152] and the references therein for further investigation.

# Bibliography

[1] Alizadeh F, Goldfarb D. Second-order cone programming. Mathematical Programming. Series B, 2003, 95: 3–51.

[2] Anderson J. Regression and ordered categorical variables (with discussion). Journal of the Royal Statistical Society. Series B, 1984, 46: 1–30.

[3] Andrews S, Tsochantaridis I, Hofmann T. Support vector machines for multiple instance laearning. Advances in Neural Information Processing Systems 15, MIT Press, 2003: 561–568.

[4] Angulo C, Català A. K-SVCR, a multiclass support vector machine. Lecture Notes In Computer Science, Vol. 1810 // Proceedings of the 11th European Conference on Machine Learning, 2000: 31–38.

[5] Angulo C, Ruiz F J, Gonzalez L, Ortega J A. Multi-classification by using tri-class SVM. Neural Processing Letters, 2006, 23: 89–101.

[6] Bazaraa M S, Sherali H D, Shetty C M. Nonlinear Programming: Theory and Algorithms. New York: John Wiley and Sons, 1993.

[7] Belkin M, Niyogi P. Laplacian eigenmaps for dimensionality reduction and data representation. Neural Computation, 2003, 15: 1373–1396.

[8] Belkin M, Niyogi P. Using manifold structure for partially labeled classification. Neural Information Processing Systems: Natural and Synthetic. Vancouver, Canada, December, 2002.

[9] Ben-Tal A, Nemirovski A. Lectures on Modern Convex Optimization: Analysis, Algorithms and Engineering Applications. SIAM, Philadelphia, 2001.

[10] Ben-Tal A. Conic and Robust Optimization. Lecture Notes for Course, Minerva Optimization Center, Technion-Israel Institute of Technology, University of Rome "La Sapienza", 2002. http://iew3.technion.ac.il/Home/Users/morbt.phtml.

[11] Bertsimas D, Sim M. Tractable approximations to robust conic optimization problems. Mathematical Programming, 2006, 107: 5–36.

[12] Bi J B, Vapnik V N. Learning with rigorous support vector machines // Proceedings of the 16th Annual Conference on Learning Theory (COLT'03), 2003.

[13] Bian Z Q, Zhang X G. Pattern Recognition. Beijing: Tsinghua University Press, 2000.

[14] Blanchard G, Bousquet O, Massar P. Statistical performance of support vector machines. The Annals of Statistics, 2008, 36: 489–531.

[15] Bonnans J F, Shapiro A. Perturbation Analysis of Optimization Problems. New York: Springer-Verlag, 2000.

[16] Borgwardt K M, Ong C S, Schonauer S, Vishwanathan S V N, Smola A J, Kriegel H P. Protein function prediction via graph kernels. Bioinformatics, 2005, 21: i47–i56.

[17] Boyd S, Vandenberghe L. Convex Optimization. Cambridge University Press, 2004.

[18] Bradley P S, Mangasarian O L. Feature selection via concave minimization and support vector machines // Proceedings of the 15th International Conference on Machine Learning (ICML'98), 1998.

[19] Bradley P S, Mangasarian O L and Street W N. Feature Selection via Mathematical Programming. INFORMS Journal on Computing Spring, 1998, vol. 10 no. 2: 209-217.

[20] Cao W H. Optimization technical methods and MATLAB. Beijing: Chemical Industry Press, 2005.

[21] Chang C C, Lin C J. Training $\nu$-support vector classifiers: theory and algorithm. Neural Computation, 2001, 13: 2119–2147.

[22] Chang M W, Lin C J. Leave-one-out bounds for support vector regression model selection. Neural Computation, 2005, 17: 1188–1222.

[23] Chang W C, Lee T Y, Shien D M, Hsu J B, Horng J T, Hsu P C, Wang T Y, Huang H D, Pan R L. Incorporating support vector machine for identifying protein tyroine sulfation sites. Journal of Computational Chemistry, 2009, 30: 2526-2537.

[24] Chapelle O, Sindhwani V, Keerthi S S. Optimization techniques for semisupervised support vector machines. Journal of Machine Learning Research, 2008, 9: 203–233.

[25] Chapelle O, Schölkopf B, and Zien A. Semisupervised Learning. Cambridge, MA: MIT Press, 2006.

[26] Chen W J, Tian Y J. $L_p$-norm proximal support vector machine and its applications. ICCS 2010, Procedia Computer Science, Volume 1, Issue 1, 2010: 2417-2423.

[27] Chen Y W, Lin C J. Combining SVMs with various feature selection strategies. Feature Extraction, Foundations and Applications. New York: Springer, 2005: 319–328.

[28] Chen Y, Bi J, and Wang J Z. MILES: Multiple-instance learning via embedded instance selection. IEEE Transactions on Pattern Analysis and Machine Intelligence, 2006, 28(12): 1931–1947.

[29] Cheung P M. and Kwok J T. A regularization framework for multiple-instance learning // Proceedings of the 23rd International Conference on Machine Learning, Pittsburgh, PA, 2006, 193–200.

[30] Chu W, Keerthi S S. New approaches to support vector ordinal regression // Proceedings of 22nd International Conference on Machine Learning (ICML-05), 2005: 145–152.

[31] Chu W, Keerthi S S. Support vector ordinal regression. Neural Computation. 2007, 19: 792–815.

[32] Chu W, Ong C J, and Keerthy S S. An improved conjugate gradient method scheme to the solution of least squares SVM. IEEE Trans. Neural Netw., 2005, 16(2): 498–501.

[33] Chua K S. Efficient computations for large least square support vector machine classifiers. Pattern Recognition Letters, 2003, 24(1-3): 75-80.

[34] Comon P. Independent component analysis—a new concept? Signal Processing, 1994, 36: 287–314.

[35] Cortes C, Vapnik V. Support vector networks. Machine Learning, 1995, 20: 273–297.

[36] Cox T, Cox M. Multidimensional Scaling. Chapman & Hall, 1994.

[37] Crammer K and Singer Y. On the learnability and design of output codes for multiclass problems. In Computational Learning Theory, 2000, 35–46.

[38] Crammer K and Singer Y. On the algorithmic implementation of multiclass kernel-based vector machines. Journal Machine Learning Research, 2002, 2: 265–292.

[39] Cristianini N, Shawe-Taylor J. An Introduction to Support Vector Machines and Other Kernel-based Learning Methods. Cambridge University Press, 2000.

[40] Deng N Y, et al. Unconstrained optimization computation methods. Beijing: Science Press, 1982.

[41] Deng N Y, Zhu M F. Optimization methods. Shenyang: Liaoning Education Press, 1987.

[42] Deng N Y, Tian Y J. New methods in data mining—support vector machines. Beijing: Science Press, 2004.

[43] Deng N Y, Tian Y J. Support vector machines—Theory, Algorithms and Extensions. Beijing: Science Press, 2009.

[44] Denis F, Gilleron R, and Tommasi M. Text classification from positive and unlabeled examples. In Proceedings of the Conference on Information Processing and Management of Uncertainty in Knowledge-Based Systems (IPMU 2002), 2002, 1927–1934.

[45] Denis F, Gilleron R, and Letouzey F. Learning from positive and unlabeled examples. Theoretical Computer Science. 2005, 348(1): 70–83.

[46] Diao Z Y, Zheng H D, Liu J Z, Liu G Z. Operations Research. Beijing: Higher Education Press, 2001.

[47] Diederich J. Rule Extraction from Support Vector Machines: An Introduction, Studies in Computational Intelligence (SCI) 80, 3–31, 2008.

[48] Dietterich T G, Bakiri G. Solving multiclass learning problems via error-correcting output codes. Journal of Artificial Intelligence Research, 1995, 2: 263–286.

[49] Dietterich T G, Lathrop R H, Lozano-Pérez T. Solving the multiple-instance problem with axis-parallel rectangles. Artificial Intelligence, 1997, 89(1–2): 31–71.

[50] Duda R O, Hart P E, Stork D G. Pattern Classification. New York: John Wiley and Sons, 2001.

[51] Elisseeff A, Weston J. Kernel methods for multi-labelled classification and categorical regression problems. Paper presented to Advances in Neural Information Processing Systems 14.

[52] Fan R E, Chen P H, Lin C J. Working set selection using second order information for training SVMs. Journal of Machine Learning Research, 2005, 6: 1889–1918.

[53] Fan R E, Chang K W, Hsieh C J, Wang X R, Lin C J. LIBLINEAR: a library for large linear classification. Journal of Machine Learning Research, 2008, 9: 1871–1874.

[54] Fletcher R. Practical Methods of Optimization(Second Edition). New York: Wiley-Interscience, 1987.

[55] Fung G, Mangasarian O L. Proximal support vector machine classifiers // Proceedings of International Conference of Knowledge Discovery and Data Mining, 2001: 77–86.

[56] Fung G. and Mangasarian O L. Multicategory proximal support vector machine classifiers. Machine Learning, 2005, 59(1-2): 77–97.

[57] Fung G, Mangasarian O L, Shavlik J. Knowledge-based support vector machines classifiers. Technical Report 01-09, Data Mining Institute, Computer Sciences Department, University of Wisconsin, Madison, Wisconsin, November 2001. http://ftp.cs.wisc.edu/pub/dmi/tech-reports/01-09.ps.

[58] Fung G, Mangasarian O L. Knowledge-based support vector machine classifiers, Neural Information Processing Systems NIPS 2002, Vancouver, December 9-14, 2002.

[59] Fung G, Mangasarian O L. Knowledge-based nonlinear kernel classifiers, Neural Information Processing Systems NIPS 2002, Vancouver, December 9-14, 2002.

[60] Fung G, Sandilya S, and Rao R B. Rule Extraction from Linear Support Vector Machines via Mathematical Programming, Studies in Computational Intelligence (SCI) 80, 83-107, 2008.

[61] Fung G P C, Yu J X, Lu H, and Yu P S. Text classification without negative examples revisit (sic). IEEE Transactions on Knowledge and Data Engineering, 2006, 18(1): 6–20.

[62] Fürnkranz J, Hüllermeier E, Mencia E L, Brinker K. Multilabel classification via calibrated label ranking. Machine Learning. 2008, 73: 133–153.

[63] Gao T T. $U$-support vector machine and its applications. Master thesis, China Agricultural University, 2008.

[64] Goldfarb D, Iyengar G. Robust convex quadratically constrained programs. Mathematical Programming, Series B, 2003, 97: 495–515.

[65] Guyon L, Weston J, Barnhill S, Vapnik, V N. Gene selection for cancer classification using support vector machines. Machine Learning, 2002, 46: 389–422.

[66] Han J W, Kamber M. Data Mining: Concepts and Techniques, Morgan Kaufmann Publishers, Inc, 2001.

[67] Hastie T. Principal curves and surfaces. Laboratory for Computational Statistics, Stanford University, Department of Statistics Technical Report, 1984.

[68] Hastie T, Stuetzle W. Principal curves. Journal of the American Statistical Asssociation, 1989, 84: 502–516.

[69] He H B, Garcia E A. Learning from Imbalanced Data. IEEE Transactions on Knowledge and Data Engineering, vol. 21, no. 9, 2009: 1263-1284.

[70] Henikoff S.,Henikoff J. G. Amino acid substitution matrices from protein blocks. Proceedings of the National Academy of Sciences, USA, 1992, 89(22), 10915-10919.

[71] Herbrich R, Graepel T, Bollmann-Sdorra P, Obermayer K. Learning a preference relation for information retrieval // Proceedings of the AAAI Workshop Text Categorization and Machine Learning, Madison, USA, 1998.

[72] Herbrich R, Graepel T, Obermayer K. Support vector learning for ordinal regression // Proceedings of the 9th International Conference on Artifical Neural Networks, 1999: 97–102.

[73] Herbrich R. Learning Kernel Classifiers: Theory and Algorithms. The MIT Press, 2002.

[74] Herbrich R, Graepel T, Obermayer K. Large margin rank boundaries for ordinal regression. Advances in Large Margin Classifiers, 2000: 115–132.

[75] Hoegaerts L, Suykens J A K, Vandewalle J and De Moor B. A Comparison of Pruning Algorithms for Sparse Least Squares Support Vector Machines. Lecture Notes in Computer Science, 2004, 3316: 1247–1253.

[76] Hsu C W and Lin C J. A comparison of methods for multiclass support vector machines. IEEE Transactions on Neural Networks, 2002, 13(2): 415–425.

[77] Hu X Q. Methods of supervised feature extraction for high-dimensional complex data sets. Master thesis, China Agricultural University, 2007.

[78] Huang H X, Han J Y. Mathematical programming. Beijing: Tsinghua University Press, 2006.

[79] Jaakkola T S, Haussler D. Exploiting generative models in discriminative classifiers // Advances in Neural Information Processing Systems 11. MIT Press, 1998.

[80] Jain A K, Murty M N, Flynn P J. Data clustering: a review. ACM Computing Surveys, 1999, 31: 264–323.

[81] Jiao L C, Bo L F, Wang L. Fast Sparse Approximation for Least Squares Support Vector Machine. IEEE Trans. Neural Netw., 2007, 18(3): 685–697.

[82] Joachims T. Estimating the generalization performance of an SVM effi-
     ciently // Proceedings of the 17th International Conference on Machine
     Learning. San Francisco, California: Morgan Kaufmann, 2000: 431–438.

[83] Jolliffe I T. Principal Component Analysis (Second Edition). New York:
     Springer-Verlag, 2002.

[84] Keerthi S S, Shevade S K. SMO algorithm for least-squares SVM for-
     mulations. Neural Computation, 2003, 15(2): 487-507.

[85] Khemchandani J R, Jayadeva R K, and Chandra S. Optimal kernel
     selection in twin support vector machines. Optim. Lett., 2009, 3(1): 77–
     88.

[86] Khemchandani J R, Chandra S. Twin support vector machines for pat-
     tern classification. IEEE Trans. Pattern Anal. Machine Intell. 2007,
     29(5): 905-910.

[87] Kim H C, Pang S, Je H, Kim D, Bang S Y. Constructing support vector
     machine ensemble. Pattern Recognition, 2003, 36: 2757-2767.

[88] Kim J H, Lee J, Oh B, Kimm K, Koh I. Prediction of phosphorylation
     sites using SVMs. Bioinformatics, 2004, 20(17): 3179–3184.

[89] Klerk E. Aspects of Semidefinite Programming. Dordrecht: Kluwer Aca-
     demic Publishers, 2002.

[90] Korenberg M J, David R, Hunter I W, Soloman, JE. Automatic clas-
     sification of protein sequences into structure/function groups via paral-
     lel cascade identification: a feasibility study. Ann. Biomed. Eng., 2000,
     28(7): 803-811.

[91] Kuhn H W. Nonlinear programming: a historical note. History of Math-
     ematical Programming. Amsterdam: North-Holland, 1991: 82–96.

[92] Kumar M A and Gopal M. Application of smoothing technique on twin
     support vector machines. Pattern Recognit. Lett., 2008, 29(13): 1842-
     1848.

[93] Kumar M A and Gopal M. Least squares twin support vector machines
     for pattern classification. Expert Syst. Appl., 2009, 36(4): 7535–7543.

[94] Lee M D. Determining the dimensionality of multidimensional scaling
     models for cognitive modeling. Journal of Mathematical Psychology,
     2001, 45: 149–166.

[95] Lee D, Seung H. Learning the parts of objects by nonnegative matrix
     factorization. Nature, 1999, 401: 788–791.

[96] Lee W S and Liu B. Learning with positive and unlabeled examples using weighted logistic regression. In Proceedings of the Twentieth International Conference on Machine Learning (ICML 2003), Washington, DC, 2003, 448–455.

[97] Leslie C, Eskin, E and Noble W S. The spectrum kernel: a string kernel for SVM protein classification // Proceedings of the Pacific Symposium on Biocomputing. New Jersey, Singapore: World Scientific, 2002: 564–557.

[98] Li D C, Fang Y H. An algorithm to cluster data for efficient classification of support vector machines. Expert Systems with Applications, 2007, 34: 2013–2018.

[99] Li Y G, Lin C, Zhang W D. Improved sparse least-squares support vector machine classifiers. Neurocomputing, 2006, 69(13-15): 1655–1658.

[100] Liu B G. Nonlinear programming. Beijing: Beijing University of Technology Press, 1988.

[101] Liu B. Web data mining: Exploring hyperlinks, contents, and usage data. Opinion Mining. Springer, 2006.

[102] Liu B, Dai Y, Li X, Lee W S, and Yu P S. Building text classifiers using positive and unlabeled examples. In Proceedings of the 3rd IEEE International Conference on Data Mining (ICDM 2003), 2003, 179–188.

[103] Lodhi H, Shawe-Taylor J, Cristianini N, and Watkins C. Text classification using string kernels. Journal of Machine Learning Research, 2002, 2: 419–444.

[104] Mangasarian O L, Musicant D R. Successive overrelaxation for support vector machines, IEEE Transactions on Neural Networks, 1999, 10: 1032–1037.

[105] Mangasarian O L, Wild E W. Multiple instance classification via successive linear programming. Journal of Optimization Theory and Application, 2008, 137(1): 555–568.

[106] Mangasarian O L, Wild E W. Multisurface proximal support vector machine classification via generalized eigenvalues. IEEE Trans. Pattern Anal. Mach. Intell., 2006, 28(1): 69–74.

[107] Mangasarian O L. Nonlinear Programming. SIAM, Philadelphia, PA, 1994.

[108] Mangasarian O L, Wild E W. Multisurface proximal support vector classification via generalize eigenvalues. IEEE Trans. Pattern. Anal. Machine Intell., 2006, 28(1): 69–74.

[109] Martens D, Huysmans J, Setiono R, Vanthienen J, and Baesens B. Rule Extraction from Support Vector Machines: An Overview of Issues and Application in Credit Scoring, Studies in Computational Intelligence (SCI) 80, 33–63, 2008.

[110] Molina L C, Belanche L, Nebot A. Feature selection algorithms: a survey and experimental evaluation // Proceedings of the 2002 IEEE International Conference on Data Mining (ICDM '02), 2002: 306–313.

[111] Nash S G, Sofer A. Linear and Nonlinear Programming. McGraw-Hill, USA, 1996.

[112] Nocedal J, Wright S J. Numerical Optimization. New York: Springer-Verlag, 1999.

[113] Núñez H, Angulo C, and Català A: Rule Extraction Based on Support and Prototype Vectors, Studies in Computational Intelligence (SCI) 80, 109134 (2008)

[114] Osuna E, Freund R, Girosi F. Improved Training Algorithm for Support Vector Machines // Proceedings of the IEEE Neural Networks for Signal Processing, 1997: 276–285.

[115] Pechyony D, Izmailov R, Vashist A, and Vapnik V. SMO-style algorithms for learning using privileged information // Proceedings of the 2010 International Conference on Data Mining (DMIN10), 2010.

[116] Pechyony D and Vapnik V. On the Theory of Learning with Privileged Information. In Advances in Neural Information Processing Systems, Curran Associates Inc., 23, 2010.

[117] Peng X. TSVR: An efficient twin support vector machine for regression. Neural Networks, 2010, 23(3): 365–372.

[118] Platt J. Sequential minimal optimization: a fast algorithm for training support vector machines. Advances in Kernel Methods-Support Vector Learning. MIT Press, 1999: 185–208.

[119] Qi Z Q, Tian Y J, Shi Y. Robust twin support vector machine for pattern classification. Pattern Recognition, http://dx.doi.org/10.1016/j.patcog.2012.06.019.

[120] Rahmani R and Goldman S A. MISSL: Multiple-instance semisupervised learning // Proceedings of the 23rd International Conference on Machine Learning, Pittsburgh, PA, 2006, 705–712.

[121] Rifkin R, Pontil M and Verri A. A note on support vector machine degeneracy. Lecture Notes in Computer Science, 1999, 1720: 252–263.

[122] Rousu J, Saunders C, Szedmak S, Shawe-Taylor J. Kernel-based learning of hierarchical multilabel classification methods. Journal of Machine Learning Research, 2006, 7: 1601–1626.

[123] Roweis S T, Saul L K. Nonliear dimensionality reduction by locally linear embedding. Science, 2000, 290: 2323–2326.

[124] Schölkopf B, Smola A J. Learning with Kernels–Support Vector Machines, Regularization, Optimization, and Beyond. MIT Press, 2002.

[125] Schölkopf B, Smola A, Muller K R. Nonlinear component analysis as a kernel eigenvalue problem. Neural Computation, 1998, 10: 1229–1319.

[126] Schölkopf B, Smola A, Williamson R C and Bartlett P L. New support vector algorithms. Neural Computation, 2000(12):1207-1245.

[127] Settles B, Craven M, and Ray S. Multiple-instance active learning. In Platt J C, Koller D, Singer Y, and Roweis S, editors, Advances in Neural Information Processing Systems, MIT Press, Cambridge, MA, 2008, 20: 1289–1296.

[128] Shantanu G, Sunita S. Discriminative Methods for Multi-labeled Classification. PAKDD 2004, LNAI 3056, 2004: 22–30.

[129] Shao Y H, Zhang C H and Deng N Y. Improvements on Twin support vector machines. IEEE Trans. Neural Networks. 2010(22):962-968.

[130] Shao Y H, Deng N Y. A coordinate descent margin based-twin support vector machine for classification. Neural Networks, 2012, 25: 114–121.

[131] Shao YH, Deng N Y, Yang Z M, Chen W J, and Wang Z. Probabilistic outputs for twin support vector machines. Knowledge-Based Systems, September 2012, 33: 145–151.

[132] Shashua A, Levin A. Taxonomy of large margin principle algorithms for ordinal regression problems. Technical Report 2002-39. Leibniz Center for Research, School of Computer Science and Engineering, The Hebrew University of Jerusalem.

[133] Shashua A, Levin A. Ranking with large margin principle: two approaches. Neural Information Processing Systems, 2003, 15: 937–944.

[134] Shen J, Zhang J, Luo X, Zhu W, Yu K, Chen K, Li Y, Jiang H. Predicting protein-protein interactions based only on sequences information. Proc Natl Acad Sci U S A, 2007, 104(11): 4337-4341.

[135] Shien D M, Lee T Y, Chang W C, Hsu J B, Horng J T, Hsu P C, Wang T Y, Huang H D. Incorporating structural characteristics for identification of protein methylation sites. Journal of Computational Chemistry, 2009, 30(9): 1532-1543.

[136] Sinz F, Chapelle O, Agarwal A, Schölkopf B. An analysis of inference with the universum // Advances in Neural Information Processing Systems 20: Proceedings of the 2007 Conference, Cambridge, MA, USA: MIT Press, 2008: 1369–1376.

[137] Steinwart I. Consistency of support vector machines and other regularized kernel machines. IEEE Transactions on Information Theory, 2005, 51: 128–142.

[138] Suykens J A K, Brabanter J D, Lukas L, and Vandewalle J. Weighted least squares support vector machines: Robustness and sparse approximation. Neurocomput., 2002, 48(1-4): 85–105.

[139] Suykens J A K, Lukas L, Vandewalle J. Sparse approximation using least squares support vector machines. Proc. 2000 IEEE International Symposium on ISCAS, Geneva, Switzerland, 2000, 757–760.

[140] Suykens J A K, Tony V G, Jos D B, Bart D M, Joos V. Least Squares Support Vector Machines. World Scientific, 2002.

[141] Suykens J A K and Vandewalle J. Least Squares Support Vector Machine Classifiers. Neural Processing Letters, 1999, 9(3): 293-300.

[142] Tan J Y, Wu L Y, Deng N Y. Comparison of different encoding scheme on Prediction of Post-translational Modification Sites. Submitted. 2011.

[143] Tan J Y, Zhang C H, Deng N Y. Cancer Related Gene Identification via $p$-norm support vector machine. The International Conference on Computational Systems Biology (ISB2010). 2010, 7.

[144] Tang Y C, Zhang Y Q, Chawla N V, Krasser S. SVMs Modeling for Highly Imbalanced Classification. IEEE Trans Syst Man Cybern B Cybern, 2009, Feb, 39(1): 281–288.

[145] Tenenbaum J B, Silva V(de), Langford J C. A global geometric framework for nonlinear dimensionality reduction. Science, 2000, 290: 2319–2323.

[146] Tian Y J. Support vector regression and its applications. PhD thesis, China Agricultural University, 2005.

[147] Tian Y J, Deng N Y. Support vector classification with nominal attributes. Lecture Notes in Computer Science, 2005, 3801: 586–591.

[148] Tian Y J, Yu J, Qi Z Q, Shi Y. Efficient Sparse Least Squares Support Vector Machines for Pattern Classification. 2012 9th International Conference on Fuzzy Systems and Knowledge Discovery (FSKD2012), 714–718.

[149] Tian Y J, Yu J, Chen W J. $l_p$-norm support vector machine with CCCP. 2010 Seventh International Conference on Fuzzy Systems and Knowledge Discovery (FSKD), 2010: 1560 - 1564.

[150] Tsang I W, Kwok J T. Distance metric learning with kernels // Proceedings of the International Conference on Artificial Neural Networks. Istanbul, Turkey, June, 2003.

[151] Tsoumakas G, Katakis I. Multi-label classification: An overview. International Journal of Data Warehousing and Mining, 2007, 3(3): 1–13.

[152] Tsoumakas G, Katakis I, and Vlahavas I. Mining Multi-label Data. Data Mining and Knowledge Discovery Handbook, 2010, Part 6: 667-685.

[153] Tveit A and Hetland M L. Multicategory incremental proximal support vector classifiers. Lecture Notes in Computer Science, Springer-Verlag, 2003, 386–392.

[154] Vanderbei R J. Linear Programming: Foundations and Extensions (Second Edition), Kluwer Academic Publishers, 2001.

[155] Vapnik V N. Estimation of Dependences Based on Empirical Data. New York: Springer-Verlag, 1982.

[156] Vapnik V N. Estimation of Dependences Based on Empirical Data. 2nd edition Berlin: Springer Verlag, 2006.

[157] Vapnik V N. The Nature of Statistical Learning Theory. New York: Springer, 1996.

[158] Vapnik V N. Statistical Learning Theory. New York: John Wiley and Sons, 1998.

[159] Vapnik V N, Vashist A. A new learning paradigm: Learning using privileged information. Neural Networks, 2009, 22: 544-577.

[160] Vapnik V N , Vashist A, and Pavlovitch N. Learning using hidden information: Master-class learning. In F. F. Soulie, D. Perrotta, J. Piskorski, and R. Steinberger, editors, NATO Science for Peace and Security Series, D: Information and Communication Security, IOS Press, 2008, 19: 3–14.

[161] Vishwanathan S V N, Borgwardt K M, Schraudolph N N. Fast computation of graph kernels. Technical Report, National ICT Australia (NICTA), 2006.

[162] Wang R S. Functional analysis and optimization theory. Beijing: Beijing Aerospace University Press, 2004.

[163] Wang S, Mathew A, Chen Y, Xi L, Ma L, Lee J. Empirical analysis of support vector machine ensemble classifiers. Expert Systems with applications, 2009, 36: 6466–6476.

[164] Wang Y J, Xiu N H. Nonlinear programming theory and algorithms (2nd Edition). Xi'an: Shaanxi Science and Technology Press, 2008.

[165] Weiss G M. Mining with Rarity: a Unifying Framework. ACM SIGKOO Explorations Newsletter, 2004, 6(1): 7–19.

[166] Weston J, Collobert R, Sinz F, Bottou L and Vapnik V. Inference with the Universum // Proceedings of 23th International Conference on Machine Learning, 2006.

[167] Weston J, Elisseeff A, Schölkopf B, Tipping M. Use of the Zero-Norm with Linear Models and Kernel Methods. Journal of Machine Learning Research 3, 2003: 1439–1461.

[168] Weston J, Gammerman A, Stitson M O, Vapnik V N, Vovk V, Watkins C. Support vector density estimation. Advances in Kernel Methods–Support Vector Learning. Cambridge. MA: MIT Press, 1999: 293–305.

[169] Wong Y H, Lee T Y, Liang H K, Huang C M, Wang T Y, Yang Y H, Chu C H, Huang H D, Ko M T, Hwang J K. KinasePhos 2.0: A Web server for identifying protein kinase-specific phosphorylation sites based on sequences and coupling patterns. Nucleic Acids Res, 2007, 35 (Web Server issue), W588–94.

[170] Xie J X, Xing W X. Network optimization. Beijing: Tsinghua University Press, 2000.

[171] Xie J X, Xue Y. Optimization Modeling and LINDO/LINGO softwares. Beijing: Tsinghua University Press, 2005.

[172] Xu C X, Chen Z P, Li N C. Modern optimization methods. Beijing: Science Press, 2002.

[173] Xu L, Neufeld J, Larson B, Schuurmans D. Maximum margin clustering // Advances in Neural Information Processing Systems, 2004, 17.

[174] Xu L, Schuurmans D. Unsupervised and semisupervised multiclass support vector machines // Proceedings of the 20th National Conference on Artificial Intelligence, 2005.

[175] Xu Y, Wang X B, Ding J, Wu L Y, Deng N Y. Lysine acetylation sites prediction using an ensemble of support vector machine classifiers. Journal of Theoretical Biology, 2010, 264: 130–135.

[176] Yang X W, Lin D Y, Hao Z F, et al. A fast svm training algorithm based on the set segmentation and $k$-means clustering. Natural Science, 2003, 13.

[177] Yang Z X. Support vector ordinal regression and multiclass problems. PhD thesis, China Agricultural University, 2007.

[178] Yang Z X, Deng N Y. Multi-instance support vector machine based on convex combination. The Eighth International Symposium on Operations Research and Its Applications (ISORA'09), 2009:481–487.

[179] Yang Z X, Deng N Y, Tian Y J. A multiclass classification algorithm based on ordinal regression machine // Proceedings of International Conference on CIMCA 2005 & IAWTIC 2005, Vienna, Austria, 2005, 2: 810–815.

[180] Yang Z X, Tian Y J, Deng N Y. Leave-one-out bounds for support vector ordinal regression machine. Neural Computing and Applications, 2009, Volume 18, Number 7, 731–748.

[181] Yoo P D, Ho Y S, Zhou B B, Zomaya A Y. SiteSeek: post-translational modification analysis using adaptive locality-effective kernel methods and new profiles. BMC Bioinformatics, 2008, 9:272.

[182] Yu H, Yang J. A direct LDA algorithm for high-dimensional data with application face recognition. Pattern Recognition, 2001, 34.

[183] Yuan Y X, Sun W Y. Optimization theory and methods. Beijing: Science Press, 1997.

[184] Zanni L, Serafini T, Zanghirati G. Parallel software for training large scale support vector machines on multiprocessor systems. Journal of Machine Learning Research, 2006, 7: 1467–1492.

[185] Zeng X Y and Chen X W. SMO-based pruning methods for sparse least squares support vector machines. IEEE Trans. Neural Netw., 2005, 16(6): 1541-1546.

[186] Zhang C H, Tian Y J, Deng N Y. The new interpretation of support vector machines on statistical learning theory. SCIENCE CHINA Mathematics, 2010, Volume 53, Number 1, 151–164.

[187] Zhang X D. Matrix Analysis and Applications. Beijing: Tsinghua University Press, 2004.

[188] Zhang J Z, Xu S J. Linear programming. Beijing: Science Press, 1990.

[189] Zhao K. Unsupervised and semisupervised support vector machines for binary classification problems. PhD thesis, China Agricultural University, 2007.

[190] Zhao K, Tian Y J, Deng N Y. Unsupervised and semisupervised two-class support vector machines // Proceedings of the 6th IEEE International Conference on Data Mining Workshops. Hong Kong, December 18-22, 2006: 813–817.

[191] Zhao K, Tian Y J, Deng N Y. Unsupervised and semisupervised lagrangian support vector machines // Proceedings of the 7th International Conference on Computational Science Workshops. Beijing, China. May 27-30, Part III, LNCS 4489, 2007: 882–889.

[192] Zhao K, Tian Y J, Deng N Y. Robust unsupervised and semisupervised bounded C-support vector machines // Proceedings of the 7th IEEE ICDM 2007 Workshops, 2007: 331–336.

[193] Zhao Y M. Robust classification and feature selection of Gene expression data. Master thesis, China Agricultural University, 2008.

[194] Zhong P, Fukushima M. A new multiclass support vector algorithm. Optimization Methods and Software, 2006, 21: 359–372.

[195] Zhou Z H and Xu J M. On the relation between multi-instance learning and semisupervised learning // Proceeding of the 24th International Conference on Machine Learning, Corvallis, OR, 2007, 1167–1174.

[196] Zhou Z H, Zhan D C, Yang Q. Semisupervised learning with very few labeled training examples. Twenty-Second AAAI Conference on Artificial Intelligence (AAAI-07), 2007, 675-680.

[197] Zhu J, Rosset S, Hastie T, and Tibshirani R. 1-norm support vector machines. In S. Thrun, L Saul, and B. Schölkopf, editors, Advances in Neural Information Processing Systems 16, pages 49–56, Cambridge, MA, 2004. MIT Press.

[198] Zhu X. Semisupervised Learning with Graphs. PhD thesis, Carnegie Mellon University, 2005a.

[199] Zhu X. Semisupervised learning literature survey. Computer Sciences Technical Report 1530, University of Wisconsin–Madison, 2005b.

[200] http://archive.ics.uci.edu/ml/datasets/Heart+Disease.

[201] http://archive.ics.uci.edu/ml/datasets/Iris.

# Index

For Product Safety Concerns and Information please contact our EU
representative GPSR@taylorandfrancis.com Taylor & Francis Verlag GmbH,
Kaufingerstraße 24, 80331 München, Germany

Printed and bound by CPI Group (UK) Ltd, Croydon, CR0 4YY
08/05/2025
01864366-0015